Japan's
Southward Advance
and Australia

Japan's Southward Advance and Australia

From the Sixteenth Century to World War II

Henry P. Frei

UNIVERSITY OF HAWAII PRESS

HONOLULU

Published in North America by
University of Hawaii Press
2840 Kolowalu Street
Honolulu, Hawaii 96822

Published in Australia by
Melbourne University Press
Carlton, Victoria 3053

Printed in Australia

Library of Congress Cataloging-in-Publication Data

Frei, Henry P.
    Japan's southward advance and Australia: from the sixteenth
century to World War II/Henry P. Frei.
        p.   cm.
    Includes bibliographical references.
    ISBN 0-8248-1311-1
    1. Japan—Relations—Australia. 2. Australia—Relations—Japan.
I. Title.
DS849.A8F74   1990
303.48′252094—dc20   89-20654
                                                              CIP

To Francis

Contents

Preface

JAPAN AND AUSTRALIA are antipodal island countries in the Western Pacific, unequal in size, resources, and population; disparate in language, culture, and religion; yet both have modern big cities, well developed economies, and today enjoy a mutual complementarity in trade that has benefitted both countries tremendously in the post-war period. This was not always so. Before World War II political dissonance tended to overshadow their relations as Australians grew increasingly uncomfortable about Japanese expansion in Asia and in the Pacific toward the South. Ever since Japan's rise as a Pacific power in 1895, there was a strong and persistent response in Australia to Japan's gradual and seemingly threatening southern advance. 'Was Japan a threat to Australia?' is the basic question this book asks, as it uses a timeframe that reaches back to the age before Japan isolated herself for two-and-a-half centuries.

In writing the book, I first of all had in mind to contribute new findings to the history of Japanese–Australian relations; more specifically, I wanted to ascertain how, over the centuries, Japan had been perceiving the southernmost continent on the farthest fringes of the *nan'yō* (South Seas) region. Taking a long view would at the same time provide a broad historical evaluation of those relations up until World War II as a basis for better understanding the increasingly close post-war ties between two stable and forward-looking Pacific Basin countries. But trying to read the

Japanese mind about Australia proved of little value if done without delving deeper into the history of Japan's so-called *'nanshin'* or 'southward advance'. By telling about Japan's early southern involvement in the Western Pacific, I hope to narrow a gap in Western historiography (which has hardly begun to treat the significance of Japan's early interest in the Pacific region) and to offer new insights relevant to the continuing historical search for the causes of Western decline in the Pacific during the interwar years.

Moreover, by reaching back to an earlier age of once bustling Japanese activities in southern waters, I should like to provide the conventional Japanese *nanshin* studies—which invariably pick up the thread in the mid-nineteenth century—with a new perspective. Account must be taken of both precedent and similarities in the long history of Japan's interest in the south from the Age of Discoveries until the Pacific War. Japanese works furthermore appear in a new light when looked at from the Australian angle. For present historical studies on the *nanshin-ron* (southward advance school of thought) have tended to focus primarily on Japanese involvement in and response from Southeast Asia, then a region under European colonial control that busied itself with other matters. They have largely ignored Australia's organized and continuous adverse response that had been aflutter to Japan's southward advance ever since the mid-1890s.

The documents upon which I draw are diverse: old Japanese world-maps and geographies, books and pamphlets of early *nanshin-ron sha* (Japanese 'southward-ho!' protagonists) in the modern period, monographs, histories, biographies, memoirs, magazines and newspapers; Japanese government, army, and navy position papers; and Australian diplomatic source material. This bold march through the events of four centuries has by no means exhausted all of the potential source materials. It presents one interpretation, set out in a chronological and straightforward way.

Acknowledgements

$\mathbf{M}$Y WORK was done in Japan, and I should like to thank the institutions that helped me. A scholarship from the Japanese Ministry of Education enabled me to do research from 1982 to 1985. I am also much indebted to the Institute of International Relations for Advanced Studies on Peace and Development in Asia at Sophia University in Tokyo, where from autumn 1986 to 1988 I was fortunate to work as a research assistant in a congenial climate that allowed me to spend most of my time doing research to complete this study. I thank all the faculty for their kind consideration and the stimulus provided at the Insititute in the heart of Tokyo.

Portions of this book have appeared elsewhere in earlier versions: in English as 'Japan Discovers Australia: The Emergence of Australia in the Japanese World-View, 1540s–1900', in *Monumenta Nipponica*, Vol. 39, 1984, and as a much abbreviated Research Report in *Transactions of the International Conference of Orientalists in Japan*, No. 33, 1988; in Japanese as 'Kindai Nihon to shintairiku Ōsutoraria' in Shimizu Hajime, ed., *Ryō tai senkanki Hihon-Tōnanajia kankei no shosō*, (Ajia Keizai Kenkyūjo, 1986).

I am particularly indebted to Professor Miwa Kimitada, former Director of the Institute of International Relations, Sophia University, Tokyo, for his unfailing patience and his constant encouragement to break new ground by clarifying the history of Japan's historical relations in the Pacific with its closest continental neighbour, Australia. I would also like to express my deep gratitude to the late Tokyo Professor Emeritus Iwao Seiichi, and to thank in particular Dr Michael Cooper, editor of *Monumenta Nipponica*, and Dr Charlotte von Verschuer of the École Pratique des Hautes Études, Paris, for their invaluable instruction in pre-*sakoku* Japan. I have also benefitted immensely from the younger historians who have taken up the study of *nanshin-ron* and who gave generously of their knowledge—especially Senior Researcher of the Institute of Asian Economies, Shimizu Hajime, and Associate Professor Hatano Sumio of Tsukuba University. Further thanks go to Professor Unno Kazutaka, Osaka University; Assistant Professor Lin Tong-yang of Tunghai University in Taichung, Taiwan; and Ms Suzuki Junko of the Geography Room of the Diet Library, Tokyo, for their precious guidance in Oriental geography before and during the Tokugawa period.

For their kind help and many salutary comments received at various stages of my research, I warmly thank Professor Royama Michio of Sophia University; Professor Mark Peattie of the University of Massachusetts; Professor John J. Stephan of the University of Hawaii; Dr Peter Drysdale, Director of the Australia–Japan Research Centre, Australian National University, Canberra; Professor Hirano Ken'ichirō of Tokyo University; Professor Shiozaki Hiroaki of Junshin Women's College, Nagasaki; Professor Miyake Masaki of Meiji University; Associate Professors Takahashi Hisashi and Akagi Kanji, and Captain Hirama Yōichi of the National Institute for Defense Studies, Tokyo; Colonel Tazaki Hideyuki; and fellow historians Tokito Hideto, Kurosawa Fumitaka, and Ito Masanori, all formerly of Sophia University, who guided me in penetrating Japanese history and the Japanese language.

I am most grateful for the invaluable information gained in interviews with Professor Okakura Koshirō of Daitō Bunka University, Tokyo; Professor Tsurumi Kazuko of Sophia University; Professor Mizuno Suzuhiko of Chūkyo University, Nagoya; former Major Yamamoto Masayoshi in Kyūshū; and former Commander Sanagi Sadamu in Tokyo. The combined efforts of these scholars and direct participants in history have assisted me in completing the work and avoiding many mistakes, but I remain responsible, of course, for all its inadequacies. My special thanks go to my friend Dr E. Bruce Reynolds of San Jose University, who improved the manuscript with stimulating scholia as a consistently valuable critic; to my compatriot Professor Thomas Immoos of Sophia University, who made my long stay in Japan possible by kindly standing surety at the immigration office for me and my family; and to my wife Chun-fang, for her humour and patience, and for giving countless hours of her time to processing the manuscript.

Glossary of Japanese Terms

adakebune 安宅船 feudal warships.

A-Gō kyōeiken 亜豪共栄圏 Asia–Australia Co-Prosperity Sphere.

Azuchi-Momoyama period 安土・桃山時代 (1573–1603).

bakufu 幕府 (Tokugawa) shogunate (1603–1867).

bushi 武士 warrior, knight, soldier.

Daitōa kyōeiken 大東亜共栄圏 Greater East Asia Co-Prosperity Sphere, a Japanese grand policy for the Asia–Western Pacific region in the early 1940s.

Gō-A chichūkai 豪亜地中海 Australasiatic Mediterranean; a late 1930s term to denote the region that connected the Asian mainland with Australia.

gozabune 御座船 feudal warships converted into ornamental state boats after the issuing of the seclusion policy in the seventeenth century.

hakkō-ichi-u 八紘一宇 the eight corners of the world under one (Japanese) roof; the entire world as one family.

hokushin-ron 北進論 the 'advance in the north' school of thought.

hokushu nanshin 北守南進 defence in the north and advance in the south.

Kaigun seisaku oyobi seido kenkyū chōsa iinkai 海軍政策及び制度研究調査委員会 First Committee, established in March 1936 to formulate 'the empire's national policy and to speed up concrete plans for southern development'.

Kamakura period 鎌倉 (1185–1333).

katakana 片仮名 the square Japanese syllabary.

kōdō shugi 皇道主義 the Imperial Way doctrine.

Kokusaku no kijun 国策の基準 'Fundamentals of National Policy' approved on 7 August 1936 by the Five Ministers' Conference, 'to develop nationally and economically, *vis-à-vis* the southern area'.

kyōnichibyō 恐日病 'fear of Japan' illness.

Meiji period 明治 (1868–1912).

Muromachi period 室町 (1336–1578).

nanban 南蛮 the South; a loan word from China where it signified 'those who live outside the southern periphery of China'. In Japan it came to mean all those living on the southern fringes outside Japan, i.e., mainly the Southeast Asian region.

nanboku heishin ron 南北併進論 the 'simultaneous southward and northward advance' school of thought.

Nankō 南興 the Nan'yō Kōhatsu Kabushiki Kaisha 南洋興発株式会社 South Seas Development Company.

nanpō 南方 'southern region', which in the late 1930s could include any region south of Japan between Africa and South America.

nanshin 南進 southward advance.

nanshin-ron 南進論 the 'southward advance' school of thought.

nanshinron-sha 南進論者 Japanese 'southward-ho!' protagonists.

nanshu hokushin 南守北進 defence in the south and advance in the north

nan'yō 南洋 the South Seas.

Nan'yō Bōeki Kaisha 南洋貿易会社 South Seas Trading Company.

Nan'yō chō 南洋庁 government bureau, seated in Palau, that administered Japan's mandate territories from 1922 to 1945.

Nihon machi 日本町 Japanese settlements in the Western Pacific region until the mid-seventeenth century.

rangakusha 蘭学者 Dutch scholars, Dutch learning.

sakoku 鎖国 period of national isolation (1639–1853).

samurai 侍 warrior.

sankin kōtai 参勤交代 system of 'alternate attendance'.

seikatsuken 生活圏 living space.

Showa period 昭和 (1925–1989).

shuinjō 朱印状 'red-seal' permits, personal letters to the governments of those countries with whom the Japanese were trading in Southeast Asia.

shuinsen 朱印船 'red-seal' ships in the sixteenth and early seventeenth centuries.

sōtokufu 台湾総督府 naval governorship on Taiwan.

soto nan'yō 外南洋 'outer' South Seas, a geographical concept standing largely for the Southeast Asian region during the inter-war period.

Tai nan'yō hōsaku kenkyū iinkai　対南洋方策研究委員会　Policy Study Committee for the South Seas Area, or Tainanken　対南研　for short, established in July 1935.

Taishō period　大正　(1912–1926).

Teikoku gaikō hōshin　帝国外交方針　'Guidelines of Imperial Diplomacy' which defined the South Seas area as 'indispensable for industrial development and defence' at the Four Ministers' Conference, 7 August 1936.

Teikoku kokubō hōshin 帝国国防方針 Imperial National Defense Policy.

tōyō　東洋　eastern region.

uchi nan'yō　内南洋　'inner' South Seas; it spread from Taiwan in the South China Sea to the Marshalls, Marianas and Carolines in the Central Pacific.

wakō　倭寇　pirates.

yume monogatari　夢物語　'dream stories', a literary form that veiled direct criticism of the government.

A NOTE ON JAPANESE NAMES

The Japanese custom of giving the surname before the personal name has been followed throughout: for example, in Shiga Shigetaka, Shiga is the surname.

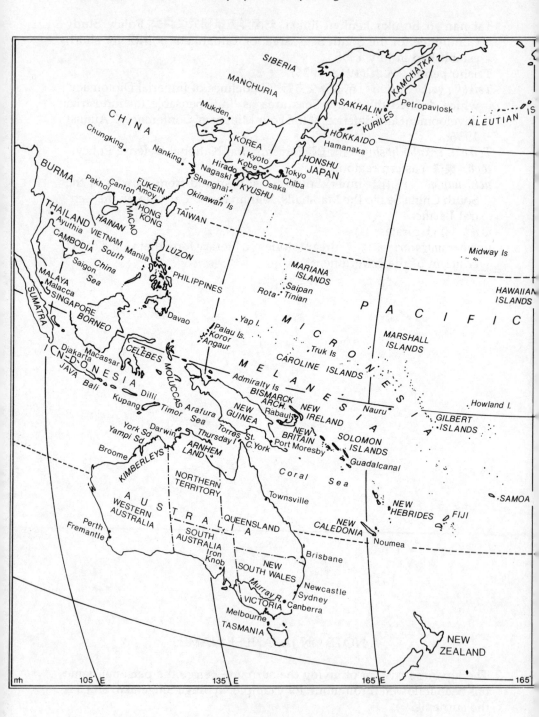

Map of the Pacific Region

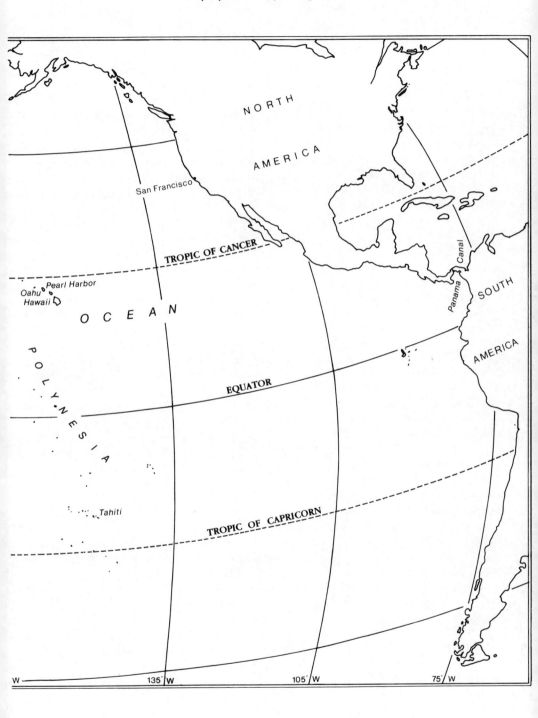

Introduction

IN JANUARY 1935, a small number of Japanese officers and bureaucrats gathered to discuss Japan's future policy in the South. From the middle-ranking echelons of the army, navy, and foreign ministry, they formed the 'Club of 1935' with the intention to sound out Japanese military and government circles about adopting a more forceful policy towards the Western colonial empires south of Japan. Their probing talks were not without effect. In June the following year, the Japanese navy successfully had the national defence plan (Teikoku kokubō hōshin) changed, targeting for the first time as a potential enemy the British Empire with its large colonial holdings in the South. Two months later the Japanese Government adopted a policy of 'southern advance' to step up Japanese emigration to southern countries and increase economic penetration of the southern region.

It was also in 1935 that E. L. Piesse drew Australian attention to the numerous Japanese books on expansion and control of the *nan'yō*. In a tract published under the assumed name of 'Albatross', the former director of Australia's military intelligence warned: 'In Japan the countries to the south are grouped under the name "Nan-Yo", the "South Seas". Nan-Yo covers the islands of the central Pacific [also Malaya and Indonesia] and sometimes Australia'. With regard to the Japanese navy's ominous presence in the Pacific, Piesse wrote: 'How far . . . views of annexation of Australia prevail in the Japanese Navy it is impossible to know . . . There may be plans or there may be none. If there are, we may at least say that they can be connected with ideas that have long been prevalent in Japan'.

Piesse was then one of Australia's most knowledgeable men about Japan. And his suspicion of that rising power was symptomatic of Australian distrust of Japan not only for that particular decade but for half a century. Australian uneasiness, in fact, reached back to Japan's victory over China in 1895; in the following year, Japan was made the major target of an Australian immigration restriction bill which extended to all coloured races. After Japan's second surprising victory, over Russia, Australians founded a league for national defence in 1906. It was an organization which favoured compulsory military training, with consequences that soon were to touch every Australian household. It would be wrong to argue that fear of Japan was the only factor determining the evolution of Australian defence policy and foreign political *Weltanschauung* in the first half of the twentieth century. But Australian scholars have pointed out the important Japanese element in Australian federal decisions leading to the introduction of compulsory military service in 1911, the building of the Royal Australian Navy in the same year, and the establishment of an embryonic Australian foreign office in the form of the Pacific Branch Bureau which functioned from 1921 to 1923.

Australia's Japan syndrome extended its influence into the realm of international politics. The most notable impact was in 1919 at the Paris Peace Conference when Australian Prime Minister William M. Hughes successfully defeated Japan's insertion of a racial equality clause in the preamble of the League of Nations. After Japan occupied Manchuria in 1931, Australia increasingly favoured appeasement of Japan. The Australian Government followed this policy throughout most of the decade and was instrumental in persuading Great Britain in 1940 to close temporarily the Burma Road as the Japanese wished. Australian attitudes towards Japan for over half a century are well known. Australian historian Neville Meaney has conveniently labelled the period 1905 to1941 as 'the Japanese phase' in the history of Australian foreign relations.

Much less well known are Japanese attitudes toward Australia. And considering the weight given the 'Japan threat' in Australian political opinion-making until the mid-twentieth century, it is somewhat surprising that Japanese strategic writings on the *nan'yō* were never seriously analysed in Australia with a view to evaluating the logic of Australia's fear toward Japan as a rising Pacific power. This study throws light on the subject by examining Japanese attitudes toward Australia in the 1930s leading up to the Pacific War, and by analysing the literature on Japan's southward advance. For the most effective way to find out about those attitudes was to analyse the indeed copious *nan'yō* literature mentioned by Piesse and to trace the story of Japan's southward advance with a view to ferreting from it any information pertaining to Australia.

This was a straightforward task for the well-documented years from 1936 to the early 1940s. Apostles such as Murobuse Kōshin with his propagandist work *Nanshinron* (Thoughts on southward advance), 1936, were then ushering in a boom-period of writings on the South. Australia, too, appeared increasingly as a topic in this literature, creating enough interest to generate scores of books on that country alone. Two months into the Pacific War, Australia's north, east, and northwest coasts were attacked by Japan, and apprehension of a northern invasion dominated Australian foreign policy and the public mind. It was in those early 1940s, when Australian fear of Japan reached a peak, that most Japanese books on Australia were published.

One must look carefully into that prolific literature. It would be easy to concoct a conspiracy theory to suggest that Japanese indeed had long wanted to encroach on Australian territory. All one need do is pick a stray sentence from Yoshida Shōin's writings about colonizing part of Australia in 1854, combine it with Japan-invasion stories that flourished on and off in Australia since the mid-1890s, add chauvinism from Australia-bashing books that appeared in the early stages of World War II, say by Madarame Fumio or Wada Shunji, mix in facts such as the Darwin raid, and spice it all with documents of early-1942 invasion discussions in the Navy General Staff led by firebrands such as Tomioka Sadatoshi, Nakahara 'King-of-the-South Seas' Yoshimasa, or Ishikawa Shingo. It would make a splendid plot, though one far from the truth.

To understand Japan's true intentions towards Australia it is necessary to enquire into the sum total of Japanese knowledge of the South that informed the southward advance school of thought. Why did the Japanese want to go out in the first place? On what dreams and aspirations was the 'go-south' wish founded? Unto which shores did their southern stars shine? Where was the aggregate of Japan's *nanshin-ron* or 'southward advance'? What visions fuelled the southern policy of the navy? Why did the navy at certain times support the status quo in the Pacific and not at others? Why did Japan have to build such a big navy? To do what with, and why?

In searching for the answers, we note that Japan's advance never proceeded south in isolation. It went hand-in-hand with Japan's 'northward advance' or *hokushin*, ever since the sixteenth century shogun Tokutomi Hideyoshi had conquered part of Korea while threatening the South (*Namban*); Japan's omnidirectional push was even more evident in modern history, when Japan made both northern and southern territorial gains in the Sino–Japanese War and the two ensuing World Wars.

That southern drama is a colourful spectacle to watch. Japanese navy interests took centre stage when the first training sloops begin to explore the Pacific in the 1870s, then again in the aftermath of World War I when navy commanders pointed out the necessity of southern bases for the Japanese navy in the central Pacific, and of course at the time of Pearl

Harbor. In another act it is all business, with erstwhile northern protagonist Inoue Tsuyoshi urging a southern advance with money in 1913, and later, in the mid-1930s, with sugar barons and rubber entrepreneurs in Southeast Asia and Micronesia stealing the show in the unfolding drama of the *nanshin* story. Waiting in the wings all the while are the *nanshin* ideologues, ready to take the stage for propaganda purposes whenever required to do so. They performed strongly in the second half of the 1930s, with Murobuse's clarion-call echoing an earlier *nanshin*-riser, Takekoshi Yosaburo. He had already made up the slogan 'Minami e! Minami e!' (To the South! To the South!) in his 1910 southern shocker *Nangokuki* that connected and led into a period of intense interest in the South just before and during World War I.

On whatever act the curtain rings down, the various actors invariably take their cues from the Meiji period (1868–1912). It was an interesting age, and not only because of ample material on early southward advance protagonists (*nanshin-ron sha*) such as Hattori Toru, Suganuma Teifu, or Shiga Shigetaka—the first batch of those who kindled the fire of modern *nanshin-ron*. More specifically, I came across early and abundant material that deals with Australia. Interestingly, Shiga, who emphatically calls the Australians his 'southern brothers' in his book *Nan'yō jiji* written in 1884, offers five chapters on Australia alone. Other early writers about Australia included Mishima Kazuo and Watanabe Kanjūrō. It was illuminating to sift their material and see how their perceptions of future Japan–Australia relations compared with what actually happened later. A hundred years of those relations confirmed their worst suspicions as much as they surpassed the Meiji men's brightest hopes.

But even in the Meiji period, where usually the thread in the history of Japan's southward advance is picked up, I could not be satisfied that from these protoypal southward-ho! protagonists could be derived a fair judgement of the southward advance school of thought and its implications for Australia. It was difficult to resist harking further back, if only to chase an interesting whiff of continuity which emanates from the yellowed pages of the late Tokugawa thinkers to settle itself more eloquently in an evolved form in the books of Meiji *nanshin-ron sha* two or three generations later. Ideas on the South found in the late Tokugawa works of Honda Toshiaki, Satō Nobuhiro, or Yoshida Shōin, for example, reappear in surprisingly similar form in the writings of Meiji *nanshin-ron sha* such as Yokoo Tōsaku, Sugiura Jūgo, or Suganuma Teifu.

It is curious to see how these late Tokugawa thinkers also displayed in their books a keen awareness of how Japanese in an earlier age had travelled in the South, traded there, and even settled down in the tropical regions. Honda Toshiaki, for example, tells with pride in 1798 of the Japanese ships which long ago used to ply the southern oceans to Vietnam, Cambodia, and beyond the Equator to the islands even further south; they speedily carried goods, were useful to their country, and were in no way inferior to the ships of the foreigners. That memory was also kept in songs, popular in the Tokugawa period and passed on through the ages; they tell of faraway southern lands, the Philippines and Cambodia, where once the Japanese roamed and played an active role.

It is no use pretending that odes to the *nan'yō* and to the glory of Japanese settlements remembered in songs by fishermen have any deeper meaning; and how much of the memory of the South was preserved during the Tokugawa period of isolation is a moot point. And yet it is revealing that, at the end of a long period of seclusion, Japanese people from simple fisher folk to intellectuals still retained an inkling of their forebears' activities in the South—and this despite the great discontinuity wrought by the long period of isolation.

Reaching back before Japan's period of self-imposed isolation, I discovered a country recovering from a century of internal feuds and making rapid progress in shipbuilding and navigation. I knew little of that period. But I came across Iwao Seiichi's engrossing works on early Japanese settlements and their sprightly 'Red Seal Ship' trade in what roughly constitutes today's ASEAN region. Between 1604 and 1635 an estimated 100,000 Japanese left their country to expand trade, and between 7,000 and 10,000 of them took up permanent residence in the numerous Japanese settlements then dotting Southeast Asian fringes of the Western Pacific. To neglect that age was to ignore an important basic element in the history of Japan's southward advance.

Japan's assertion in the Pacific in the twentieth century can better be understood in the light of the memory of her once bustling activities in the southern port towns of the Western Pacific in the late sixteenth and early seventeenth centuries. It is not that there is continuity in Japan's southward advance; the Tokugawa period signifies too great a break and invalidates any such tempting exercise in historical determinism. But I venture to say that observing Japan's earliest maritime and migratory experiences in the Western Pacific offers a telling simile with which to better comprehend the character and scope of Japan's advance at its later stage.

Earliest Connections,
before the 1630s

1

Japan in the Western Pacific

ISLANDERS ON Japan's southern ethnic fringes had already been advancing far into the Western Pacific at the advent of the Age of Discoveries. It is true that they did not contribute to the events that later gave that period its name. But it is well to remember that when Portugal's Prince Henry the Navigator (1394–1460), who stands at its beginning, was knighted at Ceuta on North African soil three hundred miles from home, the tiny island kingdom of Ryūkyū (Okinawan Islands) was regularly despatching diplomatic missions to Malacca three thousand miles away.

When the Portuguese 'discovered' Japan in the 1540s, that country was already actively engaged on the sea and expanding its presence in East and Southeast Asia, a process which lasted until 1635. Japan, by then, could look back on an eventful history of diplomatic, religious, and commercial relations that reached back to the first century. The Chinese records tell us about a Japanese envoy in the Chinese metropolis as early as 57 A.D., diplomatic visits to the Chinese governor in Korea (who resided near present-day Seoul) between 238 and 247, and embassies to the Chinese Sung court at Nanking 421–479. Then there were the formal diplomatic missions to China, the *Ken-Zui-shi* and *Ken-Tō-shi*, beginning with Ono no Imoko in 607, which for three hundred years involved considerable commercial, religious, and other cultural exchanges between the Asian mainland and Japan.

9

Furthermore, the annals tell us of early Japanese military contacts, particularly Japan's corner foothold on the Korean peninsula in Mimana from the late fourth until the mid-sixth century. Japanese of the mid-sixteenth century could even look back on the forerunner of an early seclusion policy. Enacted tamely under the Engi government (900–922), it petered out in the mid-eleventh century under the influence of Taira no Kiyomori (1118–1181), with his keen eye for the importance of seaborne trade. In the ensuing four centuries, a lively and direct commerce sprang up between Kamakura and Muromachi Japan and Sung, Yuan, and Ming China. It is in the first hundred years of this period, from the mid-eleventh to the mid-twelfth centuries, that the Japanese historian, Mori Katsumi, has pinpointed an incisive stage in the process of Japan's familiarization with the seas around her. In the intervention of those years, the Japanese idea of the sea underwent a great transformation and 'the advance of Japanese ships abroad may be said to have started'.

The appearance of the Japanese pirate or *wakō* further contributed to the transformation of the Japanese idea of the sea. East Asian pirates are mentioned in Japanese records as early as the eighth and ninth centuries. When in the twelfth century Japanese merchant ships were increasingly drawn into the domestic disturbances in Korea, Japanese ships equipped with arms began to appear in larger numbers. In the 1220s, the so-called *Matsuura-tō* (i.e. drop-outs and small landlords in Western Kyūshū and from the island of Tsushima) appeared as the first organized pirates to threaten the Korean coast. Later, in the mid-fourteenth century, the Japanese gained notoriety as pirates up and down the coasts of eastern Asia. Soon they ventured as far as the Malay Archipelago, to Vietnam, Cambodia, and the southeastern islands of the Philippines, Borneo, and Bali. By the end of the sixteenth century few harbours remained in Southeast Asia that they had not visited.

The Japanese crews of these marauding vessels have been compared with the freebooting bluejackets of Francis Drake and John Hawkins, glorified a century later in the Elizabethan Age. Their depredations reached a high point in the mid-sixteenth century when their raids became actual invasions. Pirates set upon inland cities in Chekiang, went up the Yangtze sacking towns on both shores, or attacked Hangchow and went overland to menace Nanking. By that time, however, *wakō* crews consisted in large part of Chinese; and Japanese harassment of the South China coast declined drastically with the political reunification of Japan in the late sixteenth century. But it is unnecessary to dwell on this issue. The important point is that certain Japanese were venturing deep into the Western Pacific and contributing to the expansion of the Japanese world-view.

More significant still is the transfer of technology that probably took place via the *wakō*. According to Mori, they contacted Chinese pirates in the coastal province of Fukien and bought foreign ships. These were remodelled into 'double deckers' and their bottoms tapered so that they cut through water well. They were, moreover, equipped with compass, which made them less dependent on wind direction. The innovating activities of these picaroons during the thirteenth to the sixteenth centuries thereby also helped improve Japanese ship-building and navigational skills.

For to all outward appearances, Japanese ship construction had lain idle during the first millenium. Japan's valiant embassies to Tang China had sailed on boats fashioned after the Korean ships, the *kudarasen*; with hulls fragile, masts insecure, and their bottoms flat, they made the journey to China extremely hazardous and long. The long period of prohibition from going abroad in the tenth century had further retarded Japanese naval development. The outlaw-contacts mentioned above, and even more significantly Japan's increasingly close contacts with Sung traders in the eleventh and twelfth centuries, were now finally wakening Japan from her naval stagnation.

These Chinese traders owed much of their advanced naval arts to Arabian merchants who had been arriving in China since the sixth and seventh centuries. By the ninth century Mohammedans had established a sizeable community of around 100,000 in Canton. Learning their ship techniques, the Chinese used hemp or tung oil for caulking (instead of the plant *tansuisō* used by the Japanese) and erected five different masts to take advantage of tail and cross winds. They also knew how to use the seasonal winds, how to sail by the sun during the day, by the stars at night, and even under an overcast night-sky with the use of a compass, called 'south pointing needle' (*shinanbari*). Where it had often taken the Japanese more than one month to cross the East China Sea, Sung traders covered the same distance in three to eight days.

The adoption of Chinese methods swiftly improved Japanese navigation, and the revolutionary use of nails in the Muromachi period greatly enhanced ship construction. From around 1401 to 1547, Japan sent seventeen embassies to China in ships that came to be known as *kenminsen*. These could carry from 150 to 200 men and had a cargo capacity described in contemporary sources as ranging from 500 to 2,500 *koku* (approximately 49–246 tons); they appear in pictures as decked two-masters with cabins and matted square sails. Later, in the sixteenth and seventeenth centuries, when the large ocean-going *shuinsen* (vermillion seal ship) appeared, the bamboo leaf sail gave way to the European-style square rigged cloth sail. And with the expansion of a lively overseas trade with southern countries under Portuguese, Spanish, and Dutch tutelage, Japanese shipbuilding techniques characteristically combined the shape of the Chinese junk with that of the Western caravel. The Japanese also started to use the European navigation system. Under Oda Nobunaga (1533–1582) they moreover experimented with novelties such as armour-plated battleships, and in the early seventeenth century built two English-style ships of around 80 and 120 gross tons under the direction of Will Adams.

During the Muromachi period, more information about foreign countries reached the Japanese in the course of their trading with Ming China, raising further a lively interest in the regions to their south. Long before the introduction of Portuguese atlases reshaped the narrow Japanese world view, the monk Bussho Zenji (the founder of the Ritsukyokuan monastery in Tōfukuji) returned in 1279 with an unusually comprehensive regional world map. It depicted China in the center, India in the west, Manchuria and Korea in the north, Japan in the east, and Champa (the eastern parts of Sumatra) and Java in the south. Ships from Java and Sumatra (with an elephant from Palembang for the 'Japanese King') were now also arriving at the province of Wakasa in 1408 and 1412, at Tomaritsu (near Kagoshima) in 1419, and elsewhere on the coasts of Kyūshū; and a growing number of traders from the Ryūkyūs and the 'South' were sojourning in southern Japanese port cities such as Hakata and Sakai, stimulating curiosity about foreign lands.

As a result of such contacts, a new geographical term *nanban* (the South) was added to the traditional Japanese idea of the world hitherto restricted to Nippon, Kara (China), and Tenjiku (India). A loan word from China, *nanban* signified 'those who live outside the southern periphery of China'. In Japan it came to mean all those living on the southern fringes outside Japan, i.e., mainly the Southeast Asian region. Interestingly, it included the early Europeans—the Portuguese and the Spaniards—who came to Japan in the sixteenth century, since they arrived from their southern trading posts in Macao, or the Philippines.

Something akin to the roving Iberian spirit was certainly manifest in the Japanese between the mid-sixteenth and early seventeenth centuries, when their history registers an unmistakably expansive mood. For example, Toyotomi Hideyoshi, who launched military campaigns in Korea in 1592 and 1597, was also attracted by the south or *nanban*. Declared he in 1586 and 1592: 'Not only Ming [China], but Tenjiku and Nanban, too, must be conquered at the same time'. In a comparative study of European and Japanese history of the period, moreover, the sociologist Katō Hidetoshi sees basically the same drive for colonial spoils at work in the European eastern advance as in Japan's southern advance, both converging upon the Southeast Asian region. He argues that world history might have taken a different course had British–Japanese or Dutch–Japanese naval battles been fought in the South China Sea or in the Indian Ocean already in that era (predating the Pacific War by four hundred years). While Katō's views are based on conjecture, it is a fact that in the early seventeenth century a significant number of Japanese were drifting south and rubbing elbows with the Europeans in what today constitutes the ASEAN region.

Several reasons explain Japan's increased interest and presence in the Western Pacific. With the coming of the Europeans to Asia in the mid-sixteenth century, Japan's trade, hitherto restricted to East Asian waters, began now to assume a world-wide character, with imports reaching her from various parts of Southeast Asia, India, Persia, and Europe. The drawn-out civil disturbances that had marked the Muromachi period were just then being brought to an end by strong leadership that led toward the reunification of Japan. And as order was being restored, the growth of towns was giving birth to a new class of merchants who invested their money in profitable foreign trade. Some of this trade supplied goods which began to be consumed on a large scale by a people adapting to peacetime luxuries.

Silk was being imported in vastly greater amounts. Silk fabrics were then an important part of the ceremonial clothing of the feudal lords and raw silk had become an indispensable asset in the feudal economy. A textile industry for high quality fabrics had developed in Kyoto in the fifteenth century. Aspiring to meet the more discriminating demands of the citizens in the Momoyama period (1568–1603), it expanded to Sakai and Hakata at the end of the fifteenth century, when kimonos changed from simple to elaborate and splendid styles. Unable to satisfy this demand with domestically produced high grade silk, the industry had become greatly dependent on raw silk imported from China. When Ming China, due to the *wakō* raids, ended her relations with Japan in 1547, Japanese traders were compelled to pursue their silk purchases secretly from the Chinese at ports in Formosa, the Philippines, and the Indo-chinese peninsula. Alternatively, they bought Vietnamese, Bengali, and Persian raw silk as substitutes at Southeast Asian ports, thereby further stimulating the development of Japanese trading activities in the Western Pacific.

This silk was being paid for in silver. Gold and silver had been impor-tant for military spending by feudal lords or as gifts for their retainers during the civil disturbances. With this currency a greatly coveted item, the daimyos now turned to greater exploitation of their silver and gold mines. More than fifty gold mines and thirty silver mines were developed in the second half of the sixteenth century. The amount of silver that the Japanese began to pour into foreign trade was stupendous. Europe lacked and badly needed precious metals for her development, and Thomas Muns was promoting the free trade of gold and silver in his work on *British Wealth Through Foreign Trade* (1664). It is estimated that from 1615 to 1625 Japan supplied the world with silver exports amounting to 130,000–160,000 kilograms, the equivalent of 30 to 40 per cent of total world silver production. No wonder Japanese trade was much sought after by European merchants in the Asia–Pacific region.

If Japanese could now increasingly be found travelling and also living abroad, this was due to the adoption of a distinctively outgoing official government policy established in the early years of the seventeenth century. After the decisive battle of Sekigahara (1600) when Tokugawa Ieyasu consolidated his power, he was eager to establish friendly relations with all countries and make Japan the greatest commercial center in Asia. He openly encouraged Japanese traders to sail into the world, develop commerce, and establish settlements to that end. For the international protection of their ships (*shuinsen*), he instituted in 1602 the system of *shuinjō* (red-seal permits), which were personal letters to the governments of those countries with whom the Japanese were trading in Southeast Asia.

Japanese foreign trade thereby expanded rapidly in the early seventeenth century. Detailed studies reveal that between 1604 and 1635, 356 Japanese merchant ships set sail under that system. In some years as many as thirty ships sailed from Japan to foreign countries, calling at some nineteen ports from Formosa to Indochina and the Malay islands, visiting the main economic and political centers of the region in Siam, Annam (Vietnam), Java, Sumatra, the Philippines, Cambodia, Borneo, and Macao. It is true that this growth took place in the shadow of the activities of European merchant vessels, estimated then, perhaps generously, at 25,000 by the French mercantilist Jean Baptiste Colbert in 1650. But Japan's reaching out in the early seventeenth century nevertheless marks a significant period in Japanese overseas affairs; one that is often overlooked in Western historiography, mainly because it was so short-lived.

Japanese not only sailed south into the Western Pacific, they also began to reside abroad and settle down. The Japanese historian, Iwao Seiichi, has done careful studies on the *Nihonmachi*, or 'Japanese cities, camps, colonies, or quarters' as these settlements came to be called in the European writings of the seventeenth century. The principal settlements were located in Dilao and San Miguel (now part of Manila) on the Philippine main island of Luzon, at Faifo and Tourane (now Da Nang) in middle Vietnam, Pinhalu and Phnom Penh in Cambodia, and in the suburbs of the Siamese capital of Ayuthia; others thrived in Tainan on Formosa, Batavia (Djakarta), and Macao. Situated near major ports or capitals, their administration was generally autonomous or semi-autonomous. These Japanese towns enjoyed particular prosperity in the years from 1615 to 1625.

The Japanese who populated the *Nihonmachi* were mostly men, but women went abroad, too, and often entire families settled down in some foreign port. Around 100,000 people may have left Japan between 1604 and 1635, usually for business purposes.

Most of them returned to Japan, such as the trader Sumiya Shichirōbei. His extremely detailed and advanced regional map, which he used on his travels and is still preserved, depicts in masterful fashion the entire Western Pacific region, including Japan, China, Annam, Luzon, Siam,

Cochin China (Indochina), Borneo, Malacca, and the Indonesian isles as far as Macassar. It has all the places that Sumiya visited carefully marked with needle holes from Kyūshū to Annam.

However, between 7,000 and 10,000 people are estimated to have taken up permanent foreign domicile. One such man was Wada Rinzaemon, a famous merchant, and active particularly in the 1650s between Japan, the Philippines, and Tonkin in Vietnam, where he resided permanently. Another reputed businessman of that age was Naya 'Luzon' Sukezaemon, who established himself in Luzon in 1593. He is known to have sold luxury articles from the Philippines to Toyotomi Hideyoshi, who put the items on display in Osaka. In 1607, Naya sailed to Cambodia, where he helped the Japanese community establish a burgeoning link with Japan, and lived out his life.

Other emigrants were fallen samurai, who after the battle of Sekigahara and the Tokugawa conquest of Osaka Castle took up the meandering life of the masterless warrior (*rōnin*). Showing up in the streets of the *Nihonmachi*, sword in belt, many of them became mercenaries who fought in the services of the Dutch, Portuguese, Spanish, and Southeast Asian kingdoms. The best known adventurer of this epoch, though probably no samurai, was Yamada Nagamasa. Born in Shizuoka, he went to Siam in 1611, where in the capital of Ayuthia there was already a sizable Japanese quarter. He soon became the head of its community and is said to have sent his merchant vessels as far as Malacca and Batavia; he also sent gifts there and letters to the Dutch Governor-General Jan Pieterszoon Coen in Batavia. He distinguished himself in the army of the Thai king, who bestowed on him the official rank of chief of the military forces and governor of the southern provinces. After the king's death, Yamada became involved in court intrigues and perished at the hands of his enemies in 1630. His life was indeed extraordinary and inspired later generations to see in him the prototype of a 'southern hero', fit for emulation whenever Japanese renewed their interest in the Western Pacific between the early Meiji period and the eve of the Pacific War.

Yet the average Japanese who went out and settled abroad in the early seventeenth century fall into more ordinary categories. Iwao Seiichi gives an interesting glimpse of the common lifestyles that Japanese settlers led, for example, in Batavia. Home to the government-general in the Dutch East Indies, this Dutch capital enjoyed close trade relations with Hirado and Nagasaki. From 1613 onward, the Dutch also regularly began to reinforce their labour and military forces with shipments of emigrants each year from these Japanese port towns. At first the Japanese settlers were mainly employed fighting in the Dutch army in various regions, or working as sailors on board Dutch vessels, or were hired by individuals in cottage industries. But once they had retirement payment and savings in hand, most of them stayed on. Many found suitable occupations. Some bought Crown land in the urban areas for various profit-making purposes. The notarial deeds related to Japanese emigrants—preserved and today still kept at the archives in Djakarta—testify to the kind of elevated lifestyles many of them were commanding. Iwao found 309 notarial cases which deal with agreements concerning purchases, sales; and leases of land and houses; agreements concerning loans and slave trade; and various documents regarding suits, some criminal cases, testimonies, liberation of slaves, and wills.

These legal documents are an invaluable indicator of the kind of life that the Japanese adapted to in their new surroundings. The tabulated data on Japanese marriages, mostly interracial, is revealing. Most tied the knot between 1637 and 1646. Those ten years coincide with the enforcement of the national seclusion policy, which compelled the unmarried Japanese on Java to give up hope of returning to Japan. Most stayed on and married. Other documents linked to Japanese concern money-lending, bondmen, inheritances, and land contracts—not only of home lots but also of subcontract agreements, farms, forests, and orchards. All testify to an increasingly complex lifestyle some Japanese were becoming accustomed to abroad.

As a small number of Japanese were approaching an international lifestyle, it is interesting to reflect on the kind of influence they might have had on their country had this period of international intercourse been permitted to continue. For one thing, those Japanese who left their country in the early seventeenth century were not the acrobats, prostitutes, pearlers, and showtroupers that left Japan at the lifting of the seclusion policy in the mid-nineteenth century. Rather, they were from respectable social classes: merchants and entrepreneurs with capital, craftsmen, and disbanded soldiers of the samurai class. If this small but vigorous and enterprising sector of Japanese had been allowed to continuously move out and become cosmopolitan in the port towns and marketplaces of Vietnam, Siam, or the Philippines, their intermingling with Chinese, Filipinos, Malay, and other Asian races, as well as with Europeans, might have had a considerable, and salubrious, impact at home. The Japanese *Volksgeist* would surely have recognized more readily their unexceptional membership as one link in a world made up of different peoples. One can also surmise that Japanese might have learned more easily to understand better the Judaeo–Christian mind and the motivations which caused Europeans to go out and build colonial empires. Had the Japanese continued to give their outpouring of energies into foreign lands a free rein, as the Europeans were then doing, Japan might have drawn even with the Western powers at a more natural pace, and the hasty 'catch up' expansion which occurred after the Meiji Restoration would have been unnecessary.

At any rate, one can assume that between 1610 and the 1630s a growing number of Japanese were learning rapidly about 'international society'. And could it not have been that the Japanese might have begun to learn in the 1630s what they imported with alacrity only in the 1860s? For example, many Japanese emigrants were already then being fully exposed to the Western legal mind in places such as Batavia. Through this sort of cultural–official exchange, something of Grotius and the spirit of international law might have filtered back and fallen on fertile soil in Japan. A Dutch jurist in the service of the United East India Company of Holland, Hugo Grotius, was just then completing his main work *De jure belli ac pacis* (1625). It was precisely his company's experience in South-east Asia that taught him how Dutch administrators in the Netherlands East Indies were disregarding the rights of native rulers. This motivated his widely acclaimed treatise on extending the rule of law to benefit all peoples, without distinction of race or creed. It is conceivable that an increasing number of Japanese well-placed in Dutch colonial society might have learned through his writings about the European way of thinking and the legal problems of international relationships. Had Japan remained an open country, it is possible that through them some of the European *Weltanschauung* might have been transmitted back to Japan and influenced the adaptable Japanese mind bent on competing with the European powers in the Western Pacific waters.

But to ponder how the Japanese would have responded to the idea of international society existing as a legal community governed by a law described as 'the law of nature or the law of peoples' remains an exercise of the mind. Japan turned her back on such a revolutionary concept just as it was beginning to provide the framework for the Western world view. In 1633 the shogunal provisions strictly forbade any vessel to leave Japan for a foreign country without a valid licence; and those Japanese living abroad were threatened with the death penalty if they returned. In 1635, Japanese ships were prohibited from making voyages abroad and the death penalty was prescribed for Japanese subjects if they left the country. The final maritime prohibition (*kaikin*) issued in 1639 disallowed all foreign intercourse; except with Chinese and Dutch ships through Dejima, the tiny artificial island port at Nagasaki.

Japan's seclusion was now fully implemented. It ushered in a unique period that affected not only Japanese, but world history. The Japanese diaspora were gradually assimilated, the last Japanese marriage in Batavia being registered in 1659, and all the Japanese quarters, colonies, and settlements fell into total oblivion. The once strong and active Japanese presence in the Western Pacific region was forgotten to the extent that it would appear after two-and-a-half centuries as if the Japanese had never sailed out and settled abroad. Ostensibly, Meiji history was destined to start at the year zero as far as foreign affairs were concerned.

Why did the Japanese enforce the near-total seclusion of their country and thereby throttle a period of promising intercourse? Three reasons stand out in the ongoing discussion: to forestall the influence of Christianity; strong pressure exerted by profit-seeking Japanese silk monopolists who, under the expanding influence of the so-called *ito wappu*-system, advised Tokugawa Ieyasu to stop Japanese vessels from carrying trade from abroad; and the influence of the Dutch, who wanted to counter Portuguese trade competition by accusing Portuguese priests and mariners of wanting to impinge upon Japanese territoriality.

But this is not the place to examine the reasons behind the *sakoku* policy. Our aim here has been to provide a background for the main body of this study which deals with Japan's southern advance and the Australian response in the nineteenth and twentieth centuries. It is well to remember the Japanese three-masters that once criss-crossed the Western Pacific before the closing of their country. For it appears that historians have lost sight of a significant brief time-span in the overall evaluation of Japan's southern involvement. The occasional entry on Japan's southern advance in Japanese historical dictionaries and lexicons often tells only about its official movement from 1936 onwards. A few book-length Japanese and Western studies do deal with the history of Japanese southern involvement from the beginning of the Meiji period in 1868 onward. These are essential reading for a deeper understanding of the historical process of the rise of Japan in the Pacific in the twentieth century and concomitant European decline. But it is useful to look at the process of Japan's southward advance from an even longer perspective, encompassing pre-*sakoku* times. Just as Greece did not disappear from the earth when Rome became the center of historical narrative, neither did Japan vanish when the European powers started to take over the Pacific between the seventeenth and nineteenth centuries. It is well to bear in mind that Japan's interest in the Pacific did not start with the Meiji period, but has a legacy that reaches further back.

2

Geographical Notions of Australia

DESPITE THE wide-ranging activities of early Japanese traders, the Australian continent did not figure in their early regional world-maps. From ancient to medieval times, the Japanese concept of world geography limited itself strictly to Asia, and the depiction of India, China, and Japan adhered to a Buddhist-oriented 'Three Country' view of the world. These earliest Oriental notions of the world reflected none of the Western, Aristotelian theories that there had to be land in the south to act as a counterweight to the Eurasian landmass in the north.

It was only after Japan's first direct contacts with the West, with the arrival of the Portuguese in the 1540s, that traces of a southern continent can be discerned in Japanese cartography. The maps and globes brought to Japan by Portuguese traders and missionaries in the late sixteenth century greatly expanded the Japanese world-view. They taught a people eager to learn the spherical nature of the earth with its four great continental landmasses (North and South America, Eurasia, and Africa). In addition, they had inscribed a fifth, somewhat mysterious-looking mass of land encircling the lower part of the globe, barely separated from the southern tips of the African and South American continent. Locked inside this hardly known southern landmass lay the Australian continent with its northernmost contours already visible; for although the South-land was drawn differently on each map, parts of its outline remained

19

fixed. Without too much imagination, we can recognize these as the prototypal shapes of Northern Australia's Arnhem Land, the Gulf of Carpentaria, and New Guinea protruding out of the southern mass of land. Between the mid-sixteenth and mid-seventeenth centuries, the Australian continent presented itself to the Japanese mind for the first time in this hazy outline.

The second stage is characterized by the influence of Matteo Ricci's Mappa Mundi, which dominated much of Japanese cartography until the nineteenth century. In 1602, by order of his employer the Chinese court, the Jesuit missionary drew, for China, a revolutionary new map, the *K'un-yū wan-kuo ch'uan-t'u* (The complete map of the world). Based on reports of Italian and Portuguese voyages to different parts of the world, Ricci's map was widely esteemed for its accuracy and scientific exposition, and copies of it were sent from Nanking to various parts of China, to Macao and, almost immediately, to Japan. As this map was transmitted to Japan mainly for scholarly purposes and was written in the familiar Chinese script, it reached a wider audience of Japanese intellectuals and cartographers than did the contemporary world-maps from Portugal, Spain, and Holland, which were either gifts for the shogun or passed into the hands of unappreciative shogunal officials.

The influence of Ricci's map of the world was, accordingly, more penetrating and lasting. It served as an important basis for the making of Japan's first printed world-map in 1645, which, meant for popular education, had all place names spelled in the easily readable square Japanese syllabary (*katakana*). In this new world-map, the Southland, or 'Magellanica', still extended around the entire lower part of the globe, not far below the Tropic of Capricorn. But its shape was now drawn with greater consistency, almost as an even strip of land: except for three or four major protrusions in the places where there was now definite geographical evidence concerning the Australian continent.

These protrusions were repeated on every Ricci-type map, almost to the point of stylization. Jutting out of the Southland was the shoulder of Western Australia, which, to the east, fell abruptly into the overdrawn shape of the Gulf of Carpentaria. Further east, the gulf's eastern coastline swung upward almost to the equator to form the west coast of New Guinea, which in its square peninsular-form, remained grafted on to another, much larger block—the northeastern promontory of Australia. This extended eastward, far into the South Pacific, before its eastern coastline dropped down sharply below the Tropic of Capricorn, to rejoin the Southland's even line around the globe. Into what is Arnhem Land today, Ricci wrote: 'Recently a boat from Castilla, driven by storms, reached this land. It is said to be immense and to produce nothing'.

The Ricci-style maps were copied well into modern times, freezing for two centuries popular Japanese notions about the world's southernmost regions. The version of Nagakubo Sekisui is best known and it went through several editions. Drawn around 1788, the year when the first British settlers were already taking possession of the Australian continent at Sydney Cove, Nagakubo's map came to represent the geographical concept of Australia and the world in the popular imagination until the end of the Tokugawa period.

In a partly parallel third stage, however, the Japanese were also beginning to learn about Australia's shape from other, more scientific world-maps introduced by the Dutch between the late seventeenth and early nineteenth centuries. Most of Australia's north, west, and south coasts had by then been explored by the Dutch East India Company's servants. These valiant men charted accurately two-thirds of the Australian coast line between 1606, when Willem Jansz made the first authenticated landing in Australia in the Gulf of Carpentaria, and 1643–1644, when Abel Tasman sailed along the coasts of west and south Australia as far as Tasmania and even New Zealand. Dutch mapping of Australia took place just at the time when Japan was closing her doors to all Westerners except the Dutch. They were the only Westerners allowed to trade at Nagasaki during the following two hundred years. Therefore, when François Caron, the head of the trading station at Nagasaki, provided the shogun Tokugawa Iemitsu with maps and globes in the early 1640s, the Dutch were the most qualified to teach Japan about Australia. For almost two centuries their influence predominated in the advanced sections of Japanese cartography, although Ricci-style and Buddhist-oriented world-maps continued to be produced.

For about a hundred years, however, Dutch geographical enlightenment remained the privilege of comparatively few Japanese. The Japanese seclusionist policy prevented the widespread dissemination of outside knowledge among the ordinary people. Only after 1720, when the shogun Tokugawa Yoshimune began to encourage the importation of Western scientific learning, did Dutch geographical knowledge come within the reach of the average educated Japanese.

Scholars versed in the Dutch language, the *rangakusha*, now began to translate and popularize Dutch cartographical material, especially in the last quarter of the eighteenth century. The new geographical perspective that they were then copying from Dutch world-maps was originally derived from the master map of Joan Blaeu, 1596–1673, as drawn in Amsterdam around 1640 and amended by Nikolaus Visscher in 1678. That map had left little of the Ricci-style Southland. 'Magellanica' had vanished down into the polar spheres. In its stead, about two-thirds of Australia stood faithfully revealed as constituting a huge island continent in the South Pacific. This more accurate depiction of Australia became a hallmark of world-maps drawn by the scientifically oriented Tokugawa scholars, and was copied well into the nineteenth century.

Some of the confusion about what to make of the various renditions of the Southland, Magellanica, or New Holland which derived from the basic drawings of the Ricci and Blaeu maps, is evident in two important geographical works of the Tokugawa period by Arai Hakuseki (1657–1725) and Yamamura Shōei (1770–1807). Arai, the political advisor-savant to the sixth shogun, Tokugawa Ienobu, was probably the first person in Japan to deal with the five continents. But the five continents he described were Europe, Africa, Asia, South America, and North America. He distrusted the contours of 'Magellanica': 'The Westerners are eager to ascertain the existence of this continent, but it is not yet clearly known'. He ignored 'Magellanica' in his widely-read work on geography, *Sairan igen* (Collection of strange things), preface written in 1713, and none of the five volumes carried maps.

Most of Arai's knowledge of world geography was based on his reading of Matteo Ricci's world-map, but he also had access to Joan Blaeu's world-map *Nova Totius Terrarum Orbis Tabula*, which was kept at the government library. With regard to New Holland, as Australia was then called on the Blaeu map, Arai wrote that it was not occupied by the Dutch. They had only discovered that southern land. He had his doubts as to whether Blaeu and Ricci were actually drawing the same continent: 'There is a Southland. But whether it connects to a "Magellanica", I do not know and cannot confirm.' Arai may have been sceptical about 'Magellanica' because his main informant, the captured Italian Catholic missionary Giovanni Battista Sidotti (1668–1714), kept pointing out to him the superiority of Joan Blaeu's over Ricci's world-map.

Even more confused about the exact whereabouts of the southern continent was Yamamura Shōei. He had made it his lifework to correct Arai's study in *Teisei zōyaku sairan igen* (Collection of strange things revised and enlarged) published in 1802. But when he added ten pages to Arai's half-page description of the southernmost continent, he again identified Australia with Magellanica: 'The Latin name for *Nanpō no chi* (Southland) is *Terra Australis* or Magellanica, first discovered by Magellan in 1519. Later the Dutch sailed there and its shape slowly became known', he wrote. News of the beginning of British settlement of Australia fourteen years earlier had apparently not yet reached Japan, and Yamamura's comments were limited to place-name descriptions and vague remarks about the nature of the southern lands gathered from Dutch encyclopaedias and Chinese missionary maps.

These had led him to believe that there existed *two* Southlands. For in addition to the Ricci and Blaeu maps, he used the penetrating geographical works by two Jesuits in China which had greatly influenced the dissemination of Western geographical knowledge in that country: Julius Aleni's (1582–1649) *Shih-fang-wai-chi* (Geography of the outer world), 1623, and Ferdinand Verbiest's (1623–1688) *K'ouen-yu-t'iuan-t'ou* (A complete map of the world), 1674. Verbiest's world-map depicted not only the Australian island contours as in the Joan Blaeu map, but continued to show Magellanica encircling the tip of the southern hemisphere as a separate entity and as a sort of huge sixth continent. Following

Verbiest's lead, Yamamura accepted the idea of two separate South-lands. In the six hemispherical maps appended to his first volume, he clearly marks Magellanica at 40 degrees southern latitude, protruding out of the Antarctic opposite South Africa, while placing a separate Australia in the South Pacific.

But the Dutch rendition of Australia was still an incomplete view. They had not been able to discover the passage which separated New Guinea from Australia. Nor had they sailed along Australia's east coast, which remained an uncharted terra incognita until Captain James Cook's arrival in 1770. Furthermore, Tasman had seen only parts of Tasmania and New Zealand, and had not actually circumnavigated them as islands. Thus, for a long time Japanese scholars drew Australia double its actual size, with New Guinea always shown as part of Australia. Often New Zealand was also incorporated into Australia, as, for example, in Shiba Kōkan's celebrated world-map, *Chikyū-zenzu*, 1792.

In that same year of 1792, however, amid all the diligent copying of outdated Dutch world-maps, a new map reached Japan from Russia. In the fourth and last stage, now, of Japan's cartographic discovery of Australia, it revealed, probably for the first time, the correct shape of the Australian continent. An up-to-date and precise world-map even by European standards, it had been printed on a Russian copper-plate press as recently as 1791. It is named after its translator, the *rangakusha* Katsuragawa Hoshū (1751–1809), who reproduced the map in 1794 with the collaboration of Daikokuya Kōdayū. And here it is worth digressing to recount the circumstances which had allowed this advanced world-map to reach Japan from Russia. For its prompt transmission owed much to the Japanese castaway Kōdayū and his repatriation in 1792.

In 1783 Kōdayū and his crew of the small freighter *Shinshō Maru* from Shirako Bay in Ise province were shipwrecked on one of the Aleutian Islands. As a result, Kōdayū spent ten years at various places in Russia, mostly at Irkutsk, where he was fortunate to find a protector and teacher in Eric Laxmann, a professor of natural sciences who had a deep interest in Japan. On their various journeys together, Kōdayū is known to have copied Russian world-maps and drawn maps of Japan.

There is another reason why Irkutsk must have been a congenial place for Kōdayū to learn about the outside world. It was there, in 1779, that Major M. Tatarinov had compiled an important new world-map based on material that had only just come from Captain Cook's two exploration ships anchored for five months in the same year at Petropavlosk on Kamchatka. As Britain at that time was well disposed toward Russia, and the Russians held the British explorer Cook in the highest regard, detailed accounts of Cook's voyages had been publicly available in Russia since the early 1780s. Without too much conjecture, we may assume that Tatarinov's cartographic scholarship must have further benefited Kōdayū's geographical studies.

After much pleading and an audience with Catherine the Great in

1791, Kōdayū was finally repatriated. He arrived back in Japan in 1792 with Laxmann's son, whose mission was to establish diplomatic relations between the two countries and whose party carried official presents from Catherine, including the remarkable world-map. This did for Japanese cartography what Cook's charts had done for world geography, namely, fill in the missing east coast of Australia, which was then revealed as the true 7,682,300-square kilometre island continent it is. The Japanese are said to have begged the Russians for the map, and it is quite conceivable that Kōdayū's closeness to Laxmann was a factor in their finally obtaining it. Kōdayū's crucial role in the transmission of this superior map ought not to be underestimated, especially when we consider a world-map that the Russians brought to Japan in 1804. When Nikolai Rezanov visited the country in that year on a higher-ranking diplomatic mission to follow up the limited success of the Laxmann expedition, the map which he gave the Japanese was an older version, for Japanese copies of it still depict the Southern Continent with its eastern coast entirely missing.

The 1792 world-map, which accurately depicted Australia's true shape, was only one in a series of ten regional maps that Kōdayū brought back to his country. With the latter's indispensable help, Katsuragawa copied and translated all of them into Japanese; he then submitted them to the *bakufu*, together with an eleven-volume study, *Hokusa bunryaku* (Things heard about Russia), based on Kōdayū's information-gathering in that country. But these new maps did not advance Japanese cartography in the way that Dutch ones had done, for they were kept virtually secret for sixteen years and only Katsuragawa was allowed to keep a copy. The Tokugawa shogunate, then, chose not to foster the dissemination of popular geographical knowledge and in fact did its best to impede it. In the same year, 1792, the regent Matsudaira Sadanobu had another noted cartographer, Hayashi Shihei, arrested and his maps destroyed because he had dared to write a book on the precarious state of Japan's coastal defences.

Only in 1810, with the threatening appearance of British and Russian ships off the west and east coasts of Japan, and one year after Katsuragawa had died, did the *bakufu* instruct the director of the shogunate's astronomical observatory, Takahashi Kageyasu, to compile a world-map for official publication. In drawing it, this noted geographer not only seems to have based himself on the Katsuragawa Map; he also used the advanced material of the British cartographer Aaron Arrowsmith (1750–1823) and the French explorer Jean François La Pérouse (1741–1788); both showed Tasmania detached from the Australian mainland. As a result, the general public in Japan could finally view the authentic shape of the Australian continent on a Japanese world-map.

Basing his work on Takahashi's epochal map and updating it with a

French world map of 1835, Mitsukuri Shōgo (1821–1847) compiled in 1844 the *Shinsei yochi zenzu* (A new complete map of the world). He published it together with *Kon'yo zushiki* (Explanatory notes on the world map), which looms as the third major world geographical commentary in the Edo period following Arai Hakuseki's and Yamamura Shōei's works.

In this outstanding work, Mitsukuri paid particular attention to the continents of Africa and Australia, which others had neglected: 'Coming to Australia, hardly anyone has made mention of that continent up to now, despite the fact that it lies on the other edge of the ocean that faces Japan'. 'Australia', the name Flinders proposed for the fifth continent after circumnavigating it in 1802–1803, now appeared boldly over the conventional name of New Holland in Mitsukuri's map. But traces of the French map from which Mitsukuri also copied were clearly preserved in the southeastern part of Australia; Mitsukuri kept it as 'Napoleonland', the name given it by the French explorer Thomas Nicolas Baudin (1754–1803) on his voyage to that area in 1801.

Mitsukuri filled in the blanks of Takahashi's map by adding scores of new geographical place names in *katakana*, labelling all the known spots along Australia's vast coast line. His entries on Australia proper in the twenty-six-page report on the Australasian region in his commentary far surpassed those of his predecessors. Although not always correct, his observations give an interesting idea of how that still mysterious continent was presented to the Japanese on the eve of the lifting of the national seclusion policy:

Australia is a foreign word and means 'Land in the South'. Australia belongs to the African-Asian region. Scores of islands dot like stars the Australian region, which Westerners also call the 'island world'. Its largest island is New Holland, which is bigger even than Europe . . . It has a temperate climate which is suitable to man and animal husbandry and is very fertile. No people live in its interior, so we do not know what the inner lands may yield. On its eastern side runs a vast mountain range from North to South with steep slopes falling into the eastern coast. The reefs there pose a great danger, denying ships an easy approach.

At last we are beginning to learn more about that country of three million and seven hundred thousand people, thanks to clever Magellan, who was the first to explore the Marianas as part of the Australian region 325 years ago. The natives are of slim stature, but have strong bodies. Their faces, very black, display coarse mountain features. The men and women are almost all naked and smear their bodies with oil. Some wear thin animal skins, others a nose ring which makes their speech difficult and nasal. They fish and hunt, but do not eat grilled food. They live in tiny houses which they must enter on their knees. Some live in the holes of trees, others just by the way-side . . . The Carpentaria bay region has big ants; these construct their huge ant-hills better than the Aboriginals build their homes . . .

The eastern part of Australia is called *Shin nan waruresu* (New South Wales). In 1787, the British sent there about eight thousand criminals [the actual number was around 750] and domestic animals. The people gradually increased to twenty thousand. Their capital is now Sydney with a population of 2600. Ships from various countries call at this port city to trade . . .

The Australian continent becomes very flat towards the West, where there are great deserts . . . Diemensland [Tasmania] lies south of New Holland. It is very cold and the population numbers 3214. They all fish and hunt . . .

Despite the increase in information about Australia, a certain regression in cartographic knowledge set in when Japan cautiously began showing interest in Western countries in the 1850s. For example, to satisfy the sudden demand for easy instruction in popular world geography, Nagakubo Sekisui's simplistic world-map (based on the Ricci map) was reissued and widely copied on colourful wood-block prints. This meant that many Japanese were then still learning about Australia as Ricci's 'Magellanica' drawn grossly out of shape. In addition, Ricci's inscription of 1602 was faithfully reproduced in this Southland and still read: 'Few people have come here, so not much is known about the people and products of this land'. It is interesting to reflect on the fact that Japanese popular world-maps were imparting this information in the 1850s, at a time when rapidly urbanizing Australia had long passed the pioneering stage of its history and was importing Asian labourers by the thousand from the ports of Amoy, Macao, and Hong Kong.

With such backward materials abounding, it is hardly surprising that the Sydney whaler *Lady Rowena*, whose crew destroyed the fishing village of Hamanaka in Hokkaido in February 1831, was subsequently identified in Japanese documents as a ship of Russian provenance. And as an example of more learned nescience, Yoshida Shōin (1830–1859), the influential thinker and educator, described Australia in 1854 as a country straddling the equator:

South of Japan, separated by an ocean but not too distant, lies Australia, with its latitudes situated right on the middle of the globe. Australia's climate is fertile, its people rich and prosperous, and it is only natural that various countries compete for the profit of that territory. England cultivates only one-tenth of it as a colony. I have always thought that it would be most profitable for Japan to colonize Australia.

Thus wrote he in *Yūshūroku* (A prison notebook), and the final sentence of this quotation seemed to hold out ominous prospects for the future of Australia. In fact, Yoshida's account is of greater interest in its mistaken belief that Australia was a free-for-all territory than for its expansionist overtone, for in his more detailed writings on strategy, Yoshida concerned himself strictly with Japanese expansion onto the Asian mainland and the acquisiton of Formosa and the Philippines in the south. But as an early Japanese perception of Australia written before the Meiji Restoration, it is a rare little observation. For Yoshida's notable older colleagues, such as Honda Toshiaki (1744–1821), Satō Nobuhiro (1769–1850), Watanabe Kazan (1793–1841), or Hayashi Shihei—scholars with a deep interest in national defence and world geography—had little worthwhile to say about Australia in their writings. 'Magellanica is the fifth of the big continents', wrote Satō, the thinker of the late Edo period, and Watanabe, the illustrious scholar-painter, stated: 'Because Britain's navy is strong, she was able to colonize and dominate New Holland (Australia)'.

It was *Sekai kunizukushi* (A glimpse of the countries of the world) by Fukuzawa Yukichi (1834–1901) which finally made Australia popularly known in Japan for the first time. Published in 1869, this widely circulated book described in short paragraphs the world's continents and countries in the easily memorized seven-five-seven meter style, in which much of the information of the *terakoya* elementary school-textbooks was then set out. Geographical etchings adorned its pages, showing Sydney and Melbourne, and Fukuzawa introduced Australia to his readers in this fashion:

> Westerners studied geography and navigation, and then ventured into the Pacific where in the south a large continent lay. The Dutch discovered it first and called it New Holland. But then the British came, occupied it, and called it Australia. It now has a population of 1,400,000. People seldom visit its interior, but Australia has many natural resources; its newly discovered gold mines are incomparably rich, surpassing even those of California . . . Necessities enter Australia through the busy import/export markets of Sydney and Melbourne, which bustle with activity in the South Sea like a new world with a prosperous future.

But none of Fukuzawa's three world trips in the 1860s had taken him to Australia. He knew about that continent only from encylopaedias picked up abroad. His brief passage nevertheless marked the end of the 'Dutch' period in Japanese learning, after which Dutch works came to be replaced by English and other European countries' sources of study.

The maps and books had not always put together correctly the puzzle that was Australia, but they had managed over two-and-a-half centuries to convey something of the vastness, emptiness, mystery, and uniqueness of the fifth continent, a territory that would develop into the farthest borderland of Japan's *nan'yō* concept. The 1860s also marked the beginning of direct knowledge of Australia when, in December 1867, twelve

Japanese nationals performed as acrobats and jugglers at Melbourne's Princess Theatre and were reported as probably the first Japanese seen in Australia.

This signalled a new age that would once again see Japanese ships roaming the Western Pacific Ocean, eventually in full battle strength. And as Japan's hand strengthened in the Western Pacific at the turn of the century, Australians became increasingly concerned with Japan's expansive mood. How the Japanese southern advance developed from the Meiji period until the outbreak of the Pacific War, and what weight it would accord the large, but increasingly exclusivist white southern land of Australia, is the focus of the following chapters.

Japan's Re-emergence
1850s–1895

3

Return to the Western Pacific

WHEN THE Japanese Government
was forced to open the country again in the 1850s, the Japanese looked
onto another world. Great changes in world-order had been under way
since Japan had recoiled from intercourse with the Western powers in the
mid-seventeenth century. Empires had risen and fallen on a global scale
for the first time in history, following Pope Alexander VI's decision in
1494 to award Spain the western half of the world and Portugal the
eastern half. The Spanish acquisitions were contested a century later by
the French and British, who began to settle parts of the Americas, while
the Dutch went after the Portuguese and wrested from them most of their
power in the Far East between 1601 and 1667. The Dutch, in turn, were
soon superseded by the British, builders of the grandest of empires in the
nineteenth century. By that time the Russians, too, had expanded
overland into the Far East, and the Pacific islands had all been charted
and systematically added to the substantial colonial empires of Spain,
France, Holland, and England, or to the lesser empires of Germany and
Portugal.

One important key to the control of imperial changes in world-order
had been the development of the basing system. The Portuguese had
stumbled on this geopolitical novelty in a rather unplanned way. When
in 1510 they had opened their first 'factory' in Goa on the Indian subcontinent, as a trading facility and replenishing base for their expeditions

31

east, they soon learned that in order to keep a 'factory' they had to protect it with a permanent garrison against the natives and foreign naval intruders. For this reason, and even in defiance of his home government, Portugal's Governor of India, Affonso Albuquerque, had proceeded to occupy Goa permanently as a colony under direct Portuguese rule. The Portuguese soon set up similar key bases at Aden, Hormuz, Diu, Malacca, Mozambique, and Macao. There they asserted themselves in an already existing trade network that had previously been in the hands of Moslem merchants in the Indian Ocean, and Japanese and Chinese buccaneers in the China Sea. But Portugal's oceanic empire was quickly outdone by Holland, whose small flotillas, based in a world-wide network of *points d'appui*, connected the Dutch seaborne empire from India to Guinea, Brazil, the West Indies, South Africa, Formosa, and the East Indies.

Over a period of several centuries, the British eventually loosened the Dutch grip on sea power. What is more, they established world-wide dominance of overseas basing points, mostly by successful wars, precisely at a time of Japanese withdrawal from world affairs. Just when Japan was further restricting from seventy-three to thirty the annual number of Chinese vessels allowed to trade at Nagasaki, Great Britain expanded into Gibraltar, Minorca, and large parts of Canada by the Peace of Utrecht in 1713. And in the reign of the feeble ninth shogun, Tokugawa Ieshige, Great Britain further established effective control over all of India, pocketing more of Canada, Cape Breton Island, Florida, St Vincent, Tobago, Dominica, and Grenada in the Peace of Aix-La-Chapelle in 1748. In a final geopolitical masterstroke, Britain put herself in control of most of the world's important coaling stations. This assured her not only the vital supplies for an early version of a rapid naval deployment system, but gave her substantial leverage over the movements of other navies, too.

Vastly changed was the world to which Japan was returned at the muzzles of Commodore Matthew C. Perry's black gun-boats in the mid-nineteenth century. And Japan, too, had undergone a significant conversion which groomed her favourably for an imperial age of intense nationalism. For unprecedented political unity during the 214 years of her policy of seclusion had fostered several dynamic developments under the reign of the authoritarian Tokugawa. The long peace had enhanced agricultural innovation, which benefitted increased land cultivation. City life had evolved, attracting a continuous flow of surplus labour to the towns. Manufacturing had begun to vie with farming, as greater production of foodstuffs and the handicraft industry stimulated the opening of new markets in a population that was growing apace. Free markets and guilds had been established and the weights, measures, and currency systematized, as the merchant class began to compete in economic and political power with the military caste.

The central regime of the Tokugawa was held together by the *sankin kōtai* system of 'alternate attendance'. This ingenious sytem of feudal control obliged the feudal lords from all over Japan to spend a part of each year with the Tokugawa shogunate in Edo (Tokyo), together with their next of kin; these they had to leave behind in the capital as hostages for the rest of the year, when they tended to the administration of their fiefs in person. The *sankin kōtai* was a mixed blessing. It guaranteed the Tokugawa family unprecedented power, as it transformed an outward-looking country into an inward-looking one, strictly controlled from the central seat of power in Edo. At the same time, the forced processions to Edo imposed on the daimyos formidable expenditures to keep up appearances in the capital; these drew the feudal lords into a nation-wide economy which greatly enhanced domestic financial circulation and led to the expansion of road, river, and coastal networks linking the four main islands from Hokkaido to Kyūshū in a highly developed system of communications. Prolonged peace furthermore spawned a peculiar culture, formalistic in essence, that rested on the accepted orthodoxy of Neo-Confucianism. Emphasizing human loyalties eminently suited to the feudal society of Japan, it provided a uniform secular code by which the Tokugawa could maintain social order in all their domains.

Moulding the country thus for over two centuries, the Tokugawa system allowed for an undisturbed outpouring of domestic energy in the social and economic domains. The Japanese may have been unaware of the Peace of Westphalia which laid the seeds for the building of nation states. But their long period lived in seclusion familiarized them in a natural way with two important features in modern nation building: unification and centralization. It unwittingly prepared Japan in a dynamic way for the age of nationalism and imperialism—an era which would force Japan to renounce her policy of isolation and join the comity of nations outside the East Asian world as a formidable country to be reckoned with.

In one fundamental aspect Japan did not change. Throughout the Tokugawa period, Japan's shogun had deigned himself superior to the king of Korea and equality with China was always emphasized. When Japan emerged from isolation, her leaders quickly realized that to survive at the top in the world of Western power politics they would have to become champions of Western concepts of prestige. The Western powers might pride themselves in sliding open the Japanese door by force. They were, however, approaching not an impuissant country, but a vigorous one that had chosen to live in isolation voluntarily: Japan was a state that had been progressively strenghtening—not relaxing—its policy of seclusion, as is evidenced in the final reinforcing edicts of 1791 and the 1825 *Bunsei uchiharai no rei* (Law of firing upon and driving away foreign ships in the Bunsei era). Japan, moreover, was a country with a history of expansion of its own, though few Westerners may have been aware that two hundred years earlier, Japan had established many prosperous trading settlements in the Asia-Pacific region from Formosa to the Moluccas, and from the Philippines to the Malay Peninsula. And how many of the Western governments did then foresee that once Japan dropped her policy of seclusion and wholeheartedly adopted the Western way of empire building, they would have a formidably centralized newcomer among them, a nation capable of quick and intelligent adaptation? Indeed, Japan was to revert with astounding single-mindedness to its former spirit of enterprise. It would swiftly strive to recapture its former outgoingness, and eventually throw down the gauntlet to eliminate Western encroachments in a region it had once intimately known. Japan's sense of being subordinate to none remained unchanged.

Such pride required, of course, that Japan match the power of those nations which pressured her into opening the country. Russia, Britain, and France were all expanding nations; even libertarian America had revealed herself in the Mexican War as an expansionist power *par excellence*. Japan would have to emulate these colonial powers to survive in the world of the 1850s. This idea is a common thread that runs through the writings of many important Japanese thinkers contemplating the resumption of foreign intercourse in the second half of the nineteenth century—from Yoshida Shōin's simple prescription 'to colonize or be colonized' to Fukuzawa Yukichi's call to civilize Korea and demonstrate Japan's superiority in war with China; Japan could thus do as the British were doing in India and China, and even wrest power from the British in East Asia.

The Japanese were as familiar with expansionism and the rule of strength as had been the Greeks and the Romans or the Han Chinese. Ever since the legendary exploits of Sujin (98?–30 B.C.), Himiko (third century), or Jingū (late fourth century), they had had a number of kings and queens to look back on for inspiration, and several shining knaves. In April 1592, Toyotomi Hideyoshi had invaded Korea with around 200,000 men in an attempt to conquer China. He also sent letters to Formosa and the Philippines demanding submission and tribute, and threatened that he would turn his attention to the Philippines after the conquest of Korea and China. After his first debacle in Korea, Hideyoshi issued orders again in 1597 for the conquest of the Asiatic mainland, this time with a better navy. But the campaign tapered off at the news of his death in 1598. In 1616, Tokugawa Ieyasu ordered the Governor of Nagasaki, Murayama Tōan, to invade Formosa with a fleet of thirteen vessels and around 4,000 men. Only a hurricane thwarted this effort and forced their early return. Also, Tokugawa Iemitsu is on record for twice having wanted to conquer the Philippines to stop the illegal flow of missionaries from Luzon to Japan.

But the kind of expansionism which the late Tokugawa thinkers urged on their government in the nineteenth century was informed more of strategic expediency and national pride. It was motivated less by individualistic Hideyoshian dreams of self-aggrandizement, the wish to deflect domestic political grievances, or the idea of punitive expeditions. It was prompted rather by the wish to check the Russian southward advance, and nurtured by a strong desire to gain international standing commensurate to Japan's increasing power in the concert of nations in the second half of the nineteenth century.

Already in the middle of the Tokugawa period, Russian ships had begun to appear off the Japanese east coast and had effected landings in the provinces of Awa and Mutsu (in today's prefecture of Chiba and the Tōhoku region). The Cossacks had by then already explored eastern Siberia (1632–1650) and reached Kamchatka (1679). Lieutenant Martin Spanberg in 1739 had scouted the shores of Sakhalin, the Kuriles, and Ezo (Hokkaido) for the House of Romanov.

Japanese scholars then thought of Ezo as lying outside Japan proper. The historian Tokugawa Mitsukuni (1638–1700) in his *Dai Nihon shi* (History of Great Japan), Nakai Riken (1733–1817), and Hayashi Shihei (1738–1793), for example, all classified it as a foreign territory, just like China and Korea. Roused by the menace of Russian inroads into Japan's neighbouring islands to the north, the historian and noted thinker Nakai advocated that Ezo be left as it was—a buffer zone of wilderness between Japan and Russia. But his contemporary, Kudō Heisuke (1738–1800), physician and administrator of the middle Edo period, argued forcibly in his *Aka Ezo fūsetsu-kō* (Reports of the Red-Ezo [i.e., Russians]), 1781, that the Japanese Government develop and fortify Ezo first to stave off the Russian onrush. Then Japan should open up trade relations with the Russians and sell them the agricultural produce of Ezo. This trade, together with the exploitation of the island's suspected gold mines, would finance the dearly needed extension of national fortifications. Kudō's writings greatly influenced Hayashi Shihei, an expert on administrative and military affairs, who was arrested for the views he expressed in *Sangoku tsūran zusetsu* (An illustrated survey of three countries), 1785, and in *Kaikoku heidan* (Talk on the defences of a maritime country), 1786. Both books blamed the *bakufu* (Japanese Government) for not adequately fortifying the country against the impending Western threat. Hayashi strongly urged his government to absorb Ezo and establish control over that land and people before the Russians did.

He was of like mind with Honda Toshiaki, another leading nationalist and thinker of his time. Honda suggested that Japan seize not only Hokkaido, but Kamchatka too. His writings impart most plainly the other ingredient in modern Japanese expansionism: the desire to restore national prestige. He counsels the *bakufu* to move the capital to Kamchatka at 51 degrees northern latitude, and on the neighbouring island of Sakhalin build a strongly fortified city at 46 degrees northern latitude. Those are the latitudes of London and Paris. The geographical advantages that made those two world cities powerful would thus enable Japan to establish effective control over an empire that eventually would spread from Kamchatka to the southern end of the Japanese island archipelago and be known as 'Great Japan'.

Another well-known intellectual, agronomist, and scholar, was Satō Nobuhiro. Like Honda an early advocate of Greater Japan, Satō taught that Japan could match up to the Western colonial powers only by going out to trade as quickly as possible, then acquire territories, develop, colonize, and exploit them as the West was doing. To countermand the Russian advance, Japan must exploit Ezo, capture Kamchatka and the region of the Okhotsk Sea, and establish control over Eastern Siberia by military conquest. Yoshida Shōin, the father figure of modern Japanese nationalism, said as much in his prolific writings and added a fair amount of strategic advice: Japan must build battleships, provide herself with the necessary weapons and ammunition, and conquer Manchuria as a national base for the mastery of the continent. If Japan pursued these policies, she could advance in the world and prove that she was able to maintain her national standing, 'For unless our country, too, assumes an aggressive attitude towards the outside, it will surely be destroyed'. Hashimoto Sanai (1834–1859), a political activist and Yoshida's companion in death, reiterated the need for well-trained armies and navies to fulfill Japan's desire for national prestige, as he called for the annexation of the Santang districts in Manchuria and all of Korea.

But when Japan expanded again, the age of Conquistadores, mounted cossacks, free-roving buccaneers, and the prosletyzing priests who had sallied forth with their marines to set up the first colonies for Christ and fortune, had long passed. Japan was late. How could a dynamic country that had withdrawn from the colonial race in the age of discoveries reassert herself in a world already divided up among the Western powers?

Pretexts adapted to a new age were needed to spur Japan's metamorphosis into a member of that select circle which controlled the international politics of the neo-Imperialist age. Trouble with Korea gave Japan the necessary licence to expand northward in the mid-1870s: partly to meet there the Russian threat, partly because it was the region of least resistance, and partly to rid herself of the last vestiges of the ancient Chinese world order.

When in 1867 the Japanese emperor replaced the shogun to assume actual shogunal powers as head of state, the Korean king refused to accept such notification. In the traditional Asian world-view, to recognize Japan's internal political change would have been tantamount to Korean subordination. The king had always felt himself equal to the shogun. He could not profess peerage with a Japanese emperor, and loyal he would be to the Chinese emperor only. To rectify the situation in Korea, therefore, the leader of the faction in Japan that favoured rapid reforms, Kido Takayoshi (1833–1877), advocated the deployment of troops in 1869. But Japan still lacked adequate strength.

The time to upbraid Korea came in 1874, when Ōkubo Toshimichi (1830–1878) despatched gunboats to survey coastal waters in the Korean capital's fortified zone. Promptly fired upon, they seized the area, creating the *Kangwha* Incident. The Japanese Government then sent a mission escorted by six warships to negotiate and employ the lesson learnt at the hands of Commodore Perry. An unequal treaty was won, which gave Japan extraterritorial rights in Korea and allowed her to transform the Pusan harbour area into a modern concession to stop the Russian southward advance.

Japan's glaring presence in Korea, justified by the largely self-serving aim of wanting to modernize the country, soon led to widespread anti-Japanese feelings. In 1882, the Japanese legation in Seoul was destroyed and a Japanese army instructor killed. When Japan prepared to send in soldiers, Chinese troops stole a march on her. The *Imo* uprising, as this incident came to be known, greatly affected the East Asian situation. Henceforth, Japan regarded China as a hopelessly anachronistic foe, whose remaining influence over its tributary, Korea, had to be absolutely eliminated.

Yamagata Aritomo (1838–1922), the architect of the modern Japanese army, reminisced about the year of 1882: 'It became clear then that army and navy expansion could not be put off for another day . . . If reforms had not been instituted at this time, the Sino-Japanese War, without a doubt, could not have been planned for at all.' In 1885, Fukuzawa Yukichi wrote his famous tract *Datsu-A-ron*. It commended Japan's spiritual departure from the Asian mainland which would enable the Japanese to treat China and Korea as the Westerners were doing. In this way, Japan pushed herself steadily into imbroglio on the mainland: by argument, first, from 1867 to 1873, arrogating the right to draw her line of defence in Korea and act as the reformer of the Chinese world order; then by physical show of force, acquiring special territorial rights in Korea between 1874 and 1882; and finally by challenging outright Chinese supremacy and preparing for the future showdown in 1894.

It was the development of a navy that again made possible expansion on the mainland, and returned Japan to the Asian–Western Pacific region. This was not the first time that the Japanese had shown themselves competent masters in establishing military marine expertise. Promising signs of a viable Japanese navy had emerged before the turn of the sixteenth century. Oda Nobunaga is known to have experimented with the building of iron clad warships. Toyotomi Hideyoshi strengthened the navy after severe defeats during Japan's first invasion of the Asian mainland at the hands of the Korean Admiral Yi, and won over a strong Korean fleet in 1597 in the second invasion. And Tokugawa Ieyasu developed a strong merchant marine, and invited the Governor of

Manila to send Spanish naval architects to work in Japanese ship-yards.

But this naval growth had come to a sudden end with the announcement of the Tokugawa Government's stringent naval restrictions in 1635 and the edict that Japanese ships were forbidden to make voyages abroad. The strictly enforced law had the effect of a naval disarmament, unique in history in that it was entirely unilateral and self-imposed. The feudal warships (*adakebune*) of the lords from the maritime strongholds of the western (Kyūshū) and central fiefs were completely dismantled or converted into ceremonial barges. Ornamental paraphernalia replaced cannons and armaments. The ensuing long national peace created a new type of ship, the *gozabune* or *omeshisekibune*— the most splendid of these show boats being the *yusanbune*—which the daimyos were allowed to ride only as far as Osaka, whence they had to proceed overland to Edo (Tokyo) to serve their time in 'alternate attendance' at the seat of the Tokugawa shogunate.

In their outward appearance of strength these splendid ships marked the shift from an efficient navy to one totally void of power. The once highly organized fighting patterns developed during the Warring Period, and the fleet formations doggedly rehearsed under Oda Nobunaga, were completely forgotten. Because they were no longer allowed to build three-masted ships or anything ocean-worthy of more than 49 tons (500 *koku*), Japanese shipping declined after 1635 into a mere coastal cargo service.

After the opening of the country in 1854, the establishment of a navy developed again with unusual speed. The strong call between 1853 and 1855 to relax the laws of feudal attendance at Edo, spearheaded by Matsudaira Shungaku (1828–1890) of Fukui, induced a reform of the *sankin kōtai* system, and in September 1853 the law was relaxed to allow the building of bigger ships. Already in 1856, the Tokugawa Government had welcomed twenty-two Dutch naval instructors, who between 1855 and 1859 founded the first naval school (*Kaigun denshūjo*) at Nagasaki, where the first dockyards were built between 1856 and 1861. After the Dutch presented the naval training ship *Kankō Maru*, the *bakufu* purchased two more warships from Holland in 1857 and 1858.

The Japanese Government was quick to learn. Realizing that Holland was no longer supreme, the Japanese effectively ignored the Dutch on a technical mission to Europe in 1865. It ended the traditional Dutch–*bakufu* relationship. Japan now turned to the two naval superpowers Great Britain and, especially, France, with whom the *bakufu* fostered close ties through the French Minister to Japan, Léon Roche. But the demise of the *bakufu* in 1867 eliminated French naval influence, and Britain, which had strong ties with the rising Satsuma clan, became the favoured model for the Japanese navy.

In July 1873, Commander Archibald Douglas arrived with 33 officers to teach young Japanese men, selected from all clans and attired in uniforms styled after those of the Royal Navy, the practical side of naval affairs at the Naval College at Tsukiji near Tokyo. By 1882, the British advisors had left and the Japanese fleet had grown from 17 vessels, grossing 13,812 tons in 1871 to 28 warships, 19 of which were built in Britain, aggregating 57,600 tons. On the eve of the Sino-Japanese war, a well-trained and unified Japanese fleet of 32 warships and 23 torpedo boats, manned by 13,928 men, faced the numerically superior but decentralized four Chinese fleets which consisted of 65 large ships and 43 torpedo boats. Japan's resounding victory over the Chinese fleet in major sea battles on 25 July and 17 September 1894 set her on a northern course onto the mainland.

Although rapid naval development immediately made possible Japan's northern advance, the Japanese navy in the long run became identified with Japan's southern advance. A significant step in this direction was the institution of naval training cruises to explore the Pacific. The first such expedition sailed in 1875 to Hawaii and San Francisco; the second one took the graduating cadets and officers on the *Tsukuba* as far as Australia in 1878. Before long, civilians began to ride on these naval cruises as observers. One early such passenger was the political geographer, Shiga Shigetaka (1867–1924). The procedures by which these private men came to travel on military vessels is not clear in all cases; but in Shiga's instance he is known to have requested permission from the Minister of Navy, Admiral Saigo Tsugumichi, to join the ten-month cruise of the *Tsukuba* to the Carolines, Australia, New Zealand, Fiji, Samoa, and Hawaii. Upon his return he published the important work *Nan'yō jiji* (Current Affairs in the South Seas) in 1887, in which he sought to add a new dimension to the dichotomous world-view of East and West —or backward and advanced countries—then so prevalent in Japan. Shiga not only introduced political facts about the South Sea Islands and their significance for Japan, but combined this material with valuable geographical, economic, and cultural data about the South Pacific region. His book aroused considerable attention and exerted a strong influence on subsequent writers about the *nan'yō*, or South Seas.

Yet it is difficult to gauge the exact extent to which Shiga lit the *nan'yō* interest that sparked a boom in the so-called Meiji 20s, those crucial years from 1887 to1894, when the south fever was particularly acute in the Meiji period (1868–1912). Around about the same time that his book appeared, a number of other authors took up the same topic to write about Japan's potential in the Western Pacific. A similarly enthusiastic writer on the south was Hattori Tōru, who harped on the theme of Japan's need of a policy for commerce, trade, settlement, and colonization of the southern islands in *Nihon no Nan'yō* (Japan's South Seas), 1888. His second book, *Nan'yōsaku* (Policy toward the South Seas), 1891, focused on the Philippines, Marianas, Carolines, Marshalls, and Gilbert

Islands. Suggesting that Japan learn by example, Hattori described an interesting plaque that he had come across on one of his voyages in the islands and reproduced its full text: 'This southern group of islands has been explored & taken in possession of by Commander J. Kelly & officers of the U.S. ship *Plymouth* under orders of Commodore M. C. Perry on behalf of U.S. of N.A. This 30 Day of October 1853.'

Japan should not only wake up, but stand up, implored Suzuki Tsunenori, in three books that sought to revive the once-flourishing Japanese spirit of adventure, which had floundered on the rocks of the seclusion policy. He wished to rouse Japanese interest in the Micronesian and Melanesian island worlds through his own travel experiences put down in *Nan'yō tanken jikki* (A true story of exploration in the South Seas), 1892. The first in this two-volume work treats the Marshall Islands, and the second Honolulu, Samoa, Fiji, and Tahiti (by hearsay). In *Nantō junkōki* (Report on a cruise in the southern islands), 1893, Suzuki urged his countrymen to occupy the Solomons which he believes are still 'no-man's' land [discovered by the Dutch in 1721–1722, they had, in fact, already been taken in possession by the Germans in the 1880s; the British annexed them in 1893] with bright prospects for sugar production.

'Japan should import raw materials from Australia . . . and industrialize herself to augment our nation's economic potential', suggested Inagaki Manjirō (1861–1908) in the Japanese version of his Cambridge graduation thesis, *Tōhōsaku* (Eastern policy), 1891. The two countries were island countries; they had to develop their sea lanes and Japan must augment its navy, he explained in another geopolitically oriented book, *Nan'yō chōsei dan* (Talk on an exploration deep into the South Seas), 1893. He wrote it after travelling from Nagasaki to Hong Kong, Vietnam, Singapore, Townsville in Queensland, Thursday Island, New Caledonia, Sydney, Melbourne, Adelaide, Albany in Western Australia and up the coast to Java, Sumatra, Macao, and Taiwan. Inagaki regarded British occupation of Singapore, New Guinea, and the Gilbert Islands as a threat to the Japan–Australia line of communication. Upon hearing in Sydney of the fears of the Governor of New South Wales, Sir Henry Parkes, that Japan would occupy China and use Chinese soldiers—just as Britain was using Indian soldiers—to come to Australia, Inagaki noted: 'We have to think about that, too'.

The thoughts of these and many other early protagonists of southward advance in the Meiji period have been researched in the works by Irie Toraji in the 1940s, and re-introduced and enlarged upon in the post-war period by Yano Tōru.

Although the latter has rated poorly the connection in the flow of southward advance thinking from the end of the Tokugawa period to the modern age, there are in fact many direct connections between the thoughts of the expansionist thinkers of the late Tokugawa period and those of the 'southward-ho!' protagonists of the Meiji 20s. The necessity to send out Japanese immigrants, to move and be active, and to create a militarily strong country lest others take all and Japan whither away, as urged by Yoshida Shōin in *Yūshūroku* (1854), was expressed very similarly forty years later in Watanabe Shūjirō, *Sekai ni okeru Nihonjin* (Japanese in the world), 1893. Like Yoshida, who pressed for expansion both north *and* south (to Taiwan, the Philippines, and Australia), Watanabe advocated territorial expansion in the Pacific 'to obtain the nan'yō . . . up to Australia, to go out and do as the Europeans were doing; why should only we be governed by scruples in international affairs?'. But Watanabe fell short of suggesting any appropriation of Australia.

In like vein, what the late Tokugawa scholar Honda Toshiaki had broached in 1798, Yokō Tōsaku, a government official who proposed the establishment of a 'South Sea Society', refined into more elaborate plans in 1886. In *Seiiki monogatari* (Stories about Western lands), Honda had prescribed a large-scale Japanese colonial administrative scheme, down to the islands of the southern region in the mid-Pacific, for the sake of expanding Japanese trade and to remedy overpopulation. Similarly, Yokō devised a grand scheme of colonization from the islands south of Ogasawara to the Philippine archipelago and the Caroline and Marshall Islands. His primary intention was to move Japan's surplus population there, but the promotion of trade was an offshoot in mind. Yokō furthermore suggested that some of the islands thus colonized serve as outlets for Japan's criminal population (which he represented in 1885 as totalling 320,410).

This, again, was an idea that harked back to Satō Nobuhiro, who in *Bōkaisaku* (Naval defence policy),1809, had thought of the use of prisoners to develop the southern islands. Such continuity in Japanese southern interest is perhaps best reflected in the train of thoughts that connect the ideas of this Tokugawa man with three prominent exponents of southward advance in the Meiji 20s: Hattori Tōru, Sugiura Jūgo, and Suganuma Teifu.

In *Kondō hisaku* (Confounding secret policies), 1823, Satō Nobuhiro wrote that the Japanese should sail forth and gradually make the southern islands Japanese. Using fifty to sixty ships with five to six thousand sailors, they should develop the uninhabited islands in the south and exploit their products. Satō had in mind particularly the Philippines with its seven to eight hundred large and small islands. Few of them were inhabited, he claimed, and they offered fabulous produce. But it was not so much to acquire these that Satō prodded his countrymen to go south; rather it was for the defence of Japan, to protect Edo (Tokyo) and to defend the sea lanes. Japan had to build defences against England—who, having defeated Holland and with many ships in India, was pressuring the Philippines and now wanted all of Asia. Japan must construct ships, and push full-steam into the no-man's islands in the south. Japan must invade the Philippines, occupy them, and cooperate with the Ryūkyū Islands. Japan must send her soldiers to Luzon and to Palawan Island to protect the natives from other peoples and make a basic plan for the *nan'yō*. And then Japan must despatch more vessels to Java and Borneo, to either administer them or befriend them, and thereby benefit both sides.

Much of this thought is similarly reflected in Hattori Tōru's advice to send agricultural settlers to the Philippines—to forestall there, not the British, but the Germans—to gradually tie the Philippines economically and politically to Japan. Or in Sugiura Jūgo's call to send 90,000 sturdy immigrants of the *Eta* class (a sort of outcast group, now usually called *burakumin*, or 'hamlet people'), with their families, to lead a revolt against their Spanish masters in the Philippines. Their overthrow would liberate the backward Filipinos from Spanish despotism and give the *Eta* new-found glory and a respectable place to settle.

The ideological writings of Suganuma Teifu reflect even more overtly Satō's ideas on the Philippines. Like Satō, Suganuma urged an advance south primarily to prevent further white encroachment in the Asia–Pacific region. Japan should search for new territories in the Philippines and despatch there a hundred battleships and soldiers to overthrow the Spanish. Japan must then befriend the natives and send agricultural emigrants, supervised and assisted by an emigration company, to the island of Luzon and especially to the thinly populated provinces of Cagayan and Isabella. The islands' products would be developed, industries would prosper, and a strong trade spring up with the building of commercial ships. Promoting Japanese interests in the Philippines should be part of a plan to expand further into Micronesia, notably into the Caroline Islands.

One may ask why it was left to the *nanshin-ron sha* of the Meiji 20s to gather up and further develop the 'southward-ho!' ideas of their late Tokugawa forebears? Why did they appear just then, in the mid-1880s, and not earlier, say in the 1870s, or the 1860s?

Several retarding factors appear to have conspired to make the Meiji 20s an auspicious decade for the *nanshin* boom. To begin with, those who were writing again about southward expansion were for the most part men who had been able to go out and see for themselves the conditions in the South. But they had had to wait until 25 June 1866, when the right to travel freely abroad was granted all Japanese in the Tariff Revision Treaty and Convention. Also, the naval training cruises on which a number of the early *nanshin-ron sha* sailed south were instituted only in the mid-1870s. At any rate, in the 1860s the Japanese were intensely caught up in first finding out about the West; the government sent officials and experts on seven fact-finding missions to Europe and America between 1860 and 1867. Moreover, the restive years which followed were consumed with putting down domestic strife: the Hakodate campaign

(1868), the Saga disturbance (1874), the Formosan expedition (1874), the Korean affair (1875–76), the Hagi insurrection (1876), and the Satsuma rebellion (1877).

Other factors combined to spur the *nanshin-ron* boom in the second half of the 1880s. After the Japanese had finally been granted a long-sought constitution in 1881 (which came into effect in 1890) and a parliament fashioned on the Western model, opinion-makers were searching the horizon for new topics to write about. They found more leisure to contemplate the South. It may also be that Fukuzawa Yukichi's influential advice—in his widely read 1885 tract *Datsu-A-Ron* (Departure from Asia)—to cold-shoulder China and Korea, join the Western camp of civilization, and do as the Europeans were doing, prompted ideologists to scrutinize the Western Pacific with a quickening of the spirit. That vast region was sure to hold out unclaimed living space which Japanese could search for territories to colonize, and thereby emulate the West. It was Foreign Minister Inoue Kaoru who said in 1887, the year that *Nan'yō jiji* appeared: 'Let us change our empire into a European-style empire. Let us change our empire into a European-style people. Let us create a new European-style empire on the Eastern sea.'

There was public uproar over the Japanese Government's fruitless talks with the foreign powers in the mid-1880s on revising 'unequal treaties' which imposed limitations on the full exercise of Japan's sovereignty within her own territory. It seems to have fueled the *nan'yō* writers. Some of them plainly used their works as platforms from which to vent their displeasure at the government's failure to gain fiscal and judicial independence from the Western treaty powers. Grieving for the shackled South under European domination, they clinched their point. Demands for independence for the Philippines from Spain, for Australia from Great Britain, for Samoa from Germany, and for the New Hebrides from France were made by Sugiura Jūgo, Suganuma Teifu, and Shiga Shigetaka in their 'dream stories' (*yume monogatari*). This literary form veiled direct criticism of the government, but sought to drive home the point that Japan, too, should throw off Western treaty-bondage and assert herself more. Shiga, for example, has the Samoan god Tangaroa appear to him during a nap at Apia, and say: 'Let not the Japanese experience the fate of Samoa. Don't trust the Western powers and never depend on them'. His insights were probably guided by the observations that in 1871 a German consul was stationed in Samoa, in 1877 the Germans concluded a treaty with Samoa that gave them the right to establish a coaling station and naval depot there, and in 1889 a conference in Berlin declared a tripartite (United States, British, and German) protectorate over Samoa. Europe was usurping the South. And Shiga feared a similar development taking place in Japan from the time of the installation of Western consuls in 1854 until 1887—the year that he published his book—a time of particular restiveness due to the disputes with the foreign powers over the unequal treaties.

In addition, these Meiji men who further developed the southern notions of the late Tokugawa thinkers, emerged just at a time of the establishment of four outward-looking institutions. One was the prestigious *Tōkyō Chigaku Kyōkai* (Tokyo Geographical Society). Organized in 1879, it was infused with the spirit of Prince Kitashirakawa's words: 'Geography is indispensable to economics, politics, and military defense . . . geography is navigation, trade, and attack'. Another was the *Tōkyō Keizaigaku Kyōkai* (Tokyo Economic Association), 1887, with its call for English laissez-faire doctrines advocating free trade through the eighties and nineties. A third institution was the *Tōhō Kyōkai* (East Asian Society), 1890. Its objective was the study of conditions in the East and South Seas with a view to producing 'reference materials for emigration and navigation enterprises to help carry out our country's domestic policy and our nation's duty'. The fourth and most engaging of these institutions was the *Shokumin Kyōkai* (Immigration Society), founded in February 1893 by influential people under the leadership of Enomoto Takeaki (Foreign Minister, May 1891–August 1892). In the objectives of this society one can perceive most clearly Japan's desperation to catch up with Europe's three-hundred-year advantage of colonial mastery in the Pacific:

> Emigration, to-day, is one of the most pressing tasks for Japan . . . As soon as the European Powers had started undertaking emigration projects, they eagerly planned national enrichment. Therefore, Japan must plan such an enterprise . . . if Japan will not hurriedly search for land abroad, other countries will occupy them ahead of Japan . . . Japan should search for suitable lands and build colonies through peaceful means . . .
>
> If Japan wants to secure command of the sea, Japan must extend her trade routes . . . If Japan wants to strengthen her navy, marine enterprises must accompany her emigration. The navy is useful not only in war time, but also during times of peace . . . one of the important activities of the navy is to help emigrants and to protect ships. Therefore, with the flourishing of emigration and navigation, Japan would feel the need of enlarging her navy . . . If Japan would have colonies abroad, not only would the [Japanese] ask for Japanese goods, but they would also introduce them to foreigners. Commerce and trade would prosper . . .
>
> The mind of the Japanese people has become narrow as a result of their long period of isolation . . . emigration enterprises would lift the Japanese spirit . . . and broaden the people's mind . . . Thus, emigration is urgent and must truly be a national policy of Japan . . . This Society is not satisfied with desk arguments only, it plans to carry them out by considering ways and means [to attain them] . . .

Something was now definitely astir. Japan had been 'open' to the world for thirty years without any tangible foreign political results to the nation's credit. Many were pushing for more and pushing outward. And with the rising of Japan's sun over the Western Pacific went an impending awareness of challenge to European hegemony in the Pacific. One can sense this, for example, in Robert Louis Stevenson's novel *The Beach of Falesa* completed on Samoa in 1891, in which he subtly questions the white man's fitness to invade and colonize the Pacific. Around about the same time, Shiga Shigetaka was writing in the magazine, *Nihonjin* (The Japanese people):

> Every year, to comfort the long line of our imperial ancestors, on February 11 and April 3—the anniversary of Emperor Jimmu's accession and the day of his passing—we should ceremonially enlarge the territory of the Japanese Empire no matter what, however little. Our naval vessels should venture forth on these days and hoist the Rising Sun on unoccupied islands. If there is no island, rocks and stones will do. Some will say this is child's play. It is not. This would not only be a valuable exercise for the navy, more significantly, it would instill an expeditionary spirit in the Japanese people who have been living in the confinement of their islands. We must go in for the action by all means.

Yet there was also something strangely out-of-place in the anachronistic dreams many Japanese harboured when they believed that at least some of the Pacific territories were still unclaimed for. The Anglo-Saxon-inspired liberal economist Taguchi Ukichi (1855–1905) still believed in 1890 that, although the European countries had expanded into the South Seas, they did not yet effectively control all the islands due to a lack of European settlers. Japan was therefore free to go to these islands, buy lands from the chiefs, settle down, and trade. And historian-philosopher Miyake Setsurei (1860–1945), a leading popular journalist, who like Shiga Shigetaka had sailed on a naval expedition to Guam, New Britain, Australia, New Caledonia, New Guinea, the Philippines, and Hong Kong, reminisced later about how they had searched in vain for the tiny Grampus Island marked 'unclaimed' on their English sea map in the hope of acquiring it for Japan: 'At that time the desire for colonies, especially in the South Pacific, was strong ... We felt Japan had to acquire territory.'

Alas, Japan was at least a hundred years late. Gone were the years when, for example, Samuel Wallis could annex Tahiti in the name of King George III in 1767, Louis Antoine de Bougainville claim the same islands for France in 1768, Captain Cook re-claim them for England in 1769, Don Domingo de Boenechea claim them for Spain in 1774, Captain Cook again re-claim them in 1777, and Captain Abel du Petit-Thouars finally establish a French protectorate over the group in 1842, for good. And it must have been a vexing time for Shiga, Taguchi, and Miyake to

write about their frustrating island searches, when Japan already possessed a navy that in a few years would smash the larger Chinese one;
and when non-entity powers such as New Zealand were throwing pro-
tectorates over South Pacific islands (Rarotonga), with beachcombers
such as Shirley Waldemar Baker framing and rewriting the Tongan constitution for the fourth time, and the *New Zealand Herald* trumpeting that
it was New Zealand's destiny to become the emporium of the South
Pacific. Nor were the Japanese intellectuals then witnessing only British
Imperialism at its most rampant. Bismarck was beating the British to the
islands named after him and annexing New Britain, New Ireland, and
the northern province of Eastern New Guinea in 1884 as part of his
programme for German colonial expansion; the United States was
annexing the Philippines and Hawaii in 1898–99; and the German
Government was buying the Mariana and Caroline Islands wholesale
from Spain for U.S.$4.5 million.

That annexations needed the support of adequate naval power was not
lost on the Japanese writing at that period. But many also embraced the
notion of 'peaceful' expansion, although they were at a loss to explain
how such expansion was possible in the face of the Western colonies'
stringent immigration and customs laws. They appeared oblivious to a
reality that dictated no guns, no expansion! One prominent politician,
Ōishi Masami, after a trip to Europe, urged in his book *Fukyōsaku* (On
enriching and strengthening the nation), 1891, that substantial pro-
grammes be undertaken for peaceful expansion. Overseas emigration to
South America and the South Seas should be encouraged, the navy
augmented, the merchant marine expanded, and shipping companies
developed so that Japanese could dominate trade routes in Asia and the
Pacific. He advocated that Japan should wake up and plan a hundred
years ahead. Another book published in the same year, *Kaigai shokumin-
ron* (On overseas colonization), explained that colonization did not mean
territorial annexation. It simply meant working and settling abroad,
trading, fishing, and engaging in any activities necessary for livelihood.
The author Tsuneya Seifuku, a prominent economist, contended that
Japanese colonization and expansion were essential to check Western
expansionism. He concluded that for reasons of suitable weather and soil
conditions, lenient native government regulations, and locations within
the orbit of their homeland's naval patrols, South America, Australia,
and the islands in the South Pacific were the best sites for Japanese emigration.

The South, then, was as much on the Japanese mind as was the North
when the Japanese expanded again in the late nineteenth century. Returning to world affairs in the mid-1890s, to claim rights to which as a
nation of their standing they deemed themselves entitled, many
Japanese held that the destiny of their country lay as much south as north
of the home islands. Professor Iriye Akira has even suggested that, while

it has been customary to consider Japanese expansionism in this period as directed primarily toward the Asian continent, the thrust of expansionism, as revealed in the writings of the period, lay elsewhere. That is to say, until the outbreak of war with China a strong undercurrent in Japanese expansionist thinking wished Japan to pick up the threads where they were left before isolation: in the South, where Japan should compete again with the Western powers in the task of developing the tremendous possibilities that the Pacific region was still believed to hold for any nation daring and industrious.

This pre-war importance accorded the South is evident, for example, in Tokutomi Sohō's (1863–1957) writings. Although this eminent historian and influential journalist later became a typical proponent of continental expansion after victory over China pushed Japan's destiny onto the continent, the lucid little book he wrote just before the outbreak of hostilities in 1894 rings out like a *reveille* for southern involvement: 'There will be established new Japans wherever the waves of the Pacific wash, the lights of the southern polestar reaches, or the warm Black Currents envelope ... If Japan had Taiwan, the nation would be provided with a base from which to penetrate the South Seas: the Philippines and the Dutch East Indies. Japan would then be in a position to compete with Britain in the region.'

A strong consciousness of the *nan'yō* had evidently re-developed along with Japan's re-emergence in the Western Pacific on the eve of the Sino–Japanese War. It was a time when Japan stood poised for her first major expansionary move which would establish her both north (in Korea) and south (on Taiwan) in 1895. Sprawling on the other side of the *nan'yō* lay the large and little-populated continent of Australia.

4

Japanese Visitors' Perceptions of Australia

IT WAS ONLY after the easing of the ban on foreign travel in 1866 that the first eyewitness accounts about life in Australia began to seep into Japan through information provided by Japanese sailors, acrobats, and pearlers. Among them was a sailor, Nonami Kojirō, from Hirose in Shimane prefecture, who took his discharge at Sydney and then found his way up to Thursday Island on the northeastern periphery of Australia in 1878. There he made a name for himself as a competent pearl diver and attracted other Japanese and their kin (many from Wakayama prefecture); Nonami became the first in a line of much sought-after Japanese contract pearlers in the 1880s. Their early impressions of Australia were of a mixed kind; while some described their Australian employers as unfeeling and lacking in humanity, and medical facilities as unsatisfactory, others returned to their native country with considerable savings, thus contributing to the belief that fortunes could be made in Australia.

Probably the earliest official introductions to the continent are two reports written by Hashimoto Masato and Sakata Haruo, who were commissioned by their government to go to the Australian Intercolonial Exhibition in Melbourne, 1875–1876, and the World Exhibition in Sydney, 1879–1880.

Hashimoto was a seventh-ranking official (subsequently promoted to the fifth rank on his return from Australia) in the Department for

48

Industrial Promotion. The first volume of his two-volume work, *Fu Gōshū Meruborun hakurankai kikō* (An account of the trip to the Melbourne exhibition), describes in diary form the Japanese mission's venturous journey to Australia and its experiences at the Melbourne Intercolonial Exhibition. Hashimoto was accompanied by Sakata Haruo, two agricultural experts, and Robert Page, an English resident of Tokyo who acted as their guide and interpreter. From their departure from Tokyo Station on 1 June 1875 until their return to Yokohama on 8 February 1876, Hashimoto provides a vivid account of the mission's adventures. After sailing via Hong Kong, Singapore, Java, and Timor, the party first set foot on Australian soil at Somerset Harbour in Queensland on 12 July. There Hashimoto's reaction to the dark complexion of the Aborigines was not unlike William Dampier's and James Cook's earlier entries about the 'coal-black savages' and 'wretchedest people on earth', for Hashimoto likened them to 'black devils'.

In Melbourne, the Japanese were wined and dined by local politicians, shown around by foreign dignitaries of consular rank, and given a tour of the University of Melbourne, the Public Library, and the prison by Sir Redmond Barry, the president of the exhibition. The author was particularly impressed by the innovative spirit of a Mr Thomas Mort, the operator of a 'Meat Preserving Company': 'Mr Mort showed us the two-year-old carcasses of sheep which still looked fresh ... and in Melbourne's Athenian Club we were served beef which was already eight weeks old, but hadn't changed its taste at all'. Hashimoto concluded from this that Mort's 'freezing chambers', packed with Australian beef, could be shipped safely thousands of miles across the equator to East Asia, and return loaded with salmon and wild game from Japan and North China for the Australian market.

Emphasizing conditions in Victoria, Hashimoto's longer second volume is heavy with statistics on Australia's climate, population, agriculture, industry, and her intercolonial and international imports and exports. It also touches on Victoria's political emancipation from New South Wales in 1851, and describes the Victorian education system, Australian election laws, the handling of immigration, and the sales procedures of Crown land. In its final section, Hashimoto discusses the under-developed sea routes between Japan and Australia, and foresees huge profits for Japan once communications between the two countries are better established. In many respects, Hashimoto's pertinent observations about his novel experiences are reminiscent of Vice-Ambassador Muragaki Awaji no Kami's *Kōkai nikki* (Diary of a sea voyage), which records the first Japanese mission to the United States in 1860. A more exhaustive study of Hashimoto's first volume would undoubtedly yield a wealth of useful material for anyone researching the early history of Japanese–Australian relations.

A similarly structured work, but with more facts and figures, is

Sakata's one-volume *Gōshū Shidoni fu bankoku hakurankai hōkokusho* (A report on Sydney's World Exhibition), 1881. The book recounts in great detail Japan's participation in the World Exhibition in Sydney, the first to be held in Australia. It is especially perceptive in its final section, which deals with Japan's future relations with Australia. An official of the Ministry for Home Affairs, with Australian experience as a member of the Hashimoto team, Sakata submitted his report to Finance Minister (and later Prime Minister) Matsukata Masayoshi in August 1881.

In Part One, Sakata describes the various products from Australia's six colonies, the United States, and different European countries on display in Sydney's most spectacular building, the Garden Palace. This huge edifice was built for the World Fair, and Sakamoto provides a diagram with the exact measurements of this large domed structure. Other chapters discuss the opening and closing ceremonies (on 17 September 1879 and 20 April 1880), attendance at the fair with its profit and loss sheet, and the various manufacturing and sales costs of the exhibits. The report ends by commenting on how well Japanese products had done, particularly tea, then regarded as Japan's most promising export commodity.

Part Two of Sakata's book provides statistics for the years 1876–1878 and covers much of the same ground as Hashimoto's earlier work. But it allots equal space to the individual colonies, includes New Zealand, and describes the history and geography of each territory. Having traveled to Australia twice, Sakata was struck by the country's relative closeness to Japan; if a direct route to Australia were established, Sydney would be as close to Japan as was San Francisco. Australia, moreover, was only about half the distance between Japan and Europe. Convinced that Japanese business with the Southern Continent would soon flourish, he added, 'We must let the Australians know quickly what we produce'. He foresaw a prosperous two-way trade in which Japan would sell to Australia tea, rice, tobacco, soybeans, malt, sake, fans, paper, silk, and ceramics; on a lesser scale, Japan would buy from Australia wool, coal, oil shale, and possibly meat. The meat trade would soon expand, he believed, if live cattle were shipped, as practised in Europe.

Sakata warned, however, that the Japanese should not wait for the Australians to launch this new trading venture. They should themselves take the initiative, 'lest the white people get all the trade', for the unequal trade agreements played into the Westerners' hands. It was imperative not to allow those agreements to interfere with Japan's commercial dealings with Australia. The Japanese government could beat Western rivals by dispatching either a regular consul to Australia or a special envoy trained in commercial affairs; the duties of such an official would be to inaugurate a profitable trade by informing Japanese merchants about products that could be marketed in Australia or imported from there.

The report notes with consternation that the government had already

entrusted 'somebody' in Melbourne with these duties. This is a reference
to the Melbourne businessman Alexander Marks. He had been installed
as Japanese Honorary Consul for Victoria in 1879, the same year that
Sakata arrived in Sydney. Sakata criticizes this step severely, opining
that the employment of honorary consuls to assist the Japanese in trade
matters was admissible only when Japan's relations with a particular
country were already well established and on firm ground. With Australia, however, Japan had as yet only superficial relations; it was insufficient and a meddlesome nuisance to engage there an honorary consul at
this stage. In any case, the report continues, if Japan did employ one, he
should be based in Sydney rather than Melbourne. Sydney was closer to
Japan, its harbour better able to accommodate Japanese vessels, and the
port taxes were lower; New South Wales's resources were also superior,
as were that colony's political system, educational institutions, and even
the people's character and stability. Compelling reasons enough, the
writer concludes, to make Sydney Japan's future trade bastion in
Australia.

Sakata was ahead of his times, for it was only in 1897, sixteen years
after the publication of his book, that Japan opened a regular consulate in
Sydney. How promising the situation for Japanese entrepreneurs in that
city really was, once the glamour of the international exhibition had
faded, is a moot point. When, for example, Shiga Shigetaka, whose work
is discussed below, visited Sydney seven years later, he described the
forty or so Japanese men and women peddling their talents in Hyde Park
as a sample of Japan's lowest social class—vaudeville actors, tea girls,
impoverished geishas, and puppet showmen. Nor was Shiga more impressed with the two or three Japanese traders doing petty business on
the third floor of a Sydney hotel.

Invaluable introductions to Australian affairs as both Hashimoto's and
Sakata's books were, their simple format and rudimentary binding
(Sakata's publisher is unknown) give the impression that the reports
were intended more as guidelines for internal circulation in government
trade bureaux than as information for the general public.

Popular information about Australia began to reach Japan through
Japanese naval explorations initiated in 1875. Civilian observers ap-
pointed by the government usually participated in these voyages into the
Pacific, and their reports eventually gave rise to a new genre of political-
geographical literature about the *nan'yō*, or South Seas. As already
mentioned, in 1886, Shiga Shigetaka was given permission to join
the *Tsukuba* on a naval expedition into the South Pacific. His book,
Nan'yō jiji, published in the following year about his first-hand observations of sea, land, and people south of the equator, devoted five
chapters to Australia alone.

Shiga drew attention to Australia's southern location *vis-à-vis*
Japan:

Japan's neighbouring countries are America to the east, China to the west, Russia to the north, and Australia to the south. As regards the first three countries, Japan has long since engaged in trade and active relations in the public as well as the private sector. But how odd it is that until today we have paid no attention to our southern neighbour, Australia . . . The Australians are the bravest and most audacious among the Anglo-Saxons. It is incomprehensible why we have so far had no dealings with this flourishing and civilized people close to us in the south.

He describes the 5,300-mile journey to Australia as an easy run that could be completed in 35–50 days by taking advantage of the trade winds:

Only Japan can benefit from these northeast and southeast winds . . . Since they are constant, a ship's speed is also constant. Steam-sailing vessels can even save on their coal, but if they use both coal and sail, they will travel even faster and gain time, while still saving on their coal . . . We would be foolish, nay, sinning against heaven, if we did not make the most of this gift.

Sailing from Yokohama on a southeasterly course, a ship could reach the equator within a few days. At 5 degrees south, the sea lanes divided into three different routes, and a ship sailing via the Bismarck Islands would reach Sydney within about a month. 'There', notes Shiga with satisfaction, 'the ship's arrival will be announced in Sydney's evening papers. The bravery and adventure of the Japanese will be praised, they will be hailed for their speed and single-mindedness, and their goods will be sold in no time.'

Shiga is at his most prophetic when he draws attention to the various advantages of a prospective trade flow between Japan and Australia (which in fact became the world's seventh largest bilateral trade-flow ninety years later). He recommends that Japan first of all sell Australia machine-polished rice. Silk and crepe will also be in demand for the Australians are rich, he observes, their salaries being seven times that of Japanese; for example, Irish maids earned U.S.$50 a year, English maids $75, but Australian maids $180, which only went to show that people in Sydney, even the maids, were affluent. And as Australian women were dressier than their menfolk, profits in the silk trade would be very large. While admitting that Australia's population, together with that of New Zealand, amounted to only about four million, Shiga points out that Australia's purchasing power was eighty-four times that of Japan. By multiplying four million by eighty-four, he concludes that Japan would be trading with Australia as if the latter country had a population of three hundred million.

As for Japanese imports from Australia, Shiga suggests coal, which could be bought from Newcastle in New South Wales and sold at about half the price of Japanese coal. He sees even brighter prospects for Australian wool, which he found cheap and of better quality than the American or British product. He had read a lot in the local newspapers about Australia's search for a good wool-market in Japan; to that end, there had been an important meeting in April of that year in Melbourne, at which Australian merchants had put up £75,000 sterling as capital for the establishment of a wool cloth company in Japan, with another £25,000 expected to be raised by Japanese merchants. This, Shiga felt, was a promising start, for yarn cloth was becoming popular in Japan and even the lower classes were wearing it. If it were imported, demand would grow, and if Japanese women were employed in the textile industry for the production of carpets, underwear, socks, and hats, immense profits could be made.

Here he cautions Japanese entrepreneurs to pay attention to the antipodal climate differences in Japan and Australia. He advises Japanese manufacturers to take advantage of this difference, since seasonal items such as straw hats (then all the rage with Westerners) could thenceforth be sold all the year around, with the opening of the summer market in Australia at the approach of the Japanese winter. If such goods were manufactured and sold throughout the year, not only would the Japanese craftsmen's skill improve along with the quality of their goods, but greater quantities could be produced to meet a bigger demand, and production costs would fall on account of greater efficiency.

Shiga was hopeful that if Japan and Australia engaged in such profitable trade, mutual understanding would result and its rewards spill over into non-commercial spheres. At the same time, he deplored Japanese indecision and admonishes: 'Time flies, people live only until the age of fifty—Japan must be more adventuresome!'

He goes on to discuss the political problems encountered by the Australian colonies on their way to independence. Pointing out, as Hashimoto had done, the strong rivalry between the dominant colonies New South Wales and Victoria, he thought it expedient for Australia to raise a joint capital to unite the two colonies and to serve as a rallying-point for the others on their way to independence from Great Britain. Australian unity was necessary, he reasoned, to forestall the French threat. France had already occupied New Caledonia and was now planning to take over the New Hebrides, with Great Britain merely standing aside, just as she had done the year before when Germany had annexed the Bismarck Islands in 1886. Shiga believed that within fifty years most Australian citizens would have become oblivious of their British bonds. He looked forward to the day when all Australians would peacefully emancipate themselves from Britain. One of the twentieth century's most significant regional historical events, he predicted, would be the federation of the *nan'yō* Anglo-Saxons under the flag of a new republic (*shinkyōwakoku*) in the South Pacific.

Shiga's penchant for social Darwinism is manifest as he enlarges on the theme of Australia acquiring independence:

Australia is like an egg. An egg is hatched, from which the young is born; it begins to think on its own, and then becomes an adult; colonies likewise evolve into independence. The Australian colonies are a good example. Their progress has been rapid, taking other countries by surprise . . . Not only is Australia becoming enormously wealthy, but its population has grown and large cities have sprung up . . . The child is obviously now becoming an adolescent; as it begins to have a mind of its own, it is searching for its own national identity, distancing itself from its mother country Britain . . . Australian nationalism is now harking to the motto, 'Australia for the Australians,' as propounded by Sir Thomas McIlwraith, leader of the National Party, who is pitted against Sir Samuel Griffith, his strong opponent of the Liberal Party.

But whatever the internal political differences, Shiga believed fervently in Australian independence and ended enthusiastically:

And should the Nationalists and Liberals all pass away, the undying principle of colonial evolution [*shokumin shinka*] will remain. The Australian states will unite and become independent of Britain—such is the intention of the gods and nothing can stop it. The god of evolution will protect you, my southerly neighbours, my good brothers.

For all that, Shiga's Australiophile outbursts were in fact a good deal more euphoric than the situation of many Japanese immigrants actually warranted. In the same year that Shiga was collecting his data in Australia, the Foreign Ministry in Tokyo, acting on its consul's warning about the often miserable working conditions of Japanese pearlers in Australian employ, was instructing Japanese contract labourers in north-eastern Australia's fisheries to return to their country. Ironically, the ministry had designated the very *Tsukuba*, on which Shiga was then making his discovery of Australia, to rendezvous on that voyage with the unhappy Japanese diaspora in northeastern Australia for repatriation.

Nevertheless, until the end of the century, Shiga's work set the optimistic tone of the handful of Japanese who looked south and wrote about Australia. Inagaki Manjirō, for example, echoed him in his influential *Tōhōsaku* (Eastern policy), 1891: 'It has often puzzled me why Japan does not have closer relations with Australia, especially since that country is becoming one of our most important neighbours in commerce . . . Together, the two countries will hold in the future the key to Pacific trade.' And Mishima Kazuo, a young journalist for the *Mainichi Shimbun*, who like Shiga had been privileged to sail on a naval ship to the South Pacific and even as far as India, introduced Australia in as entranced terms as

Shiga had done, although he added more detail since he had been able to spend nine months traveling inside Australia. Published on his return in 1891, his 300-page book *Gōshū oyobi Indo* (Australia and India) deals mainly with Australia, which is described as a huge market center and Japan's future trading partner.

Devoting as much space to the interior exploration of Australia and the discovery of gold there as he did to the whole of India, Mishima advised his fellow countrymen in his main section, 'A General Survey of Australia', to export fish, oil, candles, green tea, and matches, and import Australian leather, racehorses, and cattle. In another chapter, he tells his readers about the Australian Seamen's Union's general strike in August 1890. It not only crippled Melbourne but also afflicted the entire continent and its export business, since all transportation, including trains, came to a standstill for lack of coal from Newcastle. Although the strike had caused much hardship, Mishima appears to have been impressed by the unionists' solidarity and their show of strength when bargaining for shorter hours and higher wages. He also admired Australia's banking and insurance systems and the Western custom of deferring payment for thirty days, and he exhorts Japanese businessmen to establish good credit standing through sound references and hard work. Elsewhere, he notes the fertility of the soil in Queensland, where farmers could easily find work with official permission and free transport to their work places.

Other writers, such as naval Sub-Lieutenant Hirose Takeo (1868–1904), asked more soberly in the early 1890s:

> Australia is rapidly on its way to independence . . . it may well become a second America in the Southern Hemisphere. How shall we Japanese react? What position are we going to adopt *vis-à-vis* Australia? I am not a politician but a military man, and I am much concerned about this.

Hirose had noted this down in Melbourne on 20 January 1892 in his diary, *Kōnan shiki* (Personal record of a southern voyage), while on a seven-month cruise on the *Hiei* into the South Pacific. His entries about Australia take up fifty-eight pages and reflect the views of a trained naval officer. He rates Sydney Harbour as a formidable natural fortress, finds the Australian colonies' navy rather small, and includes statistical information about the organization of army units in the three eastern colonies. He is surprised that the country's monthly output of ammunition does not exceed 250,000 rounds and that, despite existing dock facilities, Australians do not build warships of over 3,000 tons. From this last piece of information he concludes that Britain was not eager for Australia to acquire a strong navy and armament industry, because it did not want its colony to be as powerful and independent as the United States had become.

The 1890s were the decade in which expansionism, whether 'peaceful' or imperialistic, onto the Asian mainland or into the *nan'yō*, had become a cardinal theme in Japanese political literature. And with underpopulated Australia bordering on the *nan'yō* at its farthest point, one might have expected that country to have figured as a rich prize somewhere in this literature. But times had changed since Yoshida Shōin had broached Japanese colonization of Australia as an academic question. Australia's colonial status as part of the British Empire was not challenged. And in marked contrast to the *nan'yō* literature of the late 1930s, the more important *nan'yō* books published in the 1890s mentioned Australia only in passing, preoccupied as they were with Japanese penetration of Oceania *per se*, and advocating Japanese expansion into the Micronesian and Melanesian island world by way of trading and emigration.

Eighteen months after Hirose queried the future of Japanese-Australian relations in his journal, a man set out specifically to find out what policies Japan should adopt toward Australia in the future. Traveling alone, the Japanese roamed the Australian countryside between Darwin and Sydney from August to December 1893, jumping ports along his way down the northeastern coast. He visited the goldmines at Pine Creek, the coalfields at Charters Towers, and wandered through the sugar plantations from Cooktown to Brisbane. Talking to many people, he extracted every kind of information about Australia and the problems facing Japanese immigrants. Never revealing his identity or purpose, he often became a temporary labourer by mixing with the Asian workers in the bush or in the fishing grounds, or else he passed for a Japanese merchant in the larger cities. After a brief trip to Melbourne, he embarked at Sydney and arrived back in Japan in mid-January 1894. The man was Watanabe Kanjūrō, employed by the Foreign Ministry to draw up an accurate report about Australia, and this he submitted to the Foreign Minister, Mutsu Munemitsu, on 3 May 1894. Watanabe's *Gōshū tanken hōkokusho* (Report on the exploration of Australia) was intended primarily to provide accurate data for any future government talks with Australia on the immigration question; secondly, it was published by the Foreign Ministry to serve all those directly involved with Australia, such as officials, businessmen, journalists, and prospective immigrants.

Supported by the latest statistics, illustrated with pictures showing how people lived and worked in Australia's northeast, and appended with four maps, Watanabe's 289-page book was Japan's first exhaustive and exact study about Australia. Literati such as Shiga and Mishima may have given free rein to their imagination in their travelogues about Australia. Watanabe's coverage was more sober, better informed, sociologically oriented, and geographically accurate. His work is divided into three parts, the first of which deals with the country in general, with chapters on its history and geography, Aborigines, trade, shipping, external relations, agriculture, industry, mining and fisheries, and the situation of the Japanese and Chinese immigrants. The second and third sections focus under similar headings on the Northern Territory and Queensland (where the bulk of Japanese immigrants were employed), but in greater detail as regards regional politics, religion, education, police and society, as well as the legal system with its implications of land possession, the protection of immigrants, and the situation of the Japanese in particular.

Until 1893 it had been difficult for Japanese to obtain an equitable share in Japan–Australia trade, wrote Watanabe, because the Japanese did not understand the foreign way of trading. They had incurred great losses through the system of money exchange which worked to the disadvantage of Japanese merchants: 'Australians with 10,000 pounds capital do business worth 20,000 pounds, whereas Japanese with 20,000 pounds capital do business worth 10,000 pounds'. But with the determined trader Kanematsu Fusajirō finally entrenched in the wool-export business in Sydney, prospects were beginning to look brighter. They would further improve if sugar and frozen meat were exported to Japan on the conveniently short and cheap shipping route. To realize this growing market potential, it was imperative for Japan to expand her shipping in the South Pacific by training competent men who knew about loss and gain in international shipping, and who could deal with the many problems of unloading Japanese cargoes onto the wharves of Australian ports.

If Shiga and Mishima had introduced Australia as a country that held out much hope for Japanese industrial and agrarian enterprise, Watanabe dispelled these illusions in his report. Other than Queensland and the Northern Territory, he saw little else of Australia suitable for Japanese immigration. Chinese already occupied vegetable and fruit farming, and there was no promising land for rice cultivation or cotton growing. In addition, the Queensland and Northern Territory governments prohibited foreign land-ownership, and even mine leasing by Asians in the Northern Territory (then administered by the South Australian Colonial Government) had been rescinded by a decree of 12 December 1893. Australians apparently feared the Japanese, observed Watanabe, and had begun to curb the influx of Asian labor: 'The Japanese actually feel more rejected in Australia than they do in America'.

But not all was hopeless. Japanese could still promote their fortunes in Australia in two profitable areas. One was the pearling industry. As Japanese were acknowledged experts in advanced techniques, Watanabe urged his fellow countrymen to enter Australian fishing grounds in greater numbers and set up new fisheries. If they operated with seagoing vessels that could weather the oceans to Europe, they would be able to sell their pearls directly in London at high profit. The other area in which Japanese could expand their labor activities was the sugar plantations. Although Japanese could not own farmland in Australia, they were at least allowed to lease plots of land. Watanabe therefore suggested that capitalists make use of this concession by immediately re-engaging on Japanese-leased land any indentured caneworkers at the end of their contracts, thereby sustaining the immigrant labour force in Australia for the benefit of Japanese-leased sugar plantations.

Although Watanabe found the situation of Japanese contract labour in Queensland generally satisfactory, he pointed out many shortcomings still existing in the contracts and working conditions of Japanese immigrants. The main purpose of his mission was to shed light on immigration problems, and Watanabe discussed this matter at some length. Japanese contract labourers for Australia were then handled by Nippon Yoshisa Immigration Company, formed in 1890. The company saw to the workers' transport as far as Australia. There they were contracted to the Australian trading company of Burns Philp, which in turn negotiated the immigration procedures and their allocation to various work places within the country. Watanabe strongly criticizes Yoshisa Co. for merely collecting the labourers and their fares, and then packing them off to Australia without the slightest regard for their working and living conditions there. He also deplores the fact that Yoshisa Co. let foreign immigration recruiters, who were often no more than inexperienced Australian interpreters, manage their Japanese immigrant customers in Australia. This deprived the Japanese government of any direct control over its subjects. It also gave Australians the impression that Japanese labourers lacked their government's support.

This final remark offers an interesting Japanese perception about immigration to the Southern Continent. Watanabe noted with wonder that although Britain had done little more than send convicts as immigrants to cultivate Australia, even these wretched creatures had always enjoyed the strong backing of their motherland. How different it was for the Japanese. The British could own land in Australia, but the Japanese could not. The latter could go and work there only as contracted worker immigrants, and were often regarded as little more than slaves. Watanabe therefore strongly emphasized the importance of the Japanese and Australian governments improving the existing contract systems, and concluded his perceptive report with the suggestion that frequent government-to-government talks be held to solve these and other problems between the two countries.

Two other Australia-related publications appeared shortly after Watanabe's report. The first was Hattori Tōru's *Nankyū no shin shokumin* (A new colony in the southern hemisphere), 1894, a short book focused on the circumstances in which approximately five hundred Japanese were living on Thursday Island. It introduces the territory's geology, climate, and vegetation, and provides a general description of the island's political, educational, religious, and sanitary systems, as well as its trade and communication links with the outside world. The book concentrates on the origin of Japanese immigration to Thursday Island and the conditions under which the pearlers were making their living there. It also recounts the vicissitudes of the local shell-fishing industry and the relations between the Japanese (the largest ethnic group on the island) and the other residents, made up of Caucasians, Filipinos, Malays, and Chinese. Hattori pleads for stronger self-government by the already powerful Japanese Club (*Nihonjin kurabu*) which looked after Japanese interests. But despite his book's provocative title, the author makes it clear that the island's territoriality lay under the jurisdiction of Queensland, and that his understanding of the term 'colony' was simply a place for Japanese to emigrate to, where they could live and work lawfully and in peace.

The other, even shorter, volume was published in 1895 and was an official Australian price-list, translated and produced by the Tokyo Trade Council. Titled *Gōshū sanbutsu kōtei daikahyō*, it lists in detail the various merchandise that Australian producers from Victoria had brought to Japan for display, and gives the prices of many items, such as mutton and bacon, eucalyptus extract, champagne and brandy, and Christmas plum pudding. Australia had truly emerged.

By the 1890s the Japanese had come a long way in their discovery of Australia since their copying of the Southland from Matteo Ricci's world map. Shipping companies, such as the Peninsula & Orient and Nippon Yūsen Kaisha were providing regular services between the two countries. Japan was beginning to buy Australian coal and wool, while Australia was receiving a constant trickle of Japanese immigrant laborers to work her pearling industry and the Queensland sugar plantations. Small Japanese shops had opened in major cities, and in both Melbourne and Sydney Japan had participated in international exhibitions. By the second half of the 1890s Japan was operating either regular or honorary consulates in every Australian colony except Western Australia (where the first Japanese consulate was opened as late as 1910 in the pearling center of Broome). Prospects for the future of Japanese–Australian ties looked bright.

However, two policies had intensified, one in Japan and the other in Australia, which in combination were to keep the two countries at arm's length until the mid-twentieth century. One had its immediate roots in Japan's prestigious victory over China in 1894–1895, which set Japan on a course of assertive foreign policy and made her appear to Australian observers as an increasingly imperialistic threat to that continent's underpopulated shores. The other owed its origin to the movement within Australia toward the creation of a 'White Australia' by extending restrictive immigration laws (hitherto limited to Chinese labour) to all Asian people. By the time of Australian federation in 1901, it had resulted in an effective exclusion of practically all coloured immigration, including the Japanese. Gaining momentum in the years 1896–1900, these two alienating trends portended a much subdued climate for future Japanese–Australian relations.

Imperial Japan Faces White Australia 1896–1923

Japanese–Australian relations during this period were often tense and erratic, hinging as they did on a distinct Australian feeling of geopolitical insecurity towards the growing regional power of Japan. After a hundred years of preponderantly British settlement, Australia still had a population of only four million in a country twenty-two times the size of Japan. To remedy an acute labour-shortage in the mid-nineteenth century, Australia had started tapping the workforce of the Australasian region by the introduction of indentured labour, and had invited Chinese immigrants to work the fields and tend the sheep. But when due to the goldrush in the colony of Victoria their numbers jumped from 2,300 in 1854 to 17,000 in 1855, Australians passed the first Restriction Act on Chinese Immigration.

After Japan defeated China in 1895, Australian concern about living close to the proverbial hordes of Asia's teeming millions began to focus on Japan. The image of the 'yellow menace' became an ever sterner element in the discussions that carried Australians to federation at the turn of the century. The feeling of threat deepened after Japan's victories over Russia in 1904–1905. It was at the same time complicated by Japan's alliance with Great Britain in a political tie that took into account world affairs in the Northern Hemisphere only, and made Australians painfully aware of their isolated situation in the Southern Hemisphere.

A significant sector of Australians believed that Japan was standing by to sail across the Pacific and invade Australia. This was an amazingly undifferentiated view. It was stimulated, it seems, more by pangs of doubt about the righteousness of closing the Australian continent to anyone but white people than by insight into Japan's true interests in the *nan'yō* or by a deeper grasp of *realpolitik* in the Asian–Pacific environment.

5

Japan's 'Southward Advance' School of Thought

THE FOREIGN political events that reshaped the East Asian world in 1894–1895 sent ripples as far as Australia. Two months into the Sino–Japanese war the British Minister at Tokyo, Le Poer Trench, warned his government and the Australian colonies in December 1894: 'A strong Japanese navy might at any time constitute a menace not only to Hong Kong and Singapore, but also to the Australian colonies and Canada'. Major-General Sir Edward Thomas Hutton (1848–1923), commander of the New South Wales military forces, advised his colonial government in 1895: 'The sudden rise of Japan to the position of a naval and military power of the first magnitude has placed the importance of the defence of the Australian continent . . . in the light of necessity'. Australia now had at her door a maritime power whose fleet had transported and was maintaining an army of 200,000 men through a difficult and bloody campaign. And while George Cathcart Craig studied with apprehension Japan's occupation of Taiwan (then Formosa) in his book *The Federal Defence of Australia* (1897), Australia's annual military exercises in 1895 had the theme of repelling Japanese vessels trying to enter Sydney harbour. Australia was put on guard.

Yet Australia need not have been alarmed unduly. It is true that the capture of Taiwan was a step closer to Australia. It established Japan's first base in the *nan'yō*, and her victory over China signalled an important

65

turn in the development of Japan's 'southward advance' school of thought (*nanshin-ron*). But it also marked the beginning of Japanese differentiation of the *nan'yō*, a process that by 1923 would clearly locate Australia outside Japan's specific spheres of interest in the South Seas.

To nineteenth century men such as Satō Nobuhiro, Mitsukuri Shōgo, or Shiga Shigetaka, the South Seas had meant the Philippines, Micronesia, and the tropical islands beyond in the South Pacific. Into that vast and yet undefined area of the unknown *nan'yō*, southward expansionists in the middle Meiji period had urged, in a haphazard way, commercial enterprise and expansionism. This yet undirected southern interest championed by progressives and liberals—intellectuals out of power—and free traders, was now given political direction for the first time and routed along the South China coast by government interests entrenched on Taiwan from 1896 onwards.

Katsura Tarō (1847–1913), the second governor-general of Taiwan, wrote to Tokyo in July that Taiwan commanded the South China coast just like Kyūshū commanded the approaches to Korea: 'Japan should make haste to commandeer the China Sea in order to be in touch with the coastal region of South China and the South Seas islands'. In June 1899, Kodama Gentarō (1852–1906), the fourth governor-general, dictated in more detail the development of the South China coast in a fourteen-point memorandum which placed special emphasis on the province of Fukien, opposite Taiwan, and its important harbour of Amoy. And his Chief of Civil Administration, Gotō Shimpei (1857–1929), advised the opening of an Amoy branch of the Bank of Taiwan as a 'precursor of imperial southward advance'. All three stressed the necessity of further southward advance and that this should take place via South China. Therefore, Japan's southward advance developed noticeably after the Sino–Japanese war, but in a direction that ignored Australia.

The Russo–Japanese war gave Japan's southward advance another push. Japan's victory over a European nation, coupled with substantial northern territorial gains, also affected her southward interests in terms of pressing for greater trade expansion in South China and penetration into the region further down the coast. It also intensified discussions concerning the national strategies of *hokushu nanshin* (defence in the north and advance in the south) vs. *nanshu hokushin* (defence in the south and advance in the north). After cabinet approval of Yamagata Aritomo's 'Plan for Imperial National Defence' in 1907, *hokushin-ron*, the school of thought for northward advance, onto the mainland and directed against Russia, came to be associated with the army. As a corollary, *nanshin-ron*, the school of thought for southward advance, towards the southern isles and aimed against the Pacific Ocean power America and other colonial powers in the Southeast Asian region, became the preserve of the navy.

These discussions waxed against the backdrop of a host of economic problems, political turmoil, and strategic rivalry in Northeast Asia between 1906 and 1913. Japan's postwar finances were burdened by foreign loans and imports to restore the nation's economy and maintain her military prestige. Railroads had to be built, embankments constructed, and large expenses budgeted for battleships to respond to the United States's policy of 'big guns and big ships' and for the creation of two army divisions to control the northern Far East. Korea was absorbed into the Empire in 1910 and the Chinese Revolution broke out in the following year. Fierce international rivalry in Manchuria further aggravated the situation, as Britain, France, America, and Russia were all jockeying for economic and strategic positions in what Japan believed to be her rightfully staked-out sphere of interest in the North. Japan's multitude of problems in the North Asian region put a brake on her southward advance.

Interestingly, it was in this very period of intense Japanese preoccupation with Korea, Manchuria, and China that Australia decided to establish an army and a navy to forestall a Japanese invasion. After Japan's momentous victory over Russia, Japan was ever more talked about in the Australian parliament as an aggressive and expansionist power in the Pacific. Her presence demanded 'a bold and well-defined plan of Australian defence', said William Hughes, the outspoken Labor member for West Sydney, who moved a resolution in 1906 to support conscription. Lieutenant-Colonel Bridges was promptly ·despatched round the world to Berne to study the Swiss compulsory and universal military training system, while Prime Minister Alfred Deakin and his Director of Naval Forces, Captain W. R. Cresswell, devised plans for a separate Australian naval force consisting of a local flotilla of destroyers and torpedo boats. When the Admiralty in London criticized the scheme as imperfect and its cost as out of proportion to the protection it offered, Cresswell defended it as indispensable, given Australia's vulnerability to a Japanese invasion. Japan had a population problem and needed room to expand; the White Australia policy was an affront to that nation which cast longing glances on Australia's empty lands. The 1909 Defence Bill secured both an Australian navy and an army based on compulsory service.

Yet Australian threat perceptions were quite divorced from the international political realities that faced Japan. It is true that Yamagata Aritomo was able to engineer the creation of two new divisions for Korea in 1911–1912, and that the heated discussions on whether to expand north or south reached a peak in an extra edition of the popular journal *Taiyō* (The Sun), issued in November 1913, under the captivating title of *Nanshin ka, Hokushin ka* (Southward or northward advance?). But Japanese perceptions of moving southward were worlds apart from Australia's narrow preoccupation with a direct Japanese invasion of her shores.

Japan in the late 1900s revealed a complex mentality of pride and doubt about being a first-rate power. 'Our empire has now become a first-class power in the world. But does any power go with it?' asked Uchida Kakichi, the Chief Civil Administrator of Taiwan, in his book on Japanese overseas development policies. It reflected Japan's pervasive feeling of uncertainty that lasted until the outbreak of World War I. It was difficult to measure up to the Chinese shopman or the white colonist in the *nan'yō*. Although Japan had defeated China, Chinese traders were still dominating the *nan'yō*. Japan may have risen to being a first-class power by victory over Russia, but that had not changed the fact that white people still controlled the South Seas, the *nan'yō* that Japan would have liked to regard as her own backyard. Unable to change the situation, Japanese continued to take an interest in restoring their finances and putting economic development first. At the same time, they urged non-territorial advance into the South Seas by way of free trade and peaceful economic advance. Their commercial interests were shifting from the Southwest Pacific region and down the South China coast to converge on the Malay Peninsula with its rubber plantations, the Dutch East Indies, and the Philippine islands.

At this stage in the development of Japan's southward advance, politicians and scholars who are better known for their mainland-directed Asian views, began to take an interest in the south also. Inukai Tsuyoshi, Prime Minister at the time of Japanese expansion into Manchuria, believed after the Russo–Japanese war in 1905 that there should be no further advance north. At Nagoya he pronounced that Japan should now shift her attention to the region of South China and Southeast Asia and expand in a peaceful way, with money, into Vietnam, Thailand, Australia, the East Indies, and the Philippines. The renowned liberal scholar, Nitobe Inazō, also showed a marked interest in the South at this time. He would later rejoice over the annexation of Korea and see Japan's outer limits as growing naturally in concentric circles to South Manchuria, Sakhalin, and North Manchuria as far as Chichihar and Harbin. But in 1907, he picked up the folk tale of Momotarō (The Peach Boy) as a tool with which to stir Japanese popular interest in the southward advance. In this thirteenth century tale, Momotarō, born out of a peach to a childless couple, sets out with the help of a dog, a monkey, and a pheasant to chastize the ogres on an island far out in the sea and retrieve their stolen treasure. Nitobe recommended the fable as an effective instrument of national expansionism: 'I believe that the folklore of Momotarō's overseas expedition expresses without doubt Japan's interest in the outside world and her marching spirit . . . Until 1895, Taiwan was the Island of Ogres . . . Momotarō of today will expand to conquer toward the Island of Ogres further [south].'

Nitobe's new look at the simple thread in the old story was worked on by other scholars and eventually found its way into the national primary reader compiled by the Ministry of Education in 1910. Little thought seems to have been given an old warning of Fukuzawa Yukichi: 'If Momotarō went to take away treasure which belonged to someone else, then he was a wicked robber. If he had gone simply to punish the demons for being wicked and troublesome that would have been very good.' Some scholars have pointed out the frontier spirit which came to be stressed in the Momotarō fable and have even likened it to such theories as the Manifest Destiny of the United States. Others maintain more bluntly that the Momotarō Doctrine developed over the years into the Japanese doctrine of aggression which grew into an invasion of China in the 1930s and of Southeast Asia in the early 1940s. Whatever the emphasis, for our purposes it is relevant to state that Australia was never targeted to become the Island of Ogres; not even as the enactment of the fable reached its climax in an adaptation to Malay and Chinese Opera for the Japanese military authorities in Singapore, where *Momotarō* was performed many times as a propaganda piece in the war years 1942–1943.

Another important book that whipped up enthusiasm for the southward advance before World War I, was Takekoshi Yosaburō's *Nangokuki* (An account of southern countries) published in 1910. It contained miscellaneous essays on the history, manners, and customs of Southeast Asian countries and southern China. That it sold well was probably due more to its rousing foreword in which the noted economic historian aimed at drawing Japanese attention away from the mainland to the southern regions. He dismissed the development of Manchuria as a hopeless venture. The international loan agreement of 1911 showed that already too many powers were meddling in Manchuria, and Japan could not hold it. Under the ringing slogan of 'Southward-ho!' (*Minami e! Minami e!*), a call that Murobuse Kōshin was to repeat in exactly the same words and with the same fervor in 1936, the author developed a number of themes in which he deplored that the Japanese had forgotten the South. Japan was an island country; it was unnatural for trading people to go north, they must seek the South. There lay Japan's future, especially in the plantation business of Malaya and Indonesia. In Mackinderian vein, Takekoshi explained that he who dominates the tropics, controls the world. But he also denied military aggression and undue exploitation of colonies, and severely criticized the plundering of Taiwanese customs revenue for Japanese government coffers. Australia was entirely outside the scope of the book.

After the Russo–Japanese war, World War I was the next important turning point in the *nanshin-ron* of this period. On 9 August 1914, Japan cast her lot with the Allies when she posed an ultimatum to Germany 'as a voluntary expression of friendship toward Great Britain under the Alliance', in the words of Foreign Miniser Katō Takaaki. What long had eluded the southward protagonists, global war now swept into their hands. It brought about significant changes in Japan's southward advance, as the nation acquired territory, wealth, and greater freedom for its citizens to move about in the South Seas region. For when Japan's navy moved to confiscate the German island possessions in October that year, her economy, too, began to fill the commercial vaccuum created by war. With the outflow of Japanese exports into the entire region, including Australia, Japanese manufactures quadrupled, heavy industry developed, the Japanese merchant fleet grew from 1,557,000 gross tons in 1914 to 2,840,000 in 1919, while at the same time her debts of around 1.3 billion yen turned into foreign assets of the same amount. Japan's swift decision to take sides had paid off handsomely.

Detailed studies of the early Taishō *nanshin-ron* (approximately World War I period; Emperor Taishō reigned from 1912 to 1925) by Shimizu Hajime, show how the thought structure of southern advance at this time became suffused with pan-Asianist thought of the *hokushin-ron* school. By the early stages of the war, the *nanshin-ron* advocates were accepting continental Asia as a logical extension of the Japanese Empire. The *hokushin-ron* advocates, on the other hand, incorporated the acquired Micronesian islands into their blown-up concept of the *tōyō* (eastern region), already vastly extended by the inclusion of Korea and South Manchuria. Fitting Micronesia into their idea of Eastern Empire somewhat blunted the edges of the ideological dispute. It also led to a division of the geographical *nan'yō* concept into *'uchi'* (inner) *nan'yō* and *'soto'* (outer) *nan'yō*. The 'inner' *nan'yō* spread from Taiwan in the South China Sea to the Marshalls, Marianas, and Carolines in the Central Pacific. From these oceanic bases, Japanese southern interest was to direct itself into the 'outer' *nan'yō*, a geographical concept standing now largely for the Southeast Asian region.

To stand up to the economic success of the Chinese and compete at the same time with the colonial powers entrenched in Southeast Asia, the Japanese began to assert themselves with a consistent policy backed by tight-knit national organizations. Where the Chinese had used unions, guilds, and clubs to unite expatriate Chinese from the same provinces and clans, the Japanese, in a more nation-directed way, began to draw on the patriotic concepts of 'country' and 'national people'. They established information organizations and human resources training centers in Japan, and in Southeast Asia Japanese elementary schools, Japanese-language newspapers, and a regional Japanese Chamber of Commerce to cultivate a sense of belonging and raise the consciousness of being a member of the Japanese nation. In this process of nurturing the Japanese idea of the Imperial subject advancing south as a loyal Empire member, much of the heavy symbolism in the Asianist's *hokushin-ron* came to infuse the *nanshin-ron* with spruced-up concepts of medieval and classic times: *hakkō ichiu* (the eight corners of the world under one roof; the entire world as one family), racial expansionism based on the ideas of *kōdō shugi* (the Imperial Way doctrine), and *dōbun dōshu* (members of the same race sharing a similar culture or using similar writing systems). The theme of Japan's mission as self-professed leader of the Orient in liberating Asians from Western control, came to be thought of as singularly applicable to the peoples living in the Southeast Asian region, too. The resources of that region were now often called Heaven's blessings (*tenkei*) or Heaven's riches (*tenpu*): blessings that were given to all people equally, riches on 'unowned land waiting to be developed'.

As the *nanshin-ron* began to lend itself to the new concept of *nanboku heishin ron* (simultaneous southward and northward advance), it was imbued with the principles of *Dai Nihon shugi* (Greater Japanism). Peculiarly *sui generis*, this brand of Japanese imperialism was considered 'moral' and therefore different from European and U.S. Imperialism. An important trendsetter of this ideology was Tokutomi Sohō, who promoted the idea of Japanese advance as a 'national family' with the Imperial Household placed at its center. His two books, *Jimu ikkagen* (My views on current affairs), 1913, and *Taishō no seinen to teikoku no zento* (Taishō youth and the Empire's future), 1916, greatly influenced the prolific, but otherwise stereotypical literature of the southward advance protagonists. They also supplied the Taishō *nanshin-ron* with widely used buzz words such as *kokuze* (national policy), *shimei* (mission), *tenshoku* (divine calling), and *hakubatsu* (white clique). This is vocabulary better known for having fired the Japanese imagination at the time of conceiving the Greater East Asia Co-Prosperity Sphere. But interestingly the essence of this ideology was already produced in the early Taishō period, although afterwards war-weariness and the meeker spirit of the age of Taishō Democracy caused its submergence for nearly a generation.

Other than the numerous books on the *nanshin-ron*, many journals discussed the southward advance—periodicals such as *Shokumin zasshi* (Journal of Colonization), *Shokumin Kōhō* (Official Bulletin of Colonization), *Jitsugyō no Nihon* (Industrial and Business Japan) which often issued special issues about the South Seas, *Tōkyō chigaku kyōkai zasshi* (Journal of the Tokyo Geographical Society), *Taiyō* (The Sun), or *Nan'yō kyōkai zasshi* (Journal of the South Seas Society). The latter was the organ of a society established in January 1915 by influential businessmen, politicians, and bureaucrats 'to investigate conditions in the South Seas and endeavour to develop the area', described in their journal as a boundless treasure house a million square miles wide, from Java, Sumatra, Borneo, and the Celebes to the Philippines, waiting to be developed by all nations.

The same enthusiasm reverberates in the pages of *Nan'yō yūki* (Travel sketches of the South Seas), 1917. Written by Tsurumi Yūsuke upon his return from an extended expedition to the tropical islands, it capped perfectly the *nanshin*-fever of those years. The authoritative liberal thinker wished for a strategy of economic advance into the South Seas, coupled with Japanese understanding of the rising nationalism in the colonies of Southeast Asia. But he emphasized a *nanshin-ron* void of military aggression or naked territorial ambition.

Although most Japanese books on the South Seas promoted an aggressive spirit, they refrained from suggesting southern advance by force. They were full of the entrepreneurial spirit, with sights set high. But they urged peaceful advance, and in doing so were naive only in that they were blind to the fact that World War I and the resulting mandate system would actually strengthen, not weaken, Western immigration control of most Australian, United States, and European-held territories in the Western Pacific—quite to the detriment of Japan's roving southern drive. After a two month political exploration trip in the South Seas in 1918, for example, House of Councillors member Yamamoto Teijirō commented optimistically on the business potential in British Malaya and the Dutch East Indies and urged that Japan should divert all her energy to the southern region. While he did observe the difficulty of freely entering those British- and Dutch-held territories, the Philippines, and Australia, he nevertheless believed that Sumatra, Borneo, Celebes, a part of New Guinea, and some other islands, still offered room for anyone venturesome. Managing the South Seas meant to him, above all, putting up capital and providing technology. Japan should also install more consulates in the region and extend the sea lanes to the East Indies. Yamamoto's report in his party organ *Seiyū* was one of many similar articles published at that time. No longer did they simply introduce marvellous and unheard of countries in the South, as had been the case in the Meiji period. Basking in the expectation that Japan would soon play an important role in developing the abundant region, the reports were now full of practical information and written with an over-abundance of optimism.

While there was not much about Australia in this specific literature on the *nan'yō*, outside the *nanshin* genre a number of books told in a detached way of developments on the southern continent. These now treated Australia in an informative and business-like way, the once prevailing enthusiasm of the mid-Meiji period having long since been stifled by the enforcement of the White Australia policy in 1901. Most writers still summed-up that policy in a critical vein somewhere in their pages, but they appeared largely resigned to White Australia as a *fait accompli*. Australia was just another country, deep in the *nan'yō*, about which much could be learnt, but which held out neither a hand for friendship nor any special hope for close economic ties.

Australia, then, remained largely outside the discussion of southward advance. The continent's existence as a British dominion was neither questioned nor challenged. Paradoxically, although victory over China in 1895 had put Japan both on a northern and a southern course of advance, her interests had been moving in a direction *away* from

Australia. Japanese southern interest in economic and demographic advance did not follow the sea lane envisaged by the mid-Meiji *nanshin* advocates—which would have developed rapidly into a direct course of lively communication between Japan and Australia on the shortest way possible, via the Philippines, the Solomons, Australia's northeast, and to the prospering cities in Queensland, New South Wales, and Victoria. After 1895, Japan's focus in the South Seas instead moved south via Taiwan, along the South China coast, eventually coming to rest on the Southeast Asian region in the late 1910s.

By then, the Japanese were distinguishing between the 'inner' South Seas or *uchi nan'yō*, and the 'outer' South Seas or *soto nan'yō*. The 'inner' South Seas was defined by Japan's territorial possessions in the South China Sea and the Central Pacific. From there, on Taiwan and the Micronesian islands, the Japanese now looked onto the 'outer' South Seas with great expectations. Interestingly, however, Australia had by then been moved beyond even this 'outer' South Seas, which in the interwar years came to be identified largely with the Southeast Asian region. According to a 1933 source, published at a time when the notion of *soto nan'yō* was well established, the 'outer' South Seas comprised the region from the Philippines to Java, West Borneo, Celebes, Sumatra, the Lesser Sunda Islands, Moluccas, Dutch New Guinea, British North Borneo, Malay Peninsula, Siam, French Indochina, and the Chinese mainland. Placed in the *nan'yō* of the Polynesian island world, Australia had drifted into the horizons of a threefold concept of the *nan'yō* that defined her far outside the sphere of Japanese interests. Australia really had no reason to be alarmed.

6

White Australia,
and a Shield Forged

EVERAL YEARS before Japan was to become imperial and Australia white, the two countries were beginning to glare at each other over immigration issues on the North Australian littoral. In one of the earliest indentured labour contracts with a foreign country, the Japanese Foreign Ministry in 1883 had negotiated a contract with the manager of the Australasian Pearl Company, Captain J. A. Miller, that allowed for the hiring of thirty-seven Japanese to work the pearl-beds of Thursday Island off Queensland. They were to join compatriots already diving there and at Darwin, some of whom were contracted from boarding houses of itinerant Japanese in Hong Kong. Industrious and reliable, most pearlers did well. Similar contracts followed, the Japanese community grew, and by 1893 they were the largest national group employed in the pearling industry at Thursday Island. On 2 April 1894, however, Alexander Marks, Japan's Honorary Consul in Australia, warned the Japanese Vice Foreign Minister, Hayashi Tadasu, that too many Japanese in Torres Strait were becoming a burden to the State of Queensland. Thousands were unemployed because of a depression in trade, particularly at Thursday Island (which could employ only a limited number of men for pearl-shell fishing), and because white labour organizations disliked competition. Marks regretted that caution had not been displayed by those engaging labour on the Japanese side.

A month later, he informed Hayashi that Queensland was debating the imposition of a poll tax on Japanese. He was going to Brisbane to try to prevent this and suggested that a war vessel be sent, which 'would have a great moral effect upon the Parliament and people of that country'. Hayashi directed Marks to keep up his efforts, but regretted that the battleship *Kongo* could not be despatched because hostilities with China had already begun 'in consequence of the Corean affair'.

Darwin, too, was beginning to build its white walls, although Japanese numbers had not increased particularly in that tiny colonial outpost, then administered by South Australia. In December 1894 there were still only around thirty Japanese in Darwin, and three of them were ship masters. But this small number was beginning to be felt as a threat, fed by fear that the more numerous Japanese boat-owners at Thursday Island would in the future extend their activities to Darwin. Already in autumn 1893 the junior member for the Northern Territory, W. Griffiths, introduced an act into the South Australian Parliament to extend the Chinese Immigration Restriction Act of 1888 to exclude all persons of Asiatic origin.

As the Sino–Japanese war unfolded, more warnings about a Japanese increase on the North Australian coast-line reached Brisbane and Adelaide. On 3 March 1894, a report issued by John Douglas, the Government Resident at Thursday Island, stated that whereas two years earlier not twenty boats had been owned and manned by Japanese, there were now around seventy boats. Thirty-eight (of a total of 153) of those were owned by Japanese; this merited the serious attention of the Queensland Parliament. At Darwin, a year later on 25 April, six white boat-owners sent a petition to the South Australian Parliament warning of an Asian monopoly and urging it to grant pearling-boat licences to whites only. This was just one week after China had signed the peace terms at Shimonoseki, and whether the petitioners were influenced by Japan's momentous victory is an open question. It was at the same time that the New South Wales free-trader Henry Willis asked the Colonial Treasurer in the Legislative Assembly: 'In view of the warlike events in the East, and the great success attained by the Japanese nation, will the Government consider the advisability of immediately introducing legislation to prevent Japanese immigration into New South Wales similar to that passed into law against the influx of Chinese?'

On 31 July 1895, with still no sign of an increase in Asian boat-owners of licences sought by them in Darwin, or of the amount of shell raised, W. Griffiths led a debate in the South Australian House of Assembly, asserting that 'very great harm was being done to the Northern Territory's pearl industry owing to the increase of Japanese engaged'. The Government at first declined his petition to restrict the Japanese. They thought it desirable to develop the industry, and the Japanese were doing it very well. But when rumour circulated of an onrush of Japanese boats from Thursday Island to Port Darwin, it abandoned its position.

And after a similar canard was spread on 4 October, the South Australian Government advised the Premier of Queensland to inform the Japanese on Thursday Island that they would be issued no more licences for pearling in the Northern Territory.

This all played into the hands of the Premier of South Australia, Charles Cameron Kingston (1850–1908), a prominent lawyer and radical liberal who had played a leading part in putting into effect the Chinese Restriction Act of 1888. He had longed to extend the Act to all Asian labour, but had lacked the support of his cabinet and had always been blocked by the New South Wales Government. With a more amenable cabinet behind him, Kingston took this opportunity—at a time when all colonies were debating whether or not to join the Anglo–Japanese commercial treaty—to call for an Intercolonial Conference at which to decide these two prime issues for Australia. Kingston was the driving force behind the conference, and his urgent call on 30 September to participate was at last heeded by the colonies. New South Wales Premier George Reid (1845–1918), leader of the oldest and probably most influential of the five Australian colonies, scheduled it for 4 and 5 March 1896 in Sydney. The other colonies had been none too enthusiastic about the summoning of an Intercolonial Conference to consider Japanese questions only—and Reid tried to shield them from 'undue prominence' by proposing that federal defence be the leading subject. But the unanimous and far-reaching decision which emerged from the talks was to extend the Immigration Restriction Act to all coloured people.

To be sure, a number of factors unrelated to Japan's victory over China had converged in the years 1893–1896 to create the influx of Japanese into Australia which was now accelerating the problem of immigration restriction. One was the new frontier spirit fostered by organizations such as the Tokyo Geographical Society and the Colonization Society in the early 1890s. We can only guess at how many Japanese were induced by their pamphlets to emulate frontiersmen who already in the 1870s had sought glory and fortune in the shell-beds on the Australian coast. And there can be little doubt that government reports—such as Watanabe Kanjūrō's 1894-briefing on Australia, with his hopeful comments on opportunities in the fishery and sugar-growing industries—gave Japanese immigration a strong push. (A generation later, Japanese Vice Foreign Minister Hanihara Masanao would tell an Australian government official that it was mainly the inducements offered by the Queensland sugar planters in the early 1890s that had caused a large number of Japanese workers to sail to Australia.)

Hattori Tōru's enticing description of Thursday Island in *A New Colony in the Southern Hemisphere*—written as a challenging 'how-to-build-a-colony' book—could have been further incentive for someone yearning to escape the poverty of a Japanese fishing village. Significantly, Hattori's 'colony' idea was supported by other disinformation, whether deliberate or just naive we do not know, provided by Japan's Honorary Consul in Melbourne. On 20 March 1896, Alexander Marks told the Japanese Foreign Ministry that for two years he had been trying to obtain an island in Torres Strait for a Japanese colony and a large concession of territory from the Queensland Government. He had not done anything about it yet, however; his friend, Jacob Goldstein, editor of the *Australasian Hebrew*, on whom he was relying to win this deal for him in governing circles, had put his scheme off for some time, because 'the Conference of Premiers in New South Wales decided to extend the Chinese Restriction Act to *all* Eastern races, and, apparently they were especially afraid of the people who went to Torres Straits Concession'.

Another important factor, unconnected but coincident with the Sino–Japanese war, which put pressure on the colonies to extend the Immigration Restriction Act was the invitation to join the Anglo–Japanese Treaty of Commerce and Navigation. The British Government had sent copies of the treaty to the colonies in December 1894. Its most important points for Australia, Articles I and III, conferred the right of residing in the contracting parties' territories and the freedom of commerce and navigation between the subjects of the signatory powers. These were heatedly debated topics and were lumped together with the immigration restriction question at the Intercolonial Conference at Sydney. They touched on two paramount issues which to many Australians appeared to be a choice between national survival and profit: they could have special trade privileges with Japan only if they allowed greater tolerance on the immigration question. The pressure of having to give London an answer by 25 August 1896 greatly exacerbated the argument.

Although fundamentally unrelated to Japan's defeat of China, the two issues conjoined, as Australians came increasingly to view Japan, rather than China, as the major threat to their country. The *Straits Times* had noted on 15 November 1895: 'The new treaty between Britain and Japan now arouses close attention in Australia . . . The Japanese there stir up greater antipathy than the Chinese, and the Japanese are indeed looked upon as more dangerous from their highly insinuating ways and greater intellectual powers'. Negative traits previously ascribed to the Chinese were now attributed to the Japanese:

Japanese coolies stick together, save, and get on, until they settle on the soil and compete with Australian producers at such cheap rates that rivalry becomes almost impossible. But their immigration is only just beginning and the problem is how best to stop the evil at the outset. The new treaty terms between Britain and Japan facilitate Japanese immigration, but do not apply to the Australian colonies unless they intimate acceptance before a specific date. That date is drawing near . . . Trade advantages cannot countervail the accompanying disadvantages of cheap Japanese labour competition against the colonial working classes. A Conference will be held at Sydney in December next.

Although mistaken on the conference date, the article sums up well the mood which led to refusal of the treaty by all the colonies in March 1896.

To understand the significant conclusions reached at the Sydney conference in 1896 (and it is generally emphasized that no notes have survived it), one cannot ignore the roundabout way in which the fear of Japanese, fostered in Australia's northeast in the mid-1890s, jumped from the pearling communities of Thursday Island to Darwin, with its festering racial animosities, and thereby to South Australia. There Charles Cameron Kingston, Asianophobe and skilled legalist, at last found an opportunity in 1895 to urge an Intercolonial Conference at which to press upon the doyen of the premiers, Reid, the imperative need for Asian all-out exclusion. When this was unanimously accepted in 1896, Kingston had achieved his aim. From there on, the all-embracing immigration law was in the hands of the New South Wales Government, which—one presumes for political reasons since neither Japanese nor Indians nor Afghanistans threatened the social structure of that colony— pressed immigration restriction with great fervor. It became the model colony for racial immigration legislation until the first constitution of the federated Commonwealth of Australia established its standards nationwide.

While several scholars have, commendably, shown the various views that existed in Australia at that time, it is difficult to go along with one overall conclusion that Japan's victories in 1894–1895 'did not greatly influence Australian thought'. It has given rise to the assumption that Japan at that time was scarcely perceived as a future defence threat to Australia. The conclusion is in part based on the fact that Japan's victory had no impact on defence expenditures. Certainly it does appear unusual that the Australian colonies in the period after that war decreased, not increased, their military expenditures. Comparison with the sudden rise of the Australian defence budget after the Russo–Japanese war in 1905 can tempt one to accept a current impression that Japan in 1895 was at most perceived as a 'social threat' (because of undesirable immigrants), not as a strategic threat. But what is a 'threat'? Is one nation a defence threat to another only when it causes that nation's defence budget to increase?

It must be remembered, that Australia in the 1890s was sufficiently protected by the British navy. Japan had only just achieved her first stunning victory, for which the little-known Asian nation won surprised admiration as a David among nations. There was little reason to raise Australian military expenditures. It must also be noted that separating the 'Japan threat' problem from 1896 to 1904 and 1905 to 1914 into the neat categories of 'Japan as a racial or immigration threat' and 'Japan as a defence or strategic threat', as is sometimes done, hinders analysis. The two issues defy such prim classification. Immigration and defence were very much inter-related topics in the Australia of those years, when the White Australia policy was being conceived as something of a national security policy. Under the umbrella of Great Britain's all-powerful navy, Australians did not need to raise their defence budget. It then sufficed to meet the Japanese threat simply by extending the Immigration Restriction Act to all coloured people.

The close relationship of defence and immigration is evident in the speeches of the Grand Old Man of Australian politics, Sir Henry Parkes, a rousing speaker for 'Asian immigration restriction', for 'uniting the whole of the forces of Australia into one army', and for Australian federation built on the pillar of these two issues. When in the late 1880s and early 1890s he warned that 'the Chinese must be restricted from emigrating to any part of Australasia . . . I do not wish to see the Chinese element increasing in our midst', he stressed that:

> It will not be by the bombardment of one of our rich cities—it will not be by an attack upon our sea-borne commerce—it will not be by any attempt to lay us under a ransom to protect our property and our lives, but it will be stealthily, so far as movements of this kind can be made stealthily, effecting a lodgement in some thinly-peopled portion of the country, where it would take immense loss of life and immense loss of wealth to dislodge the invader. I think that the new form of warfare from which we may suffer is almost certain to take that form.

In the parliamentary debates following the Intercolonial Conference of 1896, one finds the same line of argument by men like Reid or Robert Homburg of South Australia. Only this time it was no longer the Chinese, but the Japanese who were pointed out as a threatening lot trying to entrench themselves in some remote part of Australia. They constituted a defence threat which could lead to intervention of a powerful nation on behalf of its overseas nationals, and only the preventive legislation of immigration restriction could remedy it. In a heated debate in London in July 1897, Reid stressed the need for the total exclusionist bill in the interest of international amity and for absolute protection against the formation of a Japanese minority.

Thus the Australian defence budget of those years is a questionable indicator of whether or not Japan was perceived as a strategic threat. Australia clamped down on the spectral Japanese threat in the most effective and diplomatic way that the times afforded. It was then still possible to fight the Japanese racial, strategic, or whatever threat by the simple extension and refinement of the Australian Immigration Restriction Act. It was effective and cheap. No guns were needed to keep out the Japanese or any other coloured peoples who might have threatened Australia. A piece of paper at the customs office served the purpose; any undesirable immigrant could be made to write out an often ridiculously phrased dictation of fifty words in English or any other language, as for example:

> The academician, versed in chronological data and geological antiquities, expert in synthesis and the constructions of exegesis, to whom the differential calculus was arithmetical simplicity personified, who could startle philosophy with subtle theses on occult and abstruse sciences, or involve a tortured labyrinth in philological polemics, illustrated by simile and metaphor, and phrased with vocabulistic plenitude and grandiloquent exuberance.

But this perfidiously efficient exclusion system became law only in 1901. In 1896, the decision reached by all colonies at the Sydney conference was neither binding nor carried royal assent, and did little to diminish the trickle of Asian immigrants. Paradoxically, Queensland, with the largest influx of Japanese immigrants, repealed it a few months later.

In Queensland, the Japanese immigration question was a complex problem. The colony's vast sugar plantations and rich pearl-beds had been attracting the largest number of Japanese immigrants in Australia. Not surprisingly, it was there that a strong complaint against Japanese immigration had originated, from John Douglas, Governor Resident on Thursday Island and former premier of Queensland. He represented the capitalist class of Australian pearl masters who, depending less on the Japanese, felt themselves threatened by the growing number of Japanese masters of pearl luggers. But the encumbent premier, Hugh Nelson, enjoyed close links with the more numerous and important financiers and plantation owners on the mainland who desired coloured immigrants in great quantities as a cheap source of labour. And when Nelson found it politically possible to strike a deal with the Japanese Government that would give Queensland commercial advantages while allowing it to regulate the immigration of Japanese labourers, he did not hesitate to abruptly drop the Sydney resolutions in the very month of his re-election in May 1896.

There was as yet no consensus on the immigration question among the individual colonies. Even inside a colony such as Queensland, questions persisted on how to deal effectively with immigration from Asia, particularly from Japan. When the Premier was attending the Colonial Conference in the London summer of 1897, Brisbane newspapers criticized the lack of government control over Japanese immigration. Despite a separate protocol signed with Tokyo in the belief that it would have a controlling effect on the influx of Japanese labourers, Japanese numbers had risen unabated from 2,225 in 1896 to 3,247 in 1898. It was keenly felt that Government Resident John Douglas's warnings were going unheeded and that Thursday Island was in danger of becoming a Japanese colony. The *Brisbane Courier* reported in May 1897:

> Up to the late successful war with China his [the Japanese] presence in Australia was so occasional as to excite no alarm. The war has made a mighty difference . . . They have leaped at one bound to an advanced place among the nations, and they do not mean to hide their light under a bushel . . . the Hon. John Douglas declaring that there is every appearance of Thursday Island and the vicinity becoming a Japanese colony.

The *North Queensland Register* warned:

> If the pearl-shelling industry remains open to the Japanese for another 3 years it will be theirs entirely, and Thursday Island, except for the intermittent support of passing steamers, will practically become an appanage of the Mikado . . . The diminutive alien in the pearl-shell industry, and in many others, notably domestic service, is invincible. He is sober, fairly intelligent, hard-working, and the proverbial aroma of an oiled rag keeps him in the pink of condition. The hard working but heavy drinking, big eating white, the indolent aboriginal or the careless colored men from Manilla, the South Seas, and the Malayan Peninsula, are helpless before the incoming tide of little yellow men, and unless something is done, and that quickly, the worst foreboding of the Hon. John Douglas will certainly be realised . . .
>
> The economic alien is so patriotic that there is no room for European labourers . . . He ousts them all and imports per *Omi Maru* and other Japanese vessels, direct from his native country. Hitherto we have been assured the activity of the Japanese Empire since the war, would check the emigration of the pigmies to Australia, but Mr. Douglas' figures are too ominous to permit of that belief being entertained.

During Nelson's absence, the influx of Japanese was also debated in Parliament. 'Mr. John Douglas has sounded a warning note to all Australia', cautioned Acting Premier Sir Horace Tozer in his ministerial statement. Member of Parliament John Hamilton protested the Japanese presence on Thursday Island in sharper vein: 'We are not afraid of them on account of their vices, but on acount of their virtues. Take the pearl-shell business . . . More energetic men you cannot find. These men are the Scotchmen of the East, and some action should be taken to regulate them.'

Vigour and confidence on the part of the Japanese in Torres Strait spoke indeed from a breezy message to the Queen of England in 1897. Carried by the *Torres Straits Pilot* on the occasion of her birthday, it was composed by the leader of the Japanese community on Thursday Island, Satō Torajirō:

Having learnt through England's arbitration system how to add 300 million dollars to her treasury and Formosa to her possessions, [Japan] also learnt how to become the strongest of Pacific powers; inspired by the knowledge of the great power possessed by a good and effective navy, she trusts some day to be the England of the east and play her part in international politics . . . The friendly relations of Great Britain and Japan have been like those of a kind mother and well beloved and good tempered daughter, and we trust that these relations will continue throughout all time . . . The Japanese of Thursday Island sincerely express their love and respect for Her Majesty, and have attempted in these Jubilee celebrations to show genuine and heartfelt enthusiasm, and they are particularly gratified that their lot is cast among such loyal subjects of Her Majesty's in this colony as Thursday Islanders.

Torajirō Satō

But by this time, a regular Japanese consul posted at Townsville in the sugar-plantation district of Queensland's northeast coast, who had been monitoring the political barometer for one year and was now sensing the urgency of popular apprehension, cabled Foreign Minister Ōkuma Shigenobu: 'Forbid temporarily Japanese emigrants coming to Thursday Island, for pearl-shell diving. Particulars by mail.' Ōkuma reacted quickly in his reply to his consul in Sydney: 'Immigration of Japanese to Thursday Island has been suspended. Inform Nakagawa [at Townsville] of this.' The prompt self-restriction had a salutory effect on the pearlers' situation on the island off Queensland, where Japanese immigration stopped and even began to dwindle.

Japanese immigration to the mainland of Queensland, however, continued unabated, as the other colonies kept a close watch on how the renegade colony's special agreement with Japan was working out. When Queensland demanded that passports be issued for Japanese immigrants, and stipulated that they needed prior job sanction from the Queensland Government, Japan protested unsuccessfully. There followed 'disagreeable collisions' and protracted correspondence, as Queensland complained about labourers entering the colony with false credentials under the pretence of being 'merchants'. Finally, in 1900, the government set a ceiling, allowing no more than 3,247 Japanese to reside in Queensland at any time. Other measures which Queensland felt itself forced to adopt in this trying period limited the issue of new pearling licences to British subjects (1898), denied Asians the right to employ Aborigines, and restricted government subsidies to sugar mills that employed only white labour. As a result it appeared to the other colonies, which were establishing the White Australia policy, that Queensland's adherence to the Anglo–Japanese Treaty had not been leading to the expected harmony, and its example was not followed.

In London, therefore, at the Colonial Conference in 1897, the

Australian premiers were directing their discussions towards the enforcement of a White Australia policy in the face of reluctance by the British Government. The Colonial Secretary, Joseph Chamberlain's attempts at deflating the problem met only with intransigence on the part of the Australian colonies. And it is a triste irony that in the heated debates, the essence of the argument shifted from the human *right* of coloured people to freely enter Australia, to the *method* by which to restrict Asian immigration in the most humane way possible.

If this shift of discussion saved face for Japan, it also disguised the nature of the Immigration Restriction Bill, which actually became more stringent than originally conceived. In order to save Japan's *amour-propre*, the Japanese Minister in London pressed the Marquis of Salisbury to urge the Australian premiers to adopt the educational 'Natal formula', the method which regulated immigration into British Natal on the southwest African coast by way of a dictation test. The Australians agreed to submit the formula for discussion in their parliaments. On 7 October Reid concurred and, in November, New South Wales replaced the blunt 'Coloured Restriction Bill' with the 'educational' Immigration Restriction Bill. It bore a less odious title. But this second bill went much further: it excluded all coloured people by means of a notorious dictation test, whereas the former, although it refused immigrants directly, had nevertheless exempted tourists, students, missionaries, and merchants.

The new bill now effectively sealed the White Australia policy. It became the model federal bill adopted by all the colonies. On 17 January 1901 at Maitland, Australia's first Prime Minister, Edmund Barton, announced that White Australia was the first plank in the federal government's platform. All parties pledged themselves firmly to this policy and maintained it without much change for the next half-century.

The immigration dispute with Australia from 1897 to 1921 fills nine thick volumes of documents in Japan's Diplomatic Record Office. Five volumes alone deal with the problem of establishing a white Australia between the years 1897 and 1902. It comes as an anticlimax, amid all the acerbic correspondence which then passed between Japan and Australia, that the Anglo–Japanese Alliance, announced suddenly after secret negotiations in February 1902, was, on the whole, received in Australian political and commercial circles 'with marked expressions of approval'. The Alliance was seen as a check against a Russian fleet from Vladivostok or a German fleet from the Chinese Sea, and as a guarantee to the trading interests of Australia in the Far East.

Another positive development in 1902 was New South Wales's opening of a permanent commercial agency at Kobe. J. B. Suttor managed the posting without interruption until 1922, with considerable success under a White Australia policy that in the first few years barred even Japanese businessmen from entering the southern continent. Furthermore, in 1904, Australia's second prime minister, Alfred Deakin, relaxed the Immigration Restriction Act *vis-à-vis* Japanese nationals. The passport agreement that he concluded with Japan—in the Australian Commonwealth's first direct negotiations with a foreign power, independent of the usual British diplomatic channel—now allowed Japanese merchants, students, and tourists to enter Australia without restriction, as long as their passports specified the purpose and duration of their visit.

But it was neither philanthropy nor the effect of Japan's successful war against Russia that led Deakin to this step. Commercial advantages were foremost in his mind, an argument pushed time and again by Suttor in Japan, who complained about the handicap placed on Australian products because of the discrimination against Japanese merchants. In 1905, Deakin tried in further direct talks with Japan's Consul-General in Sydney, Iwasaki Mitsuo, to obtain the same commercial preferences in Japan that other signatories of the Anglo–Japanese Commercial Treaty enjoyed. But the talks failed because Australia was not prepared to admit even restricted numbers of Japanese labourers and artisans.

In any case, the slight loosening of Australia's immigration restriction by the more lenient passport agreement did not much improve the situation of those Japanese already in Australia. In June 1904, a Japanese labour inspector travelling in Queensland's sugar-plantation district was ordered by a train guard to change into the special wagon reserved for coloured passengers. Swiftly apprised of this incident, Japan's Consul at Townsville, Tayui Rinzaburō, complained forcefully to the tramway company and the Government: 'There is no country in the world where travellers are carried in separate compartments of train or tramway according to the race'. The company apologized and explained that it was changing its discriminatory policy. Tayui also advised Foreign Minister Komura Jutarō to demand an easing of re-entry procedures, the adoption of a Japanese language test for Japanese subjects, and permission for labourers to bring their families to Australia. Japan's victory over Russia was making a big impression in Australia, he observed, and speculation was rife about where Japan's new-found might would lead her next.

Australia was living in uncertain times. Japan's remarkable defeat of Russia in 1905 coincided with the withdrawal of Britain's five battleships in the Pacific to redress the naval balance against Germany in the North Sea. It sounded an alarm bell and brought with it far-reaching policy consequences. Three weeks after Japan's rout of the Baltic Fleet in the Battle of Tsushima, Australia's Prime Minister Alfred Deakin, chief architect of her defence and foreign policy from 1903 to 1910, was interviewed by the *Melbourne Herald*. For the first time, Japan was officially pointed to as a defence threat. Australia was now within striking distance of sixteen naval stations, he said, the strongest of which was Yokohama.

Australia had to learn a lesson about the feasibility of long sea-expeditions (such as that undertaken by the Russian Fleet around Africa) and from what had happened to it at Port Arthur: 'What we have to learn is, that we require to be ready both to give and to receive just such blows'. Similarly, Allan McLean, a former deputy prime minister, warned: 'We have been living in a fools' paradise. Japan has astonished the world . . . We now find one of the great naval and military powers within a very short distance of our shores. That puts us in a very different position from that which we considered we occupied before.'

The renewal of the Anglo–Japanese alliance in the same year was viewed with much less equanimity, now that the strategic arrangement had left Japan in charge of Pacific defence. Minister for Defence George C. Pearce thought it a foolish thing to take the alliance to be a guarantee for all time: 'Japan has shown that she is an aggressive nation. She has shown that she is desirous of pushing out all round. What has always been the effect of victory and of conquest upon nations? Do we not know that it stimulated them to further conflict? To obtain fresh territory? Has not that been the history of our own race? . . . Is there any other country that offers such a temptation to Japan as Australia does?' Such logic pressed upon the Australian mind the need for one's own defence forces which one could always rely upon and be in sole charge of.

Voluntary associations sprang up in this gathering year of crisis to kindle the spirit of strategic and racial defence. One was the National Defence League, founded with the support of Labor and Liberal politicians such as J. C. Watson, W. Hughes, A. Deakin, and Thomas T. Ewing. Its first president, the chancellor of the University of Sydney, Sir Normand Maclaurin, proclaimed on inauguration day in September: 'We know not when the din of battle and clash of arms just ceased in the East, would be at our doors'. Its journal, the *Call*, pointed out the serious danger of invasion by a colonizing army from Asia: 'Japan is the possible, if not probable, enemy of the future'.

Another association that Watson and Deakin helped establish that year was the Immigration League which can, in a sense, be viewed as Japan's Colonization Society in reverse: it organized people not to go out but to come in, and only white people, please. Its main aim was to stimulate vigorous immigration, preferably from England, and then from the rest of Europe. The League's first president, Dr Richard Arthur, called for a strong migration program in response to the threatening rise of Japan and the withdrawal of the British battleships: 'Let us make any sacrifice to increase our numbers . . . We must have our own Australian Fleet. The withdrawal of the British battleships from China has put a different complexion on affairs . . . Our ideal should be that twenty years hence we should find the Australians twenty millions strong . . . with 250,000 men trained to use the rifle.'

One of the few who resisted the racist frenzy of those years and spoke up for Japan was Senator Edward Pulsford. A free trader, he moved a motion of friendship between Japan and Australia in the Senate on 28 September 1905, and proposed a treaty that would arrange all questions of emigration and immigration. 'Japan, successful as she has been on the battlefield, is much more anxious to be recognised as the exponent of peace and civilisation, than of war and conquest . . . though originally Asiatic, the Japanese have stood apart in their islands for centuries . . . and are now no more Asiatic than they are European', read his pamphlet *The British Empire and the Relations of Asia and Australasia: Immigration Restrictions in Australasia* which he published and circulated at the same time. But Pearce condemned the pamphlet as 'a greater disgrace to Australia than the Immigration Restriction Act', and demolished Pulsford's motion in the course of the debate.

Another lone voice, but one in foreign pay, was E. H. Foxall, the private English secretary to the Consul-General in Sydney. By 1907 he had grown so exasperated with the bad press Japan was getting in Australia, that he wrote to the Japanese Foreign Minister, Viscount Hayashi, offering to write pro-Japanese articles under a pseudonym:

> It appears to me that a great number of those who favour the exclusion of Japanese from Australia, do so from considerations of which they are more or less ashamed . . . Their real reasons being insufficient to justify their attitude, they attempt to justify it by misrepresenting Japan as a Menace to Australia. While this misrepresentation is eagerly published, it is practically impossible to secure publication of a reply . . . Therefore I take the liberty of making the following suggestion to your Excellency: I am prepared to write articles upon this question from time to time, exposing the unfairness of the journalistic methods adopted in the manufacture of racial prejudice, and severely criticizing, in some cases, the individuals who adopt them. My identity as the author of the articles, in view of my connection with your Consulate-General in this city, need not be disclosed. But if they could be published, as I should write them, in the columns of some Japanese newspaper printed in English—say, the Japan Times, Japan Mail, Kobe Chronicle—I should then be able to obtain a number of copies of such newspapers, and send them, marked, to the principal newspapers in the Commonwealth and in England.

When he submitted his first such contribution, 'Impressions of Australia', to the Consul-General for approval, he signed it 'Tetsu Gakusha', a homonym for philosopher in Japanese.

But such effort was futile. The transformation of the strategic situation in the Pacific wrought by Japan's victory over Russia in 1905, strengthened inexorably the move in Australia to establish a regular army and a navy (which would be part of Britain's Eastern Fleet) to combat and overcome any Japanese enemy force. Prime Minister Alfred Deakin became the prime mover, who forged the costly shield through three governments, from the first announcement of his defence scheme in December 1907 until its final presentation to Parliament in November/December 1909.

Deakin was well served by his Minister of Defence, the Asianophobe T. T. Ewing, whose speeches were peppered with paranoia: 'We passed an Immigration Restriction Act with one idea in view—to keep . . . away . . . the silent invasion of these people . . . I refer to the yellowmen to the north. We have virtually kicked these men off our doorstep; we have slammed the door of Australia right in their faces . . . I am dealing with the great battle of Armaggedon, which has yet to be fought between the yellow and the white man . . . If a nation were to legislate that no Australian could land—if we were virtually turned out of a country—should we not seek the first opportunity for revenge?' In 1908, he introduced Deakin's Defence Bill, a measure 'designed to keep Australia intact and white'.

Nor was the 'shield' a bipartisan issue in the interim, when Deakin was briefly out of power in 1908–1909. It was seized upon with alacrity by the Labor Party, which in 1908 proposed an even larger naval program for twenty-three destroyers at the cost of 2.3 million pounds. Its Defence Minister, another effective Japanophobe, Senator G. F. Pearce, warned that Australia was in a very dangerous position owing to the nearness of Japan which was the fourth naval power in the world: 'We should not be safe until we have twenty million standing behind the guns'.

In 1909, the Defence Bill was back again with Deakin for the final touch in his Fusion Government. And it was then clear to all whom his new Defence Minister, Joseph Cook, was talking about, when he called upon Parliament on 21 September to establish an Australian navy and to legislate for compulsory military service to protect Australia. He cited:

> . . . the existence, far from our shores, of two or three million of the best trained troops in the world. They belong to a nation whose ideals are, in many respects as unlike our own as possible for them to be . . . Australia is the most vulnerable part of the British Empire. Half-a-dozen mighty kingdoms could find accommodation on this continent, and we are surrounded by nations hungering for room and breathing space . . .

Both Houses passed with little debate a scheme that proposed the compulsory training of males between fourteen and twenty years of age to provide a first- and second-line military force of 66,000 men by 1915. The naval scheme was also put into effect, pushing up defence expenditures by more than 200 per cent. The Admiralty in London was asked to arrange for the construction of the new navy's flagship, a 19,200 ton

Dreadnought, H.M.A.S. *Australia*, and the first recruits marched into adult compulsory camp in July 1912. The shield was forged.

It was little wonder that, in the year of the vote on the Australian defence scheme, spy stories were rife again. The press paid particular attention to a report about four Japanese who allegedly had been spying out Northern Queensland disguised as 'showmen'. Defence Minister Pearce backed the story without hesitation, and drew the indignation of Consul-General Ueno K. in the *Australian Star*: 'Is not Japan an ally of Great Britain? . . . is it likely that Japan would be spying on a friendly and allied nation?'

More sensational were the *Sun's* headlines on 6 March 1911: 'Only 900 Miles Away! New Caledonia's Colony of Japanese. Why they Are There! What They Are Doing!! Spies in the Island. Japanese Who Wear Military Overcoats and Carry Arms. COULD TAKE THE ISLAND TOMORROW. Possible Naval Station and Coal Depot.' Excerpts from the text, serialized in three instalments, read:

> If the Japanese already on the Island were to take it into their hands to rise to-morrow, the people of New Caledonia could no more stop them than they could stop the sun rising . . . There are at least 2,000 Japanese known to be in New Caledonia to-day . . . At least 2,300 more will follow before long. The last shipment of 1,036 Japanese are working in the mines. Not coolie laborers, but intelligent and skilled. Nearly all fought in Japanese-Russo war. Many still wear military cloaks and carry revolvers . . . It is admitted that there are Japanese secret service spies in the island. [This] provides food for immediate thought and careful action on the part of the Commonwealth authorities if they desire to effectually prevent New Caledonia from becoming a Japanese colony, from which hordes of the little brown men may swoop down upon Queensland any fine day . . . The Japanese brain is a curious product of latter-day education and of profit by example . . . He is a sphinx.

The bland statements induced the Japanese Consul-General's immediate despatch to A. Frey, the manager of La Société 'Le Nickel' company in New Caledonia, who employed most of the Japanese miners: 'It has occurred to me that it might be both possible and advisable for you to make some statement, the publication of which might tend to counteract the pernicious effects of the misrepresentations which are now being indulged in'. No response is listed in the diplomatic correspondence.

The 'Yellow Peril' syndrome affected not only the press in those years, it also found its way into Australian novels, poems and plays. In the *Lone Hand*, a widely read monthly magazine close to Deakin and the tenets of compulsory military training and Australia's own navy, the titles speak for themselves: '"Our" Pacific Ocean', 'A Japanese Pond', 'From the Oldest World: Japan's Ju-jitsu Diplomacy', 'The Asiatic Menace: Japan the Gamester', 'The Asiatic Menace: The Awakening of the Dragon'. Other stories about Japanese invasion of Australia appeared in 1910–1911 under the titles of 'The Deliverer', 'Command of the Air', and 'First Blood'. In F. R. C. Hopkins's *Reaping the Whirlwind*, the play has a Japanese naval deployment force proceed on Sydney in 1915. The marines overcome every obstacle in their way, until the shilling-shocker ends dramatically: 'The Asiatics will enter this country without firing a shot! Oh! My God!'

But the best known piece, with a smattering of literary merit, was 'The Commonwealth Crisis' serialized in the *Lone Hand* in 1908 and published as a book in 1909 under the title *The Australian Crisis*. In this story, Japanese are secretly landed on the unpopulated shores of Australia's Northern Territory in 1912. When found out, Japan apologizes. Both look to England for help, but British wealth and the upper classes side with their Japanese allies. The British navy withdraws its warships, and by blockading Australian ports forces the Northern Territory under direct Imperial control. A 'White Guard', commissioned with recruits from as far as Canada and America to do battle for 'Aryan ideals', is helpless before the numerous and well-organized foe, and the Japanese are allowed to increase on Australian territory under nominal British control. The story shows a deep Australian suspicion of the British–Japanese connection. It was written by C. H. Kirmess, alias Sir Frank Fox, *Bulletin* journalist, editor of the *Lone Hand*, and friend of Prime Minister Deakin, who praised Fox's first two issues: 'I am genuinely surprised at the variety and general excellence . . . Total effect of both numbers far beyond my expectations'.

With the 'Japanese are coming' syndrome now pervading press, literature, and government circles, it is not surprising that even shrewd Australian foreign policy analysts had no deeper wells to draw from in their strategic appreciations of Japan. When in an important speech on 17 March 1914 Winston Churchill asked for Australian and New Zealand Dreadnoughts to strengthen the decisive theatre in Europe, he based himself on the premise that Australia was adequately protected by the Anglo–Japanese alliance. Australian leaders, however, were flabbergasted by Churchill's implication that the Pacific was to be made safe by the treaty with a nation whose people they did not admit to their shores.

The most spirited reply to Admiralty and its First Lord, Churchill, came from Frederic Eggleston, a Melbourne lawyer, the leading brain in the Round Table movement and widely revered as a trenchant foreign policy analyst, whose public ripostes in the months before the outbreak of World War I are still generally regarded as 'well-informed and sophisticated opinion' based on 'rigorous analysis'. The treaty was weak, maintained Eggleston, because Japan did not need the alliance. From this he deducted that Japan could simply not be trusted if Australians permitted their fleet to go to Europe: 'there is nothing in the Anglo–Japanese treaty which prevents Japan from raising the question of making a demand upon England that Japanese subjects shall be admitted to Australia'.

But by asserting that Churchill had wrongly assessed the security afforded by the Anglo–Japanese alliance, Eggleston took upon himself the dunce's cap. A war erupted that for four years tested his fallacious assumptions based on the sum-total of an Australian knowledge that was preoccupied with its whiteness and had never cared to search in a consistent and systematic way for a deeper understanding of Japan. Eggleston's brilliance was a victim of his environment, and his article shows that even the most lucid and rigorously presented analysis can, if deeper knowledge does not inform it, be as untutored as a fuzzy piece of writing based on expertise. Australians had done their Latin and French, when they should have done Japanese. In the event, Admiralty demonstrated a sounder grasp of global strategy: the escalation of German naval aggression was indeed best met by dominions and allies entirely at the disposal of the naval command in London, and Japan revealed herself a loyal ally. Churchill, who later was to be blamed with more justification for many things, in 1914 proved himself right in premising the security in the Pacific on the guarantee of the Anglo–Japanese alliance and its 'strong continuing bonds of interest'.

7

Relations During and After World War I

WHEN WAR broke out in August, Australia had the beginnings of a small fleet. Her Dreadnought cruiser, four light cruisers, three destroyers, and two submarines stood by in the Southwest Pacific. But Japan had ten times as many vessels in the North Pacific, a matter of deep concern for Australia.

Ironically, two months later, the cruiser *Sydney* (5,600 tons), built to repel Japanese ships from launching an attack on Australia, found herself side by side with the powerful Japanese battle cruiser *Ibuki* (10,000 tons), chasing after the light cruiser *Emden* (3,600 tons) of their common German enemy. It happened on the occasion of one of the most gigantic convoys in naval history, when thirty-eight vessels transported 30,000 troops with military equipment and 7,843 horses from the Australian to the African continent, escorted by one British, one Japanese, and two Australian war vessels. As the ships were passing the Cocos Island group in the Indian Ocean on 9 November, they sighted the *Emden*. The *Sydney* dashed off to fight her. The *Ibuki*, being the strongest battleship in the convoy, wanted to follow suit, but was restrained by the leading ship *Melbourne*, whose captain told her instead to take the *Sydney*'s position for flank protection.

In an encounter that lasted one hour, the *Sydney* sank the *Emden* in what became the Allies' first naval victory. It was a proud event for the newly created Australian navy. The *Emden* had been a dangerous ship, having sunk or captured nearly 100,000 tons of allied shipping between Calcutta and New Guinea, besides bombing Madras and raiding Penang Harbour. The naval battle also demonstrated a fine co-operation between the Australian and the Japanese navies. Goodwill had only slightly been strained by the concern of the *Ibuki's* captain, Vice-Admiral Katō Kanji, at having been kept back and having received little information during the sea-encounter. But congratulations poured in from all sides as the convoy proceeded safely across the Indian Ocean, landing at Alexandria in December, six weeks later.

During the war years, a great part of patrolling the Australian coastline and convoying of troops between New Zealand, Australia, and Europe was done by the Japanese navy, which already in 1914 proposed to have a naval liaison officer placed at Sydney. From December 1914 to January 1915 the light cruisers *Chikuma* and *Yahagi* patrolled the coast off North Queensland. From May to July, the light cruisers *Aso* and *Sōya* completed visits to Rabaul and Fremantle. In the same year, Japanese and Australian ships were attached to the China station controlling the Malay archipelago, where in February 1915, Japanese marines helped suppress an Indian mutiny at Singapore. The following year was quieter, with visits by the light cruisers *Azuma* and *Iwate* between Fremantle, Brisbane, and Auckland. Also, Britain again requested Japanese assistance to protect the sea lanes between Australia and Aden. In 1917, Japanese protection of Australia was increased due to Germany's all-out submarine warfare. Three Japanese cruisers and eight destroyers escorted troop ships across the Indian Ocean in March. From May to June, the light cruisers *Izumo* and *Nisshin* escorted cargo from Fremantle to Colombo. And from April to December, the modern light cruiser *Hirado* and her sister-ship, *Chikuma* were employed directly in the defence of Australia in the absence of Australian ships serving elsewhere. In March 1918, the *Yahagi* visited Fremantle, and from May to October helped patrol the northeastern coasts of the continent with Australian ships. As Australia's official history of the war has it: 'The most cordial relations prevailed between the visiting Japanese squadrons or ships and the naval authorities in Australia, and the Japanese admirals were supplied with all necessary information'.

But it was not always plain sailing. The official history is silent on the incident of 20 November 1917, when the *Yahagi*, moving in to dock in Fremantle port, was shot at from an Australian naval artillery stand overlooking the harbour. Port authorities had been advised the day before of the *Yahagi's* arrival, and as she sailed in at six-thirty in the morning a pilot had already boarded her to bring her in. The shot was fired without warning at 6.58 and missed the ship. After berthing, Captain Miyaji Tamisaburō demanded an explanation from the officer in charge of the port, Captain Clare. The next day, Clare explained that it had been meant as a simple warning to the *Yahagi* for not hoisting the code flag that was supposed to be shown as she entered the Australian port. Miyaji protested that they had correctly answered the signal lamps and announced themselves by morse dashes. He informed Admiral Ōguri Kōsaburō, commanding officer of the Indian and Western Pacific Ocean squadron, who conferred with Tokyo. Ōguri then told Miyaji not to pursue the incident with Clare, but to take it up directly with the Australian naval ministry in Melbourne. As a result, Australian Governor-General Sir Redmond Munro Ferguson went to Perth and personally told the Japanese captain on 25 November that the shot had been unintentional: 'It was an unfortunate accident for which I apologize'. Three days later, the Australian Naval Board, too, sent an official apology, and the incident was closed.

Political distrust of Japan added friction to the strange feeling of being protected by a rival Pacific naval power against whom Australia had built her own navy. The Australian Prime Minister William M. Hughes epitomized such suspicion in his observations from London, where he went in 1916 at the invitation of the British Government to observe first hand the Empire's plight. His letter of 21 April to Acting Prime Minister George Pearce may have reversed what little goodwill might have sprouted between Japan and Australia in the war years:

My dear Pearce,
I hardly know how to begin to tell you the story of what is going on in England ... all our fears—or conjectures—that Japan was and is most keenly interested in Australia are amply borne out by facts ... [Foreign Secretary Sir Edward] Grey believes Japan will stand behind Britain—he admits however that there is a large and growing party in Japan who look askance at the alliance and with favour on Germany. It is to me quite clear that in the event of even a temporary reverse to the Allies, the Japanese Government might not be able—even if they so desired—to keep Japan behind Britain ...

The position is aggravated ... by the fact that Britain has approached Japan with a view to obtaining naval (and, or, military) assistance—say in the Mediterranean—and that the Japanese Government, while ready enough to grant this, ask for some evidence of Britain's friendliness towards her in order possibly to justify her action or placate the opposition ...

I told Grey that Australia would fight to the last ditch rather than allow Japanese to enter Australia. Upon that point we were adamant ...

My dear Pearce believe me things are *not* going well here ... I feel very depressed and missing Australia and all of my colleagues and friends more than I can say.

Hughes feared two things: that Japan was trying to use the alliance as a means by which to gain access for products and people into Australia, and that Japan would change sides and join Germany if there were reverses on the side of the Allies.

On the first point, it is true that Atlee Hunt, Secretary of the External Affairs Department, twice had talks with the Japanese Consul-General: in June 1915 with regard to a Japanese request for a 'Treaty of Commerce and Friendship', and in February 1916 about waiving the twelve-month limit on passports for merchants. But these negotiations did not take place at the end of the muzzle of a rifle as is sometimes intimated. In his reports, Hunt stresses the sincerity that informed these talks, held in good faith. It would be well to consider Japanese hopes with regard to removing 'any very limited [immigration] restrictions', Hunt wrote, because during the fourteen years since the beginning of White Australia 'there has never been any indication that the Japanese Government wished to force their labouring classes on us'. Likewise, Australia's man in Japan, J. B. Suttor, had persistently spoken in favour of Australian adherence to the Anglo–Japanese Commercial Treaty, and suggested securing the treaty against uncontrolled immigration with a 'gentleman's agreement', as Canada had done in 1906, 1911, and 1913. He also advocated a modification of the White Australia policy to encourage Japanese businessmen to engage in Australian trade.

Hughes's other fear, that of Japan switching sides to join Germany, reinforced his obsession to keep Australia white. His tortured views had a pernicious effect on public opinion in Australia, where the people were kept in the dark by a strictly enforced censorship and were highly susceptible to what their Prime Minister heard abroad and said at home.

A reading of Count Ishii Kikujirō's comments about the allegation that Japan would join the Central Powers sheds light on the atmosphere of suspicion that probably deepened Hughes's Japanophobia in the spring of 1916. Soon after Japan had thrown in her lot with Great Britain and declared war on Germany on 26 August 1914, Britain, France, and Russia promised in the London Declaration of 4 September not to make a separate peace with Germany. Ishii, then Japan's Minister at Paris, immediately urged his government to sign the declaration, too. But Foreign Minister Katō Takaaki refused, probably from fear that this might entail despatch of Japanese troops to the European war front. Only when Ishii became foreign minister in the following year did Japan become a signatory, and the government announced this formally on 19 October 1915.

It provoked an unexpected and stormy controversy, exciting interpellations in the Diet which gave rise to the widespread supposition that Japan had an understanding with Germany. Some politicians decried signing the Declaration because it precluded the possibility of a separate peace. But the government replied that a separate peace with Germany was anyway out of question by virtue of the Anglo–Japanese alliance. Signing the Declaration guaranteed Japan a seat at the peace table at the end of the war: that was the government's main concern. Ishii believed that Allied doubts about Japan's loyalty in 1915–1916 was only a sign of their lack of knowledge of Japanese politics. As he explained to a correspondent of the London *Times*, the Diet interpellators had merely been seizing upon the diplomatic problem to create a partisan issue at home, since the question provided good ammunition for assailing the government.

It may be that arriving in London when this controversy was still fresh put Hughes in 'a state of some alarm'. At any rate, Hughes's suspicion, vented freely in his speeches upon his return, about being threatened by 'a thousand millions of coloured people', fueled the Labor Party's attitude against Japan from 1916 onward. The anti-Japan issue soon carried over to affect the referendum for sending conscripts abroad. Hughes stressed the importance of providing a monthly quota of 16,500 soldiers to fight in Europe in full support of Great Britain because her help would be needed at the end of that war when Japan would turn to attack the White Australia policy. However, his opponents countered that sending conscripts abroad was draining the country of manpower and inviting an influx of Japanese labour that would leave Australia prostrate. The conscription debate elicited a strong statement from Japanese Consul-General Shimizu Seizaburō: 'The whole of Australia is now agitated upon the conscription issue . . . the references to Japan are awkward and unpleasant from both sides, and I may add baseless . . . I think and hope that those who are most voluble upon this subject will yet live to see and acknowledge their error'.

All through the war years Labor alarm was a festering issue in the Party paper *Labor Call*, alleviated none by the yellow journalism of leftist liberal Kayahara Kazan. Translated excerpts from his cabalistic article 'America and England Are Forcing Suicide On Japan' were circulated at the State Conference of the Australian Labor Party at Perth in June 1918 and quoted at length by a delegate in the South Australian Legislative Assembly on 31 July 1918. Published in October 1915 in the monthly bulletin of 'The Third Empire', and probably introduced to Australia through German agents, Kayahara's call for Japan to take Australia, New Zealand, and Tasmania to relieve the nation's problems of over-population and lack of space did much damage as it continued to provide grist to the Labor mills.

A further note of discord that reverberated through the war years was the question of the final allocation of the Micronesian Islands. It reflected general misunderstandings on both sides of the Western Pacific, and a growing sense of confidence on the part of the Japanese as their southward advance began to clash with the more latent Australian northward advance.

Soon after the outbreak of war with Germany, a British squadron had bombarded Yap and eliminated its powerful wireless station that connected the German island possessions with the Chinese mainland at Tsingtao. On 19 August, the Admiralty suggested that an Australian expeditionary force occupy Rabaul and the three wireless, coaling, and phosphate islands of Yap, Angaur (in the Palau island group), and Nauru. Australia seized only Rabaul. Vice-Admiral Sir George E. Patey, the commander of the Australian Fleet from 1913 to 1915, replied early in September that, while they might also take Yap, 'Angaur and Nauru should not be occupied . . . Occupying them will entail our feeding the inhabitants as well as the garrisons . . . and become an anxiety to ourselves'.

Trifling with the occupation of German islands north and south of the Equator would prove a serious mistake. It would prevent Australians effecting the surrender of all Micronesia—a surrender which on 17 September the Germans had conceded to the Australian Commander in charge of the capitulation of Rabaul (seat of the German administrator for all the German island possessions in the Pacific Ocean)—and result in a long period of futile anticipation.

On 26 August, Japan entered the war to help eliminate the German navy in the Pacific and on 7 October, Japanese marines took Yap. At that time they were quite prepared to hand over the island to Australian occupation forces. But Patey, who was then on Suva, replied that his ships were busy chasing after the *Geier, Prinz Eitel Friedrich,* and *Cormoran;* he even suggested that Japan provide escort ships herself to convoy Australian occupation forces to take over Yap and other islands.

Had the Australians then gone northward right away with a force of sixty officers and men to transfer to Australia the surrender of these islands—which, in the words of the Admiralty, 'closely affect the whole question of the naval defence of Australia in the future. They are of great strategic importance'—they would have acquired Yap and probably Angaur, too. It would have changed the post-war strategic situation and given the entire question of Japan dominating the northern Pacific and Australia the southern Pacific a different turn. Yap would not have become an exasperating issue at the Paris Conference, where the United States delayed recognition of Yap as a Japanese mandate and continued to press Japan for submarine cable privileges on that strategically located island.

As it was, Australian leaders showed complacency, when it would have been wiser to act quickly and decisively. This attitude contrasts greatly with their later adamant insistence on Australian proprietorship of the islands. There may also have been a serious misunderstanding as to exactly what the Japanese were prepared to hand over in October. George Pearce was clearly mistaken when he understood that Japan's intention to transfer Yap and other islands meant transferring all the other Micronesian islands to Australian forces. Hunt was closer to the truth when he wrote to Minister for External Affairs P. McM. Glynn: '[The Japanese] do not say anything about the Carolines and I should not be surprised if they desired to keep them . . . They are a little out of our beat and their possession by the Japanese cannot but be harmless.' At any rate, by the time an Australian expeditionary force was fitted out— even down to the printing of postage-stamps bearing the inscription 'North West Pacific'—and ready to take possession of the Micronesian islands at the beginning of December, it was too late.

By then Japan had participated in what had already become her most active and successful three months of the war. Japanese troops had taken the German Shantung concession on the Chinese mainland and the Japanese navy had successfully helped in the hunting of the German fighting squadrons all over the Pacific. She had proved herself an indispensable ally and a decisive factor in the conduct of war against Germany. But Japan had also grown confident after the capture of Tsingtao on 7 November, and riots erupted in Tokyo when it was learned that the government was prepared to hand over the Micronesian islands to their allies. The commotion caused the Japanese Government to re-tract its earlier offer, and on 23 November Britain asked Australia not to proceed to any islands north of the Equator. In addition, British Colonial Secretary Lewis Harcourt explained a week later to Australian Governor-General Sir Ronald Munro Ferguson that 'for strategic reasons' the Palau, Mariana, Caroline, and Marshall Islands were to be allowed to remain in Japanese occupation, 'leaving whole question of future to be settled at the end of the war'.

A top secret 'My dear Ronald' letter spelled out in greater detail the reasons why 'it seemed to us here undesirable that the Australian Expedition should proceed anywhere north of the Equator'. He des-cribed how in the beginning they had believed that Japan's active participation in the war would be confined to the capture of Kiachao on the Chinese mainland:

> But later on it was found necessary by us to ask them to extend their activities. Our fleets were so fully engaged in the North Sea, Atlantic, Mediterranean . . . that we could not spare enough to deal with the Pacific . . . . All this has changed the character of the Japanese participation and no doubt of their eventual claims to compensation . . .
>
> You ought in the most gradual and diplomatic way to begin to prepare the mind of your Ministers for the possibility that at the end of the war Japan may be left in possession of the Northern Islands and we with everything south of the Equator. I know that they won't like this . . .

Ferguson did so on 24 January 1915 in a letter to his prime minister: 'Japan has dealt with the German posts North of the Line; two of her squadrons have patrolled the whole North Pacific; and she has assisted us in the South Pacific & Indian Ocean. —We have not therefore very good grounds for objecting should Japan eventually desire to hold the Islands North of the Line.'

Ferguson assured Harcourt in May that he anticipated no effective objection by the Fisher Government to the continued occupation by the Japanese of the islands north of the Equator at the end of the war. And one year later, after a change in government, Prime Minister Hughes wrote as much to Pearce from London: 'I told [Foreign Secretary] Grey . . . that . . . we were prepared to consider favorably the Equator as a line of demarcation, giving us control of all Islands to the South'.

When Germany redoubled its effort to sink Allied ships in early 1917, Britain bartered post-war assurances for the help of Japanese destroyers to combat German submarines in the Mediterranean, with the two cruisers *Nitaka* and *Tsushima* thrown into the deal for action off the South African Cape. At the same time, the new Colonial Secretary, Walter H. Long, made sure that the Australian Government would back these British asssurances, and was satisfied of Prime Minister Hughes's unequivocal consent on 10 February 1917. Accordingly, London informed Tokyo that 'His Majesty's Government accede with pleasure to the request of the Japanese Government for an assurance that, on occasion of any peace conference, they will support Japan's claim in regard to the disposal of Germany's rights in Shantung and her possessions in the islands north of the Equator'.

On the eve of the Armistice, however, Prime Minister Hughes tried to retract all former pledges given by the Australian Government during the war. In a long letter to British Prime Minister David Lloyd George on 4 November 1918, he sought to revive in their place Australia's claim to *all* Germany's former island possessions:

> It is necessary to remind you of Australia's deeply rooted mistrust of Japan, and to enter an emphatic protest on behalf of the Commonwealth against Japan's right or even claim to . . . the Marshalls, Caroline, and Ladrones. . . .
>
> The islands are most important to Australia from the point of view both of defence and of possible offence . . .
>
> I am aware of course that certain communications relating to these islands have passed between the British and Commonwealth Governments, and certain conversations took place between the representative of Japan and the present. But since then much water has run under the bridges, and I need not remind you what Japan's attitude towards the Empire in this war has been . . .

Hughes need not have reminded Lloyd George. The British Prime Minister would have none of it. In his icy reply two months later on the last day of the year, he stated:

There can be no question that the British Government will enter the [Paris Peace] Conference having given a pledge to Japan to support her claims to the German rights North of the Equator—a pledge to which the Australian Government was a consenting party. I presume that if you wish any further discussion of this question you will raise it at the Imperial War Cabinet.

There the matter rested.

'[We shall] come to the ship and have the melancholy satisfaction of taking our farewell on the day of your departure', wrote the Premier of New South Wales, W. A. Holman, to Shimizu Seizaburō shortly before the Japanese Consul-General's return to Japan. Looking back over the long years of a not-always-easy association during the war, Holman enclosed in his letter a long memorandum that evaluated in sixteen points the development of Japanese–Australian relations during the war. Point 8 read:

The Australian attitude towards Japan has been enormously changed by the war. (a) The appearance of Japan on the scene as one of the great powers, (b) the part she has played in policing the Pacific, and (c) the protection afforded by her Navy to our troops on their passage to battlefields have enormously affected the Australian imagination. Japan's dignity and prestige are now realised to a degree that was impossible before.

But Holman's kind evaluation in 1919 belied the hostile mood between Japan and Australia at Paris. At the Peace Conference the two countries' delegates were just then locked in bitter disagreement about the insertion of a racial equality clause in the charter of the League of Nations. Baron Makino Shinken's three proposals met with three blank refusals engineered by Prime Minister Hughes; the Australian managed to persuade the attending heads of state to reject even the most watered-down Japanese amendment in the preamble of the Covenant: 'by the endorsement of the principle of equality of all nationals of States members of the League'. Having refused Japan all and sundry, United States President Woodrow Wilson, who was chairing the discussions, was unable to prevent the cession of Shantung to Japan in the next vote. Major E. L. Piesse, Director of the Pacific Branch of the Prime Minister's Department, lamented in Melbourne: 'How much better it would have been to accept the Japanese amendment in one of its least noxious forms . . . As it is we have been perhaps the chief factor in consolidating the whole Japanese nation behind the imperialists'.

Another issue that consumed much of the two countries' energies at the Peace Conference was the question of the disposal of the German territories in the Western Pacific. Both Australia and Japan wanted annexation. On this point Hughes was most outspoken: 'Strategically the Pacific Islands encompass Australia like fortresses . . . [They are] as necessary to Australia as water to a city . . . In the hands of a superior power there would be no peace for Australia.'

Hughes's refusal to place the former colonies under an international trusteeship galled not only Prime Minister Lloyd George, who sought a compromise with America, but also President Wilson, whose Fourteen Points ran counter to colonial acquisitions. Wilson's objections appear to have been guided even more by strategic calculation than by idealism, for Hughes's insistence on annexation ran counter to United States regional strategic appreciations. If permitted to annex the islands, Japan could fortify Micronesia and so menace United States strategy in the Western Pacific. As Wilson told a Conference member after a heated confrontation with Hughes on 30 January: 'These islands lie . . . athwart the path from Hawaii to the Philippines and . . . could be fortified and made naval bases by Japan'. Wilson did not trust the Japanese and was infuriated with Hughes because Australian intransigence played into the hands of Japan's geo-strategic interests in the Pacific.

Indeed, by the end of the war the Japanese navy was finally catching up with the popular Meiji *nanshin-ron* spirit of Suzuki Tsunenori, Hattori Toru, and the like, when the Japanese naval commanders realized that by securing Micronesia, Japan was adding more to the empire than just a few useless islands. A naval position paper, prepared in early February 1919 for the negotiations at Paris, stressed the value of the Micronesian islands. Japan had to keep them, because they were well placed as a link into the regions of the Philippines, the Dutch East Indies, New Guinea, and Polynesia. However much Australia and the United States protested, it was Japan's right to hold on to them, because it was the Japanese navy that had expelled the German enemy from the Pacific and Indian Oceans, and kept open the sea lanes throughout the war.

This position paper had been conceived in Micronesia by Commander Matsuoka Shizuo, who after the war left the navy and became a renowned scholar of the Pacific peoples with numerous ethnographies to his credit. Matsuoka challenged the assumption that the expeditionary forces despatched at the beginning of the war had the right to claim for their countries the territories from which the Germans were expelled. If that rule were followed, 99 per cent of the former German island territories in the Western Pacific would go to Australia and New Zealand, and only 1 per cent to Japan. The United States, with its long-standing interest in Samoa, would have to drop its claim to that island. Japan thoroughly resented the way in which Australians were about to curtail Japanese economic enterprise by extending north to New Guinea their White Australia policy. It was only natural that the Japanese should keep Micronesia, obtain Nauru, and strongly protest New Guinea and the Bismarck Islands being put under Australian rule. Above all, Japan should for the sake of regional development establish her central administration on Palau, a pivotal island at the hub of a large sphere that reached from the Philippines to Borneo, the Celebes, and New Guinea.

At the receiving-end of such naval coaching, the Japanese delegates in Paris—old Prince Saionji Kimmochi and the genteel Makino Nobuaki— were, alas, no match for the cantankerous Hughes and his biting oratory. The Australian Prime Minister insisted on Australian jurisdiction over trade, navigation, and defence matters in all former German island possessions in the Western Pacific south of the Equator: 'Commonwealth Government cannot agree to grant Japanese subjects any rights . . . in regard to the Islands . . . We are starting with a clean slate.' And in morbid fear of Japan, the obdurate Hughes fought rabidly for the right to enforce Australia's Immigration Restriction Law in the islands on grounds of defence.

It is interesting here to see how the old Henry Parkes syndrome sprouted again, this time with wider claims staked out in the Southwest Pacific. The old fear about an Asian minority settling in a remote part of Australia and creating an 'incident', which Parkes had brought up in 1888 with the Chinese in mind, and which Reid had kept alive in 1896 with regard to the Japanese on Thursday Island, was resurrected in 1920 and extended to the danger of Japanese accumulating on an island in the former German possessions south of the Equator. If there they were given 'equal opportunities for trade and commerce', an Australian delegate contended, 'a Japanese population would quickly flood the islands—other Asiatics would also come in large numbers. On a suitable occasion an "incident" might occur which would have the gravest results.'

It would be wrong to assume that only Australia desired to annex territory. The interested continental powers of the Council of Ten all did. But they allowed Japan and the British Dominions— Hughes in particular —to lead the fight in the Council. South Africa's General Jan C. Smuts introduced the A, B, and C Mandate plan. After a last-minute amendment of the paragraph for the C-type Mandate, thrashed out by the Australian delegation on 29 January, and a change to which Colonel Edward House (Wilson's assistant) agreed, Lloyd George adopted the revised version as the British Empire delegation's final solution. It became Article 22, and the mandates were officially issued in December 1920.

By first demanding annexation and then settling for the C-Mandate (which was the same except for the non-fortification clause) Australia had won the case not only for herself but for Japan as well. For Japan this proved a pyrrhic victory, however. While on the one hand Japan gained all of Germany's former island possessions in the Pacific north of the Equator, on the other she lost all access to those south of the Equator.

There would be no more commercial equality in the islands, no more thirty-year land leases over large areas such as Japanese residents in New Guinea had enjoyed until the outbreak of war. Moving Australia's Immigration Restriction Act to the Equator put up an effective barrier against Japanese enterprise in the Melanesian parts of the Western Pacific. And when Japanese delegates opined that it was unacceptable that Japan's having helped defeat Germany had resulted in the abridgement of rights once freely enjoyed by her nationals in German territories, a British Empire delegate reminded Japan that the administration of the former German possessions was the responsibility of the mandatory power—to the establishment of which Japan had herself subscribed.

Ironically, Japan after the war entered a narrower world in the Pacific region. Just at a time when this eastern nation had caught up with the West after a fifty-year struggle and now ranked third among the world's great naval powers; just when she had won prestige in victorious wars and made considerable economic gains, the doors were closed to her subjects by new immigration restrictions on the American west coast in 1924 and were strongly bolted even against Japanese enterprise in the vast Australian-controlled area of the southwest Western Pacific. Already in 1917, Australia had frozen the Japanese population at its existing level in New Guinea and had refused permits for Japanese companies to trade between New Guinea and Australia, and Rabaul and the Solomons. In lengthy negotiations in 1920, the Australian Government fought tooth and nail against the 'open door' principle and Japanese acquisition of any commercial rights in its sphere. Japanese lost their right to obtain, own, and operate copra plantations at Rabaul, and there was to be no more loading and unloading by foreign ships there, as: 'The Commonwealth Parliament will have the same unfettered discretion as it has on the mainland of Australia'. Finally, the Navigation Act of 1919–1920 excluded virtually all foreign shipping between Australia and its Mandates, although ironically it soon had to be suspended because of a lack of Australian shipping.

But the rules Australia laid down in the aftermath of the war needed to be backed by military power commensurate with the claims which the Australian Government was staking out over its island empire in the Southwest Pacific. So, back home, when Prime Minister Hughes introduced the Treaty of Versailles for ratification in the Commonwealth Parliament on 10 September 1919, he called for an Australian Monroe Doctrine in the South Pacific: 'The Monroe doctrine . . . lays down that no European Power can meddle in any matter affecting either of the two American continents, North or South . . . It is proper that a like doctrine should be promulgated on behalf of Australia . . . the Pacific . . . too, is covered by a doctrine that is for us to settle, and for nobody else'. It was a sweeping demand to be made by a continent that lacked naval strength to press for such a doctrine. After all, U.S. President James Monroe had pronounced his Doctrine in Congress in 1823 with a certain sense of confidence in United States military means against any meddling in the New World by European powers. But it was entirely to Europe that Hughes looked for the defence of an Australian Monroe Doctrine.

He was lucky, however, to find an ally in Lord Jellicoe, who was then touring the world to advise the British Dominions on their individual naval policies. When the acting Prime Minister of Australia asked Jellicoe for more specific strategic advice, the former First Sea Lord, against the instructions of the British Government, eagerly volunteered his opinion in a report on the future source of danger to the Empire. Jellicoe never much appreciated the part Japan had played as an ally during World War I. In his report he identified Japan as the future source of danger to Empire, and especially to Australia whose policy of exclusion could only be a thorn in the side of the Japanese. Japanese expansion was pointing to China, the Philippines, and the Dutch East Indies. Any foothold in the Indies posed a serious threat to Australian sea communications. To be able to meet the threat of the Japanese Fleet, Lord Jellicoe recommended the permanent stationing in the Pacific of at least eight battleships and eight battle cruisers.

Hughes and his Defence Minister Pearce seized with alacrity Lord Jellicoe's report as a guideline for military considerations in the post-war era. At two conferences summoned in January and February 1920, the Commonwealth's most senior military officers appreciated the mere suppositions of the British navy man as positive assertions:

> The maintenance of a White Australia is easily capable of being made a *casus belli* . . . There is reason to believe that the shipping available to Japan would enable the concentration of sufficient mercantile shipping to transport an army of 100,000 men fully equipped in one convoy . . . Japan . . . could land troops at almost any place desired on the Australian coast, continue to reinforce them, and supply them with fresh munitions and other requirements . . .

It was agreed that 'Japan is the only potential and probable enemy'.

On 12 April 1920, the Council of Defence approved 3.6 million pounds for 'the maintenance of the existing Naval Unit as an efficient fighting machine', 3.5 million pounds for land forces, and 1.1 million pounds for the provision of a nucleus of an Air Force. All in all, defence appropriations for 1920–1921 rose to nearly twice the amount approved for 1913–1914—to give Australia a 'sporting chance' of holding out until British command of the Pacific could be established. The Prime Minister also announced that, in connection with Lord Jellicoe's recommendation, he would urge the British Government to station certain capital ships at Singapore.

Spy stories blossomed again in these early post-war years, imbued with suspicion of Japanese foul designs. Japanese ships' officers on leave while ashore in Australia were reported running up high taxi bills along the strategic area between Sydney and the coal mines of Newcastle. One Japanese ex-sea captain was reported as having established himself as a stationery agent at Newcastle. The perfect spy, so it appears from the reports of those days, was a Japanese with sketch book in hand. A Japanese posing as a cook had been seen sketching the coast. Another one ran a boarding house at Woy Woy near the vital Hawkesbury Bridge on the northern railway line between Sydney and Newcastle; his only boarders were Japanese who devoted much time to sketching the surroundings. One more Japanese selling writing materials, who also set up a drapery and millinery shop in central Newcastle, was providing the sketch paper, and yet another stationer, a Mr Kuwata, was suspected to be the chief co-ordinating agent in the Sydney–Newcastle area.

A considerable file on Japanese clandestine behaviour was created, built on the evidence of dock workers, the general public, press, and such zealous Japanese agent hunters as Commander J. G. Fearnley. Their reports continue to haunt impressionable Australians although, after the war, Major E. L. Piesse, who headed Military Intelligence during much of World War I, played down the Japanese spy-scare:

> There is little or no evidence to connect these Japanese . . . with the Government of Japan . . .
>
> They are an alert, inquisitive people, and everywhere they go they ask questions and take photographs and make notes, to satisfy their own curiosity . . . Let us remember that the collecting in another country of information . . . does not necessarily mean that plans are being made to conquer that country.

The Japanese Consul-General had a hard time refuting the embarrassing invasion scare stories. When, on 2 February, the *Sydney Morning Herald* reported a commercial traveller as having seen thousands of Japanese land on offshore islands and on the mainland between Townsville and Darwin during the previous twelve months, Consul Tamaki Katsusaburō retorted two days later in the same paper:

> The incomprehensible malevolence and persistent frequency with which it is hinted, insinuated, or openly stated that Japan has sinister designs upon Australia is one of the greatest marvels of the 20th century, and those who hold such an opinion appear to have deliberately closed their minds to all evidence to the contrary . . . Can it be possible that this is a sign of an uneasy conscience? It has been pointed out many times that, if Japan cherished any animosity towards Australia, the time to have gratified it was during the recent war, when, even by simply remaining neutral, she could have left Australia in a condition of the greatest danger at German hands . . . It becomes necessary to remind some Australians that

they had no better nor more faithful friend and ally than Japan during the war.

Negative post-war assessments of Japan engendered such animosity in Australia in the three or four years following Armistice Day that, on the occasion of celebrating the Emperor's birthday at the Japanese consulate in Sydney on 1 November 1920, a high political dignitary, R. W. Caldwell, felt an apology in place:

> I avail myself of this opportunity to express my deep regret and shame at the recrudescence of anti-Japanese prejudice, which has taken place in Australia since the conclusion of the late war. So many of the prognostications of anti-Japanese prophets were disproved by the faithful performance of her treaty obligations by Japan during that great struggle ... They deny that Japan did anything at all during the war, or assert that, if she did, she did it from interested motives ...

Acting Consul-General Tamaki added: 'Should there be any conflict of opinion as to whether we have done our duty or not, there is but one way of settling such a question, and that is by an appeal to the facts'.

To counteract the negative wave, men in Japanese pay were driving home these facts to the Australian elites in speeches and pamphlets. In June 1919, Oliver Bainbridge wrote to Acting Prime Minister W. A. Watt:

> The co-operation of the Japanese Navy during the war, which has been cordial, complete, and uninterrupted from the very outset ... should shame the alarmists into facing the realities of the situation. P.S. It is my intention to give a dinner to Members of Parliament and other public men in Melbourne and Sydney and tell them what I know of Japan and the value of the Anglo–Japanese Alliance.

At such a dinner on 20 June 1919, Bainbridge addressed the members of the Empire Literature Society in Sydney, in a speech issued as a booklet by Sydney's Vale & Pearson Printers, *Our Ally Japan*:

> The co-operation of the Japanese Navy during the war has been cordial, complete, and uninterrupted from the very outset. Japan declared war on Germany on 23 August 1914. Four days later Kiao-chow was blockaded. The British battleships 'Triumph' and the destroyer 'Usk' were placed under the command of the Commander-in-Chief of the Second Japanese Fleet ...
>
> We owe it to the loyal and effective co-operation of Japan upon the seas that the troops brought from India and the Anzacs from Australasia were transported in unmolested security to the European battlefields ... I am sure the Japanese Navy took great pride in escorting the Australians ...
>
> It is somewhat of an illogical assumption that Japan sits with a jealous

eye upon Australia. It would be rank madness for Japan to offend the greatest Powers of the world by attempting to invade the white man's country.

We cannot appreciate what is best in the Japanese folk unless we understand them; Japan is not dumb . . . She has many eloquent spokesmen and possesses a noble literature. Her language is, unfortunately, difficult to acquire and little known among us. One would hope that Britishers who have an eye to the future distribution of influence and opportunity on this planet will see to their boys learning Japanese.

All Bainbridge's dinner expenses at the Menzies Hotel in Melbourne, for example, or at the New Palace Emporium in Brickfield Hill, Sydney, were taken care of by Japanese Consul-General Shimizu. The speaker, moreover, was paid handsomely, as his surviving receipts reveal for 16 July: 'Dear Mr. Shimizu, I thank you for your kind present of 150 pounds. Part of the expenses of dinners in Sydney and Melbourne. Oliver Bainbridge;' and for 25 July: 'I have received from Mr. Shimizu the following presents. 100 pounds Honorarium & 180 pounds Lecture & distribution'.

A more spontaneous, because unremunerated, and therefore more credible friend of the Japanese cause was R. A. Hornabrook, a parliamentarian from Adelaide, who also made speeches and wrote to editors and ministers on behalf of Japan. He defended Japan in the same vein as Bainbridge: 'Japan convoyed Australian ships; Japanese destroyers in the Mediterranean more than once saved Australian troops in transport. Japan will always play straight.' Hornabrook was a former ship's surgeon and officer and especially concerned with the continuation of the Anglo–Japanese Alliance. He warned: 'If we break our alliance with Japan we will force her into an alliance with Russia, against her own will. Of all the countries in the world not to desire to break the alliance, Australia should be that country.' In his long letters to Prime Minister Hughes, the editor of the *Times* in London, and others, he lambasted the United States: 'The U. S. A. . . . . think that someday they may have trouble with Japan . . . They must have some place of safety for the repairs of their ships and for bases in the Pacific. So they say to themselves, let us coquette with New Zealand and Australia—tell them their interests be with ours—work for the breaking of the Anglo–Japanese Alliance and all will be well with us (the USA)'. He emphatically denounced United States scheming and declaimed: 'As long as the Anglo–Japanese Alliance remains in force we have absolutely nothing to fear in the Pacific. We lose nothing by the maintenance of the Alliance, but by the breaking of it we stand to lose everything.'

Hornabrook frequently reported the points he thought he had scored to Tamaki, and sent him also a copy of his letter to Prime Minister Hughes on the eve of the leader's departure for London. Hornabrook proudly stated that he had won over to Japan's cause eight hundred at the Socialist Hall. W. F. Massey, the Prime Minister of New Zealand, and Jellicoe were with him now, he wrote, and Hughes had learnt common sense. In reference to Hughes's speech in which the Prime Minister pledged himself to the promotion of the Anglo–Japanese Alliance, Hornabrook gasconaded: 'The voice of Hughes—the words of Hornabrook'.

But Hughes needed no prompting from Hornabrook in this matter. Already in 1911 he had understood the salutary effect of renewing the Anglo–Japanese Alliance when he commented in the *Argus*: 'This gives us breathing time, and . . . makes distinctly for the maintenance of peace'. Now at 10 Downing Street, on the morning of 21 June 1921, Hughes told the representatives of the United Kingdom, the Dominions, and India:

> To Australia, as you will quite understand, this Treaty with Japan has special significance . . . I think from every point of view that it would be well that the Treaty with Japan should be renewed. Should we not be in a better position to exercise greater influence over the Eastern policy as an Ally of that great Eastern Power, than as her potential enemy? . . . The world wants peace. Which policy is most likely to promote, to ensure, the world's peace? As I see it, the renewal of the Treaty with the Japanese Empire.

Hughes made clear that the Australian Government refused to surrender to United States machinations of abrogating the Anglo–Japanese Alliance. New Zealand's Prime Minister Massey backed him entirely: 'To preserve peace in the Pacific, there is no better way than having the Japanese as an ally . . . because they are a strong nation, army and navy, but their navy is best'. Together with Massey, Hughes put up an impassioned stand to have the alliance extended.

It was somehow curious to watch the man who in the past had spoken out so virulently against Japan, especially at Paris, now making every effort, in London and upon his return in September 1921, to preserve the Anglo–Japanese Alliance system and 'live in peace and friendship with Japan'. Hughes was wearing a new hat, and Japanese Consul-General Suzuki Eisaku remarked that the kindly tone in Mr Hughes's speeches created very friendly sentiments in Japan, adding: 'These speeches will do much to remove misunderstanding between Japan and Australia. Every word spoken by Mr. Hughes . . . is followed with keen interest by my nation'.

Yet Hughes was also aware of the reports in the United States that Great Britain, as the ally of Japan, could be involved in an American–Japanese war through British obligations in the Anglo–Japanese Alliance. Thus, if the alliance were to be renewed, it would have to be modified so as to 'be acceptable to Britain, to America, to Japan, and to ourselves'. Hughes and Massey therefore urged the convening of a preliminary Pacific conference, to include America and Japan, to ascertain what would be mutually acceptable. Most of July was spent sounding out opinion in Japan, China, and the United States about a preparatory meeting in London on Pacific and Far Eastern questions. But when Britain received an invitation from United States President Warren G. Harding to attend an armament limitation conference to be held late that year in Washington, the Pacific Conference idea was dropped and incorporated into the wider Disarmament Conference which took place at Washington from 12 November 1921 to 11 February 1922.

Although the Dominions could speak only through the British Empire delegation, the results achieved at the Washington Conference had a soothing effect on Australia. E. L. Piesse, Director of the Pacific Branch of the Prime Minister's Department and one of the two members of the Australian delegation, highly valued the Four Power Treaty which superseded the Anglo–Japanese Alliance, because '*Australia* gets from Japan a recognition of the White Australia policy'. In fact, all that Japan, the United States, Britain, and France agreed to was simply to respect one another's rights in the Pacific region with regard to their insular possessions and dominions.

Prime Minister Hughes, too, was on the whole optimistic when he presented the Washington Treaties for ratification in Parliament on 26 July 1922: 'The Anglo-Japanese Treaty merges or disappears, and the Quadruple Treaty takes its place . . . This Treaty establishes an equilibrium in the Pacific . . . It insures peace for the next ten years for Australia.' Although he cautioned that 'There is nothing in this Treaty that guarantees us any protection if we are attacked', he stressed its economic benefit: 'Were it not for these Treaties we should now be contemplating additional naval expenditure rather than be comforted with the positive assurance of a substantial reduction in our Naval Estimates. War begets war, and peace begets peace.'

More amazing was the conversion of Minister for Defence Pearce, the leading Australian delegate at Washington, who stated the following day:

We have been nervous . . . I believe that Japan is peaceful . . . Baron Kato, who was the head of the Japanese Delegation—a skilful and able diplomat and statesman—is to-day the Prime Minister of Japan. He took the reponsibility for most of the great decisions that Japan gave at the conference . . . It is a great source of satisfaction for us in Australia to know that this powerful neighbour should desire to turn away from military aggression and the policy of force and to tread the path of peace . . . While . . . I suspected Japan, I believe now that Japan is earnest and sincere . . . Japan [has] played the game with us under the terms of the Alliance . . .

I am glad that [the decisions reached at the Conference] have provided an opportunity to merge that Alliance into a Treaty which, whilst it is not an alliance, nevertheless gives us an opportunity of extending the hand of friendship to Japan . . . I am proud to have taken part in the Conference, and I invite the Senate unanimously to ratify the Treaties . . .

As a result, defence expenditures were cut by more than one million pounds. The Royal Australian Navy ships were reduced from 23 to 13 (the capital flagship *Australia* was scrapped under the rules of the Naval Disarmament Rules). Army numbers were slashed from 118,000 to 30,000; 885 professional soldiers were dismissed. Compulsory military training was shortened from 16 to 10 days and cadet training from 4 to 2 years. For a brief moment, Australia was set at ease by the pledges given at Washington.

Less positive was the closing down of essential institutions established during the war to help Australia better understand Japan. Most glaring was the elimination of the Pacific Branch of the Prime Minister's Department. Set up to monitor Japan, it had provided valuable information on the Japanese press and general mood in the country and even promised to become Australia's first embryonic foreign office. The Washington Conference was believed to have yielded such marvellous fruit that a detailed study of Japanese affairs was 'for the next few years, at least, quite unnecessary', said the Branch director, E. L. Piesse, in 1922. He retired from office in the following year and Captain Broadbent, sent to Japan to prepare himself for the continuous study of the Japanese vernacular press in the Pacific Branch, was recalled. Even the tenure of the full-time lecturer in Japanese at Duntroon College was cancelled.

No sooner was Japan believed to be inoffensive, than all effort to know more about Japan was stopped dead in its tracks. Australia slipped back into the same old kind of Nipponese ignorance that she had suffered before the war. The cancellations revealed a singular superficiality of Australian policy *vis-à-vis* Japan and her understanding of Asia, and seriously handicapped Australia in the years leading up to the Pacific War.

Between the early 1890s and early 1920s, Japanese–Australian relations were severely tested in a time when Japan was beginning to re-assert herself in the Pacific region through a series of wars that three times saw her on the victor's side. During those thirty years, Australia was growing into a federation increasingly preoccupied with the defence of its white strain in the isolated environment of the Australasian region. When Japan trounced China, Australia extended her immigration restriction law to the Japanese in 1896. When Japan beat Russia, Australia built her army and navy. Finally, when Japan helped defeat Germany in the Pacific, Australian Japanophobia rose to a crescendo at the Paris Peace Conference, where Prime Minister Hughes quashed the

Japanese racial equality clause in the League preamble and secured the former German island possessions in the Western Pacific south of the Equator as a bulwark against Japan. Australian anxiety subsided only after the Pacific powers decided at the Washington Conference in 1921 to scrap a significant part of their navies. Yet all through the din of Australian cries that vented suspicion of Japan, Japanese entrepreneurs, politicians, and intellectuals were actually charting a southern course away from Australia, down the South China coast and into the Southeast Asian region. This view of the *nan'yō* by the early 1920s defined Australia as far outside the ambit of Japanese interests in the Southern Seas.

Golden Years
1924–1935

'Japan has paid Australia a very high compliment', commented the *Sydney Morning Herald* upon the arrival in Australia of the new Consul-General, Tokugawa Iemasa, in early December 1925. To receive the son of Prince Tokugawa, who but for the Restoration would have been Shogun that day, was an honour and 'a tribute to the importance with which Japanese regard their representation in the Commonwealth'. The message which the illustrious envoy brought to Australia was as elevated:

> [Prime Minister] Viscount Kato desires to renew the glorious recollections of the time when Australians and Japanese stood together in arms for a righteous cause and for the establishment of everlasting peace . . . Japan and Australia should communicate to each other all that is best and happiest in their respective civilizations.

Prime Minister S. M. Bruce responded in like vein:

> The beginning of our history as a nation is marked by comradeship with the Japanese people in the cause of justice and right . . . The destinies of the two peoples in the Pacific lie together. Our civilisations are complementary and we shall mutually enrich ourselves in receiving and giving what is best in them. This the Australian people hope to achieve by the closest relation with your people.

The exchange may have been more diplomatic than substantive, but the subsequent decade did bring less racial disaffection, closer trade relations, and territorial consolidation by the two countries in the Western Pacific with a minimum of strategic apprehension.

Turning a new page in Japanese–Australian relations was also Mitsui Takasumi of the Mitsui Trading House who, on a tour of Australia, was taking stock of business opportunities and the future of commercial relations between the two countries. In his book published upon return, *Gōshū ryōkōki* (Travelogue of Australia), Mitsui sounds as optimistic as had Shiga Shigetaka on discovering Australia. Mitsui sailed the same route as the Meiji intellectual had once weathered on an austere war vessel in 1886; although in 1923 the journey still took a month, with deck-tennis and fancy dress parties time passed much quicker on the pleasure steamer *Yoshino Maru*. The young scion in the early twenties was doing Australia in style, with two tuxedos and riding breeches.

Mitsui was a businessman, not an intellectual, but he shared Shiga's enthusiasm for introducing Australia to Japan. Where Shiga had been exasperated about Japanese ignorance of Australia because no one yet had given much thought to the south, Mitsui was now impatient about the lingering ignorance because the political and economic ties forged for so long had yielded only mediocre results. He wrote little about the White Australia policy, but offered a succinct account of the commercial situation in the bigger cities. He dwelt on the prospects of the seventy or so expatriates employed in thirty Japanese trading, banking, and shipping buisnesses in Sydney; on rivalry, especially between the old established trading company of Kanematsu and his own Mitsui Company; and on his company's pending negotiations on meat export contracts with Japan, about which he was sanguine.

His day-to-day observations offer a rare glimpse of the travel-style of a well-bred Japanese entrepreneur as he mingled with Australian high society and members of the various Japan associations in Australia from August to September 1923. A bit of politics, economics, and general history of Australia round out his observations. But Mitsui's voice was first of all that of a trader whose company had profited through World War I. It was apolitical, largely uncritical, and carries little weight.

Of greater consequence is the comprehensive analysis of Japanese–Australian relations up to 1926 that E. L. Piesse wrote for the April issue of *Foreign Affairs*. An authority on the subject, he listed all the events which since 1896 had led Australians to believe that their country occupied a leading place in Japanese plans for future territorial expansion. Much of the Australian paranoia he blamed on the press, 'particularly those evening papers which are in unscrupulous hands'. He dismissed Japan's rising population figures and shrinking food resources as a threat to Australia: South America offered a wide-open door for Japan's emigrants, and the food resources of South Manchuria and the waters off the

Siberian coast guaranteed a ready supply of food. Piesse's conclusion is characteristic of the relaxed years in this 'golden' period:

> There is little or nothing in the past conduct of Japan to support the view which many Australians had that she will challenge the White Australia policy and that she envisages the future domination of Australia. It seems safe to conclude that we are of so little importance to her that we scarcely enter into her policy.

Nor was the White Australia policy broached in the international forums that grew up in the post-war years of Wilson's New Diplomacy, such as the Institute of Pacific Relations, of which both Japan and Australia were members. The Institute was created 'to study the conditions of the Pacific peoples with a view to the improvement of their mutual relations'. Nitobe Inazō (whose portrait today graces the 5,000 yen banknotes) was its leading Japanese member, supported by intellectual retainers such as Takagi Yasaka, Tsurumi Yūsuke, Takayanagi Kanzo, and Maeda Tamon. The Australian delegations were often led by Frederic Eggleston, and included S. H. Roberts, H. Duncan Hall, Ian Clunies-Ross, and other international-relations specialists and historians. Every two or three years, the member countries met to promote international peace by taking a scientific view toward solving the burning regional political issues of the day. Naturally, each nation had its own priorities. For example, the Japanese members criticized the British for making the China problem and Manchuria central issues on the agenda, while they themselves encouraged semi-official discussions with the Americans on immigration problems in an effort to revise the hurtful Japanese Exclusion Act of 1924. But, to the relief of the Australian delegation, the Japanese seemed unconcerned about the White Australia policy, for they did not bring it up for discussion.

That policy had become much less of an issue after the clamour at Paris. Australia was now recognized as a country that was out of bounds and accessible only to the Japanese businessman on his occasional errand to purchase wool or sell textiles. Other outlets beckoned in that decade—for example, South America and Manchuria—into which planned immigration was being canvassed, under official Japanese supervision. Attention focused increasingly on the Philippines and the Dutch East Indies, where the respective Japanese immigration figures rose from 8,000 and 3,800 in 1924, to 21,400 and 6,600 in 1935, while in the same period the figure for Japanese residents in Australia dropped from 4,200 to 3,100. But most of all, it was the sugar plantation industry in Micronesia that began to lure the Japanese in ever greater numbers into their new mandate territory in the central Western Pacific.

8

Consolidation
in the Western Pacific

THE CHARACTER of the Japanese southward advance entered a new stage between 1924 and 1935. The course of Japan's *nanshin-ron* had been separating itself from Australia, even as Japanese interests moved south, and the Southeast Asian region became the main focus of attention. In that region, Japan was now determined to play a bigger role and to involve herself in a search for raw materials to fuel her heavy industry at a level commensurate to her status as a great power at the Paris Peace Conference. As she was doing so, Japan's southward advance underwent a change. *'Minami e! Minami e!'* ('To the South! To the South!') no longer rang out. Instead, Japan's southern interest in the 1920s and 1930s became stationary, as Japanese enterprise concentrated on the outer and inner *nan'yō*. That is to say, for about twelve years the *nanshin-ron* ideology consolidated in a gestative period that endowed it at the same time with significant staying power.

This new stage in Japan's southward advance had a number of features that were strikingly similar to Japan's southward advance in the pre-*sakoku* period, as the economic historian Shimizu Hajime has pointed out in an arresting comparative study of historical continuities. His findings sustain the view that to better understand Japan's southward advance in the modern period, it is useful to look into her southward advance in the pre-modern period.

116

Shimizu draws attention to the fact that those emigrants who had left Japan in the early seventeenth century had been traders with considerable capital investments, self-employed businessmen, artisans, disbanded military of the samurai class, and the like. They differed considerably from the adventurers who again went south in the late 1860s, whom Shiga Shigetaka described as the riffraff he had chanced upon in Sydney in 1886: jugglers, actors, gamblers, and tea girls. An even larger segment were club owners, room renters, pimps, and prostitutes (*karayukisan*), who settled in the various towns of Southeast Asia along with an entourage of hairdressers, vendors of cosmetics, and other professionals catering to women's needs. With Japan's new rise to respectability, and after the Japanese government curtailed prostitution abroad from the 1910s onward, the women and related side-businesses quickly diminished or disappeared. Traders, investors, managers, and farmers replaced them completely in the 1920s, when company men set up the trading houses of Mitsubishi and Mitsui, opened branches of the banks of Taiwan and Yokohama, and established all over Southeast Asia the Nihon, Osaka, Yamashita, and Yūsen shipping lines to serve the entire Western Pacific region with a close-knit network of cargo and passenger transportation.

Basing his conclusions on the studies by Iwao Seiichi and official statistics on Japanese immigration into Southeast Asia in the 1920s and 1930s, Shimizu shows that Japanese immigration into the southern region, both in the early seventeenth century and in the interwar period, was dominated by immigrants who were preponderantly in the international trading business and continued to retain strong ties with their home country. Even the farmer immigrant between the two World Wars was closely connected with international trade, since returns from the rubber he went to cultivate on plantations in Malaya, or the flax he grew in the Philippines, depended greatly on the price fluctuations of international markets.

Moreover, in both periods the Japanese Government had a trade policy, but not an immigration policy. While international trade in the *nan'yō* was officially encouraged and supported by the Tokugawa and Showa Governments, neither took interest in organizing permanent Japanese immigration into the Southeast Asian region or lent the expatriates any government support. This is particularly noteworthy in the modern period, when policies existed for immigration to Latin America and Manchuria, but not for Japanese going to Southeast Asia. Japanese *nan'yō* interest in Southeast Asia was exclusively trade-oriented and unsustained by official programs. In this it resembled Japan's southward advance between 1600 and 1639; for then, too, the Japanese lacked the tools of empire-sustaining structures for permanent monopolistic expansion, of the kind epitomized by the Dutch East India Company and the British East India Company.

Shimizu also draws attention to the fact that the non-permanent Japanese immigrant prevailed over the permanent immigrant in both periods. Many immigrants in the early seventeenth century went abroad without a family and returned when the terms of their commercial duties abroad expired. Likewise, in the modern period, the single man who was moved to various appointments in the banks, trading houses, and transportation companies abroad [by the *tanshin funingata* system], was most often a temporary expatriate.

This may hold true for many Japanese who were involved exclusively in the *shuinsen* trade of the pre-*sakoku* period, or for the new breed of company men in the interwar years who dealt with international trade and circulated in the branch offices in the trade ports of the Southeast Asian region. Nevertheless, there were in both periods 'fixed' immigrants who emigrated with their families (or, in the modern period, started one through the 'picture'-bride system) and became permanent residents. These included, in earlier days, traders such as Luzon Sukezaemon or Wada Rinzaemon, as well as the three to four hundred Japanese immigrants who settled down permanently into urban and rural life in and around Batavia in the seventeenth century. Their modern counterparts included the sizeable community of Japanese permanent residents engaged in the hemp industry in Davao in the Philippines in the 1930s, who often brought their families and sometimes married local people. A far larger group includes the tens of thousands of Japanese who emigrated to Micronesia (an area not touched on by Shimizu in his study) and began to settle permanently in the mid-1920s and 1930s.

At Paris, both Japan and Australia had been given C-mandates over the former German island possessions in the North and South Pacific. International agreement allowed them to administer these as if the mandates were an integral part of their respective countries. In comparing how each of them went about this task, it is easy to lose one's balance, if only because the islands which became their quasi-colonies differed greatly in size and population. Japan became master over 1,400 small islands and coral reefs of the Mariana, Caroline, and Marshall Islands, totalling around 830 square miles, with small and manageable populations. Australia, on the other hand, had to rule over 110,300 square miles of island territories, consisting of the Bismarck Archipelago with New Britain, New Ireland and the Admiralty Islands, the two northern Solomon Islands, Bougainville and Buka, and one of the world's largest islands, New Guinea, which alone accounted for 93,000 square miles and was fragmented into a multitude of different native societies. The populations of Japan and Australia were directly inverse to their mandate tasks: little populated and oversized Australia should have been managing a smaller mandate territory, whereas Japan with her high population would have been less likely to dominate local peoples numerically had it administered a territory the size of New Guinea.

But these discrepancies aside, the mandate period tempts comparison. It has an obvious beginning and an end, and is clearly limited to territories in the Western Pacific, where for twenty years the dividing line of the Equator made Japan and Australia direct neighbours in the widest geographical sense. At Paris, both governments had fought with hurrah for the possession of the island territories and had started a colonial experiment under League supervision. They were given their mandates on 17 December 1920 and their tenure was ended by the Pacific War in December 1941. Later, the mandates were recast as trust territories, supervised under the authority of the United Nations' international trusteeship system. The subject still awaits detailed comparative analysis, although a number of studies have already separately treated the Japanese and Australian colonial experiences.

Ripe for comparison, and of topical interest, are the respective civilian administrations, and the labour and population problems encountered. In 1921, Japanese administrative headquarters were moved from naval command headquarters in the strategically most valuable island of Truk to Koror Island in the Palau group, where the Nan'yō-chō (South Seas Bureau) was established to govern Micronesia. Until 1924, the Nan'yō -chō stood under the jurisdiction of the Prime Minister's Office in Tokyo. Thereafter, it was primarily responsible to the Foreign Ministry, but also to the Posts and Telecommunications Ministry, the Finance Ministry, and the Commerce and Industry Ministry. Australia's civil administrative center remained at Rabaul, but was similarly attached to the Prime Minister's Office until 1923, when it became obligated to the Ministry for Home and Territories only.

Japan administered its widespread island empire through six branch bureaux on the islands of Saipan, Yap, Palau, Truk, Ponape, and Jaluit, and introduced a town council system similar to that of Japan. Village chiefs, selected from the tribal headmen, were responsible to the Japanese branch officials and had to appear in person twice a year to present their reports. By mid-1935, the number of Japanese officials in the islands stood at 944 (while Germany had governed Micronesia with only about 20 to 30 officials). The American scholar Paul Clyde, who visited the Japanese mandates at that time and published his book *Japan's Pacific Mandate* in 1936, was impressed with the Japanese administration he saw and commented that Japan had been fortunate in finding the six men of ability and judgment who had served as governor of the island empire to that time.

The Australian Government, which had to rule over a much larger territory, installed administrative centers in ten districts of New Guinea. In 1922, however, the district staff still totalled only 51 and decreased to 43 in 1924. Recruitment of able executives was a problem. Australia's immense island colony remained poorly administrated. Even though patrol cars were used to tour the region, a patrol car with one district officer, one medical assistant, and one native policeman would appear in a village only once a year to collect a head tax. On an island of 93,000 square miles—25,000 of which were still completely unexplored in 1921 —Australia could effect only a thin control and provide only a semblance of law and order. There was no steady and continuous Australian administrative influence on the population's affairs, since the limited staff was unable to establish sufficient contact to give direction at the village level.

Japan's administrative machinery was more complex, and made effective through a management-by-delegation style that had the natives' roles clearly prescribed. In the Marshall Islands, for example, native administration was carried out by two village chiefs who passed orders to sixteen village headmen. Meanwhile, in the Australian mandates, one agent had to perform various functions, so that the situation of indirect rule tended to 'no rule at all'. The Japanese had clearly defined the functions of the chief and village headmen and worked mainly through them to attain harmonious co-operation with the native populace. Australian authorities, however, made their own district staff directly responsible for the enforcement of its many requirements, thereby depriving the villagers of control of their own affairs. What is more, the Australian district staff, who did not trust the natives much, were frequently moved to new districts. Unavoidably, writes Australian historian Heather Radi, the police functions of government were dominant.

By 1924, the Australian Government became so worried about the negative side-effects of the haphazard development of its colonial policy that it engaged a native affairs expert, Colonel J. Ainsworth of the British colonial service. His report confirmed that the colonial administration was not satisfactorily staffed. He also blamed Australian authorities for a lack of planning and for depriving the *luluais* (village officials) of sufficient power. (Even under German administration, *luluai* courts had been part of the administrative judicial system.) There was no provision for these courts under the Australian administration. Most of Ainsworth's recommendations were ignored, however.

Japan not only administrated her Pacific mandate with zeal, but developed tremendously its agricultural–industrial potential. Copra production trebled, phosphate mining quintupled, a fishing industry grew up, and alcohol (for Japan) was produced as a side-product of the most important agricultural product, sugar. As copra became the first cash crop for many villages, especially in the Marshalls and Carolines, the community work it generated transformed the pace of village life and, on Palau, native copra brokers even emerged as a new Micronesian middle class in a money economy. Moreover, the vegetable and fruit markets that sprung up around Koror were so lucrative that native farmers organized joint agricultural producers' cooperatives with the South Seas Bureau.

The driving forces that moved all the goods between the islands,

Japan, and international markets were the South Seas Development Company (Nan'yō Kaihatsu Kabushiki Kaisha) and the South Seas Trading Company (Nan'yō Bōeki Kaisha). Their flourishing trade activities allowed a number of Micronesians to participate on the fringes of the business-world by setting up shop in the retail trades, selling goods and services on the native market. Others profited from a windfall in rents owing to the Japanese presence, particularly in the Marianas, where some large landowners were able to lease land to the South Seas Development Company at a good price. In a longer study on *Nan'yō: The Rise and Fall of the Japanese in Micronesia 1885–1945*, Mark Peattie concludes that the economic prosperity enjoyed by a considerable number of Micronesians during the three decades of Japanese rule was the brightest aspect of Japan's treatment of its native charges.

But the boom was accompanied by serious population and labour problems, brought about mainly by the phenomenal development of the sugar industry. The number of Japanese attracted by that industry grew rapidly from 4,000 in 1922 to 20,000 in 1930. By 1937 the total number of Japanese expatriates in the Central Pacific islands reached more than 62,000 and began to exceed that of the Micronesians. The local peoples had been found to be unreliable, too few in number, and unfit to cope with the technology of cane cultivation or sugar manufacture. In the Marianas in the 1920s, for example, Micronesians were not even hired as manual labourers. Japan's official excuse was always that there was neither time nor money to redress inborn native indolence.

The main sugar centers were located on Saipan, Tinian, and Rota in the Northern Marianas. By 1937, 21,000 Japanese labourers were employed in this industry alone, the bulk coming from Okinawa. Most of them were permanent settlers who came with their families, with women constituting over 40 per cent of the immigrant community. In that year, the Japanese became the dominant element in Micronesia, making up 55 per cent of the 113,000 inhabitants of the islands. The greatest discrepancy existed on Saipan, where 4,000 natives had to tolerate 42,500 Japanese who worked mainly in the sugar industry. Japan's swamping of her mandate with her own nationals was criticized on several occasions by the Permanent Mandates Commission. Native society was in fear of dying out. In *Labor Problems in the Pacific Mandates*, John Alvin Decker protested in 1940: 'The C-type mandate plan intended to help primitive peoples "unable to stand by themselves under the strenuous conditions of the modern world"; it did not envisage at all a situation in which the people of the mandated area would be submerged by and all the economic resources of the territory be placed in the hands of the nationals of the Mandatory Power'.

Australia's mandate problems regarding population and labour policies were opposite in nature, but they produced similar ill-effects. Australia showed too little interest in her Pacific mandate. Not enough

Australians could be found to emigrate, settle, and run the island territories. Those who went were mostly ex-soldiers, inexperienced in plantation work. No new agricultural industries were developed and copra remained the main product. Cocoa decreased in production and rubber ceased to be planted. Moreover, when rich alluvial gold was discovered at Edie Creek in 1926, many administrative officials left their jobs and planters sold their plantations to go after gold, but it was only in 1932 that gold production became a viable industry. As a result of poor, unqualified, and understaffed administration, coupled with the isolation effect of the vast territory, the natives were not brought into the mainstream, but were exploited. By 1940, New Guinean labourers had the lowest wages of all the Pacific Mandate labourers.

Unlike the Japanese, the Australian planters lacked their own labour and had to rely exclusively on the native work force. Asian workers were in strong demand, but barred by the White Australia policy. The acute labour shortage therefore caused specific recruiting problems. Ruthless recruiters tricked native men into forced labour-like conditions, and absence from their villages for two- to three-year periods caused social discord which threatened to destroy village life. However, the Japanese were also accused of using forced labour, as Japan's phosphate mines at Angaur were worked primarily by Chamorros from the Marianas, and by Carolinians from Yap, Palau, and Truk. The latter were recruited by village chiefs and headmen on special Japanese payroll, who were compensated for each 'volunteer' for the loss of tribal labour incurred. It seems that Carolinian men were often taken away from their villages against their will, to engage in exhausting open-pit mine work for periods from six months to four years. The Mandate Commission criticized both countries' contracting practices, as well as the enforcement of the White Australia policy in the Australian mandate.

Commission Chairman Lord Lugard, in particular, persistently castigated Australia's discriminatory immigration policy from 1923 to 1929, but without effect. Australia continued to value the mandates as a ring of fortress islands sheltering the white continent. Unlike Japan's profit-oriented view, that first of all sought a rapid commercial development of their territories, Australia's most important aim, after satisfying her minimum goal of making the territories at least pay for themselves, was to keep out foreigners and restrict all non-British investment.

For all their proximity, Japan and Australia might have been complete strangers but for their trade relations that enjoyed a singular boom between 1924 and 1935. Although the two countries' economies were closer linked to the European and American markets and did not favour each other with any special bilateral trade agreement, they had steadily been converging after World War I. Japan's exports to Australia had risen from 9 million yen in 1913 to an average of 30 million yen during the war years and, weathering various crises such as Australian high tariffs in 1921, the yen-decrease following the Kanto earthquake in 1923, Australia's inflation in 1929, and her policy in 1931 to import only half the amount of her exports, Japan's exports climbed steadily to 65 million yen in 1934. Over the same period, Australia doubled her purchases from Japan from 1.4 per cent of Japan's world-wide sales in 1913 to 3 per cent in 1935.

Australia's export figures to Japan are even more startling. They rose from 15 million yen in 1913 to 235 million yen in 1935. At the same time, Japan's market share for Australian products rose from 2 per cent in 1913 to almost 10 per cent in 1935, and increased Japan's trade deficit in favour of Australia from 6 million yen in 1913 to 160 million yen in 1935, totalling 314 per cent of Japan's sales to Australia.

Japan mainly bought such raw materials from Australia as wool, wheat, leather, some zinc, lead, and iron ore; she sold apparel and textiles, fertilizers, bags and baskets, chinaware, furniture, and oils and waxes in return. The years following the depression further reinforced their mutually advantageous two-way trade pattern. To solve domestic economic problems, Japan concentrated on higher industrial output, which led her to increase substantially the purchase of Australian wool, wheat, minerals, and other produce. Whereas Japan's total imports of raw wool alone more than doubled between 1929 and 1933, Japanese cotton, rayon textiles and artificial silk reached record import levels in the Australian market. The healthy trade pattern gave Australia a much-sought favourable balance which greatly helped her survive the difficult times. The whole situation revealed for the first time on a large scale how complementary were the needs of Japan and Australia. It was the kind of commercial relationship Shiga Shigetaka and Mishima Kazuo had been dreaming of in the 1880s. It also gave hope that this would lead not only to a profitable long-term interchange of goods, but to increasingly friendly diplomatic relations.

Goodwill missions were undertaken by Australian Minister for External Affairs J. G. Latham to Tokyo, and by Japanese high-ranking senior diplomat Debuchi Katsuji to Canberra. On both occasions the Australian Government declared its full support for Japan's Asia policy, and Japan received permission to develop the iron-rich Yampi Sound region southwest of Darwin on the northern coast of Western Australia.

There was now far less agreement on the 'Japan Threat' school of thought. In July 1924, the deputy leader of the Labor Opposition, Frank Anstey, denounced in Parliament Prime Minister S. M. Bruce's intention to allocate an additional 2.5 million pounds for the defence of Australia. It was a wasteful sum to spend at a time when security was provided by the League of Nations, the Washington Conference treaties, and the peaceful attitude of Japan:

> We are told that this nation [Japan], since no other enemy can be imagined, threatens us in the future. I can say to Japan, on behalf of those for whom I now speak, that there is at least one great party in this country, representing one half, if not more, of the population, that is not seeking to foster racial hatreds or to build up any kind of defensive force on that basis. We have no belief that Japan will assail us in the future, for we know that she has not done so in the past . . .

Economic circumstance as well as policy decisions gradually consigned the military to a lower level on the list of state priorities by the end of the decade. In July 1929, Prime Minister Bruce was forced to reduce defence expenditure by 540,000 pounds due to an accumulated deficit of 5 million over the previous two years. In November that year, following a change in government, Labor Prime Minister J. H. Scullin further curtailed defence expenditures and, true to Labor's declared policy to support the cause of world peace, abolished the compulsory military system, replacing it with a voluntary training scheme.

Lower military expenditures went together with a lower appreciation of Japan as a future enemy. A government paper on Australian foreign policy in 1930 stated that Australia's only direct concerns were the future ownership of the Antarctic region and the administration of the New Hebrides. It reaffirmed the principle of the Covenant of the League to limit and reduce armaments. And while the paper did say at the outset that a threat to peace in the Pacific might come from an attempt by Japan at economic or political expansion or from continuing disorder in China, the Australian representative at the London Naval Conference in the same year, J. Fenton, commented that from information received from Canberra 'Australia was not apprehensive of the designs of Japan upon Australia'.

When Japan seized Manchuria in 1931–1932, the unexpected Japanese inroads on the Chinese mainland sent everything into reverse. Old Australian fears again rose to the forefront, voiced this time against a less-manageable Japan, no longer reined in by the Anglo–Japanese Alliance. The Japanese incursion took place just at a time when Australia was enjoying excellent trade relations with Japan, and Australian military preparations were at their lowest. Making matters worse, it was still questionable whether a British Battle Fleet could arrive in time at the incomplete naval base at Singapore to assist a threatened Australia, and it was doubtful whether American help could be counted on in the case of a Japanese attack. Under the circumstances, the Australian Government felt it had only one policy option: appeasement.

The Lytton Commission, which was sent to investigate Japan's incursion into Manchuria and the establishment of the new state of Manchukuo, denounced the invasion and recommended non-recognition of the puppet regime in February 1933. When the British Government acted immediately by imposing an embargo on sales to China and Japan, it upset the Australian government, which had standing orders for all sorts of military equipment from Far Eastern quarters.

How closely Australia came to identify with Japan's plight on the Asian mainland is evident in the secret report Minister for External Affairs J. G. Latham presented to Prime Minister J. A. Lyons when Latham returned from his Far Eastern tour in July 1934. He stressed that Japan considered herself most unjustly treated and that the Lytton Report gave a completely misleading picture. China had violated treaty after treaty and led anti-Japanese boycotts. The merits of the case lay with Japan. There was not the slightest probability that Manchukuo would cease to exist. Latham urged that a formula be sought which would enable both Japan and the League to 'save face' and would get rid of the permanent source of poison that non-recognition of Manchukuo was threatening to become.

He based his findings on a long conversation with Foreign Minister Hirota Kōki in Tokyo. Latham not only took pains to put himself in Japan's position, but he touched on a number of sensitive points in regional politics. Together they had discussed the question of what Hirota referred to as the alleged 'Japanese menace'. Latham pointed to the frequent reports that Japan was fortifying the Japanese mandated islands, to which Hirota gave the prepared answer that 'Japan was not fortifying the islands, did not intend to fortify them, and recognised that she was bound by specific obligations not to fortify them'.

It was in their discussions on Japan and the South that Latham advertised Australian fears perhaps more than he should have. He explained to Hirota that if Japan contemplated any southern military adventures, these could not be on a small scale; for effect, they would have to involve the conveying of armies to occupy territory in Asia, the Dutch East Indies, or Australia. He warned the Japanese Foreign Minister that the Japanese fleet could not sail unless Hong Kong and Singapore had been put out of action first; that moving south would invite Russia to thwart Japanese might in the north; that in the case of any attack upon a white power America would not remain passive; that Japan was too dependent upon sea-borne supplies of iron, steel, rubber, oil, wool, wheat, and other resources of war; and that this being so, it was extremely unwise for Japan to engage in any war with the British Empire. Latham finally cautioned 'that if Japan were to go so far as to attempt to land an army in

Australia, and succeeded in the enterprise, she would then find that she had her hands in a very lively nest of hornets'.

In retrospect, Latham's unvarnished explications appear a little odd. Was it not off the mark to reveal such distrust on a goodwill mission at a time when there was no thought on the part of the Japanese Government or armed forces of an invasion of Australia? One wonders whether Latham was not overstepping the boundaries of diplomatic wisdom. What good was there in displaying so brazenly the fears of a cringing Australia betraying her reliance on Britain, America, and the Russian menace? The unsophisticated frankness with which Latham advertised Australian threat perceptions could only have proved embarrassing to the Eastern reserve of his host and, in a self-defeating way, might have suggested to the Japanese that if Australia really felt so insecure it might be an easy prey.

Whatever Latham may have achieved in Tokyo, the new Prime Minister Robert Menzies took his minister's concerns to heart, and to London next year where, at the meeting of British Commonwealth prime ministers in May 1935, he tried to assure his colleagues that the Japanese in Manchukuo had produced order out of chaos. If the Japanese were not allowed to expand in their own area, would they not turn to the South Pacific? He recommended that the recognition of Manchukuo would go a long way to remove any feeling of antagonism on the part of the Japanese. His companions, however, hardly saw it as Australia did. The Canadians said that Manchukuo was a matter largely determined by the League of Nations, and the British added that their country would have to act as a good member of the League.

The Australian rationale behind her policy of appeasement is most glaringly revealed in a diary entry of the United States Consul-General in Sydney, Jay Pierrepont Moffat. He relates a meeting in the External Affairs Office on 3 October 1935 at which External Affairs Minister George F. Pearce told him that 'with British naval strength reduced below the safety point, and with American aid discounted, there was no policy open to [Australia] other than trying to be friendly with Japan . . . and to rejoice (irrespective of the moral aspect) every time Japan advanced more deeply into Manchukuo and North China. He hoped that her energies would be absorbed there for a generation'.

If Japan in those years was again as much on the Australian mind as in the geopolitically sensitive years between 1896 and 1923, the Australian defense mechanism was now considerably changed. The sabre-rattling speeches that in a brighter day of *Pax Britannica* had denounced Japanese aggression, were no longer heard. The change was most evident in the behaviour of Pearce, the old pro, who in the mid-1930s was still around. He had now cultivated a very quiet, cautious, and pragmatic attitude *vis-à-vis* Japan, hoping that Australia could influence the international community into taking a benign view of Manchukuo and wishing that the menace would dissolve by itself if only Australia adopted a policy of docile appeasement.

Fewer immigration disputes marked the 'golden decade' from 1924 to 1935, and less criticism of White Australia. Although that policy remained unchanged, it was less of a thorn in the side of the Japanese, who in the interwar period concentrated on Southeast Asia while enjoying the option of sending their immigrants to Micronesia, Manchuria, and South America. These years were, above all, mutually gainful, raising the prospect of huge economic profits for both countries in times of peace. Both countries, moreover, co-existed without friction in the Western Pacific, where the Equator kept them apart and at peace. In the atmosphere of disarmament, Japan as a strategic threat was discussed in Australia with declining interest until after the London Naval Conference. The Mukden Incident in 1931—the pretext for Japan's seizure of Manchuria—did raise old fears, but Japan's focus on the North also relieved Australia as much as it invited a policy of unabashed appeasement toward Japan. Less alert and militarily unprepared, lacking the restraining influence of the Anglo–Japanese alliance, but with growing trade ties with Japan, Australia found herself in a much more fragile situation than before World War I.

Building an adequate navy to meet the strategic exigencies of the new age was regarded as impracticable. William M. Hughes, who was still holding forth in the cabinet, now as an elderly Minister for Health and Repatriation, sounded a loud warning in his book *Australia and War Today: The Price of Peace*, published in 1935. Australia's defence policy was hopelessly inadequate, he wrote; the British navy could no longer be relied on for security; a sufficient naval force was beyond Australia's resources, but an air force could be made available within a comparatively short time. It was a conclusion shared by E. L. Piesse in his 1935 booklet *Japan and the Defence of Australia*, published in the same year under the pseudonym 'Albatross': 'We cannot furnish ourselves with a navy strong enough to defend Australia . . . The air arm has all the attractions of novelty . . . the prospects of its affording adequate defence seem to grow year by year'.

At the end of this hopeful period it is interesting to encounter Piesse again, who now draws a different picture of Japan: 'No tears are shed for what might have been if the dead hopes of the 1920s had been fulfilled'. Whereas in 1926 Piesse had concluded that 'the danger to Australia from an increase of population in Japan seems remote', in 1935 he hoists a different flag. He points ominously to the neighbour's presence 'within 2000 miles of Queensland', and its immense population that increased yearly by 800,000 to 1 million people. Japan also had immense armaments and was following a foreign policy that was often in the hands of a military and naval oligarchy unlikely to be controlled by civil government, popular opinion or international ties. Japan was likely to extend her empire towards Australia, he predicted, and whether she planned to annex Australia was a question for the future. Although Japan had never shown a major interest in Australia, there had been minor questions such as the White Australia policy which she probably regarded as a minor affront, but which might be coupled with other questions such as trade. The Japanese Government might demand, for example, that Australia buy less from Britain and more from Japan; 'Trouble might occur at a time when the Japanese Navy wished to follow a forward policy . . . aided by a patriotic fury in Japan connected with the White Australia policy'.

Piesse's tract aimed at awakening Australians to the fact that in the future they might have to fight a protracted war without hope for British military support—engaged, or perhaps even defeated, elsewhere—and that developing the air and land forces was crucial to Australian defence. Always Australia's expert on Japan, Piesse's disparate comments on the same topic at the beginning and end of this golden period stand as two watchtowers. The earlier observation looked onto the new age in the 1920s with optimism; his second one closes on a note of alarm that points out clearly where Japan's road could lead in a future Pacific war.

Japan's Road to Port Darwin
1936–1942

Ten weeks after he had become the squadron hero of Pearl Harbor, Fuchida Mitsuo catapulted again off his flagship *Akagi,* this time to lead an attack on Port Darwin. Not only was he thereby fulfilling Australian predictions, he was also living out those of an obscure Japanese naval writer. For already in 1933 Lieutenant Commander Ishimaru Tōta had predicted in his military novel *Nichi-Ei hissen ron* (Japan must fight Britain) that in three years time Japan would draw the British navy into a decisive battle in the South China Sea; he foresaw not only the elimination of Hong Kong and Singapore, but also of British Borneo and the Australian north coast, notably Darwin, to prevent it from becoming a base for British consolidation.

In Ishimaru's plot, Darwin is approached by a Japanese fleet of three cruisers and three aircraft carriers. The valiant air fighters take the city by surprise in the morning, bombing the telegraph station. The population escapes pell-mell into the bush, one of the four Australian destroyers and cruisers in port is set ablaze as the other three escape, and in an air battle that lasts for forty minutes the Japanese airforce finishes off the British squadrons. The Japanese then fly on to subject the port settlement of Derby, 610 miles further south, to the same ritual, and return safely to their carriers. Ishimaru's prophetic account pointed out the weakness of Australia's exposed northern front-line protected by insufficient military forces, and gave the fictitious dates of 3 and 9 September 1936 for the declaration of war with Great Britain and the battle of Darwin.

In that year John Curtin—then the leading backbencher and a later prime minister—was emphatically drawing attention to Australia's military weakness before Parliament in a heated debate on the Defence Estimates. Pleading for a strong Australian air force, he derided the naval installations at Singapore as a waste, because the British fleet would be able neither to arrive in time to use them, nor to venture beyond to rid Australia of her most likely future enemy, Japan:

> History has no experience of the situation I am visualizing . . . The first step [of an enemy] would be the capture of Hong Kong and/or Singapore, but as long as the principal Australian ports remained intact there would remain in the mind of an enemy the lurking possibility of the eventual arrival of the British fleet to use these ports as a commencement of operations to recover step by step the losses sustained . . . The enemy would consider a major attack on Australia essential to the elimination of British sea-power . . . Hence our provision for local defence should contemplate the possibility of a major land and air attack.

To meet this eventuality, he urged preparation of efficient local defence forces and development of Australia's air force as a *striking* force. He estimated that the enemy's threatening thrust would reveal itself in a land-based air attack, rather than in a carrier-based one.

When Japan struck six years later, it was in a combined land- and carrier-based air attack. Darwin with its untested military base was as unprepared as ever. In the morning of 19 February 1942, Commander Fuchida led his 188 carrier-borne fighters and bombers on the first raid of Darwin, which destroyed much of the town, Government House, the civilian and military aerodromes, and the harbour. The post office and telegraph station received a disastrous hit, the few American P-40s (Kitty hawks) in the air were all shot down, and half of the United States and Australian naval vessels in port were sunk or heavily damaged. After forty minutes the Japanese navy planes returned to their four carriers (the *Akagi, Kaga, Soryu,* and *Hiryu*) waiting three hundred miles off the coast under the command of Admiral Nagumo Chū'ichi and the operation's mastermind, Commander Genda Minoru. The second raid was launched from the Celebes and Ambon. With pattern bombing at noon, fifty-four twin-engined Betty bombers blasted Darwin's air base 'off the face of the earth', in the words of Major-General D. V. J. Blake, the Australian officer in command. While there were acts of great heroism during the raids, they also caused widespread panic among Royal Australian Air Force personnel. It took days to reassemble the considerable number who ran into the bush, one airman fleeing as far as Melbourne.

The bombing of Darwin left 243 dead and more than 300 wounded. Darwin's commercial life ceased, the town came under military control, and the municipal administration was moved to Alice Springs. Between 4 March 1942 and 12 November 1943 there were fifty-eight subsequent attacks on Darwin and other places with military installations along Australia's north and northwest coasts. However, none approached in intensity that first major bombardment.

Yet for all its ferocity, the Darwin attack figures prominently neither in Japanese nor in Australian war histories. For Japan the raid was a minor campaign in a long war which lasted from 1937 to 1945, and in Australia the northern aggression had to compete with other weighty news at that time: the fall of Singapore four days earlier (where 15,000 Australians of the 8th Division went into Japanese captivity), Rommel's winning streak in Africa, the blazing Russian front, and the Battle for the Atlantic. According to President Franklin D. Roosevelt's special envoy dispatched to Australia, Brigadier-General Patrick J. Hurley, even sports results got more press. He reported to Washington: 'The newspapers the day after the raid . . . had much more news concerning horse-racing than they did concerning the raid on Darwin'.

But if Japanese youngsters today are not familiar with the history of the Darwin attack, in Australia the raid has not been forgotten. The Australian flag that flew on the lawn in front of Government House that day, riddled with bullets, is carefully preserved at the National War Museum in Canberra as the first Australian flag damaged by enemy action on Australian soil. Yet that day is also remembered for less than heroic deeds. Paul Hasluck, one of the official Australian historians during World War II and Governor-General from 1969 to 1974, has called the day of the raid one of 'national shame'. Two books, Douglas Lockwood's *Australia's Pearl Harbour: Darwin 1942* and Timothy Hall's *Darwin 1942: Australia's Darkest Hour*, narrate in considerable detail the losses Darwin suffered that day. Ironically, it is not so much the fierceness of the raid inflicted by Japan on an enemy of two months that these authors deplore. They provide untarnished revelations about how, immediately after the raid and for weeks thereafter, the evacuated town of Darwin was looted on a large scale by the military forces and police who were supposed to be protecting the property of those who had been evacuated.

For whatever reasons the Darwin attack is either remembered or forgotten in Australia and Japan today, the raid on that town was Japan's southernmost and last major territorial bombardment in the final stage of her southward advance. Sixty-six years after modern Japan's first move south in the punitive expedition to Taiwan in 1874, Japan's *nanshin* ground to a halt at Darwin in February 1942. In May and June came the naval reversals in the Coral Sea and at Midway, after which the Japanese navy stayed on the defensive until the end of the war. Darwin stands as the furthest milestone affected by the *nanshin* on the far fringes of

Japanese *nan'yō* designs. The Australian town had appeared as a natural target in the extension of Japanese war operations which, against expectations and in only three months, amounted to the quickest and largest seizure in modern military history; it also proved to be short-lived. When one explores how Darwin and other towns on the Australian north coast slipped into the gun-sights of the Japanese naval forces in 1942, the evidence confirms once again the stop-and-go tactics of Japan's sudden thrust after Pearl Harbor; an advance that was brilliantly conceived in its first stage, but thereafter rested more on daring and military opportunism than carefully planned grand strategy.

9

'The Empire Will Go South'

Events at Darwin in 1942 were the result of increasingly fateful policy that had its more immediate making in two ministerial conferences in the summer of 1936. That year also happened to coincide with a decline in stable economic relations beween Japan and Australia, as in May the Australian Government blunderingly started a trade war with Japan that cost Australia its lucrative sales to a market never really restored until the 1960s. Diplomatic niceties uttered at official Japanese–Australian functions tended to become more ominous or sounded hollow. 'None of us can imagine that there will come a time in the future, when the two countries will be called for to decide a difference by resorting to armed forces', said Baron Sakatani Yoshirō upon introducing R. B. Neil, editor of the Melbourne newspaper the *Age*, to the Japan–Australia Society in Tokyo in April. Five months earlier, Colonel Longfield Lloyd, Australia's new Trade Commissioner in Tokyo, had assured the audience at a reception in his honour that the personnel of His Imperial Japanese Majesty's Naval Training Squadrons that visited Australia regularly were 'very popular in Australia, and from the Admiral to the most junior Cadet, they all have made a host of friends. I take this opportunity of assuring your Excellency (here addressing Vice-Minister [Shimada Shigetarō] for the Navy) that the visits of your [Navy] are entirely appreciated'. Unknown to Lloyd, that navy was then hatching the most far-reaching southern policy in Japanese history.

135

In a fundamental way, 1936 portended far-reaching changes. For the first time in more than three hundred years, the Japanese again had an official policy that commended going south. The well-known document 'Fundamentals of National Policy' (*Kokusaku no kijun*), approved on 7 August by the Five Ministers' Conference of the Hirota Kōki cabinet (March 1936–February 1937) decreed: 'We must plan to develop nationally and economically, *vis-a-vis* the Southern area, especially the outer Southern area, avoiding provocation of other countries as much as possible. We must expand our power by gradual and peaceful means'. This call to expand southwards was reinforced later in the day by the Four Ministers' Conference in their 'Guidelines of Imperial Diplomacy' (*Teikoku gaikō hōshin*), which defined the South Seas area as 'indispensable for industrial development and defence'. For far more sombre reasons this time, the South—and there could be no way for Australians to know how far that South stretched—had once more captured official attention. Some 335 years after the Government of Tokugawa Ieyasu had issued red seal permits to Japanese merchants and exhorted them to sail and trade in the South and there expand Japan's economy peacefully, the Japanese Government once again declared the South an area of prime interest. Only this time, the Japanese navy was behind the policy and a more foreboding dash could be expected.

The events that strengthened the navy's hand to promote its southern advance policy in the second half of the 1930s were largely born of competitive dissension with the army, and departmental strife within the navy that harked back to the early 1920s. The Washington Treaty was then replacing the Anglo–Japanese alliance and a generation of Anglo–Japanese friendship. The new Treaty did not please all. It imposed on Japan a 60 per cent limiting ratio *vis-à-vis* the United States on the building of capital ships to preclude a dangerous naval race. Admiral Katō Tomosaburō, head of the Japanese delegation and Navy Minister, who viewed the Japanese navy as an instrument mainly of defence not of war, ruled out a conflict with the United States and accepted the limitation. Not so Katō Kanji, his chief naval aide, who pressed for a 70 per cent ratio on strategic grounds. Katō later went on to become chief of the Navy General Staff, and from that position he continued to hanker after the 70 per cent.

Over the years, this difference caused a widening rift between the Navy Ministry, or 'administrative group' (charged with policy matters), and the Navy General Staff, or 'command group' (charged with operational and tactical matters of the navy). Despite the untimely death of Katō Tomosaburō in 1923, his line played heir to what came to be known in the 1930s as the 'Treaty Faction' of navy moderates such as Admirals Yonai Mitsumasa, Yamamoto Isoroku, Inoue Shigeyoshi, Koga Mineichi, and Nomura Kichisaburō. At the same time, Katō Kanji continued to wield considerable influence long after he resigned in 1932 over the second failure to obtain a 70 per cent ratio at the London Naval Conference in 1930. His men of the 'Fleet Faction', such as protégés Takahashi Sankichi and Admiral Suetsugu Nobumasa, now topped the positions in the Navy General Staff and the Combined Fleet. Moreover, Katō's influence was strongly felt among the cadets he had once presided over at the Naval Academy and Navy War College in the early 1910s and 1920s. By the mid-1930s the Katō kindergarten had grown into a powerful group of middle-echelon officers, ever mindful of their teacher's saying that Japan could easily rout the combined Anglo–American fleet.

In the military–political turmoil of the early 1930s, the 'command group' managed to wrest a fair amount of power from the 'administrative group'. And in the context of historical continuities in Japan's southward advance, the 'command group''s path of usurpation is an interesting one to follow in the crucial years from the time of the world economic crisis in 1929 until 8 August 1936, when it succeeded in having Japan's defence and foreign policy rewritten to include the southern advance.

The world depression is generally regarded as an important catalyst that led to the Manchurian Incident in September 1931. It hastened the collapse of the American market for Japanese silk, then Japan's major export article to the United States. It also drove a large number of men from Japan's hardest hit regions to enlist in the army, whose Kōdōha (Imperial way) faction regarded the exploitation of Manchuria as the only solution to Japan's poverty of resources and population surplus. Defying Sino–Russian interests in the region, remedying Western barriers to Japanese emigration, and taking advantage of economic distress in England and the United States were other important factors that goaded the country into seizing Manchuria.

The effect of Japan's successful invasion was not lost on the navy. Emboldened, naval forces quarrelled with the Chinese 19th Route Army at Shanghai in early 1932. And in the May 15 Incident that year, naval officers played a significant role in the assassination of Prime Minister Inukai Tsuyoshi. Fleet Factionists had strongly resented Cabinet instructions from the Navy Ministry in the Shanghai clash. They envied the army its line of command which had allowed the army chief to direct the Manchurian campaign without restraint. Emulating the army's imperial appointment of Prince Kan'in as chief of the Army General Staff, the Navy General Staff was able to secure as its figurehead Prince Fushimi who, as expected, proved amenable to a complete overhaul of the navy's internal power structure.

The time was opportune. Although Navy Minister Admiral Ōsumi Mineo had been an adherent of Katō Tomosaburo's line, he now was easily influenced by the scheming of Katō Kanji's group. Takahashi Sankichi, the vice-chief of the Navy General Staff, ruthlessly exploited Ōsumi's non-resistance in the name of the amenable Prince Fushimi. Takahashi was, for example, decisive in effecting far-reaching changes in the 'Regulations Concerning the Mutual Jurisdiction of the Navy Ministry and the Navy General Staff', whereby the right of command over the naval forces even in times of peace were transferred from the Navy Ministry to the Navy General Staff in September 1933. Furthermore, in the so-called 'Ōsumi purge', senior officers of moderate opinion were systematically retired or placed on the reserve list during 1933–1934. This curtailed a strong segment of the navy's upper leadership and weakened considerably the moderate forces that otherwise might have exercised restraint over the Katō-Suetsugu group and, later, over the growing power of the 'command group' 's middle-echelon officers.

Other factors combined to play into the hands of the formidable 'command group' and provide a strong warrant to push south. The occupation of Manchuria was condemned in Geneva, and Japan resigned from the League of Nations on 27 March 1933. This raised the question of proprietorship over the mandates in the Pacific. The Japanese press and politicians made it clear that 'there cannot be the slightest doubt that the South Sea Islands are virtually Japanese territory'. In 1934–35, Palau, Tinian, and Saipan were militarily strengthened according to plans for harbour extensions, oil storage constructions, and the establishment of airbases for island patrol operations, a scheme in which Captain Kusakari Ryūnosuke, first section chief of aviation headquarters, was the driving force. In addition, the keels for the world's largest battleships, *Musashi* and *Yamato*, were laid, and the building of a Fourth Fleet—to be assigned to the *nan'yō* region— was decided upon in 1933.

These oil-dependent projects turned the navy's attention to the energy question. Starting with the Shōwa period, the Japanese navy had gone from coal to oil. Moreover, aircraft carriers were ushering in a new age that called for greater quantities of oil. But by 1936, Japan's oil reserves still stood at only 4 million tons of oil, 67 per cent of which came from the United States. Stockpiling 10 million tons became the navy's ambition. Other indispensable raw materials were tin and rubber. Thailand and Malaya produced these and the Netherlands East Indies had the oil. Increasingly conscious of the dire resource situation towards which Japan was moving in the mid-1930s, navy hardliners were loudly calling for the nation to rescind the last fetters of the Washington and London treaties. In 1934, Katō and Suetsugu stepped up pressure on Ōsumi and Prince Fushimi to demand absolute parity for Japan at the preliminary naval talks in London, which began in October that year. And failing to get their way at the conference table, the Japanese delegation walked out of the talks in January 1936.

This ushered in a new period in which the navy, unrestricted now by naval limitations and open to an arms race, became strongly involved in foreign-policy making. Navy middle-echelon officers, in particular, were dissatisfied with the generals' excessive say in Japanese foreign policy and the army's persistent expansion north into Manchuria and the Amur region. They wished to remedy the situation by promoting a policy for the South, believing that Japan's destiny rested on the sea and in the resource-rich areas of the tropics. To this end, they organized a number of committees, staffed with key personnel from the Navy Ministry and the Navy General Staff, to study and reverse the army's northern advance. One of these was the Tai Nan'yō hōsaku kenkyū iinkai (Policy Study Committee for the South Seas Area), established in July 1935. Its main function was to lay down basic long-range policy for Japan's southern advance.

Of more immediate importance was the First Committee (Kaigun seisaku oyobi seido kenkyū chōsa iinkai), established in March 1936 to formulate 'the empire's national policy and to speed up concrete plans for southern development'. It took particular issue with the head of the tactical section of the General Staff Office, Ishihara Kanji, who had returned from the mainland in August 1935 to wield power within the Army General Staff for the promotion of Manchuria's industrial potential as Japan's northern bulwark against the Russian menace. The committee's energetic strategists at the section-chief level were resolved to at least supplement, if not to supplant, the northern war cry with strong demand for action in the South. They believed that Japan's future depended not only on the exploitation of Manchuria's iron and coal, but even more on the critical strategic resources of oil, rubber, and tin in the South, and vehemently defied the counsel of Ishihara to postpone southern plans for another ten years.

On the military level, the navy now pushed for a revision of the Imperial National Defence Policy (*Teikoku kokubō hōshin*). Deciding on potential adversaries, suggesting changes, and laying down guidelines to cope with the strategic situation, had traditionally been the prerogative of the army. Since its establishment in 1907, the policy had always followed army recommendations in the designation of Japan's main hypothetical enemy: Russia in 1907, the United States in 1923, and the United States and the Soviet Union again in 1936. But in 1936 it was the navy that took the initiative to change the policy, and succeeded in having Great Britain singled out as a potential secondary enemy, together with China.

The navy resented the fact that the Manchurian Incident continued to give the army preponderant status and greater budgetary means. Had it not been the Japanese navy that beat off United States naval intimidation in the Western Pacific and thereby made possible the Manchurian conquest, asked Admiral Suetsugu, who judged the Manchurian and southern questions as inseparable. Any future trouble in the southern region would surely call into play the British navy, which dominated the Western rim of the Pacific from Singapore to Malaya and Australia, and was the backbone of Dutch defence in the Netherlands East Indies. From the naval strategic standpoint it was imperative to have Great Britain blazoned in the new Imperial National Defence Policy.

Talks with the army were begun in February 1936. The Emperor showed surprise when he learned in May that Great Britain was to be marked as a potential future enemy. He was not told that a possible southern grab of resource-rich territory would probably be defended by the British and therefore required the military's new evaluation of Britain as an enemy. He was only advised that precautions had to be taken against the British because they were fortifying Hong Kong and Singapore. The new Imperial National Defence Policy received imperial sanction on 3 June. Although the army's stamp on it was still strong, the navy had been able to add the Western Pacific to the East Asian defence perimeter and to have Great Britain named as a possible enemy for the first time. Ultimately this was to have repercussions as far as Australia. But in 1936 the Japanese navy kept its strategic calculations pinned strictly to Southeast Asia, Micronesia, and the Melanesian perimeter.

On the political level, the navy had broached the southern question with the army and the Foreign Ministry much earlier. In September 1934, four 'command group' echelonists, including the *nan'yō* firebrands Ishikawa Shingo and Nakahara Yoshimasa, contacted their counterparts at the Foreign Ministry, Tashirō Shigenori, Kawamura Shigehisa, and Yano Seiki, to form the Southward Advance Reformist Group. In January 1935 they were joined by army colleagues Wakamatsu Tadaichi, Yamaoka Michitake, and Katakura Tadashi. Together they founded the Rikukaigai renraku zadankai (Round-table liaison talks of the Army, Navy, and the Foreign Ministries) on 30 January, known as the earlier mentioned Club of 1935, the Shōwa Ten Club, named after the Japanese calendar year of 1935. It was an informal group and not much survives of their deliberations. But a fairly straight line of thought leads from their early exchange of ideas on southern policy to the army–navy compromise sealed in the 'Fundamental Principles of National Policy' (*Kokusaku Taikō*) on 30 June 1936, which served as the basic document for the aforementioned famous 'Fundamentals of National Policy' decreed in August 1936.

The naval members of the Jusshōkai participated also in the Policy Study Committee for the South Seas Area mentioned above and in the pivotal First Committee. The latter, as we have seen, was trying to moderate the scale of Ishihara Kanji's plans for northern entrenchment and instead win army interest for the South. In April, the First Committee produced a signal paper that clearly spelled out Navy Headquarters' preferences in the 'General Plan for National Policy' (Kokusaku yōkō): 'we will adopt as basic policy the development of the Southern areas and ... establish peace in East Asia'. It sketches the policies Japan should pursue toward Manchukuo (implant Japan's real economic power), China (induce them to be friendly), Russia (make necessary military preparations), Britain (watch and be on strict guard against), the United States (resist traditional American policy in the Far East), and raises the major point: 'The Southern countries are the areas we should regard as most important for strengthening our national defence and solving the population problem and economic development. The administration of this area is necessary to complete our policies toward Manchuria, China, and Russia'.

Ensuing political talks with the army gradually adjusted the two services' positions at the end of June. By then the Army General Staff Headquarters had drawn up its own study paper 'Fundamental Principles of National Defence Policy' (Kokubō kokusaku taikō), which sounded a horn for war preparations in the Far East and had 'Russia' written into almost every paragraph. It did not suit the navy. On 30 June a compromise was reached in which the navy carried the day for all its points. These were integrated into a joint army–navy position paper, 'Fundamental Principles of National Policy', which was forwarded to Hirota Kōki's cabinet for discussion and political implementation.

This paper furnished the content for the grave decision reached at the Five Ministers' Conference on 7 August 1936 that the Japanese people should venture south. In fact, the entire army–navy position paper was taken over *tel quel*, with only its title changed (on the advice of the Foreign Minister) to 'Fundamentals of National Policy' (Kokusaku no kijun). It is a short and general document that urges the development of Manchukuo to remove the northern threat of Russia, military prepared-ness against the latter, and close ties with China. With regard to southern policy, it stresses navy preparations to ensure Japanese naval supremacy in the Western Pacific against the United States navy. It also seeks, both nebulously and ominously, 'to develop nationally and economically *vis-à-vis* the Southern area (meaning Southeast Asia), avoiding as much as possible confrontation with other countries'.

But because the army thought that it had given in too much, a Four Ministers' Conference in the afternoon ratified a *supplementary* policy paper, entitled 'Guidelines of Imperial Diplomacy' (Teikoku gaikō hōshin). Interlarded with more detailed diplomatic prescriptions, 'Guidelines' clearly reflects the army view in its long passages that dwell on the Soviet Union and on the northern problems of China and Manchuria. While the document does not discount the South Seas area as 'indispensable for industrial development and defence', it cautions in favour of slow advance 'to avoid war with Britain and the United States as far as possible'.

The two policies must be viewed as one set, but it is the navy-inspired 'Fundamentals of National Policy' that proved the stronger. The state-ment in its opening paragraph was from then on pursued relentlessly by the navy: 'The basic policy Japan should establish is to secure the position of Japan on the East Asiatic continent in both diplomacy and national defence, and *at the same time* to advance and develop in the Southern region', ('*Konpon kokusaku wa gaikō kokubō aimatte Tōa tairiku ni okeru teikoku no jiho o kakuho suru to tomo ni nanpō kaiyō ni shinshitsu hatten suru ni arite'*) [emphasis added]. This sentence gave rise to an important new stage in Japan's *nanshin-ron*; that is, it realized at a government level what so far had been only a theory of the 'simultaneous northwards and southwards advance' school of thought (*nanboku heishinron*). The navy's involvement and success in policy formulation at this point was an important development. Henceforth, Japan's southward advance was pursued on the official level by the navy, generally with army acquiescence and with the Foreign Ministry as a by-stander.

After August 1936 the navy pressed on. When on 3 September a Japanese shop owner was killed by a Chinese mob in an anti-Japanese flare-up in Pakhoi (a city on the Gulf of Tonkin on the southern Chinese mainland), the Navy General Staff responded with alacrity. Ships were sent to investigate the incident and pressure brought to bear on the Chinese Government to apologize. Expecting little in the way of apology, Captain Nakahara Yoshimasa sprang his 'Plan to Handle the Pakhoi Incident' (Hokkai jiken shori hōshin) of 14 September 1936 on the General Staff. It called for the occupation of Hainan, the large island opposite Pakhoi in the Gulf of Tonkin, 250 miles south of Hong Kong, and the establishment of a Japanese power sphere to countermand British control in the Hong Kong–Singapore region. This would cause the Pakhoi Chinese to knuckle under and strengthen Japan's national defence in the spirit of the First Committee's 'General Plan for National Policy' produced in April. Nakahara saw the incident principally as a welcome pretext to oust the British, leading to a swift take-over of all of China by Japan.

Weapons were readied and the navy vessel *Saga* steamed into Pakhoi to investigate the incident, just as the Chinese vessel *Fukuan* moved in, too. To avoid a confrontation, Generalissimo Chiang Kai-Shek, leader of the Chinese Nationalists, at the same time wisely ordered the retreat of the 19th Route Army from Pakhoi. Even greater restraint was urged by the Japanese army, which opposed an invasion of Hainan because it would only isolate Japan further from England, America, and France. In September the crisis blew over as quickly as it had started. But the near implementation of the Navy General Staff's 'Hainan scenario' shows that one year before the Marco Polo Bridge Incident, the Pakhoi Incident held every potential for a flare-up that could have led to war between Japan and China already in 1936—a war sparked not by generals but by their counterpart-hawks in the Navy General Staff.

If in the course of events Hainan was shelved by the Navy General Staff, it was not forgotten. It made plain that control of Hainan would strengthen the position of Taiwan (whose civilian colonial administration was changed in the same month of September to a military one with Admiral Kobayashi Seizō as the new Governor-General) as a cardinal link and forward base in the onward march of Japan's southward advance. This advance would henceforth pursue a different course. Instead of following the usual route that had taken Japanese pioneers on Taiwan's eastern side to Micronesia and thence into the outer *nan'yō*, the Dutch East Indies, and the rest of Southeast Asia, the Japanese navy now thought of blazing a new trail west of Taiwan via South China and Hainan into Southeast Asia. Hainan also marked the turning-point at which the navy began to take a better look at China, to listen to the army, and to identify with its China policy.

The outbreak of the Sino–Japanese war in July 1937 finally brought the navy and the army together. The navy cooperated swiftly with army occupation operations in North China, and supplemented these with the conquest of the South China coast. Navy and army objects further entwined in the task of bringing Chungking to its knees. For the execution of this inland operation the army depended heavily on naval cooperation to cut off outside help to China through French Indochina, Hainan, and Hong Kong. Soldiers and sailors were beginning to work together. The purposeful intermingling of infantry and marines on the Chinese mainland began to harmonize the dichotomous military history of Japan's 'northward' and 'southward' policies, so much out of step since the Meiji period. In yet another new policy directive, 'General Principles for National Policy' (Kokusaku taikō), announced in January 1938, the navy now recognized Manchuria officially as Japan's important bulwark in the north. It stopped denouncing the army's 'northward advance', and in the autumn even closed its bureau in Manchuria which had been monitoring the army's movements there. And it seemingly began to curb its own interests by accepting economic development in the South pending a settlement of the China conflict. The navy adjusted so much in the first two years of the Sino–Japanese war that one can speak of a temporary shelving of the navy's 'southward advance' policy, a stratagem it had championed so fiercely the year before.

Perhaps it is better to speak of a consolidation of the southward advance in this period. Naval accommodation with the army actually served to solidify the prerogatives of the admirals, who in the interim sailed on to claim new stepping-stones in their bid for the South. When Chinese Nationalist troops threatened the Japanese settlement and naval installations at Shanghai in August, Navy Minister Yonai Mitsumasa enforced the dispatch of three divisions to Shanghai over the objections of War Minister Sugiyama Gen. The navy then lost no time in occupying Kinmon, Amoy, Nanōto, and Canton on the South China coast. It gladly sailed on further into French Indochinese waters at the behest of the army in a further effort to help contain Chiang Kai-Shek. Hainan was invaded in February 1939 and immediately put under the control of the naval administration on Taiwan. The navy's longstanding plans to seize Hainan had been reinforced in spring 1938 with the establishment on

Taiwan of a naval military office, the Bukanfu. This office exerted considerable influence over Taiwan's naval governorship, the Taiwan Sōtokufu. It also devised the occupation plans for Canton and Hainan, and produced blueprints to fuse the South Seas' administration (Nan'yō cho), seated in Palau, with Taiwan's military administration. Had the latter been realized, it would have created a single administrative centre for the entire Japanese southern islands. Micronesia, Hainan, and Taiwan would all have been ruled from Taipei under the aegis of a naval southern regional governorship, the Nanpō sōtokufu.

Although that office never materialized, the Taiwan–Hainan line grew stronger. The colonial experience gained on Taiwan, and Hainan's advantageous strategic situation, combined to distinguish Hainan as the main forward base for southern operations. Two weeks after the invasion of Hainan, the navy had Taiwan despatch experts to develop its rich iron mines. As Hainan thus passed into Taiwanese tutelage, it was earmarked by some *nanshin-ron sha* as the pilot base for future operations in the south. Japan's southward advance had reached new frontiers.

From Hainan, ardent Navy General Staffers now cast longing glances at French Indochina for new basing-opportunities. For the time being, however, Nakahara Yoshimasa's dream was fulfilled: Hainan was perfectly placed to sabotage the resented British control between Hong Kong and Singapore. To seriously impinge on continental Southeast Asian sovereignty—in Malaya and Vietnam—was still considered premature. One year had to pass before the navy was to produce that singular 'Study of Policy toward French Indochina' in August 1940. That position paper noted that forceful action would invite the curtailment of United States oil and other essential supplies on which Japan depended, and that any such reductions would compel Japan to appropriate Indonesia's oil fields and other resources-rich areas. In the first half of 1939 the navy was not yet ready for such drastic action.

The outbreak of war in Europe in September 1939 dissolved the navy's last restraints on going into Southeast Asia. It also encouraged the army to look south as a solution to the Sino–Japanese war. After all, Germany seemed about to thrash her European opponents—masters until then of most of Southeast Asia. The day seemed at hand when Japanese forces would at long last expel the old colonial countries entrenched for centuries in what Japan now regarded as her own domain in the Asian–Pacific region. As in World War I, no chance would be missed to recover ground lost since the fateful decision to close the country in 1639. Japan's 'Don't miss the bus!' reasoning, nurtured since the first German shots on the Polish border, has been described elsewhere in much detail. The navy was to cross several Rubicons with each new policy issued, as it championed the southward advance on a path leading toward war at Pearl Harbor.

'Finally the day has come. This maritime nation, Japan, should today begin its advance into the Bay of Bengal!' rejoiced Nakahara Yoshimasa in his diary on the day of the outbreak of war between Great Britain and Germany. At that time he was still captain of the *Maya*. In May 1940 he became head of the War Guidance Office (Sensō shidōhan) of the Navy General Staff. As early as September 1939 he had drawn up a concrete schedule for military operations in the South and stressed the navy's need for an arms replenishment program, the equivalent of the army's mobilization plan. Much of Nakahara's schedule was acted on by the Navy Ministry, including the assignment of the Fourth Fleet to forward (blue water) operations in the South Seas in November; but it stopped short of putting the fleet on a 'first alert' basis for the duration of the 'phoney war', that peculiar time until spring 1940 when the Western European front was quiet.

When Germany invaded Norway and Denmark on 9 April, decisions in the Navy Ministry and the General Staff continued to click on in perfect timing with military events in Europe. Conferences held on 11 and 12 April declared: 'Now is the time to occupy the Dutch East Indies'. On May 15, the day that Holland capitulated to Germany, the Fourth Fleet set sail for Palau to be on an alert for further dispatch to the Dutch East Indies and intervention, just in case Britain, France, or Germany violated the Indies' neutrality. The attached Yokohama Air Corps was ordered to proceed with war preparations as quickly as possible, and the Second China Fleet was positioned to guard the Fourth Fleet in the case of a sudden attack on the Indies. The expected opportunity to promote its southern advance did not arise, however. Dutch colonial neutrality was not breached by European powers. The navy cancelled its stand-by orders and agreed in talks with the army that 'with respect to the Dutch East Indies, for the present, effort will be made to acquire needed resources by diplomatic means'.

Meanwhile the European situation had jolted the army into action, too. The generals began to look south in earnest for the first time. On 19 May, the day that German forces broke through the Maginot Line, the Army Ministry's Military Affairs Section began drafting a grand strategic plan that would take into account the great military changes in the world. It developed into the 'Outline of the Main Principles for Coping with the Changing World Situation' (Sekai jōsei no suii ni tomonau jikyoku shori yōkō) approved by the Army Ministry and General Staff on 3 July.

The army discussed this 'Outline' with the navy on 4 July, accompanied by written explanations of war aims. Their blueprint contained practically all the final steps in the army's policies that led up to the outbreak of the Pacific War in December 1941: Japan was to rid herself of dependency upon England and America by establishing an economic sphere that centered on Japan, Manchuria, and China, and stretched from the Indian Ocean to the South Seas north of Australia and New

Zealand; Japan should not hesitate to go to war with Britain and the Netherlands, but should take advantage of America's indecision and Britain's difficulties in Europe to attack Malaya and Hong Kong and expel British forces from the Far East and the southern areas. Furthermore, the resources of the Dutch East Indies were to be brought under Japanese control so that Japan might become economically independent of England and America. 'Never in our history has there been a time like the present', proclaimed the document; 'We should grasp the favourable opportunity that now presents itself'. With this army 'Outline' the serious, but easily foreseeable step was taken, and it carried the 1936 'Fundamentals of National Policy' to a watershed in its substitution of a 'forceful' for a 'peaceful' advance.

The army was now running south ahead of the navy; in an unusual instance of restraint, the navy sought to apply the brakes to the army's sudden longing for southern action. At their July meetings with army officials, navy representatives urged them to scrap the army plan for a military invasion of the Dutch East Indies. The navy also refused to yield to Reservist General Koiso Kuniaki's demands to provide him with war vessels and marines in a show of strength for his forthcoming oil negotiations with the Dutch in the Dutch East Indies. July 1940 was a rare moment in the history of Japan's southward advance, when roles reversed and the navy was warning the army not to push south impetuously.

The navy knew from large-scale map exercises held between 15 and 21 May that an attack on the Dutch East Indies would not only lead to war with Britain and the Netherlands, but would inevitably draw in the United States and thus result in a protracted war with her navy. In July the navy was not yet prepared for this, lacking oil resources, war materiel, and budget. Before signing the 'Outline' on 15 July, the navy was therefore careful to insist that the United States be marked as military target and that war preparations clearly take this into consideration. The army yielded to the insertion that 'all necessary preparations must be made for the opening of a war against the United States'. The navy received a further concesssion in September, when it dropped its opposition to the army's resolve to sign a Tripartite Pact with Germany and Italy, and received substantial priority over the army in the allocation of war resources.

Perhaps sobered by its idle stand-by in the Dutch East Indies in May, the navy also knew that the military could not just start an attack without good reason; simply coveting Dutch oil resources in the East Indies was not a valid pretext for a strike south. The navy was aware of a need for a cause—for example, one such as would offer the notion of 'Empire encirclement' by enemy forces in an arc from French Indochina to Papua New Guinea. The policies conceived and decisions reached in the navy between August 1940 and December 1942 reveal the relentless making of this pretext. Indochina would serve as abettor, not Sumatra, Java or Borneo. Japan's ultimate Rubicon flowed in Vietnam.

The navy submitted its views to the Army and Foreign Ministries in the position paper 'Study of Policy toward French Indochina' on 1 August. The document urged the stationing of troops in French Indochina as a firm step forward in the southern advance to gain control over Thailand, Burma, and Malaya. It would also be of great strategic advantage in a war against the United States and Britain, and would help secure for Japan necessary products for defence, such as coal, iron ore, phosphorous, rubber, and rice. Should diplomatic negotiations fail to secure Japan's purposes, military power should be used and military operations could begin before November 1940: 'If . . . Japan occupies all of French Indochina, there is a strong possibility that the United States will tighten its embargo. An American embargo on scrap iron and oil would be a matter of life and death to the empire. In that event the empire will be obliged to attack the Dutch East Indies to secure oil'.

Here stood revealed for the first time officially, well before the signing of the Tripartite Pact, that peculiar, powerful, circular, perhaps even conspiratorial logic hammered out by the Operations Section of the Navy General Staff, from whose middle echelons the navy's true voice now spoke with increasing authority. It was to suck Japan, whirlpool-like, into Pearl Harbor. Japan would march into French Indochina: this would result in a total resources embargo by the United States; compel Japan to seize the life-preserving oil fields of the Dutch East Indies; and lead to war with the United States (the new protector of the Western powers in Southeast Asia since Britain was locked in battle with Germany in the Euro–African war theater). These prospects made it necessary for Japan to expand its fleet, make preparations, and place its navy on a wartime footing.

The navy did not dally in setting its peculiar circular reasoning into motion. With the United States having meanwhile placed strategic export resources under an export licensing system, the navy, independent of the army and the government, took its first step towards war with the United States by invoking the 'promotion of war preparations', begun immediately and reported to the Emperor on 21 August 1940. This led promptly to the next stage of 'preparatory fleet mobilization', issued on schedule on November 15. By March 1941 the fleet was to be put on a 'second alert' status, and in November it was to be prepared for full wartime operations. The navy would stick to its time-table.

As the navy proceeded smoothly with its 'preparatory mobilization', it got caught up in the border dispute between Thailand and French Indochina in December and January. Hoping to take advantage of the situation, the navy drew up elaborate plans to position its fleet and airforce from Japan, Taiwan, and Hainan to land seven hundred marines at three places along the French Indochinese coast: 'Our objective in dispatching troops is to overawe [the French] . . . our real intention is to use military force in central and southern French Indochina . . . The navy's hope is to secure permanent bases near Saigon and Camranh Bay, once we dispatch the marines'. Because Thailand and French Indochina accepted Japan's mediation proposals, however, the landings did not take place and the units dispatched to the area were recalled to Japan. In the aftermath of the dispute, the forces approved a new 'Outline of Policy toward French Indochina and Thailand' on 30 January. Challenging the United States and Britain, it recommended that pressure be brought to bear on French Indochina and Thailand, using force if necessary, to set up air and naval bases in French Indochina and establish Japanese leadership in those two countries.

Thereafter army and navy wrangled over how to proceed further with the southern advance. The army-inspired master plan, 'Outline of the Main Principles for Coping with the Changing World Situation' of July 1940, had evaded the problem of war with the United States. It raised the question of whether Japan should go to war, adopt a policy of concessions, or abandon its plan for military operations in the southern region, only *if* the United States embargoed Japan. In the February 1941 disputes with the navy, the army still believed that the South could be won without having to fight the United States, and that forces could advance down the Peninsula into Malaya and the Dutch East Indies by 'taking advantage of the favourable opportunity' presented by the Anglo–German war.

The navy thought quite differently. Because the United States and Britain were inseparable enemy targets, the most important thing at that stage was to prepare for war against the United States. There was to be no 'taking advantage of a favourable opportunity'. Military operations in the South were to occur only under extreme military pressure by the United States, in a situation where that country could clearly be targeted as a main enemy; for example, in the case of a complete United States embargo of Japan. Driven into a corner by the navy's obstinate, perplexing, circular logic, the army discarded its 'favourable opportunity' scheme and accepted that military operations should be undertaken only if 'absolutely unavoidable'.

To the army this semantic squabble meant giving up any further plans for southern operations, except in French Indochina and Thailand. To the navy, however, this agreement, reached on 27 March, meant a green light to go ahead with its own new 'Outline of Policy toward the South'. Discussed with the army in April, its essence stated that close relations had to be established with Thailand, French Indochina, and the Dutch East Indies. Diplomatic means were to be preferred, but if they failed— for example due to embargoes imposed by the United States, Britain, and the Netherlands—the empire would employ military means for the sake of self-existence and self-defence. This new Army-Navy Draft Policy superseded the July 1940 'Outline' and went into effect on 17 April 1941.

By this time, army and navy units were already cooperating on the beaches of Kyūshū and practising their assaults for the Malaya and Singapore campaigns. In Tokyo, members of the Navy General Staff's zealous and now seemingly all-powerful middle-echelon officers, Captains Tomioka Sadatoshi and Ishikawa Shingo, were heard saying: 'Now is the time to strike. We will not be defeated'. And late in April, the head of the Intelligence Division, Rear Admiral Maeda Minoru, was reconnoitring Thailand and Indochina to gauge the consequences of an invasion of southern Indochina. His conclusion, expressed to Prime Minister Konoe a month later on June 5, deemed it 'quite safe to move into southern Indochina'.

That same day, Navy Staff middle-echelon officers came up with yet another paper entitled 'The Attitude to Be Adopted by the Imperial Navy under Present Circumstances'. Its main theme was the 'unavoidable' war with the United States, and it recommended an armed advance into Indochina and Thailand 'without a day's delay'. It also called for 'preemptive measures' to break the 'ABCD encirclement', which purportedly was gaining strength through the political and economic consolidation of Southeast Asia under British sway and the gathering of United States forces in the Philippines. Apparently influenced by these recommendations, Chief of Staff Nagano Osami urged at the Liaison Conference of June 12: 'We must build bases in French Indochina and Thailand in order to launch military operations. We must resolutely attack anyone who tries to stop us. We must resort to force if we have to'. As he put his seal to the navy's draft policy for the drive into southern Indochina, he was heard muttering: 'This will mean war with America'. For our purposes he might have added 'and with Australia, too'.

Forty-three days later, forty thousand Japanese troops marched into southern Indochina, breathing life into the apparition of 'ABCD encirclement'. It now was real. The 'unavoidable situation' was created. The United States froze Japanese assets and imposed a total embargo on Japanese trade. Joined by Britain, the Netherlands, and other countries, such as Australia on August 6, it completed the clearly envisaged 'strangulation' of Japan by confronting the country with an oil-shortage nightmare fatefully engineered by the Navy General Staff. After another 136 days, Japan's road reached Pearl Harbor. And within two months, a side road would lead to Port Darwin.

Japanese naval minds had been largely responsible for advancing Japan south over minor rapids in the 1930s toward the main cascade at Pearl Harbor. Although they wished to expand the Japanese sphere in the *nan'yō* to the utmost, Australia had until then hardly come up for discussion. The southern continent did not figure on the list of war objectives prepared for the General Staff on the eve of the outbreak of the Pacific War. Yet already from the mid-1930s onwards, Australians had become indirectly but intimately involved with the Japanese navy's southern finagling, and were busy fending off dreaded Japanese penetration of the Australian northern sphere. This penetration was of a strategic, economic, demographic, and diplomatic kind: the strategic placing of Japanese companies dealing with the exploitation of raw materials in the southern region, expanding Japanese shipping lines in Southeast Asian waters, bidding for aviation rights, and strengthening the Japanese presence in the European colonies by immigration and the opening of consulates.

The organization that undertook the initial planning for infiltrating the Western territories in the Western Pacific was the Tai nan'yō hōsaku kenkyū iinkai (Policy Study Committee for the South Seas Area), or Tainanken for short, established in July 1935. Its twenty-two members also participated in the Navy General Staff's much larger First Committee, which produced the revolutionary 'Fundamentals of National Policy' to go south in August 1936. But whereas the latter was deliberately vague ('We plan to expand our power by gradual peaceful means . . . We will avoid superficial projects'), the First Committee's braintrust concentrated in the Tainanken spelled out in concrete policy Japan's advance into selected areas of the Outer *Nan'yō* (*soto nan'yō*), based on knowledge of the region's geography, history, raw materials, trade, industry, and strategic main points.

A central figure of the Tainanken was Captain Oka Takazumi (later Admiral and Chief of General and Military Affairs Bureau in the Navy Ministry, 1940–1944) who organized the South Seas Policy Committee and carried much weight in the First Committee. Other representative members were the omnipresent Nakahara Yoshimasa, with his Nelsonian dream of turning Japan into a Great Ocean power; and Chūdō Kan'e, who was influenced by the writings of such *'nanshin-ron sha'* as Suganuma Teifu and noted Micronesian ethnologist Matsuoka Shizuo. Chūdō considered himself and Nakahara as 'the twin gems of the Navy's southward advance'. Also involved was Ishikawa Shingo, the naval attaché in Berlin in 1935, who had published *Nihon no kiki* (Japan's crisis) right after the Manchurian Incident and who regarded the Asian continent as Japan's 'lifeline'. Unlike Nakahara and Chūdō, he was less interested in 'the South' as such, but believed that the Japanese navy simply had to expand in order to be able to stand up to the United States in the Pacific and to secure Japan's rights on the Asian continent.

The 'outer *nan'yō*' into which the Tainanken planned to direct Japan's thrust included British Malaya, Borneo, French Indochina, Thailand, the Dutch East Indies, New Guinea, the Solomons, the Gilbert Islands, and Portuguese Timor. In formulating concrete policy to penetrate these territories, the Committee paid special attention to two points. In a number of studies, it first evaluated the effectiveness of Taiwan and the Japanese Pacific mandates as relay and forward bases for advance further south. How exactly Japan would reach out from the 'inner *nan'yō*' into the 'outer *nan'yō*' was the subject of more specific studies on a second level. The guidelines which the Tainanken members established cautioned against the flaunting of Japan's naval presence. They advised, intead, the use of Japanese trading and mining companies in the *nan'yō*, and working through the European Colonial Ministries to accomplish Japan's economic and migratory purposes in the South. Naval support for the activities of the Nan'yō Kōhatsu Kabushiki Kaisha (South Seas Development Company), in Portuguese Timor in particular, illustrates how the Tainanken plotted political and economic infiltration beyond the Equator.

The Nan'yō Kōhatsu Kabushiki Kaisha, known as Nankō, had been instrumental in the development of Japan's Pacific mandates in the 1920s and 1930s. Established in 1921 by its executive director, Matsue Haruji—later nicknamed the 'Sugar King' of the South Pacific—the Nankō brought in thousands of contracted labourers from the home islands to clear the lands on Saipan, Tinian, and Rota for the cultivation of cane and the setting up of a thriving sugar industry. Under Matsue's leadership, the company became the prime economic force not only in the Marianas but throughout Micronesia. Working hand-in-glove with the Nan'yō-chō (Japan's colonial seat of government at Palau), which obliged it to cooperate in the development and administration of the mandated region, the Nan'yō Kōhatsu's sugar-related industries accounted for more than 60 per cent of the Nan'yō-chō's revenues by the early 1930s.

The Nankō fitted perfectly into the plans of the Tainanken. Matsue enjoyed the full support of the Navy General Staff's First Committee, which was well disposed to his building of a fleet of schooners and put great expectations in his company as an entirely private enterprise. On 28 May 1936, Matsue visited the Vice Chief of the Navy General Staff, Shimada Shigetarō, to discuss his company's various marketing strategies in the Arafura Sea, Thailand, and the Dutch East Indies. The entrepreneur emphasized plans that would expand electricity, banking, and coastal shipping in Portuguese Timor. Plenty of opportunities awaited the Japanese, who would be welcome on that island, Matsue said, as he requested the navy to strongly support his company's ventures on that island. On 20 July, a small committee meeting of the Tainanken issued the following directives in a 'Memorandum for the Planned Advance into Portuguese Timor':

We shall use the good offices of the *Nan'yō Kōhatsu* for concrete advance . . . and give the Company *carte blanche* to secure a footing on Portuguese Timor. With regard to entrepreneurial opportunities in the territory, we

shall meet the wishes of the local government and then gradually guide it
and the people to a pro-Japanese attitude; as soon as we have a foothold,
we shall think of the next step . . .

We shall establish power swiftly and advance by putting deeds before
words; we shall keep the intention of our pay-offs completely secret and
throw our utmost internal support behind the Nan'yō Kōhatsu K. K.

The inner workings of the Tainanken's select circle of middle-echelon
officers soon made itself felt on the Australian side and in the inter-
national arena. In April and June 1937, Mr Henry Fitzmaurice, the
United Kingdom Consul-General in Batavia, warned Australia and
England of an impending Japanese purchase of a large company in
Portuguese Timor and of the Nankō's intention to establish a
Japanese–Portuguese concern with a capital of five million yen. Australian Minister for External Affairs, Sir George Pearce, replied in August
1937: 'As you rightly surmise, this is a matter of direct concern to the
Commonwealth of Australia and any large establishment by the
Japanese at Dili or its utilisation as a base of operations for further
penetration in this part of the world cannot be regarded with
equanimity'.

Nan'yō Kōhatsu was anxious to develop the Timorese oil fields in
particular. At that time, an Australian businessman, A. J. Staughton, was
holding oil concessions in Portuguese Timor which were about to lapse
by default, because he had done nothing about them for eight years.
Others were vying to take over his concessions, notably Serge F.
Wittouck, a Belgian engineer and company promoter described as a
'most unscrupulous financier'. If he succeeded in pressuring the Portuguese Government to sell him Staughton's concessions, it was regarded
as highly likely that the Belgian would later sell out to the Japanese. To
frustrate any such deal, the Australian Government backed the Australian 'Oil Search Company' (which received government grants to
pursue its oil investigations) to take over Staughton's oil concessions. In
December 1938, Australia's Department of External Affairs cabled to
Fitzmaurice: '"Oil Search" received favourable reception [from] Lisbon
authorities and is hopeful of obtaining oil concessions. On other hand
Wittouck . . . cannot obtain Lisbon confirmation of any rights'.

In October 1939, however, despite the Australian Government's
inducement to continue, Oil Search abandoned prospecting for Timorese
oil as too risky. The project was then taken over by the Oil Concessions
Company, which received the same strong government backing. It
immediately set up the Companhia Ultramarina de Petroleo, posing as a
Portuguese company, under which name it pursued the oil prospecting
activities. Well into November, the Nan'yō Kōhatsu Company was trying to link up with the Companhia, unaware that it was an Australian
company. The oil concessions were finally granted and signed formally

on a government basis between Portugal and Australia on 22 November 1939. It provoked a strong reaction from the Japanese Minister at Lisbon, Yonezawa Kikuji, who, after 'cross-examining the Portuguese Vice-Minister for Foreign Affairs', reported to Tokyo that 'Portugal under British pressure has ruthlessly overridden existing rights of Belgian capital and has granted concessions to Australia'.

Japanese interests were not limited to oil and Portuguese Timor. They also sought metals in Australia. After the Australian goodwill mission led by John G. Latham had visited Japan in 1934, permission was given to a number of Japanese experts to inspect the Yampi Sound iron ore deposits, situated on the Australian northwest coast about six hundred miles southwest of Darwin. The Japanese showed great interest in gaining a lease over the large reserves of iron ore in that remote part of the continent. Of the estimated 250 million tons of ore in the area, Japan's absolute minimum interest was to obtain 15 million tons, shipped to Japan in yearly 1 million ton quotas over a period of fifteen years. With the express consent of the Australian Government, the Nippon Mining Company, acting through a British dummy firm, H. A. Brassert & Co. Ltd, began to develop the costly project. It spent large sums of money on land leases, had blast furnaces constructed in Japan, and ordered special machinery stored at Singapore for shipment to Yampi Sound at the time of the opening of the mines.

The project developed as planned over the next few years. When reports predicted a world steel shortage in early 1937, no warning was sounded in Australia of any impending iron ore export restrictions. In May 1938, however, there was a complete reversal of the government's policy in regard to iron ore, as sudden and unexpected as the reversal in the 'trade diversion' policy in 1936. The export of iron ore was banned as of July 1, with the explanation that new surveys had shown Australian iron ore reserves to be less extensive than previously supposed. The Australian Government took pains to explain that the new measures were not anti-Japanese in intention. To substantiate the fact that the iron ore embargo had nothing whatsoever to do with Japan, the Australian Government made known part of a report by Dr Walter G. Woolnough, the Commonwealth Government Geological Adviser. He had stated that the known deposits of iron ore in Australia capable of being mined economically were of considerably less magnitude than hitherto believed. Expressing alarm about the prospects of the Japanese Yampi Sound enterprise proceeding, he urged the government to limit or prohibit the export of iron ore pending surveys on further resources.

The relevant government papers of those years clearly indicate that Woolnough's report was more a document of expediency than an exact scientific estimation based on comprehensive observation. They reveal, in fact, that the only reason for implementing an iron ore embargo was the growing geopolitical menace of Japan. It has been suggested that the

great geographical–political changes under way on the Chinese mainland since July were an important catalyst in the Australian Government's about-face in the period between renewed official sanction for
the Japanese mining project as late as August 1937 and the sudden
announcement of the embargo in May 1938. Certainly, the effect of
Japan's gains in the revived hostilities with China was not lost on
Colonel Longfield Lloyd, Australia's Trade Commissioner in Tokyo.

Already in Spring 1937 the former military intelligence officer had sent
a message of warning to Army Headquarters in Melbourne. In it he drew
attention to the increased signs of interest with which Japanese official
circles were viewing the New Guinea, Darwin, and Yampi Sound areas.
After hostilities in China spread to the Yangtze Valley in August and
September 1937, Longfield Lloyd repeated his warnings; this time more
effectively. In a highly confidential memorandum of 6 October 1937, he
set out the Japanese system of penetration:

(1) The use of Japanese capital for economic development is a feature of
Japanese penetration and 'special interests'. It has been utilised in
Japanese efforts in China. The system has been proved to operate against
the country accepting it.

(2) Japan is always prepared to invest even in unpromising ventures to
secure a foothold.

It is to be noted also that Japanese efforts in the Philippines, Portuguese
Timor, Siam, Malaya, Dutch New Guinea, and Netherlands Indi[es] have
in recent years been supplemented by an investigating activity in the
Mandated Territory of New Guinea and Yampi, in the last two mentioned
places particularly by the Nippon Mining Company ... there is no
shadow of doubt that all this is in deliberate pursuance of the southward
expansion policy ...

The Yampi endeavour, as shown in the Brassert–Nippon Mining Agreement, is unquestionably part of the whole scheme and the operation of the
terms of that Agreement can only result in the occupancy and exclusive
right over a portion of Australian territory by Japanese interests and
personnel, upon the face of it for half a century; a hold from which these
people will not be either then or in the interim readily loosened *once the
Agreement is allowed to become operative.*

Of the three methods of prevention which might be applied to this
question:

    a. Immigration Act;
    b. Preclusion of export by declaration of insufficiency of iron for
       Australia or Empire needs;
    c. Defence Act;

method b. is diplomatically unobjectionable and should provide the
readiest solution ...

Longfield Lloyd

The memorandum was passed around for comments in the various government offices in Canberra before it came up for discussion in mid-December before the Prime Minister and his Cabinet. It must have caused serious alarm, for on 17 March 1938 the alarmist Woolnough Report was out, urging the government to stop exporting iron ore. On the same day, Prime Minister Lyons sent a secret cablegram to Stanley M. Bruce, Australia's High Commissioner in London, informing him of a forthcoming government announcement concerning the embargo of iron ore, operative in three months. He wrote to Bruce again on April 7 to clarify in greater detail the Australian Government's motivations:

> We are getting increasing evidence of [our iron ore resources'] supposed inadequacy, although admittedly there is some doubt on this point. However, the point on which there is no doubt is that we do not wish . . . a Japanese Government enterprise well installed in Northwestern Australia, close to Broome where there are already large numbers of Japanese engaged in pearl shell industry . . .
>
> We have to have good reasons for an embargo, particularly in view of the fact that for nearly two years we have raised no difficulties and may well be taken as having tacitly acquiesced in enterprise developing . . .
>
> The best line for us to take is to say that our investigations into the probable tonnage of iron ore that can be economically exploited in Australia gives us increasing concern and anxiety . . .
>
> P.S. Desire you understand we are not only concerned with preservation of adequate ore resources but also expressly wish to avoid the establishment of this Japanese enterprise in North West Australia . . .

The Japanese Government answered with the strongest protestations. There were long letters from the Japanese Consul-General, Wakamatsu Torao, in Sydney to Prime Minister Lyons in which he expressed his Imperial Japanese Government's deep regret over the drastic decision, which could only be aimed at Japan. An inequitable measure had been taken. It ran counter to world opinion that the maldistribution of natural resources had to be remedied by such peaceful means as freer access to raw materials and freer markets for exports. In London, Japanese Ambassador Yoshida Shigeru conferred with Stanley M. Bruce and handed him a long *note verbale*. In Tokyo, Vice Foreign Minister Horinouchi Kensuke made his formal protests to British Ambassador Sir Robert Craigie about Australia depriving a 'have not' power of iron ore. Also, Baron Itō Bunkichi, the president of Nippon Mining Company, visited Longfield Lloyd's office, and two days later an *aide-mémoire* from the Japanese Foreign Office followed, stating that the Yampi Sound project was regarded as important by Japanese military authorities.

The British Government, too, was vexed by the sudden turn in Australia's export policy. Britain's Ambassador in Tokyo warned against pushing the 'have not' states too far, lest one day they simply 'take' what they required. He hoped that the Japanese would be let down as lightly as possible in this affair. Combined with adequate compensation, could not a relatively small supply of iron ore to Japan over a limited period be considered as an act of grace?

The Australian Government not only remained firm, but strengthened its resolve in early 1940 when two Japanese expressed interest in mining the silver lead deposits in Western Australia. Their request put the government in a delicate spot, because 'no question' had arisen 'as to possible depletion of [silver ore] deposits'. It effected a flurry of correspondence between the Prime Minister's Department and that of External Affairs on the question of 'whether Japanese economic penetration is to be discouraged or not', bearing in mind the difficulties which 'still confront the Commonwealth Government in regard to compensation claims over the Yampi Sound leases'. In the end, nothing came of the silver project.

Having so far failed to secure iron and silver in Australia and oil in Timor, the Japanese Government now began to press the Portuguese Government for mining and agricultural concessions in Timor, and even offered to establish a shipping line from Japan to that colony. This immediately alarmed the Dutch and Australian Governments. They sought British protestations in Lisbon. But the British Government remained unruffled and the Portuguese Prime Minister, Dr A. de O. Salazar, discounted the danger. Although his Minister for Colonies, Dr F. J. V. Machado, agreed at first with Holland and Australia to strongly resist Japanese penetration, his resolve weakened when Japan threatened to use the Macao lever.

Already in December 1939, Japanese Foreign Minister Nomura Kichisaburō had suggested 'hinting in a roundabout way at pressure', using Macao to gain the remaining oil concessions in the western part of Timor. In a telegram to Yonezawa in Lisbon, he advised breaking the deadlock by threatening to cut Macao's land and water communications to create a food shortage, or occupying the coast opposite Macao. At the time of Germany's Western offensive in April 1940, the Japanese stepped up pressure when they told the Governor of Macao and the Portuguese Minister at Tokyo that, if Portugal did not satisfy the Japanese over Timor, they would make trouble at Macao and drive out the Portuguese. The upshot was Yonezawa's message to new Foreign Minister Arita Hachirō on April 17, in which he reported that Portugal's Minister for Colonies had come round to welcome Japan's cooperation in the development of Timor in three areas: the development of mineral resources throughout the island, with the exception of oil; the inauguration of a sea route to Timor; and the establishment of an air route to Timor.

Australia was strongly opposed to an air connection between Japan and Timor. Again it was Fitzmaurice in Batavia who already in September 1937 and January 1938 had informed England and Australia of the Governor of Portuguese Timor's intention to establish an air-connection for its capital Dili. A British airline was preferred, but Dutch, Portuguese, and Japanese proposals would also be reviewed. Even if the air route was without immediate profits, Fitzmaurice considered it an important one, 'largely for strategic reasons . . . and in view of the obvious undesirability of any opening developing for Japan to interest herself in air communication in Timor'. Qantas Empire Airways and Imperial Airways officials discussed in London the feasibility of including Dili on the Singapore–Darwin route, and the Australian Defence Committee looked into it, too. However, at that time they all dismissed the run as impracticable; it was too costly, involved too much of a detour, and the approaches to Dili were obstructed by very high mountains.

Australian Minister for Aviation H. V. C. Thorby raised the matter again in March 1939, amid rumours from London that the Japanese were trying to make a deal with Portugal 'under which in return for Japan's guaranteeing Macao, Portugal would adhere to the Anti-Comintern Pact, recognise Manchukuo, and grant Japan an air-base in Timor'. To forestall such a move, he exhorted the Cabinet to open an air service between Darwin and Dili as advocated by the Department of External Affairs:

> The possibility of Japanese penetration and infiltration into the Netherlands East Indies and Timor had been one of the main reasons why the Commonwealth Government has shown constant interest in Timor . . . There is a special bureau of the Japanese Foreign Office to deal with South Seas affairs and two major Japanese companies, the Formosa Development Company and the [Nan'yō Kōhatsu Company], have been established to promote the economic penetration of the southern islands . . . According to the British Consul-General in Batavia: 'Little doubt is left . . . that Japan's real interest in Portuguese Timor is but the move of a pawn in a big game of southward expansion, to be followed by moves of more aggressive pieces when the time seems propitious, Australia being the real objective . . .'
> In view of the political advantage of establishing Commonwealth interests in Portuguese Timor and of counteracting Japanese penetration, it is considered that the relatively small expenditure involved in establishing this air service is amply justified. It is therefore recommended that Cabinet authorise steps being taken to establish this service as soon as possible.

The Australian Government thereafter kept pressing the Portuguese Government to grant permission for the establishment of a weekly air service, Darwin–Dili. A draft agreement was lodged at Lisbon in August

1939. But in the face of strong Japanese bidding, the Portuguese Government proceeded with caution and gave its final approval only in December 1940. The following month, Qantas Empire Airways flying boats made their first regular stop-overs at Dili on their flight route from Darwin to Batavia.

Amid reports that Japan was planning to set up a broadcasting station and a consulate in Dili, the Australian Government decided in February 1941 to despatch David Ross of the Civil Aviation Department. He would officially administer Qantas flying services and, unofficially but more importantly, monitor and report on Japanese activities in the island. This precipitated a race for diplomatic appointments between Japan and Britain and Australia at the shanty capital of Dili. In September, Ross resignedly informed the Department of External Affairs of the impending arrival of a Japanese consul in Dili:

> It would appear that the Japanese have stolen a march on us and that the only reasonable counter measure is to appoint a British consular officer, senior in status to the Japanese . . . The Japanese consul will have a fine residence, modern motor car, and will no doubt do a great deal of entertaining. All these things make a great impression on the Portuguese . . . Against this influence . . . we have myself, a technical aviation expert masquerading as a general Government representative, and Whittaker [who joined Ross in June to assist him in his duties], a naval intelligence officer, masquerading as a civil aviation officer . . . We must accept the fact that Japanese penetration in Timor cannot be satisfactorily prevented with the means now available. I am thoroughly disgusted with the existing situation . . . I am now convinced that there is nothing more which I can do to minimise effectively the progress being made by the Japanese in the extension of their southern penetration policy, and I ask that I be relieved at the expiration of the term which I volunteered to serve here [until October] . . .

The Department of External Affairs had been reluctant to grant Ross consular status in the belief that the Portuguese Government would thereby be able to resist more easily any Japanese claim for the same right. But pressure on Macao had proven an effective lever and the Japanese soon got their consul at Dili. With tensions now escalating in the Pacific, the Australian Government urged Ross to stay on, and followed Britain's advice to make him a British consul since the British had no suitable career officer on hand who could have reached Dili in time. By the time Ross was recognized as Consul for Great Britain and Representative for the Commonwealth two days after Pearl Harbor on 10 December 1941, new Japanese Consul Kuroki Tokitarō and an entourage of seven officials had already taken up posh quarters at Dili, and Dai Nippon Airways had been granted (in October) a fortnightly service on the line Kobe–Palau–Dili.

The next day, Britain's Secretary of State for Dominion Affairs, Lord Cranborne, advised Prime Minister John Curtin in a most secret and urgent cablegram to stand by for joint action with Dutch forces to invade and take control of Portuguese Timor, so as to forestall Japanese infiltration or aggression. The Australian Government immediately acknowledged 'accord with the proposal to send a combined Australian and Dutch force into Portuguese Timor to liquidate the Japanese . . . without delay . . . [Australian] forces are expected to arrive at Koepang [in Dutch Timor] today the 12 December'.

It was five days into the Pacific War and forty thousand Timorese were to die before the handing-over ceremony on the Dili waterfront following the Japanese surrender in September 1945. Fending off Japan's *armed* southward advance would prove a formidable task for Australia.

10

To Invade
or Not to Invade Australia?

TWO HOURS ahead of Pearl Harbor, Malaya was the first country to bear the brunt of Japan's southern offensive that signalled the opening of war in the Pacific in the early hours of Monday 8 December. The Malayan Peninsula was held by Commonwealth troops from England, India, Malaya, and Australia and the latter had two battalions on guard in the southern part at Malacca and Johore. As the Australian battalions braced themselves for action, eventually to die for Empire, Fatherland, and Forward Defence in fierce fighting from December 1941 to February 1942, or to go into captivity, their country was not on the list of war objectives in stage one of Japan's basic war plan.

This first stage—initiated in the first twelve hours on an arc of some 9,500 kilometres that represented about one-quarter of the earth's circumference, from the Malayan Peninsula to Pearl Harbor—was calculated to knock out the enemy's navies and to occupy most of Southeast Asia. The intention was to annihilate or temporarily eliminate the British, Dutch, and United States naval units based in Hong Kong, Shanghai, Singapore, Batavia, Guam, Wake Island, Manila, and Pearl Harbor and to secure for the Japanese Empire indispensable raw materials from Southeast Asia, such as oil, iron, coal, bauxite, and rice. A meticulous schedule had been drawn up for this first stage: operations were to be wrapped up by April or May 1942.

In fact, Southeast Asian territories from Rangoon to Java were already in Japanese hands by the beginning of March and the Port Darwin base had been eliminated on 19 February. Accordingly, Japanese military planners suddenly found themselves grappling with how to advance into the second stage of Japan's basic war plan in the first quarter of 1942. 'It looks as if advance operations in stage one can be concluded by the middle of March', wrote Rear Admiral Ugaki Matome, the Chief of Staff of Combined Fleet, in his diary on 5 January 1942: "Where shall we go from there? Shall we advance into Australia, attack Hawaii; or shall we prepare for the possibility of a Soviet sortie and knock them out if an opportunity arises?' Whether or not to capture Australia (*Gōshū o kōryaku suru*) became a serious topic for discussion whenever its main proponent, the Navy General Staff, convened with Combined Fleet and the Army to decide the options of war aims for the next stage in 1942.

The successful southern operation in the early months of that year could no longer be easily limited to Southeast Asia. The more Japan expanded, the more she needed to expand—for 'defensive purposes', according to the age-old law of conquering nations. In the case of the Australia operation, the strategic imperative 'demanded' that Rabaul, Australia's forward-most island sentry in the Bismarck Archipelago, be seized for the sake of protecting naval headquarters at Truk in the Carolines. Securing Rabaul, in turn, necessitated the capture of nearby Port Moresby, the capital city of Australia's mandate in Papua New Guinea. And once the southern limits of the Japanese Empire extended from the Timor Sea to New Guinea in the Arafura Sea that washed the northern Australian shores, that mainland's littoral garrisons at Port Darwin and Broome had to be eliminated.

But it was not simply expansion begetting expansion that pushed Australia into Japanese gun-sights. From the Japanese point of view, Australia's northern settlements were playing host to the forces of their enemy. Broome offered safety to the Dutch escaping them in the East Indies, and Darwin a base for American fighters on the counter-attack. The proposal to invade Australia surfaced for strategic reasons. As such, it was far removed from the racist invasion scenarios conjured up earlier by Australian writers such as Frank Fox (1909) or Earl Cox (1938), who in their political novels had depicted the Yellow Peril as one day squaring off with the white race to bring Australia into the Oriental fold. Nor did Japan intend a resources grab: Southeast Asia already offered everything Japan needed. Perhaps John Curtin had come closest to the crux of Japanese intentions when he said in Parliament in 1936: 'It might be that the enemy would consider a major attack on Australia essential to the elimination of British sea-power, even if he had no intention of remaining in permanent occupation of the country'. But in 1942 it was not British but American sea and airpower that Japan was seeking to eliminate. As Britain was losing to Japan in the Western Pacific, Australia switched with unexpected speed from resolute backing of its former colonial master to reliance on the United States, pledging alliance and inviting United States forces to recover lost territory by using Australia as a huge base with an advantageous hinterland.

The chief of the Navy General Staff's Planning Section and chief champion of the Australia invasion idea, Captain Tomioka Sadatoshi, deeply feared such a disadvantageous development. He fervently believed that Australia must not become a strategic springboard for United States planes, ships, and soldiers gathering for a counter-offensive. After the war he wrote: 'War operations' first stage had gone entirely according to schedule . . . As we were moving to stage two, what I worried about most, was Australia'. They had estimated American war power to reach enormous proportions within the next two years. Aeroplanes would increase tenfold, as would war vessels and other shipping. But whatever dimensions this output assumed, as long as that equipment was pinned down on the mainland and Hawaii, nothing was to be feared. The war had perfectly shown how little air power meant without the development of air bases. If, however, the United States built up air power on the Australian continent, while at the same time applying pressure from the north, Japan could not possibly win. Australia had either to be knocked out quickly (*datsuraku saseru*), or cut off from America.

But the navy and the army did not see eye to eye on the Australia question. 'We must think quickly about invading Australia . . . the United States is now in the middle of reinforcing Australia, Fiji, and Samoa', wrote Captain Miwa Yoshitake on 6 January. 'The Army General Staff opposes navy insistence to invade Australia because it overextends the Pacific periphery', noted Major-General Tanaka Shin'ichi, Operations Section chief (and Tomioka's opposite) in the Army General Staff, one month later. The two diary entries epitomize the opposite views that characterized the numerous discussions between army and navy on whether or not to invade Australia in the winter, spring, and summer months of 1942.

The navy's idea was to keep the enemy continuously on their toes; to deny them respite for entrenchment from which to gather strength and fight back; to be on the offensive always and put pressure on the war front from Hawaii to Ceylon and Australia; and to seek swift and decisive victories, coupled with territorial gains, which hopefully would quickly bring the enemy to the negotiation table. On the southern front, in particular, Australia was increasingly seen as a real menace to Japan's occupied southern territories and the 'inner' *nan'yō*. Because of its potential for use as the main American base in the South Pacific for staging a counter-offensive, the northern Australian coast with its submarine and air bases was viewed as a strategic liability that could involve the Japanese Empire in a feared war of exhaustion at great disadvantage for Japan.

To prevent this, the Navy General Staff sought as early as December to press for control over all of Australia as a major 'stage two' war objective. This would be achieved by invading the strategically most important points on the northern and northeastern coasts of Australia. Japan would there annihilate the enemy's maritime forces, cut the American–Australian line of communication, and thereby deal the entire Australian nation a thorough blow. The Navy General Staff reckoned that this could be done with very little expenditure of men and war material. After all, Australia had only a small population and its bases on the north coast were isolated outposts facing the sea, with desert up to their backdoors. At the same time, denying the United States access to Australian bases was not the only objective. Isolating the vast continent from the British Commonwealth would also hasten Britain's downfall.

The army perceived the realities of the Pacific War quite differently. It drew attention to the nation's lack of resources with which to carry out the naval blueprints; Japan was dangerously overextending its defence lines. 'Naval plans to invade Australia do not quickly end the Pacific War, but make it the center of the next stage and overextend the limits of our offensive power in the Pacific', warned Major-General Tanaka Shin'ichi. 'We respect the plans of the navy—as long as they remain desk-plans', seconded Colonel Kōtani Etsuo, Tanaka's section chief on the war operation staff, arguing that 'They are too risky and fanciful . . . the most important thing is first to cultivate the nation's necessary war potential'. The army wished to keep and protect the Pacific perimeter. It wanted to defend, not increase, the occupied territories, exploit their raw materials for a protracted war, and aspire to the ideal of self-sufficiency as spelled out in the Japanese government's design of 'autarky for the Greater East Asia Co-Prosperity Sphere'.

Australia was too far south. The Army General Staff was more concerned about its own turf: in the north it needed its troops. War with China, then in its fifth year, was far from being settled, and the Soviet Union loomed as a constant threat. Moreover, the army kept an open mind about invading Siberia—especially after Pearl Harbor when it was feared that the surviving core of the United States Pacific Fleet was still intact and might link up with the Soviets to launch air raids on Japan from the Soviet maritime province. Believing that there might be war in March 1942 with the Soviet Union, Tanaka wished to preserve his troops for northern security, and throughout the army–navy discussions he was loath to parcel out any contingents for Australia adventurism.

At the center of discussions was the number of soldiers needed to invade Australia. The Navy General Staff calculated in its early requests in December 1941 that three divisions (between 45,000 and 60,000 men) would suffice to capture and annihilate the Australian fleet and to secure the flanks and center of the northeastern and northwestern Australian coastlines. This figure was probably quite realistic. It was the time when Australian Prime Minister John Curtin cabled both President Roosevelt and Winston Churchill: 'We would gladly accept United States command in Pacific Ocean area'. He noted: 'We are now, with a small population in only white man's territory south of the equator, beset grievously . . . we now lack adequacy for our forces of our homeland on our own soil'. The first military talks between the United States and Australia took place at Victoria Barracks in Melbourne on 3 January, where the Australian chiefs of staff jumped at the offer to have Australia reinforced with 40,000 to 50,000 United States troops.

Had Japan actually launched a limited offensive in January/February with three divisions, there is little doubt that northern Australia would have suffered the same fate as Rabaul and Ambon, where the Japanese employed a division against a battalion. Darwin was then garrisoned with a mere brigade or two of mainly militiamen, joined by 3,000 Americans at the end of February. The Armoured Division had no tanks, and the Australian naval and air forces were almost non-existent, being employed elsewhere with Australia's elite troops on the African war front of the British Commonwealth. The seven CMF divisions (over 270,000 troops, 12,000 of which were in Western Australia by mid-February) consisted largely of hastily drawn up reservists. They were assigned less for the defence of Australia's north than to hold her most vital points in the Port Kembla–Sydney–Newcastle–Lithgow area in the southeast corner of the continent, behind the so-called 'Brisbane Line' that stretched some 1,000 miles from Brisbane to Melbourne.

Luckily for Australia, however, the Japanese army always opposed as too low the navy's estimated number of soldiers needed for an invasion. Time and again the army insisted that it would take at least ten divisions (between 150,000 and 200,000 men), maybe twelve, to invade Australia. The Australians themselves expected a Japanese invasion force of eight divisions. At one time in late February, they even estimated 'that it would require a minimum of twenty-five divisions to defend Australia against the scale of attack that is possible. This would mean that ten fully equipped divisions would have to be supplied by our Allies'. The Japanese army kept telling the navy that it was not prepared to draw the required divisions from its elite troops in Manchuria, the Kwangtung Army. To the contrary, after completing stage one, it wanted to withdraw 200,000 troops from the 400,000 deployed in the South since the outbreak of war, in anticipation of a spring offensive against the Soviet Union.

The Japanese army was even more worried by the shipping problem. As Curtin pointed out correctly to Churchill at the time: 'Should Japan secure complete freedom of the seas, the only limit to the forces she could employ against us would be that imposed by the amount of shipping available to her'. The Japanese Army General Staff calculated 1.5 to 2 million tons of shipping for the support of a major assault on Australia; but to provide that amount of tonnage would destroy the basis of the nation's war economy. The army had entered the war with 2.1 million tons of shipping, requisitioned largely from the civilian sector. Of this, 1.1 million tons were scheduled to be returned to it by July 1942 to ferry back to Japan the newly gained raw materials from the southern region. Anything less than 1.5 million tons for the invasion's task force would greatly imperil the Japanese supply line and endanger the Australia operation.

This may have been a pessimistic evaluation. There was then little to set against Japanese shipping. As United States Brigadier-General Patrick J. Hurley communicated to General George C. Marshall from Australia on 21 February: 'It may be pointed out by the optimistic that Japanese landings in New Zealand and Australia would over-extend supply lines and thus enable us to break them, but when I stated this pro-position to one of our Generals, he replied "Break them with what?" Unfortunately, his question is significant'.

Nevertheless, many years later in 1968, Tomioka admitted that some of the army's caution may have been justified and that the Australia invasion might have been a reckless venture. But he defends their stand-point in the Navy General Staff by reasoning that:

> . . .once the war had started, the enemy had to be beaten and victory won. In order to win, the enemy had to be denied the use of Australia as a base, no matter what. As long as the enemy had no foothold there, Australia could be taken. But if within the next two years the United States con-centrated rapidly on aircraft production and made full use of Australia, Japan would never be able to resist the material onslaught bound to follow.

The navy not only deplored the army's lack of daring; it suspected the generals of resisting the Australia invasion and talking about caution and the coming of war with the Soviet Union only to get a bigger slice of the military budget.

In early February, the deviating opinions about invading Australia were tossed about in increasingly acerbic dispute among the powerful middle-echelon personnel of both services. The army–navy discussions grew into acrimonious meetings, which at times came close to physical violence the closer the capture of Singapore was at hand. To the army, attacking the fortress city meant experiencing the realities of a bloody invasion. To the excitedly on-looking navy, the impending fall of the British sea bastion meant Oceania laid wide-open down to the Antarctic.

The Navy Ministry put up a strong case for invading eastern Australia at the same time that Japanese forces would be seizing Fiji, Samoa, and New Caledonia, and introduced its plan formally at a conference on 6 February. Speaking for his Ministry at the 'Saturday Conference' the following day, Captain Ishikawa Shingo continued to lecture the army: 'There will be no security for the Greater East Asia Co-Prosperity Sphere, unless we make Australia the main target in stage two of our basic war plan and annihilate it as a base for the American counter-offensive'.

But the army would only disagree, and re-emphasized instead the necessity to plan for war against the Soviet Union, to defend the present Pacific perimeter, and to prepare a military structure capable of withstanding a protracted war without defeat. 'Blinded by victory, our onslaught in the Pacific is getting dangerous. We must realize our limits in the Pacific offensive', cautioned Major-General Tanaka in his always gloomy entries on the subject of Australia. On 11 February, in negotiations at the Suikōsha (Navy Club), Commander Yamamoto Yūji, Tomioka's assistant, called for energetic offensives against Hawaii, Australia, and other targets in the Pacific; his opposite number in the army, Lieutenant-Colonel Imoto Kumao, countered that even if they did invade those places, they would be hard put to hold them.

At the next 'Saturday Conference' on 14 February—one day before the fall of Singapore—army and navy section chiefs confronted each other again over the issue of Australia.

A Naval Ministry official: 'Because the results since the beginning of hostilities have been greater than expected, the war situation is now more advantageous than anticipated. Has not the time come now to take one big leap forward? This is a good chance to make a clean sweep of Australia's forward bases.'

Colonel Kōtani Etsuo: 'It cannot be said that the situation has improved.'

Navy official: 'Even if the situation has not improved, the time to advance is only now.'

Colonel Kotani: 'It is too difficult. We have no reserves.'

Captain Tomioka: 'But if we take Australia now, we can bring about the defeat of Great Britain. With only a token force we can reach our aim!'

Such talk on the part of the navy, understandable perhaps because uttered at the moment of Britain's worst defeat in modern history, deprived the navy of a sound basis for further serious discussion in the eyes of the army, and was noted down in the Imperial Headquarter's secret diary as 'so much gibberish'.

Two days after the fall of Singapore, Army General Chief of Staff Sugiyama Gen moderated the cantankerous dispute on the highest level, as he set forth his views on Australia to Navy General Chief of Staff

Nagano Osami. The situation for action in Java looked none too bright, said he. But there was hope, and following the defeat of Java the Japanese forces would be pressed to think about the next military operations. These would certainly include Australia, which stood next in the line of assault as it furnished the biggest United States and British bases from which to launch counter-attacks against Japan. Certainly it was import- ant to have an Australia policy, but, at the same time, they also had to reflect on the immense problem of how to control Australia. What they needed was a comprehensive plan that took into consideration *all* of the country, 'because if we only take one part of Australia, it will surely develop into a war of attrition. This, in turn, could escalate into total war. Unless there are in-depth plans that consider the control of the entire continent, it is useless for us to plan for an invasion of only part of Aus- tralia. On the other hand, there is no objection to plans to isolate Australia by cutting her lines of communication with the United States'. To this end, plans for invading Fiji, Samoa, and New Caledonia had great value, and Sugiyama urged that the navy proceed together with the army in a joint study of this operation along already established plans.

The army was by no means blind to the Australian danger. Ever since the navy and the army had gotten together in late December 1941 to study the Fiji–Samoa–New Caledonia project—FS Operation, for short —the army had been willing to contemplate landings on those islands, assuming that their capture would prevent the United States from establishing Australia as their main beachhead in the Pacific for the counter-offensive. Because the operation required few troops and did not handicap the army's mainland positions against China and the Soviet Union, it could be made to fit in with the army's concept of preserving the Pacific periphery. It was even deemed useful, since it would put Japan in possession of New Caledonia's mineral wealth, especially nickel.

FS Operation, moreover, functioned as a tranquilizer administrated every time the Australia controversy threatened to raise navy tempers. Already at a Liaison conference of 10 January 1942, army approval of FS Operation had deflected the navy's scheme of capturing Australia, by focusing in a joint agreement on *isolating* rather than *invading* Australia. Further talks about isolating the southern continent from British and United States forces in both the Indian and the Pacific Oceans led to a modus vivendi which stipulated, on 15 January, that 'manoeuvres against India were a matter for the army and those against Australia for the navy'. FS Operation deflated army–navy tensions again when, in mid-February, Sugiyama encouraged further study of it and Tanaka, then on the southern front, cabled from Java that the operation could start at the end of March or beginning of April, as soon as the vessels used for the Java operations were available.

Navy General Staff excitement to push on to Australia did not, of course, evolve in isolation. That elusive aim had to compete with the weightier war objectives of two other departments which carried more clout and showed little interest in the south. The army looked first of all north, and then west, to Burma, India, and Ceylon, the only places it felt expansion might be of any profit. Combined Fleet, too, looked west and certainly east, but not south. Commander-in-chief Yamamoto Isoroku by then sorely regretted not having been able to break the United States Pacific fleet at Pearl Harbor in December. Thereafter he fixed his mind on an 'Eastern Operation' which aimed at an invasion of Hawaii with the capture of Midway as its prelude. He was eager to draw out the United States and British navies in the Pacific and Indian Oceans, where he intended to eliminate them both in quick and decisive sea battles. But until the situation looked better in the east (predicted for autumn), Yamamoto concentrated with army consent on western operations. An invasion of Ceylon would destroy the British Indian Ocean fleet and secure Japan's western front; cut British communication lines between Suez, Ceylon, and China; hasten Indian independence; link the Indian subcontinent with West Asia; and hold out hope of acting in concert with the German and Italian navies in the Mediterranean.

As far as the South was concerned, Yamamoto would only commit himself to invasion plans for Lae, Salamoa, Tulagi, and Port Moresby, to which all services agreed on 29 January. He was not interested in an invasion of Australia. That was a waste of manpower and too round-about a way to end the war speedily. He was not even willing to endanger his fleet for the invasions of Fiji, Samoa, and New Caledonia, four thousand miles away from home. As long as the United States air-craft carriers were afloat, it would be difficult to hold those islands; and, besides, the United States navy could always circumvent those islands and find other routes to reach Australia.

Notwithstanding Yamamoto's antagonism to any further involvement in the South, the middle-echelon members of his Combined Fleet submitted yet another plan to the Navy General Staff at the end of January. It listed the following priorities:

One, invade Ceylon at the end of May/June; establish contact with the German forces; mission accomplished, Combined Fleet will turn toward the east.

Two, Port Darwin must be taken.

Three, Fiji and Samoa need not be taken, only destroyed.

Four, we should like to take Hawaii, if possible.

The Navy General Staff immediately criticized the planned invasion of Hawaii as pointless and risky, and insisted on landings in the FS Operation. However, Combined Fleet emphasis on securing Darwin revealed that it was divided on the Australia issue and that its middle-echelonists did not always see eye to eye with Yamamoto on the matter. Indeed, at a study meeting of the Navy General Staff and Combined Fleet on 24 February, they strongly pressed for an invasion of northwestern and northeastern parts of Australia.

About the only thing all three services could agree to with regard to Australia was the destruction of Darwin—ironically, because it had nothing to do with an invasion. The elimination of Australia's northernmost town was purely related to Japanese operations against Java and Timor. As Prime Minister John Curtin correctly advised Lord Cranborne in early January: 'The defence of Timor as a whole is closely bound up with the defence of Darwin and the Netherlands East Indies. The occupation of Timor by Japan would seriously prejudice the defence of Darwin'. However, the Japanese were going to take care of the Darwin defence before they attacked Timor. It is useful here to go back and say a few words about the further developments in Portuguese Timor after mid-December 1941.

The Dutch–Australian invasion of Portuguese Timor on 17 December, 'for the liquidating of Japanese in Portuguese Timor' had developed into a controversial affair. On the hasty promptings of Lord Cranborne in London, who gravely misread Portuguese intentions, Australia and the Dutch East Indies had sent in troops without the consent of the neutral colonial government on Timor. As it turned out, Lisbon was willing to enlist Allied support only if Japanese aggression had already taken place. After the arrival of the uninvited Dutch and Australian troops, the Governor of Portuguese Timor, M. de A. Ferreira de Carvalho, cabled the Australian Prime Minister his strongest protestations 'against the aggression, absolutely contrary to the principles of law, being carried out against this part of Portuguese territory, by Dutch and Australian forces'.

Suddenly it was Australia, not Japan, who found herself the aggressor. It upset Australian Prime Minister John Curtin and embarrassed even more the British Government, which was anxious to preserve its good relations with Portugal in the face of an imminent German invasion of the Iberian Peninsula. Lord Cranborne expressed regret to the Portuguese for the rash action taken by its Allies on the spot and implored Curtin not to mention Britain's complicity as the instigator of the landings, lest it make Gibraltar unusable and endanger air and sea communications 'from the Atlantic to Australia'. He suggested that Australian troops replace the Dutch troops, so that it would not look as if Portugal was siding with the Dutch and the British in Asia. Curtin expressed his anger in a lengthy telegram to Cranborne, telling him that Australia had no troops to spare. Could not British soldiers replace the Dutch? But this was precisely what Britain was trying to avoid. In the end, the Australian Government agreed to move two of their infantry companies stationed in the Dutch Timorese capital, Kupang, to Dili, pending the arrival of some 700 Portuguese troops, after which all Allied troops were to be withdrawn.

Meanwhile, Portuguese Timor had appeared on the Japanese military agenda, too. Disposal of this neutral speck of Portuguese territory with an enemy presence drew heated discussions in the war council. The army pleaded for withdrawal after a cleansing operation, but the navy wanted to retain Portuguese Timor as a forward base in a future attack against Port Darwin and for purposes of invasion. To this end, the Dutch and Australian presence offered a welcome pretext to establish an operational base there by force.

Prime Minister Tōjō Hideki was totally opposed to Chief of Navy General Staff Nagano Osami in the dispute that raged in the Diet and at the Liaison Conferences from 21 to 31 January 1942. As the spokesman of the government and the army, Tōjō strongly insisted that after the mopping up operations, all troops were to be pulled back; it even appears that he may already have given such a pledge to the Emperor, who disliked extending the war to neutral countries. On 31 January, the parties reached an agreement of sorts, which played into the hands of the navy: Japan would evacuate Portuguese Timor to the extent that Portugal was able to guarantee its neutrality.

With the Portuguese Timor problem thus disposed of, dates could be set for the elimination of the 'Port Darwin–Timor–Bali' line as an essential step to precede landings on eastern Java scheduled for 27 February. On 15 February, Japanese forces left Palau to take up positions for the raid on Darwin. Steaming out of the Carolines, the Japanese main task force consisted of Carrier Divisions I (*Akagi* and *Kaga*) and II (*Soryu* and *Hiryu*), shielded by four heavy cruisers and nine destroyers under the overall command of Admiral Nagumo. The commanding officer of Carrier Division II, Rear Admiral Yamaguchi Tamon, had suggested the Darwin operation to Admiral Yamamoto at the time of the Rabaul attack on 20 January. Yamamoto gave his permission on 31 January and radioed this top secret order to the carrier fleet on 9 February at 7:30 p.m.: 'to seek to annihilate enemy strength in the Port Darwin area and to intercept and destroy enemy naval and transport fleets, while at the same time attacking enemy strength in the Java area from behind. For the surprise attack on Port Darwin on February 19, the task force will advance to the Arafura Sea'.

It appears, though, that the army was left in the dark as to the timing of the Darwin strike. Major-General Tanaka Shin'ichi notes in his diary as late as 18 February that Colonel Hattori Takushirō, the second section chief of operations, reported to him that same day about his talks with the navy and their agreement to undertake a study concerning the feasibility of destroying Darwin. It was a quick study, indeed. Early next morning, the Japanese navy planes were already up and on their way to bomb Darwin. And on 20 February landings on Dili, Kupang, and Bali were effectively carried out.

After the destruction of Darwin, the question of whether or not to invade Australia was taken up again for the last time in late February and early March. At a meeting of the war operation sections on 27 February, the Navy General Staff's insistence on invading the northern part of Australia's east coast met again with the army rebuttal that this would not seal the fate of Great Britain and the United States. The army did not want to get bogged down in another war of attrition as had happened in China, nor lose its punch in the north by shifting ten divisions from the Soviet front to Australia. The army calculated that 300,000 soldiers were already lying in wait in Australia and that the number of mobilized combatants, including civilians, totalled 600,000. The Japanese army could not possibly match this number without pulling troops out of the Philippines and having at least two million tons of shipping at its disposal.

At a further significant conference on 4 March the Australia dispute was put on the back-burner for good. Australia was not dropped entirely in the resulting 'Fundamental Outline of Recommendations for Future War Leadership' (Kongo torubeki sensō shidō no taikō) signed by the Liaison Conference on 7 March and presented by Tōjō Hideki, Sugiyama Gen, and Nagano Osami to the Emperor on 13 March. But the issue of invading Australia was now definitely put aside at the highest policy level when, together with the mention of an invasion of India, it was relegated to the end of paragraph three as a 'future option to demonstrate positive warfare'—if all went well. In its diffusion of the Australia issue, the army even allowed inclusion in the text of careful consideration to a 'temporary invasion of Port Darwin', if and when the situation allowed; that is, if Chiang Kai-Shek could be brought down and the Soviet threat diminished. In reality, this meant little more than 'never'.

As the prospects faded for an invasion of Australia, isolating the continent by way of intercepting and annihilating the British and United States navies became the prime focus of Japanese strategic attention in the Pacific. A Liaison Conference on 28 February ratified the top secret document 'Consequences of cutting the communication lines between the United States and Australia, and Britain, India, and Australia' (Bei-Gō narabini Ei-In-Gō kan no sōgo izon kankei narabini kore ga shadan ni yoru eikyō) against army suspicion that 'perfect severance of Australia' was but a naval euphemism for 'invading Australia'. The document concluded that total isolation of Australia was the key to Japan's mastery of the Southwest Pacific, and that to preserve Japan's naval supremacy in the South Pacific and Indian Oceans and to isolate Australia, the strategically valuable islands of New Caledonia, Fiji, Samoa, and Ceylon had to be occupied. In March, however, Combined Fleet abandoned its plan to invade Ceylon, because it judged the island too difficult to hold and an ineffective location from which to counter-attack the British in India.

On the political level, Prime Minister Tōjō Hideki continued to support pressuring Australia into submission by way of cutting her communication lines to the United States. In a Diet oration on 21 January he proclaimed decisive defeat for Australia if she continued to fly the flag of the enemy. His intimidating rhetoric notwithstanding, he always opposed an invasion of Australia and encouraged his army operations chief on 30 January to actively pursue the plans for FS Operation, which would throttle Australia into submission by the gradual extension of Japanese control over eastern New Guinea, the Solomons, and the New Caledonia–Fiji Islands area. On the occasion of the fall of Singapore in mid-February, he again demanded dramatically that now was the time for the peoples of Australia, India, and the Netherland East Indies to surrender; any further resistance was futile. And in a further appeal to the leaders of Australia at an extraordinary session of the Diet on 28 May, Tōjō repeated his threatening lure that it was not too late to make the right decision and toe the line with the Japanese Empire.

Japan was now tightening the noose on Australia. The dates for the invasion of New Caledonia, Fiji, and Samoa were firmly set for 8, 18, and 21 July, respectively. Army and navy leaders were already squabbling over which service would get the prize of administering New Caledonia to manage and exploit its rich nickel and cobalt mines. Psychological warfare against Australia was to be stepped up at the time of the FS Operation, and Major-General Tanaka with Army Vice Chief of Staff Lieutenant-General Tanabe Moritake were searching for ways of communicating Tōjō's messages to Australia together with Japan's real intentions: 'We respect the sovereignty of Australia; all she must do is maintain a strict policy of neutrality'. Tanaka wanted the political messages conveyed either by special messenger or through the Australian consul in New Caledonia's capital, who had at his disposal the undersea cable between Noumea and Sydney. And should Australia still prove unresponsive, psychological warfare would be increased, the blockade of Australia strengthened, and political dissension planted to cause a split between the Australian Federal Government and the various Australian State governments. At the end of May 1942, the army supreme command was confident that the Australia problem could be solved.

The Battle of Midway was then only about ten days off. June had, in fact, been originally reserved for the capture of Fiji, Samoa, and New Caledonia, but the Japanese naval successes in the Indian Ocean had taken up the better part of April and necessitated the change in dates to July. Each victory had taken Combined Fleet further away from the Navy General Staff's FS Operation and made Admiral Yamamoto more dogmatic about his next move: the successful Western push had to be supplemented with an equally successful Eastern push, including nothing less than the capture of Midway and the annihilation of the United States navy.

Already in mid-March, Yamamoto had briefly informed the Navy General Staff about Combined Fleet's attack plans for Midway. Just then the Navy General Staff (with the army's support) had been studying the approaches to Lae and Salamaua in eastern New Guinea as a preparatory invasion for isolating the Australian continent by way of the Fiji–Samoa Operation scheduled for June. In early April, Yamamoto again despatched to Tokyo a staff officer, Commander Watanabe Yasuji, to explain in more detail 'Operation Midway' to the Navy General Staff. That briefing turned into a series of seething discussions, often described as a meeting that brought the two main disputants, Watanabe and Commander Miyo Tatsukichi (First Section Air Officer who represented the Naval General Staff), close to tears in angry debate over their service's aims. It is probably this dispute which the senior participant in those discussions, Tomioka Sadatoshi, refers to in his postwar reminiscences as the one that sealed the fate of Japan; for when in the uproar Admiral Yamamoto Isoroku threatened by phone to resign (as he already once before had threatened to do over Pearl Harbor) if Midway was not carried out, the Navy General Staff had little choice but to give in and postpone FS Operation to July.

What might have been an ongoing, and perhaps successful, southward advance, was thereby turned into a fatal eastward advance. After the Doolittle raid in mid-April, the army too was won over and agreed to provide a regiment for an invasion of Midway on June 5. On that day, however, the Japanese navy was routed by the Americans when the Midway Task Force under the command of Admiral Nagumo lost four aircraft carriers and 30 per cent of its veteran pilots. The Midway fiasco became a turning-point after which FS Operation was cancelled on 11 July; and thereafter Japan fought a war of retreat. Nothing more was heard of pressuring, much less of invading, Australia.

That is the case, unless one takes at face-value the headlines of the *Australasian Post* forty-three years later, 'The Soldier Who Invaded Australia', and classifies as an invasion the Japanese reconnaissance mission which set out from Timor and effected a brief landing on the north-eastern shore of Australia. Although that episode had no great significance in terms of the southward advance, it is interesting to recount for the sake of the record.

On 19 January 1944, four army officers, led by Lieutenant Mizuno Suzuhiko, landed in York Sound near the mouth of the Moran River on Australia's northwestern coast, about eight hundred kilometres south-west of Darwin, on a clandestine mission. They had left Kupang two days earlier on the thirty-five ton *Hiyoshi Maru*, equipped with machine guns, anti-submarine guns, and a crew of six Okinawan fishermen. They also had with them a living shield of ten Timorese youth, averaging sixteen, who would have been the first to die had they come under enemy-fire. They shot over an hour's reel of eight millimetre film, recorded the heights of the hills, the mountains, and the vegetation, and after an insignificant day and night in the bush, left the forbidding place on the most direct route back to Kupang, where they arrived in the evening of the twenty-first.

Mizuno reported their findings to his superior, Major Yamamoto Masayoshi. Like Mizuno a graduate of the famous Nakano Intelligence School for subversion and counter-intelligence, Yamamoto headed the Timor branch of the Matsu Kikan (Pine Tree Organisation), an espionage wing of the Imperial Japanese Army, and was responsible for the Australia mission. He had been planning and organizing the covert run out of Java and Timor since May 1943 on orders from the Navy General Staff. The Americans were then launching Operation Cartwheel and closing in on Rabaul with a two-pronged drive via the Solomons and New Guinea, whence they would leapfrog their way to the Marshall and Caroline Islands. Anxious to check the onslaught of Americans based in Australia, the Navy General Staff in mid-1943 wanted to ascertain whether the Americans were really building large bases on Australia's northwest coast near Darwin and Drysdale as rumour had it.

More than forty years later, it appears that the original order for the mission was added to as it got under way. Whereas Yamamoto today stresses the purely intelligence-gathering aspect of the operation, Mizuno maintains that it was in preparation for launching guerrilla-type warfare on Australian soil. After briefing Yamamoto, Mizuno flew to Tokyo in February to report to Imperial Army Headquarters, where he was received by Prince Mikasa, the youngest brother of the Emperor, and Field Marshal Sugiyama Gen. After listening to Mizuno, they shook his hand and congratulated him. 'Thank you. Well done!' exclaimed the Marshal, as he asked the 27-year-old officer what he thought should be their next step. Mizuno suggested that they collect about two hundred of the worst types from Japan's prisons and send them thither on small fishing boats. He would lead and land them on Australian beaches, from which they would penetrate deep into Australia. Moving from village to village, they would create panic and thereby divert Allied power away from the Japan-offensive and into the interior of the continent. With the words 'Splendid idea—please go ahead!' Mizuno was complimented out of the room and transferred for duty to another island as soon as he was back in the Western Pacific. No more was heard of 'Operation Australia', but he did receive a written congratulatory message for having persevered afloat under adverse conditions.

Australia in the
Nan'yō *Literature*
1940–1944

11

A Fleeting Moment of Truth and Fiction

WHEN JAPAN'S southward advance entered its final stage in the early 1940s, the war frenzy and Japan's first spectacular victories in the South engendered a sense of eternal victory that generated an enormous output of literature on the *nan'yō*, particularly in 1942 and 1943. As pens shunned modesty and ambiguity, the furthest countries bordering on the *nan'yō* began to be boldly discussed in an assertive tone of enforced regional brotherhood. Australia was such a country and, although it remained a marginal subject in the *nan'yō* literature, many books on Australia were issued in those years.

One might question the value of analysing Australia in the often spurious literature of a fleeting moment's censored times. Indeed, one must be cautious not to read too much into the often fervent discussions about Australia in the books and magazines of wartime Japan. But one can find also level-headed argumentation in that literature, the remarkable thing being that for once an intense interest in Australia was generated and the opinions of writers of various political backgrounds were frankly and forcefully expressed. And if there is one interesting aspect, it is the fact that several of the issues for which Australia was criticized in this literature were actually settled in the post-war period. The White Australia policy was abolished, Australia loosened her ties with the mother country England as she began to see herself more as an

Asian–Pacific regional country, and the raw materials, denied Japan in the late 1930s, were gladly sold in large quantities to fuel the Japanese economic miracle in the post-war period.

Perusing the *nan'yō* literature of that age, moreover, illuminates the years of the Greater East Asia Co-Prosperity Sphere from a different angle. The Greater East Asia concept had been unveiled in August 1940 by Foreign Minister Matsuoka Yōsuke, a spokesman who held his grandiloquent own with his counterparts in Germany and Italy. His visionary concept drew its rhetoric from all that Hitler and Mussolini stood for, and Roosevelt and Churchill deplored. Though nebulous in geographical and political application, the idea of Japan's Greater East Asia Co-Prosperity Sphere foresaw the Western Pacific region ruled by Tokyo— just as Berlin was expected to dominate Europe and Africa; Moscow the Soviet Heartland with parts of India; Washington to hold on to the Americas; and London to cede some of the Empire. The Greater East Asia Co-Prosperity Sphere was a flaunting caprice born of its time, but Japan pursued it with the historical vengeance of a desperate latecomer.

This Sphere concept is usually discussed from a short range, as the product of the turbulent war years of the 1930s and early 1940s. And many studies weigh it with all the attendant criticism of the concept because it failed utterly in its aspirations. But if the Greater East Asia Co-Prosperity Sphere idea is viewed as the culminating policy manifestation of Japan's southern interests from before her period of national seclusion, the ideas launched in the 1930s/1940s appear perhaps a little less extravagant. By taking this longer view one tries to understand the Greater East Asia Co-Prosperity Sphere chauvinism from behind its inception, so to speak. One looks at the climactic years of the Sphere concept not from the present, but rather from the recesses of a deeper past located in the century before the *sakoku* period. One seeks to understand the manifestations of the Pacific War from the vantage of an earlier point of departure in history, when the historical phenomena of expansionism were easier to understand; when in the days of Francis Drake, Richard Cox, and Yamada Nagamasa, the Japanese too had been outgoing, adventurous, curious, and profit-seeking. They too had once exhibited an expansive spirit alongside the Portuguese, the Dutch, and the British on the eve of the European appropriation of the vast expanses in the Asian–Pacific region and in the short heyday before the closing of the country in 1639, at a time when Japanese were peopling their foreign settlements in increasing numbers.

A strong undercurrent running through the peculiar literature of this period suggests that finally the day had come to make up for the fateful Tokugawa policy of isolation with its crippling effect that for centuries had thwarted natural expansionism inherent in all vital countries. Bearing this long time spectrum in mind, the copious writings dealing with

Australia in the early 1940s are particularly relevant, and arranged here according to six themes.

Australia Fears Japan

When Japan invaded Manchuria in September 1931, most of Australia's official and business circles and the press kept a low profile. It was not wise to antagonize a strong, potential enemy who, luckily, was striking north in the opposite direction to Australia. Intellectuals shared this attitude. The main paper read by Professor A. C. V. Melbourne at a gathering of prominent figures at Southport, Queensland, in October 1934, for example, gave full marks to Japan's 'great experiment in systematic exploitation' in Manchukuo. 'Japan needs room for expansion . . . The Japanese regarded the occupation of Manchuria as a matter of necessity . . . In such circumstances it is useless to talk right or wrong . . . If Japan is driven from Manuchukuo, the necessity will reappear in an exaggerated form . . . The position is full of potential danger for Australia'.

In the following year, when distinguished senior diplomat Debuchi Katsuji visited Australia, Minister for External Affairs George Pearce assured him, during their five-hour car conference while driving about the countryside near Canberra, that the Manchurian problem had nothing to do with Australia. It should be handled by the Japanese themselves. Australia was not in the least opposed to Japan developing Manchuria, or even China, added former Prime Minister Bill Hughes the next day. He was a 'realist' himself; in order to stay alive, a country had to develop in a suitable direction.

In summer 1940, Australia played an active role in urging the British Government to comply with Japan's request to close the Burma Road at the cost of Chinese security. And in the final desperate round of talks in November and December 1941 between Japanese Ambassador Nomura Kichisaburō and United States Secretary of State Cordell Hull on the eve of war in the Pacific, the Australian Government instructed its Minister in Washington, R. G. Casey, to do everything possible to prevent the negotiations from breaking down. He was to suggest that economic restrictions against Japan might be lessened in return for Japan's withdrawal from Indo-China and a general guarantee against Japanese aggression elsewhere. Casey kept up his broker services until the last moments before the outbreak of the Pacific War, hopefully carrying a proposal from the Japanese on Sunday morning 30 November to Secretary of State Cordell Hull, only to see it rejected by the Americans in the evening. In the diplomatic arena, but well within the bounds of the Canberran geopolitical world-view that denied Japanese claims to southern resources, Australia appeased Japan right up to Pearl Harbor.

One appeases that which one fears. In the case of Australia, appeasement sprang from a fear which, to the surprise of not a few Japanese writers residing in Australia, was rooted in a deeper past. Inoue Shōzō, a freelancer for proliferating tabloid magazines such as *Shin Ajia* (New Asia), was perplexed to learn that thirty years earlier a primary school teacher had been lecturing pupils about a future Japanese invasion of Australia. Writing out of Melbourne, where he lived from April 1940 to March 1941, Inoue regarded the Australians as a 'happy-go-lucky' people who lived rather blithely in the pristine splendour of their beautiful country. More introspection would stand them in good stead, lest they continue to fall prey to the Japanophobic media. He regretted that many Australians were as ignorant about Japan as they were fearful of her. Two cartoons in the Australian press had struck him in·particular. One depicted Japan as an enormous crocodile, its jaws, caricatured as the islands of Shikoku and Kyūshū, stretched wide open and salivating lustily on Australia. The other one showed a Japanese soldier stepping smartly forward out of a horizon draped as the great rising sun in the Imperial Japanese naval flag; with his boot resting on Indochina, he was marching on to Malaya, Singapore, Sumatra, Java, Portuguese Timor, and Darwin as the next stepping stones laid out on a large map of the Western Pacific region spread before him. Inoue wondered how Australians could draw a cartoon that gave the impression that only Australia could own everything between Darwin and Singapore. After his return to Japan, he compiled his essays into a book, *Ugoku Gōshū*, published in 1942.

Another Japanese resident in Melbourne, Hayashi Sōtarō, who was the Managing Director of Kanematsu Trading Company, had already noticed a growing Australian preoccupation with Japan's southward advance four years earlier in 1936. In his book on the trade problems between Japan and Australia, *Nichi-Gō tsūshō mondai,* he attributed Australia's fear to several factors that Australians were well aware of: the loss of power by the League of Nations, which could not be depended on anymore; Taiwan's governmental change in 1936 from a civilian to a naval–military administration; occasional visits of Japanese admirals to Java for 'research' purposes; Ishimaru Tōta's wide interest in the *Nichi-Ei hissen ron* (Japan must fight Britain), a book which in English translation was soon sold out despite its price; and the new geopolitical situation created by the Italian invasion of Ethiopia in June 1935. This latest crisis caused the British fleet to pass around South Africa, thus weakening Australian naval links with the motherland. The failure of the League of Nations to act in the Italo– Ethiopian crisis distressed the Australian Government because it diverted British naval attention to Africa, Hayashi observed. It strengthened the hands of the Japanese militarists and encouraged them to extend Japan's power in the Pacific. All these factors contributed to the peculiarly Australian *kyōnichibyō*, 'fear-of-Japan', illness.

Takagi Saburō, managing director of Oceania Mining Company, defined Australia's feelings towards the Japanese as having passed through three stages: in the first stage Australians had slighted Japanese; in the second stage Australians respected Japanese; now, in the third stage, Australians feared the Japanese. He illustrated these changes of attitude by the way he was treated at Australian hotels in 1919 and 1941. On his first visit he had been given a shabby room and had been seated in the restaurant right next to the noisy entrance; but the second time he was immediately ushered into superior accommodation and offered a quiet dining table near the window with a view. He now realized how deeply aware Australians were of Japan. He sensed this not only in his talks with notables such as Robert Menzies and John Curtin, but also in the shop-windows that displayed Japanese grammars, histories, and literature, next to foreboding and widely advertised titles such as *Japan's Southward Policy* and *The Coming of Japan's Devil Hand*.

Australian interest in Japan was reciprocated by the Japanese who were becoming more aware of things Australian through a growing number of translations of Australian books in the early 1940s. These included Sir George Hubert Wilkins, *Gōshū no tsuchi to hito* [Undiscovered Australia],1942; H. L. Harris, *Gōshū no seiji-keizai kōzō* (The political–economic structure of Australia), 1942; Griffith Taylor, *Ōsutoraria no chiri* (The geography of Australia) 1942; D. B. Copland, Prime Minister J. Curtin's top economic adviser, *Gōshū keizai ron* (The Australian economy), 1943; Jose Arthur, *Gōshū no jūmin to sangyō* (The population and industries of Australia), 1943; and Sir Baldwin Spencer, *Gōshū genjūmin no kenkyū* (A study of the Australian natives), 1943. The Australia boom sometimes even produced two versions of the same book by different translators, as in the case of Ernest Scott, *Ōsutoraria shi* and *Gōshū shi* (A short history of Australia), both based on the sixth edition of 1937, and translated in July 1943 and October 1944 respectively. These translations give an idea as to the kind of knowledge about Australia that was sought and disseminated in Japan; they also are of interest because in lengthy forewords and afterwords (which in the case of Scott's work could run to twenty pages) they often carried Japanese gung ho opinions about the lucky twist in history that was now finally whipping Australia into the right shape of things for common prosperity in the New Order of the Asian–Pacific region.

The numerous translations on Australia's history, economy, and government gave the Japanese reader a fairly good idea of Australian affairs and often spoke eloquently of Australia's uncertainty about her future in the Pacific. Watanabe Izō's translation of Felix M. Keesing, *Atoms of Empire*, published under the title *Taisen to Nan'yō guntō* (The Great War and the South Seas Islands), 1941, for example, describes how Japan was stretching her hands toward New Guinea and New Caledonia by extending her sea lanes in that region through a cheap-rate passage policy. Japan had not yet stated clearly how far her power sphere would extend in the region. Two big problems remained to be answered. How far would the United States commit her line of defence? What kind of southern policy would Japan adopt?

The puzzle that Japan posed and the fears she stirred in Australia were also keenly sensed by an employee of Horikoshi Shōkai company, Matsunaga Sotoo, who had resided in Australia for thirteen years. After his repatriation in 1941, he put down his memories in *Gōshū inshōki* (Impressions of Australia) in which he offers perceptive glimpses of the apprehensive Australian mood towards his country on the eve of the Pacific War. Like Inoue Shōzō, he was amazed that at a school debate, adolescents were discussing the Japan threat. They concluded that it would take Japan fifteen years to establish her rule over China; then she would turn to Australia; therefore it was necessary to build up Australia's defences to meet that future threat. This surprised Matsunaga as much as when he overheard a British cotton manufacturer from Shanghai, J. C. Summer, predict that after China fell, Australia would be next in line. And didn't Australians know that the Japanese had more precise maps of Australia than the Australians? *Kyōnichibyō*, or the Japan-threat disease, was felt even in police quarters. When Matsunaga asked his local police station for permission to travel outside Sydney, the policeman engaged him in a long conversation:

Officer: 'How long will it be before Japan launches her attack on the South?'
Matsunaga: 'Attack the South? I have no idea. I have heard it say that the nan'yō is our life-line, but I never heard anything about an attack on the South.'
Officer: 'Ever since the Manchurian Incident, beginning with China, has not Japan steadily been groping for southern territories?'
Matsunaga: 'Not at all. Until now Japan has had no territorial ambitions whatsoever. She is only interested in realizing the ideal of co-existence and co-prosperity. Look at Manchukuo and the People's Government in Nanking: Japan wants to make them prosper together and lay the foundation for the creation of a Greater East Asia.'
Officer: 'Even though Japan has pledged herself to the status quo in the Pacific Ocean, why has she been threatening the Dutch East Indies?'
Matsunaga: 'That is a big misunderstanding. The negotiations between Japan and the East Indies have only been about mutual trade.'
Officer: 'Do you think there will be war between Australia and Japan?'
Matsunaga: 'No there won't. Although the political mood in both countries has worsened, Japan is committed to solve everything

peacefully by whatever means. If a war were brewing there would not now be ambassadorial exchanges.'

At this, the police officer lost some of his reserve and asked about the suicide bombings, when three young Japanese carrying bombs on their shoulders had blasted themselves and Chinese military installations in Shanghai in 1932: 'We cannot understand such actions. What on earth does it mean?'

Matsunaga: 'It means: "To die seven times for one's country and the Emperor" [to sacrifice oneself in seven rebirths to the cause of one's nation]. [Here, Matsunaga reports the officer's admiration 'Golly, what an awesome country!'; he proceeds to question Matsunaga on the abstract principle behind Japan's recent government declaration.]

Officer: 'What is the meaning of the words *Hakkō-ichi-u*?'

Matsunaga: 'They are the words of the first Emperor, Jimmu Tennō, and manifest his wish to bring the eight corners of the world under one roof. Put simply, it signifies the ideal of making society as one family. Manchukuo offers a good example: in 1932, it celebrated its first glorious birthday and, joined to Japan, became a blissful country following the Kingly Way . . . Japan is about to form a family, she is not creating new colonies. Japan and Manchukuo are now like one family and reflect perfectly the spirit of *Hakkō-ichi-u*: Countries like yours, built on the principle of individualism, have difficulty understanding this kind of family system. Therefore you can never grasp the meaning of the *Hakkō-ichi-u* principle, which in its essence is simply an amplification of the family ties extended to embrace world society, so that all races will eventually live together as one family with a deep affection for each other.'

Officer: 'Then why does Japan bully China, England, and America?'

Matsunaga: 'All families have quarrels. It amounts to no more than brotherly squabbles . . .'

Bidding me good-bye with a smile, the police officer ended the conversation good-humouredly: 'If Japanese-Australian relations worsen and I'll have to lock you up, I shall prepare a comfortable cell for you.'

Matsunaga gives the impression that *kyōnichibyō* was groundless and lacked rationality. The Japanese did not plan to invade Australia: her fear of Japan was nothing but an old sickness that had become worse since the end of World War I when Australia had been unable to forestall Japanese territorial expansion down to the Equator; and it was small wonder that the sickness was not improving, now that Australia had turned herself into a base for the ABCD forces against whose encirclement Japan was fighting.

Matsunaga furthermore purports not to understand what all the fuss was about in Australia when, on 24 February 1941, Japan's Foreign Minister Matsuoka Yōsuke (1880–1946), told the House of

Representatives at a budget committee that 'Asians should colonize Oceania'. He could remember Matsuoka having already publicly expressed interest in Oceania as Japan's representative in Geneva in the early 1930s; how could this make headlines in Australian newspapers, now in 1941? He notes their particular concern with how far Matsuoka's Oceania extended. Did it include Australia? Some said it did not. A Washington geographer was quoted as saying that it did; and those who reached for their *Encyclopaedia Britannica* found out that Oceania stretched from the shores of Western Australia to the eastern islands of Polynesia. When the newly established Japanese legation was bombarded with questions on this issue, Minister Kawai Tatsuo evaded the question by explaining: 'At primary school our geography teacher did not tell us how far Oceania extended'.

Australia Is Part of Asia

'I may with respect suggest that you get your geography books right, so that in your schools at least they will know that Australia is not part of Asia', remonstrated Sir John Latham, Kawai's counterpart in Japan, upon assuming office in January 1941 at a reception of the Japan–Australia Association in his honour.

If most Australians agreed that their country was part of Oceania, whether it was also part of Asia was another matter. While most considered their cultural strain, the British heritage, to preclude any discussion as to Australia's affiliation, the fact that Australia was close to Asia in geographical terms registered increasingly as a truth during the interwar years. Australia was the neighbour not only of white New Zealand, America, and Canada, but also of populous Southeast Asia, China, and Japan. Asia was, in fact, Australia's most important geographical vicinity.

'The Far East is our far-North . . . Whilst racially we are Europeans, geographically we are Asiatic. Our own special immediate Australian interests are more nearly concerned with what is happening in China and Japan than with what is happening in Belgium and Holland', had said Sir George Pearce already in 1922 after serving as Australia's representative at the Washington Conference. Twelve years later, after touring Japan, Latham himself proclaimed in Parliament: 'What the "Far East" is to Europe . . . the "Near East" is to Australia'—only to be topped by Prime Minister Robert Menzies who broadcast the 'Far East' as Australia's 'Near North' in April 1939.

With the blazing war successes on the Japanese southern front working themselves down to Asia's 'Near South' in early 1942, the notion of Australia being part of Asia gained currency in Japanese geographical education. Concerned with the speed with which Southeast Asian countries were then rapidly becoming Japanese-occupied territory, the Ministry of Education decided to hold a conference in January. It no longer found satisfactory the European and American geographies of Southeast Asia relied on for so long. A new geography was needed, one that taught Japanese schoolchildren the process of restructuring the region that was coming under Japanese domination. The curriculum should pay more attention to the subject of creating a New World Order in the Greater East Asian region, preferably with an understanding of geopolitical principles. The Ministry of Education did not suggest outright that geopolitics be taught at high school. But when the new school year began in April, educators were alive to the suggestion that geopolitically trained or inspired geography teachers would henceforth be a great asset in school education.

Although German-inspired geopolitical principles had been increasingly discussed in Japan since 1940, this dialogue had failed to keep up with swift military victories that were quickly changing the regional map of Asia. Geopolitics was supposed to serve as prediction followed by action, as Hitler's Germany had clearly demonstrated. In the case of Japan, however, military action was outrunning geopolitical explanations. Malaya and Singapore were already taken before the geopolitical reason had been explained sufficiently at home in textbooks and in the mass media. With the Japanese forces now suddenly *ante portas Australienses*, it was high time to start thinking about the meaning of Australia in geopolitical terms. Australia was part of Asia; and one thought offered at this juncture to better explain why, was the idea of the 'Australasiatic Mediterranean' (Gō-A chichūkai).

'Australasiatic Mediterranean' constituted the region that connected the Asian mainland with Australia and functioned as a junction between the Indian and Pacific Oceans; it comprised the Celebes, Banda, Arafura and South China Seas, the islands therein, and part of the Indochina peninsula. Yet the new geographical concept was not one invented by the Japanese; it was taken over from German geopolitical writers such as Hans Lautensach, Kurt Wiersbitzky, and Karl Haushofer.

Haushofer's chapter on Australasia in his standard work, *The Geopolitics of the Pacific Ocean*, 1924, appears to have inspired Iimoto Nobuyuki, who enlarged on the theme, contending that the widely scattered island region that comprised the Australasiatic Mediterranean formed, despite its highly diverse cultures, a natural geological and ethnological unit. The islands had once been connected, he wrote, and acted as a landbridge on which the people from the Asian mainland had migrated into the Pacific and down to Australia. This migratory flow over long stretches of time bound the various peoples in a bond of common ancient heritage. At their migratory destinations, these people had tilled the soil as conforming and self-sufficient farming peoples under a common monsoon climate. When the Europeans then began to colonize this region in the sixteenth century, the white masters broke the unity by the principle of division of labour through exploitative plantation work which fed their capitalism and brought disorder to the region. It was the aim of the present war to restore the old unity by chasing away the European and American intruders, so that once again an agricultural society could flourish.

From this novel geopolitical viewpoint which rested on pre-historical presumptions, it was only a short step to the logic that the Australasiatic Mediterranean, including Australia, formed the natural counterpart of Northern Asia in the north–south super-sphere concept of the Axis powers. Kawanishi Masahiro, who in 1933 had denounced German geopolitics as a study of aggression in disguise, saw world affairs differently in the early 1940s. He now perceived the British power sphere, which spanned the globe in a horizontal way, as weakening and giving way to large space spheres that in the future would straddle the equator in a vertical order. These would span the globe in huge north–south units, concentrating industry and population in the northern continental halves while drawing the raw materials to fuel their industries from the less populated southern halves. The idea was borrowed from Haushofer, who had been working on this new world concept since his 1931 publication, *Die Pan-Ideen*. Now, in 1942, it looked as if a Eurafrican sphere, a North and South American sphere, a Soviet sphere in possible combination with India, and a Greater East Asian sphere with Australia, were going to fulfil his prognostications. Kawanishi opined that Australia, as the Greater East Asian sphere's complementary southern part, with its small population and abundant raw materials, satisfied perfectly the geopolitical north–south exigencies of the time.

How did those *nan'yō* writers not trained in geography use this new kind of geographical knowledge? Some dissected the word 'Australasia'. '"Austral" means "south": Southland of Asia', argued Kaneko Takanosuke and Kiyokawa Masaji, the editors of the 638-page book *Nanpō keizai shigen sōran* (Comprehensive survey of economic resources in the southern region). They derided this semantic paradox: that Australians wanted nothing to do with Asia was evident in their White Australia policy. Okakura Koshirō reminded his readers that the Europeans themselves had originally designated Australia and New Zealand as Australasia. What could this mean, asked the 29-year-old graduate of Keio University, who had specialized in India but at the height of the *nanshin* boom was told by his guiding professor to write a book about Australia. True to the sweeping spirit of his famous grandfather, Okakura Tenshin, who in 1903 had coined the phrase 'Ajia wa hitotsu' (Asia is one), Koshirō wondered: was not Australia bound to Asia in karmic relationship (*ketsuen*) through the countless islands that connected the two continents in the Australasiatic Mediterranean since times eternal?

The Kanematsu Trading Company stated in one of its studies *Gōshū yushutsu bōeki ni tsuite* (On Australia's export trade) in July 1942 that, geographically, Australia had always been part of Asia. Miyata Mineichi, who had taught at Sydney University, classified Australia as one of the South Asian countries in his work *Gōshū renpō* (The Australian commonwealth). Madarame Fumio urged Australia to 'return' and understand her position as a 'Pacific Ocean country' in the new world order. In this, he brought to mind the allusion that just as Japan had departed from Asia under the prodding pen of Fukuzawa Yukichi in 1885 but returned to her true position as the candlebearer of Asia in the 1930s, Australia, too, after long tutelage under European dominance should now realize her natural position in the Pacific and return. In a more draconian tone, he also stated that the Australasiatic Mediterranean had always acted as a connecting landbridge between Australia and Asia and that it would become Australia's duty to act as the southern supply base to fuel Japan's industry. And Inoue Shōzō offered a syllogism: Australians had to know that geographically they were as much part of the Pacific Ocean as they were of the East Asian Ocean; therefore they had to wake up to the fact that they were a Pacific country in the East Asian region.

By the 1940s, many Japanese had come to regard Australia as one of the *nan'yō* countries, and wrote in rather conclusive terms of Australia as being part of Asia. When *'nan'yō'* had begun to circulate as a new word in the Meiji period, it had still stood for everything south, in contrast to the more familiar geographical areas of Russia in the north, China in the west, and America to the east. This view changed by the mid-Taishō period, when Japan took possession of Micronesia and the regional concept of the *nan'yō* became a focal point in the mandate and fortification discussions of the League powers at the Paris and Washington Conferences between 1919 and 1922. Thereafter Japanese distinguished between the *uchi* (inner) *nan'yō*, which comprised their mandated Western Pacific island possessions down to the Equator as home territory, and the *soto* (outer) *nan'yō* (Southeast Asia): during and after World War I the Japanese generally placed Australia in neither.

After the Japanese Government announced its intention to create a New World Order in East Asia in the late 1930s, the geographical concept of the *nan'yō* became increasingly identified with the Japanese power sphere. It was also largely replaced by *nan'yō ken* 'southern sphere', or *nanpō* 'southern region', which could include any region south of Japan between Africa and South America. When Foreign Minister Matsuoka announced the plan for the establishment of a Greater East Asia Co-Prosperity Sphere in August 1940, his statement did not mention Australia specifically as a prospective member of the *nanpō*; but in September, when Japan and Germany concluded the tripartite pact with Italy, a secret agreement declared Australia (together with Malaya, British Borneo, the British and French Islands in the South Pacific, New

Zealand, and even India) as belonging in the Japanese living sphere (*seizonken*). The *nanpō* region was thereby secretly and officially connected for the first time with the core of the sphere—Japan, Korea, and Manchukuo—to form an integral whole.

In any case, *nan'yō* had by then already been incorporated into the even more collective concept of *tōyō*, the East Asian region, a current geographical expression that came to emphasize Japan's future sphere of action; it encompassed the entire Western Pacific region east of Malaya, including both the northern and southern hemispheres.

Occidental logic was here successfully entwined with the Oriental view point. In many Japanese minds, the final link that connected Australia with Asia was the widely accepted German geopolitical view that the southern half of the world had to be capped and dominated by the upper half of the northern *Herrenlander* in an encircling fashion that divided the globe into four super regions straddling the Equator in vertical Pan-spheres. The original meaning of Australasia, which the Europeans themselves had introduced between the seventeenth and nineteenth centuries, thus rounded out the logic by which many Japanese began to see Australia as part of Asia.

Empty Australia Must Be Developed

Just about every Japanese book on Australia in this period marvelled at the size of the Australian continent and the scarcity of its people. 'Australia is one of the world's virgin continents', wrote Murobuse Kōshin, an ultra-nationalist and editor of the magazine *Nippon hyōron* (Japan review) from 1934 to 1945; 'Its surface of 7,636,000 square kilometres is twenty-two times the size of Japan proper'. 'Yet only 7.8 million people live there', lamented Matsunaga, basing himself on figures of March 1941:

> I was surprised to learn that its population is about the same as that of Tokyo. If we compare Australia's 2.3 people per square mile with Japan's population density of 386 people per square mile, we realize how thinly populated that country is and why it is called 'the empty continent'. From the Japanese point of view, one cannot help saying that it is a region without people.

The Japanese comments were, in fact, matched by volumes of Australian literature that dealt with the problems of demography and immigration to Australia. 'There has been a widespread and rather uneasy interest in population problems', wrote Professor K. H. Bailey in 1933; 'Books such as Lothrop Stoddard's *Rising Tide of Colour* and East's *Mankind at the Crossways* have been in great demand in libraries'. Further titles reveal the level of discussion: *The Peopling of Australia* (1928), *The*

Peopling of Australia: Further Studies (1933), C. V. James, *The Future of Immigration into Australia and New Zealand* (1937), and W. D. Forsyth, *The Myth of Open Spaces* (1942). All these studies discussed the relationship between carrying capacity and the type of population Australia intended to acquire.

That Australia sorely needed immigrants was not concealed, nor that the nation preferred white immigrants to coloured people. But by no means did Australians want to have their living standards lowered because of problems connected with immigration. The continent could perhaps carry up to two hundred million people according to some propagandists' estimates, wrote W. D. Borrie, but the Australian people would not be willing to absorb such numbers without regard to the quality of life to which the existing population had become accustomed.

Griffith Taylor, a British geographer who had resided in Australia for twenty years, made what was probably the most scientific assessment on the peopling of Australia. He viewed racial differences as based on prejudice and regarded racial assimilation as quite feasible in Australia. He estimated that Australia could comfortably support twenty million people. This was the most generally accepted figure among Australia's demographers, then. It still is today.

Most Japanese studies believed that Australia not only had living space, but also abundant economic resource potential. They opined that Australia could contribute a lot more to solving the ills of the times, such as over-population and lack of raw materials, and concluded that Australia had to be developed. While some conceded that Australia had made certain progress in dairy farming, mining, and forestry, as well as in the textile, glass and weaving industries, they maintained that the low population level thwarted any hope for building large-scale industries which could make Australia a successful exporting country. Japan offered a way out of this predicament. She had what Australia needed: skilled labour, high technology, textiles, and light and heavy industrial products. Australia, on the other hand, could provide Japan with the necessary raw materials of wool, wheat, and iron. Here was the basis for a mutually profitable new relationship of give-and-take.

Australia had a splendid economic future before her, ran the standard argument, but for the lack of manpower. Australia's heavy industry, particularly the steel industry, was late in developing because the main iron ore deposits at Iron Knob in South Australia and Yampi Sound in Western Australia were almost inaccessible. Australians would not be able to exploit their resources without the Asian worker. Australians were idly hoarding space and raw materials. But not only Japanese held such views. British Minister of State Alfred Duff Cooper said as much to Cecil Brown, the American war correspondent for Columbia Broadcasting System, over lunch in Singapore in January 1941: 'The Australians refuse to allow immigrants to come into their country because they are afraid of unemployment. They have failed to develop their country'.

Current opinion in Japan readily accepted the view that Australia's future lay in the northern tropical parts of Western Australia, Queensland, and the Northern Territory, if worked with coloured labour. The history of Australian land development showed that Australians had needed Asian help before, wrote Kawaji Kanichi in an article on 'The Geopolitical Structure of Australia' in 1943. He cited as an example the Yampi Sound iron ore deposits which had been developed by the Japanese and were temporarily in their hands from 1934 to 1938. On the agricultural side, droughts and floods were the Australian cancer. The continent needed irrigation systems. Only the Murray River region in the south had a flood control system that could irrigate 700,000 acres of land, but that area had proven unsuitable for rice growing because of excessive rain. Perhaps Kawaji knew of the case of Takasuka, a Japanese immigrant, who since 1906 had been battling the elements trying to grow rice on the Murray River with little success; he returned to Japan in 1939, leaving his sons to continue in the tomato growing business. If, however, the Australians developed irrigation systems in the tropical northern monsoon regions, they would be able to feed the whole of Asia. The experience gained by irrigating Queensland's tropical areas would furthermore lead to a revolution in cattle breeding all over Australia. Advancing these great schemes required Japanese technology, capital, and labour power. Australia was saddled with two big problems: would she be able to develop her tropical regions without the coloured man, and would she be able to keep him out?

Yes, said J. W. Gregory, a geologist originally from Scotland, who published extensively on the physical and human geography of Australia. The northern tropics were in no need of coloured labour. White settlers could cultivate the arid land and stand the climate as well. Asia had no claim to admission and was not to be tempted to undertake the difficult task of colonizing the unoccupied areas of tropical Australia. Gregory was also a prominent author on the peopling of Australia and vociferously favoured the White Australia policy: 'If the coloured races are to hold all Asia and Africa and to be predominant in South America, it would appear only fair that the three smallest of the continents— Europe, North America, and Australia—should be assigned to the white race'.

Asking for the opening of the large tropical regions in Australia was an old grievance. As he had done in 1918, Konoe Fumimaro (1891–1945), who was to be prime minister for the second and third time in 1940–41, pointed out in the February 1933 issue of the popular magazine *Kingu* that the main cause of war was the unfair territorial arrangements between 'status quo' powers and the 'have not' nations bent on destroying the status quo. His examples both times included Australia with her vast territory, who would not admit a single Japanese immigrant. He asked: 'How can one call this a just state of affairs?' A non-militarist and a disciple of pacifist Christian scholar Uchimura Kanzo, University of Tokyo Professor of Economics Yanaihara Tadao, who in 1936 saw 'Japan's economic advance into the south-west Pacific as an inevitable and necessary course', explained a year later in his article 'Taiheiyō no heiwa to Eikoku' (England and peace in the Pacific) that the people of England, Australia, and the Netherlands had to be aware that Pacifists of whatever shade in Japan would demand the economic opening of the south-west Pacific. And Ishibashi Tanzan, the editor-in-chief of the influential economic magazine *Tōyō keizai shinpō*, argued in the March 1938 issue that, although Britain held vast possessions throughout the world, these were cruelly closed to Japan's peaceful economic advance. Could not Britain adopt a policy of opening the doors of her territories? To these commonly held strong views of otherwise liberal thinkers must be added that of Tsurumi Yūsuke, intellectual heir apparent to Nitobe Inazō, a progressive conservative (liberal in the British sense), orator, writer, and admirer of Lovelett, Woodrow Wilson, and Winston Churchill.

In the keynote chapter of the book *Gōshū no shizen to shakai* (The land and society of Australia), which he edited in January 1943 under the auspices of the Pacific Society (of which he was senior director), an interesting section outlines a grand design for future immigration into Australia. Tsurumi was much concerned about Japan's acute problem of overpopulation and captivated by the immigration question in all its aspects. In his mind there were two ways to solve the racial immigration problem in Australia. One was to abolish the White Australia policy and let Australians and Japanese freely live and prosper together in the eastern parts of the continent, even though this might result in a racial mix desired by neither.

A better way would be to allocate Japanese immigrants a special region in which they could live. It would be difficult to have the white people move out of New South Wales and Victoria, the most liveable colonies from a climatic point of view. Northern Queensland offered itself as a better place where least friction would occur. Tsurumi knew Australia from his travels (he was travelling in Australia on a World Education Council trip when war broke out in China in 1937) and notes that Queensland's ex-governor had apparently approved of Japanese immigration into that region, as had Australian Catholics, and Melbourne University Professor of Economics David B. Copland, Prime Minister John Curtin's top economic advisor, with whom Tsurumi was well acquainted.

Tsurumi had ambitious plans when it came to the number of Japanese immigrants to be sent to Australia. He calculated that one 10,000 ton ship could carry 2,000 immigrants to the promised shores, and that it could do the run six times in one year. This would amount to an annual figure of 12,000 people for each 10,000 ton vessel used; transporting 600,000 Japanese immigrants to Australia in one year would necessitate fifty ships. He lamented that even if the war were over, Japan lacked the ships for such a large scheme. At the most the Japanese could plan to send 200,000 people in available ships. But he was dreaming in terms of dispatching 10 million farmers to Australia over a period which, according to his calculation, would span 16.5 years.

This number was loftier even than the total in Prime Minister Hirota Kōki's successful petition in August 1936 for a twenty-year plan to settle one million farm families in Manchuria. It moreover reminds one of the visions of Katō Kanji (1884–1965), the farm educator and leading advocate of large-scale emigration expansionism in the 1930s. But although similar in scale, Tsurumi's outlook was worlds apart from Katō's narrow and militant agrarianist views which shunned modern technology and promoted mystical Shinto values steeped in the *kokutai* (national polity) philosophy and the return to the proven method of sickle and hoe. Tsurumi was well aware of the advanced agricultural technology in Australia, birthplace of H.V. McKay's stripper-harvester in the 1890s, the stump-jump plough, and the rotary hoe. One could not just dump masses of uneducated Japanese farmers on Australia. Experienced Japanese agriculturalists from the cotton farms and coffee plantations in the Americas would be selected to lead the Japanese immigrants and promote the development of Australia. To these would be added pastoralists from Hokkaido to enhance cattle breeding and increase the import of cheese and butter to Japan.

Nor did this Japanese thinker view Australia as the domain solely of the Yamato farmer. Australia would have to let in Chinese, Indian, German, and Italian immigrants, too. Australia's population was sadly stagnating at the 7.5 million level which even in ten years from 1943 would not change because of the unreasonable White Australia policy. This sorry condition deprived the Australians even of protecting their own land which, if opened up, could possibly carry more than the envisaged twenty million population—perhaps fifty million.

Tsurumi's project loses some of its loftiness when seen in the context of earlier Australian plans to bring in Japanese immigrants on a large scale to cultivate her northern areas. Sixty-five years earlier, the South Australian Wilton Hack, with the consent of his government which paid his trip to Tokyo, unfurled plans at the Japanese Foreign Ministry in February 1877 for the first large-scale immigration project. Hack negotiated to bring in not coolie labour but the more respectable classes —some three to four hundred farmers, skilled workers, artisans, even aristocrats—who, he was convinced, would make good colonists to help open up and develop the vast Northern Territory of Australia. And in 1896, John Langdon Parsons, Lower House Representative of the South

Australian Parliament from 1890 to 1893 and then Japan's Honorary Consul in Adelaide, discussed with the Foreign Minister in Tokyo plans to sell to Japanese capitalists land in the Northern Territory 'and to induce them to send thither a large body of Japanese settlers'. Parsons, who had been Government Resident at Darwin from 1884 to 1890, believed that Caucasians were unable to work the tropics, and championed the use of coloured labour to develop the Northern Territory.

Both schemes, however, came to naught: Hack's because the Japanese government at that time resisted emigration in large numbers to protect its nationals from exploitation and probably because of national unrest caused by the Satsuma Rebellion; Parsons's because the South Australian Government, then already committed to a White Australia, disapproved of the entirely unofficial and private enterprise of its citizen. But the Hack and the Parsons proposals lived on in Japan's Australia-related literature, and were especially seized upon in the 1940s. Hack's blueprint, in particular, got special coverage, as in Tsurumi's book, which translated S. H. Roberts's original 1924 research on the Hack scheme in full.

Australian scholars have since reviewed Roberts's findings, long-lived in English print too, and criticized him for overemphasizing the scheme's official nature. But their corrections admit that the South Australian Cabinet was 'certainly prepared to accept Japanese migrants and . . . that had Japanese immigration to the Northern Territory then taken place . . . it might have changed the whole nature of the social and economic development of Australia'.

Away with 'White Australia'!

The discussion of Australia's retarded state of development was seen as closely related to the problem of the White Australia policy. Ever since the enforcement of that policy at the turn of the century, practically every Japanese book on Australia had a chapter or section devoted to this problem. They usually conformed to highlighting in a critical way the racial policy's history, motivation, and function as an important tenet of Australian foreign policy. Japanese writers pointed out how little the Australian population had grown since retired naval officer Arthur Phillip had brought 750 convicts from London to Australia in 1788. Fifty-five years later these pioneers had increased to a community of only 6.8 million—99 per cent of whom were white and 97 per cent British—an insufficient number to develop the Australian continent.

Miyata Mineichi, in a typical chapter entitled 'Hakugō shugi' (White Australia), tells how the shut-out policy was effectively enforced by way of a discriminating dictation test which prospective immigrants could be made to take in any European language. It was a foolproof method to keep out all Asians—and even undesirable Europeans, as in the case of the Dutchman who knew seven languages but was administered the fifty-word dictation test in Gaelic. Invited by the New South Wales Government to teach at Sydney University, Miyata had lived in Sydney for several years. The dust jacket of his book, *Gōshū Renpō* (The Commonwealth of Australia), described him as a 'renowned expert of Australia' and advertised Australia as a country with land and resources that could support a population of 400,000,000, adding: 'Japan cannot think of tomorrow without knowing Australia'.

To Miyata, the White Australia policy was above all a social policy: racist, superstitious, and egotistical. He cites the Australian political leader Sir Henry Parkes's public refusal to let any 'inferior' people into Australia, and Labour leader Z. C. Watson's strong argument for bolting the door in 1901 for fear of possible racial contamination. He also quotes the Australian magazine *Britain*:

Australia opposes all Asian, African and Kanaka immigration for the simple reason that they work for lower wages; white workers would have to adjust to these and their living standard would sink; secondly, Australia would be taking in lower cultures. If these immigrants married Australian girls, the white race would become low and vulgar; their offspring would badly affect Australia, perpetuate the worst in both races and produce a hybrid mongrel race. That is why we oppose coloured immigration.

Another lecturer, of Doshisha University, Wada Shunji, who had studied geography under the prominent Kyoto University geopolitician, Komaki Saneshige, pilloried the White Australia policy as a British Machiavellan machination. Australia was fast drifting away from the motherland—already seven-eighths of her population were born in Australia—and only from pictures and books did Australians know about Great Britain. But that imperial country did not wish Australia to follow the American way of 1783 into secession and independence. British 'divide and rule' tactics were fostering separatism and disunion among the six Australian colonies, which Wada saw reflected, for example, in the various colonies' different train gauges that prevented smooth transport connections across the continent. Crossing from Sydney to Perth one had to change trains three or four times. Great Britain, moreover, supported the discriminatory immigration restrictions to prevent Asians from developing Australian manufacturing and mining industries as a sound base for an independent national defence. Australia was to be kept dependent upon Britain's factories and the navy, without whose protection she could not exist a single day. To Wada the White Australia policy was nothing but a crafty British plot to keep the continent in a lasting flutter of servitude.

By contrast, semi-official and governmental books debating the White Australia policy in the early 1940s denied themselves that range of imagination. The Ministry of Agriculture and Forestry's Research Section for Southern Resources' *Gōshū oyobi Nyūjirando ni okeru hakujin ni kan suru chōsa* (A study of white people in Australia and New Zealand), for example, was a sober study that based itself primarily on the translated *Official Yearbook of Australia 1940*; and the South Seas Economic Institute's careful statistical evaluation of Australia's immigration restrictions in *Gōshū jinko no kōsei* (The organization of the Australian people), published in January 1943, was void of the usual Greater East Asia War rhetoric.

In a finer vein of philosophical differentiation, Okakura Koshirō declared that the White Australia policy was an economic, not a social problem. The policy appeared racial only on the surface. It was fundamentally materialistic in character and lacked the spiritual base of a racial social policy. How could it be racial? Australia was still too young a country to pretend that it had the sound social cohesion of a *Gemeinschaft*. The Australian people had a long way to go before, as a people, they could lay claim to their land in the sense of the *'Blut und Boden'* (blood and soil) philosophy, which in the fascist philosophy of those years distinguished, for example, the German and the Japanese peoples.

Still, most Japanese perceptions were critical of the White Australia policy, which they thought had proved enduring only because of powerful Western backing, and which, by 1942–1943, appeared to have run its course. Izumi Shinsuke put it in a nutshell in *Gōshū shi* (A history of Australia), published in May 1942. The basis of Australia's foreign policy was to protect her White Australia policy. Living in isolation with a small population and having all she needed, she was complacently guarding her white shores. Three conditions had enabled her to protect her White Australia policy: the establishment of the League of Nations designed to abolish imperialistic wars, a Monroe doctrine in the South Pacific which kept the Australasian island world white, and the strengthening of a navy which depended on the British Empire. Interestingly, the young John G. Crawford, who after the war became the leading promoter of Japanese–Australian economic relations, said as much at the 1938 Summer School Session of foreign policy specialists, in Sydney:

Australia is a Pacific Power complete with colonies and a navy which some consider adequate. However, it is a small power with a large territory, a small population, a high standard of living, a not un-provocative immigration policy based on racial discrimination, and a comfortable feeling that, as a member of the British Empire, all these things are secure possessions.

'Australia Belongs in the Greater East Asia Co-Prosperity Sphere'

Japanese air raids on Australian coastal targets profoundly changed that comfortable feeling in March 1942. Madarame Fumio, fresh out of university and teaching history at a junior high school, was just then finishing the foreword to his remedial treatise *Gōshū shinryaku shi* (A history of the invasion of Australia). According to him, the British Empire's strength had been tested at Singapore and the spell of *Pax Britannica* that had sustained Australia was broken. But this would prove a boon for Australians, for their country had been nothing but a dumping ground of the British.

The history of Australia was a history of British invasion, he argued, and Great Britain's invasion of Australia had been an invasion of Asia for, long before the Union Jack was hoisted on those shores, Australia had been part of Asia, 'part of us'. With her snail-like world-view, Australia had been stagnating in her environment like a withdrawn escargot, her shell the Pacific and Indian Oceans. However, oceans no longer acted as 'screens', they now functioned as 'links', a geopolitical fact that was going to rewrite her history. Australia could do much better. Endowed with plenty of natural riches, she already had the best wool, ranked second in production of lead, and fifth in gold and silver. It was not that Australia was spiritless or inactive, only overly cautious, self-satisfied, and unambitious; like a senile infant. Australia had to be made right again. She had to reflect on her true geopolitical nature. What was the cure? 'Bring her into the Greater East Asia Co-Prosperity Sphere'.

When Madarame referred to the linkage concept, he was using rhetoric from the principles of the 'New Order in East Asia' policy enunciated by Prime Minister Konoe Fumimaro on 3 November 1938. That policy's ideas relied heavily on nativistic concepts supplied by the Dai Ajia Kyō kai (Greater Asia Association). But when it evolved into the 'Greater East Asia Co-Prosperity Sphere' policy two years later, the 'Sphere' proclamation was imbued with economic scientific notions advanced by members of the Shōwa Kenkyū Kai (Shōwa Study Group). Between 1938 and 1940 the stronger pull of the Shōwa Study Group's more scientifically regional outlook transformed and extended the earlier proclamation of a 'New Order in East Asia' into the 'Greater East Asia Co-Prosperity Sphere', a term first officially used by Foreign Minister Matsuoka Yōsuke in a radio statement at 12:30 p.m. on 1 August 1940. The 'Greater Asianism' championed by the 'New Order' policy aimed at a closed regional solidarity based on the notions of geographical closeness, Pan-Asianist blood relations, and anti-modern theories of the state as promoted by the Asianist Nakayama Masaru. In contrast, the Shōwa Study Group propagated an open-ended regionalism and a theory for building a mutually complementary regional economy which depended on the participation of the peoples within the region and on accommodating their nationalist desires, as proposed by the political scientist, Rōyama Masamichi.

Both 'New Order' and 'Greater East Asia Co-Prosperity' terminologies were freely used by the *nan'yō* writers focusing on Australia. Those authors who suggest that 'by undergoing a rebirth (*kōsei*), Australia would become Asia's Australia through *musubu* (tying together)', clearly reflect the emotional tone of the Nakayama Pan-Asianist school. In their view, 'Australia had to cooperate with building the New Order of the Greater East Asia Co-Prosperity Sphere because the land's original tribes had always been part of the Greater East Asian peoples'.

On the other hand, it is significant that Rōyama Masamichi, the leading intellectual force, if not the father of 'Greater East Asian' regionalism and the extended 'Sphere' idea, hardly mentions Australia as a prospective member of the Greater East Asia Co-Prosperity Sphere in his numerous writings. He was well aware that the envisaged Sphere did not exist as a coherent economic region, but was made up of two rather different north-south regions, the latter of which overlapped the economic regions of the United States and Great Britain. His prime concern was how to integrate the Southeast Asian economy into the Sphere so that it would achieve at least part of that complementarity which Japan already enjoyed with the Sphere's eastern region in Manchuria and China. He suggested first consolidating the region politically before integrating it economically, and ignored Australia in his breakdown of the Sphere's countries, recognizing it instead as belonging to the United States and British power spheres.

But the average Japanese Australianologist was less careful in the early 1940s. He was writing at a time of boom and victory whose fanfare few could resist. In 1942 it seemed that the status quo was effectively broken, never again to be mended. The future promised new 'continental configurations, in Europe as well as in the Asian–Pacific region. The establishment of a regional framework for the Greater East Asia Co-Prosperity Sphere—in 1940 only a theory which had been expected to take decades to realize—was already a military reality. The new age also promised radical changes in the racial equilibrium of the region. There was no reason to doubt the doom of White Australia after the Coral Sea battle on May 8, which the censored press reported as a great victory for Japan.

It is therefore not surprising that, in writing about Australia at a time when press reports of victory were taken at face-value, authors often got carried away with their new subject of Australia and the Greater East Asia Co-Prosperity Sphere. According to an interview with Okakura Koshirō, even had someone wanted to write a sober and factual book on Australia, he had to pledge himself to the Greater East Asia ideology if he wanted to pass the strict assessment of the Censorship Department of the Home Ministry's Police Bureau: if not in heart, at least in appearance; if not in the main text, in the forewords and afterwords. This must be kept in mind when perusing the writers' opinions in 1942–1943 about why Australia ought to belong to the Greater East Asia Co-Prosperity Sphere. There is little of the sinister in their tendentious reasoning, but plenty of opportunism, misconceptions, and a sense of righteousness in the euphoria of victory. There also are a few rare sparkles of truth.

After the fall of Singapore, one pervasive theme in Japan's Australia literature was that of historical injustice being righted. The white man's sole claim to the southern continent since its discovery in the sixteenth century was challenged. Australia was a 'new continent' and a 'new colony' only from the European point of view, but God had let coloured people live there from earliest times onward: it was not the special sphere of white people. Australians had embarked on an imperialistic policy in the Australasian island world since the 1880s and, although the Japanese navy had helped them secure their naval lines in World War I, they had shown themselves ungrateful at the end of the war, when their prime minister had spoken out vituperatively against any Japanese claims to equality at Versailles. Just as Commodore Perry's visit had once opened the eyes of the Japanese, the Japanese fire-bell was about to awaken the Australians.

Justice was now being done. War was repairing an old historical condition and Australia could not avert the great avalanche of righteousness that was now sweeping the Greater East Asian region. It is in the light of this hope of bringing to an end strongly felt racial injustice in the Asian–Pacific region, that one can understand the glee with which firebrand works (such as the Investigation Committee of the Southern Region's Industries' chauvinistic book, *Gōshū* [Australia]) predicted that Great Britain and the United States would have to give up Australia to the Imperial soldiers protected by the gods (*shinpei*). Japan was simply too strong and Australia would suffer the same fate as Corregidor. 'Ah! if only it had not been for the seclusion policy . . . the southern countries would have been in Japan's power sphere from the beginning and the British and Americans expelled long ago', mused Matsunaga Sotoo in Melbourne's Botanic Gardens, shortly before he and his compatriots were repatriated on the *Kashima Maru*. He recounts how on deck they had recited poems by Suganuma Teifu about the deeds of old Japanese adventurers such as Yamada Nagamasa, Zeniya Gobei, Takadaya Kahei, Kato Kiyomasa, and Toyotomi Hideyoshi.

Pulling out on 15 August 1941 on the same boat for officials and business executives and their families was Nishikawa Chūichirō, another long-term resident of Australia who had worked in the branch offices of Takashimaya Ida Trading Co. in Melbourne and Sydney. He sounds as bitter as Matsunaga about the forced evacuation in his book *Saikin no Gōshū jijō* (The recent situation of Australia), published in September 1942. 'Australians are haughty . . . we have been restraining ourselves, the time has now come to rectify things at one stroke . . . The Australians must surely be realizing how gravely they have been miscalculating the situation', he wrote. The Japanese were already at Rabaul; they had sunk many Australian ships, such as the *Australia*, and damaged heavily the flagship *Canberra*, in the battles of the Coral Sea and the Solomon Islands; and they had bombed Darwin and attacked Sydney and Newcastle with submarines. Australia was slowly being isolated and reduced to the wretched state of an orphan.

In fact, 'Australia, orphan of the South Pacific', was a recurring expression in the Australia-related literature of 1942. The Australian Prime Minister John Curtin had provided the root for the epithet in his public statement on 27 December 1941: 'Without any inhibitions of any kind, I make it quite clear that Australia looks to America, free of any pangs as to our traditional links or kinship with the United Kingdom'. In Okakura Koshirō's rendition, Australia begged Roosevelt to pick her up: 'Without any inhibitions', cried Curtin, 'help the Orphan of the Pacific!'

The general picture given was that of an Australia totally abandoned by her foster parents, the United States and Great Britain. The British in particular, whose collapse appeared imminent, were described as having utterly forsaken Australia. Australian troops had been badly treated in Greece, Crete, Hong Kong, and Malaya, and in Singapore they had been left to do all the fighting on one-third the salary of British soldiers, while the British had been trying to do a bolt. But with Burma about to fall and all of China occupied, there was nothing to be gained by fighting on. Australians should instead heed the warm-hearted counsel of Prime Minister Tōjō and enter quickly the Greater East Asia Co-Prosperity Sphere. They should not miss this golden opportunity; if they failed to accept it, they would regret it for a thousand years. In Matsunaga's view, the little bird, Australia, now lay prostrate at the mercy of its captor. 'Do not make him kill it!' he warned; 'Curtin! make an Australia for the Aus- tralians! Abandon Churchill and Roosevelt quickly! Is there not a Prime Minister like Pibun of Thailand in your country?'

These ideas were published in December, one year after Pearl Harbor, when Japanese writers still believed in Japanese military glory, knowing little or nothing of the draw at Coral Sea, the defeat of Midway, or the battles of Guadalcanal and the Solomons. Although deluded by cen- sored news of unbroken victories, they were informed correctly that Australia had sided with the main enemy, the United States. Australian leaders had offered General McArthur the continent as a base from which he could 'return'. This made Australia a geo-strategical liability. The southern continent had to be gathered into the Greater East Asia Co-Prosperity Sphere, if only from geopolitical considerations.

Australians had allied themselves with the enemy, wrote the Investi- gation Committee for Industries in the Southern Region (Nanpō Sangyō

Chōsakai) in July 1942. It was not permissible to let them use their continent as a future base for the main enemies, America and Britain. Australia had to be included in the Greater East Asia plans. Her absence would be as damaging as a small crack in a great dam. Even from the Australian point of view, they should join for their own good sake. Australians knew very well that as long as their country was not a member of Greater East Asia they would always have to fear the Sphere.

'Our victorious airforce has rained bombs on Darwin at long last . . . Even Commander M. Collins, the American naval observer already stationed for two years in Darwin to direct war operations against Japan, has been unable to foresee the gradual destruction of the Pacific enemy. It is news received with great emotion', wrote Miyazaki Ryō in the March number of *Shin Ajia*, one of those obscure little magazines that proliferated as the outlets for pent-up feelings of grandeur or frustration in the glorious early 1940s. Miyazaki urged Australia to give up and prove that the nation no longer supported British imperialism. Being part of the Greater East Asia Co-Prosperity Sphere would help Australia overcome her traditional feelings of distance and isolation, he argued, and instill her with a new geographical sense of being.

Much was made of Australia as an enemy base in 'triangular geopolitics'. The Tōkyō Nichi Nichi Shinbun Tōabu publication, *Daitōasen ni okeru Jūkei, Indō, Gōshū* (Chungking, India, and Australia in the Greater East Asian War), maintained that the East Asia Co-Prosperity Sphere could not be realized with Chungking (Free China), India, and Australia outside the sphere. Two of its chapters dealt with the problem of Australia as an enemy base 'soon to be embraced by the Japanese war flame'. They appraised the strategic implications of two triangular sets of bases in the Indian and Pacific Oceans perceived as threats to the establishment of the Greater East Asia Co-Prosperity Sphere.

The 'British triangle' in the West stretched from Colombo to Singapore to Sydney. The 'United States triangle' in the East ran from Hawaii to the Philippines to New Caledonia. Of these six Anglo-Saxon bases, only the westernmost, Colombo, and the easternmost, Hawaii, were still in operation. With Singapore captured and Australian vulnerability clearly demonstrated by the Japanese midget-submarine attacks on Sydney, the Western triangle was considered broken. But it appeared to be reforming in another new giant triangle that now spanned the Indian Ocean from South Australia to Colombo to Cape Town in South Africa. Likewise, the Eastern triangle was fractured, with the Philippines in Japanese hands and New Caledonia soon to be taken care of; but the new United States triangle was re-establishing itself between Hawaii, Panama, and South Africa, where it converged with the new British triangle and continued to pose a grave geopolitical threat to Japan's East Asia Co-Prosperity Sphere.

The geopolitically inclined Iguchi Ichirō, who taught journalism at

Sophia University in Tokyo, stressed the importance of Thursday Island off Australia's northernmost Cape York in his study 'Kita Gōshū no chiseigakuteki kōsatsu' (A geopolitical analysis of Northern Australia). He considered it a significant island speck that prevented the Arafura Sea (between New Guinea and northern Australia) from linking up with the Daitōakai (Greater East Asian Sea), as the Pacific Ocean was then called. The tiny island constituted a key point in the Anglo-Saxon defence line Singapore–Darwin–Thursday Island–Port Moresby, which had been greatly obstructing the construction of the Greater East Asia Co-Prosperity Sphere. But with Singapore and Portuguese Timor (on the western fringes of the Arafura Sea) finally in the hands of valiant Imperial soldiers, that defence line was now effectively broken and reduced to the minor triangle of Darwin–Thursday Island–Port Moresby. Even this configuration would not be able to hold itself much longer and would soon disappear. The Arafura Sea would then cease to be a dividing surface and turn into a bridge leading to 'the uncultivated large space region' of Australia's three northern promontories: the Kimberleys, Arnhemland, and the York Peninsula.

There was a lot of Haushofer-jargon in these Japanese expostulations of the 1940s. And had Haushofer read Japanese, he might have praised Nipponese geopolitics beyond the few kind words of 'coming very close to the level of German geopolitical scholarship'—plaudits he had once allowed a book on human geography by distinguished British geographer James Fairgrieve. For a large body of Japanese international political writing was borrowing assiduously from his renowned Munich School of Geopolitics. This despite Rōyama Masamichi's reservations about the blander shades of imperialism in Haushofer's work, or the Kyoto geopolitician Komaki Saneshige's attempt at Japanizing the German pseudo science into the Oriental *kōdō*-codex of an 'Imperial Way'.

Haushofer's language applied itself easily to the Japanese condition in the early 1940s. Bitter about his country's defeat at Versailles (because as a Major General in 1919 he had been compelled to surrender Germany's unbroken Eastern front) Haushofer thereafter concocted geopolitical theories which in the 1930s popularized concepts such as 'soil mastery', 'organic frontiers', 'shatter zones', 'spatial determinism', and 'large space struggle'. These were as truth to the Japanese in the early flush of victory in 1942, when Japan was pushing successfully into the Southeast Asian 'shatter zone', 'mastering the soil' at Khota Baru, Kuching, and Surabaya by effective assault, ever widening her 'organic frontiers' in a historic 'large space struggle'.

Authors such as Kunimatsu Hisaya, composer of numerous geopolitical text-books, discussed extensively the theory of living space in his book *Chiseigaku to wa nani ka?* (What is geopolitics?). He took great pains, though with no more success, to render more clearly in Japanese the misty content of the nebulous tenets of Germany's top geopoliticians

Karl Haushofer, Otto Maull, Erich Obst, and Herman Lautensach. To all appearances empires were on the move, the old Anglo-Saxon dominated order was dying, and Haushofer's theories were right. The colonial injustices committed by the ABCD 'have' powers, which encircled the Japanese homeland, were being swept away by the victorious Japanese liberating forces, bearers of a new order for the 'have-not' nations.

In this atmosphere of swift moves on the world-map, when German geopoliticians were speaking of Eastern Europe as lying within the 'European law of geopolitics' and Japanese geopoliticians talked about Australia as being bonded to the 'Greater East Asian law of geopolitics', it is not surprising that otherwise scholarly writers such as Itō Takashi were soon suggesting that 'just as under Mussolini Italian immigrants were successfully making the desert zone of northern Libya into a liveable area, making Australia's northern desert zone bloom would be no problem for Japanese immigrants'. After all, Haushofer had already insinuated as much in 1930 in his *Journal for Geopolitics*:

> The ultimate solution of Japan's problem of overpopulation is expansion into the spheres of least resistance . . . At this time, Japan's strategy still cautions her against a direct attack on Australia. But it should not be forgotten that the tropical north and northeast of Australia today give shelter to only a few thousand white men, although they could offer homesteads for thirty million people.

To be sure, it was not only Haushofer, his troupe of German geopoliticians, and Japanese disciples, who wrote in ever more conclusive terms about Australia. Important United States geographers, too, were inclined to settle the case in favour of Japan. A leading scholar in political geography, Isaiah Bowman, for example, wrote: 'The Japanese are tropical colonizers . . . Only the barrier of restrictive laws prevents them from figuring more largely in the population of northern Australia . . . in case of successful war, territorial control might follow'. Distinguished Professor of Geography at Clark University, Samuel Van Valkenburg, pointed out: 'In the north, reaching to the equator, is dynamic, overcrowded Japan, which could make good use of Australia as an outlet for its people . . . In the future will Australia be allowed to remain empty?'

And N. J. Spykman, towering over American geopolitics, believed in 1942 that there was plenty of room for Asian immigration into the desirable tropical zone of Northern Australia: 'The blueprint for the future is a sketch of Japanese hegemony over the Western Pacific rimland from Siberia to Tasmania in an economic empire that will include 600 million people under the military and political domination of Tokyo. Australia and New Zealand will cease to be white man's countries, they will be opened up for Asiatic settlement and racially assimilated into the new

Oriental world'. Such a blueprint, which Spykman accepted freely, could have come straight from the dust jacket of Nanpō Sangyō Chōsakai's book *Gōshū*, which had 'New Greater Asia' drawn as a huge circle spinning within the antipodes of Lake Baikal and the Antarctic, Polynesia and Madras, with the commentary: 'Incorporation of the greater nan'yō into this "New Greater Asia" is the ideal. This union would be realized in its economic, geographical, and racial aspects under the leadership of Japan. It will shake off the invading White Peril's utilitarian burden of the past'.

History was an important ingredient in geopolitical analysis. To give an historical edge of respect, old *nan'yō* writings were dug up, reprinted, and presented as if now was their day of fulfilment. For example, Suganuma Teifu's pioneering *Dai Nippon shōgyō shi* (History of greater Japan's commerce) was resurrected from the 1890s by the publishing house of Iwanami Shoten and republished in 1940 together with his previously unpublished article 'Nihon no tōnan no yume' (Dream of Japan's southern lands) that propagated Japanese aggrandizement in the Philippines and the South Sea islands. Naval hero Hirose Takeo's *Kōnan shiki* (Personal record of a southern voyage), with its interesting passages on Australia as he saw it in 1892 was reprinted in 1942. Mishima Kazuo's harmless travelogue *Gōshū oyobi Indo* (Australia and India) of 1891 was republished in January 1943; it was dressed up in the foreword and afterword to look as if already half a century earlier Mishima had been nudging Japan into the struggle of the Greater East Asia War and egging her on towards the prizes of Australia and India. Little did it matter that the early *nan'yō* writers had viewed expansion primarily in terms of trade and legal immigration. In the early 1940s they were hailed as the torch-bearers of a traditional line of expansionists whose grand dreams were finally being realized by force.

The work of Shiga Shigetaka, doyen of the 'southward advance' exponents, who stands at the beginning of modern Japan's southward march, was particularly distorted. Although his message in 1887 had indeed been expansion into the southern region, in 1942 his epoch-making work, *Nan'yō jiji* (Current affairs in the South), was depicted as a blueprint for Japanese expansion by whatever means. Completely ignored was the fact that Shiga had advocated not territorial aggrandizement and military conquest but expansion by commerce through international trade and within the defence system of British naval strength. The utterance 'Australia belongs to Asia' (*Gōshū ga Ajia no mono de aru*), which Okakura Koshirō used to frame the opening and closing phrases of his 312-page book *Gōshū no shakai to keizai* (Economy and society of Australia), was ascribed to Uchimura Kanzo, Shiga's fellow intellectual from Sapporo Agricultural College. Even Fukuzawa Yukichi (1834–1901) was credited with a flair for geopolitics, simply for having pointed out in 1869, in *Sekai kunizukushi* (A bird's eye view of the world), that Australia was a southern part of Asia. Along with Yoshida Shōin and the late Tokugawa geographer Mitsukuri Shōgo, he too was enshrined as one of the forebears of Japanese geopolitics.

A more careful perusal of the geopolitical articles about Australia churned out after Pearl Harbor gives one the impression of hastily conceived pieces fashioned by geographers and would-be geopoliticians dressing otherwise dry geographical and political matter with flashy international political jargon borrowed from the Munich school of geopolitics. There is, for example, Iguchi Ichirō's lengthy *Kita Gōshū no chiseigakuteki kōsatsu* (A geopolitical analysis of North Australia). Serialized in *Taiheiyō* (The Pacific Ocean) from March to May 1942, it either lacks the sixth chapter in the middle part or else is wrongly numbered, and introduces mainly commonplace facts about Australian geography without offering a conclusion. Other articles covered: 'My plan for Australia', 'Australian lifestyles', 'A clue for Australia', 'The isolation of Australia as seen from the shipping point of view', 'The Australian people's cultural and spiritual life', 'The Greater East Asia War and the problem of Australian naturalization of Japanese and Chinese', and 'Our bombing of strategic points in Australia'. Some of them concluded prosaically as Wada Shunji in 'The problem of developing Australia's tropics': 'settling Australia's tropical north has failed because of the climate and the White Australia policy', and 'Australia's tropics are close to the very center of the Greater East Asia Co-Prosperity Sphere and on the way to getting all the spotlight in the future'.

Others swung in the opposite direction of excessive imagination. Professor Komaki Saneshige went overboard in his lead article in the journal *Chirigaku* (Geography), 'A geopolitical overview of Greater East Asia', when he suggested renaming the continents: the Americas were 'East Asia', Africa 'Southwest Asia', Australia 'South Asia', and Europe a peninsular extension of Asia proper. He went further: 'There are no seven seas. There is only one sea and it is connected with Japan, where the sun is rising. All the oceans are henceforth to be recognized as the Great Japanese Sea'. But this was shortly after the fall of Singapore when Anglo-Saxon domination appeared doomed. And Komaki may have felt something that others had expressed before him, when in the perspective of that moment he went beyond the American Josiah Strong, who in 1900 had written that the Anglo-Saxon was destined to turn the Pacific Ocean into 'an Anglo-Saxon sea', or Lord Tweedmouth, who had said in 1907: 'The sea is the link that joins us together . . . There is one sea, there is one Empire, and there is one Navy'.

Otherwise, there is little in these geopolitical writings that would have matched invasion scenarios conjured up by Australians in the past half-century. Search as one may, imaginary scenes of Japanese fighting in Australia, such as one can find in the related Japanese literature on Hawaii, remained the soliloquy extravagance of the diarist. The naval

officer, Nakahara Yoshimasa, for example, nicknamed 'King of the South
Seas', imagined a defeated Britain bringing the Empire's remaining
troops to Australia. While Japan is occupying Borneo, Malaya, and
Indonesia, Commonwealth diehards array themselves with United
States contingents along the Western world's last line of defence—
across Eastern Australia—to give battle against the invading Japanese
soldiers.

Other than the geopolitical imperative which demanded the inclusion of
Australia in the Sphere for strategic reasons, the literature stressed that
Australia was economically dependent upon the Greater East Asia Co-
Prosperity Sphere. Blaming Australia for practising what Japan was then
establishing on a large scale, Kawaji Kanichi pointed out that Australia
since World War I had been building a closed society; she was veering
towards extreme autarky by the strict enforcement of her White Australia
policy and the Ottawa agreements of 1932, which bound her even closer
to the British Empire. Would it not be far better if Australia used her
natural resources to contribute to mankind and shook hands with the
Greater East Asia Co-Prosperity Sphere? 'Australia's raw materials are a
desirable asset', he wrote, 'But we are not calling Australia simply for
economic matters. We believe Australia will understand that participation in the East Asian Co-Prosperity Sphere is the only right way. We
shall not force her'.

   That Australia was selling much but buying little from Japan was a
common complaint. Many writers saw the White Australia policy as a
barrier which, if dropped, would allow many cheap Japanese products to
enter Australia. At the same time it would enable Australia to sell more of
her products in the Greater East Asia Co-Prosperity Sphere, the gains of
which would offset any lowering of her living standard. This well-
known Australian fear would not befall their country, wrote Okakura
Koshirō, because, by consuming the cheap goods flowing in, Australians
would be able to continue to keep up a comfortable way of life. And any
small drop would not matter too much, since the Australian living standard was extravagant anyway; people did not work hard enough, labour
costs were excessive, and Australians had a 'white man' complex which
needed to be set right. They were a materialistic people practising an
extreme form of economic nationalism, and their White Australia policy,
the guardian angel of their high living standard, was criticized even by
their own economists.

   Okakura saw Australia as having three choices: to fight to the end with
Great Britain, to become a dependency of the United States, or to rise as a
politically and economically independent 'Interstate' in union with the
Greater East Asia Co-Prosperity Sphere. Japan until the war had been
buying 73 per cent of Australia's iron, 15 per cent of her wheat, and 30
per cent of her wool. As an affiliated Sphere member, Australia could

find a huge outlet for her wheat in Greater East Asia, and with Japan's quickly growing population her wool exports could easily reach 40 to 50 per cent in the Japanese market alone. By joining, Australia would prosper and benefit the Sphere, which held a potential that her traditional British market could never offer.

Replete with statistics, Okakura's last chapter 'The East Asian Co-Prosperity Sphere and Australia' is as soberly researched as his selective few sources allowed—Frederic Bentham, *Japan or Manchester?* (London,1939), H. L. Harris, *Australia's Interest and National Policy* (Melbourne, 1938), and the *Official Year Book of the Commonwealth of Australia.* He was also writing with less restraint, now that the Pacific War had broken out in December 1941. Okakura was convinced that he had found the land which Rōyama Masamichi had been trying to designate as Japan's apanage in the South; a rich southern country that offered every complementarity Japan already enjoyed with the northern Sphere countries of Manchuria and China. He saw Australia—rather than Rōyama's choice, Southeast Asia—as the perfect complementary southern partner for Japan.

Probably the most detailed study on Australia was the monumental 600-page work *Gōshū* (Australia) published by the Japanese Trading House Kanematsu Shōten in February 1943. Notably void of the run-of-the-mill 'Greater East Asia Sphere' rhetoric, except for the obligatory ornamental pledgings in the first and last pages of the book, it is the most accurate and sober study on Australia's economic situation of the early 1940s. Supervised by the Managing Director, Hayashi Sōtarō, it analyses the entire spectrum of the Australian economy—from eucalyptus oil to Broken Hill Proprietary Co. Ltd's heavy industrial productions—with exactitude and sharpened by the company's policy of taking the long view, gained from the presence of a Kanematsu office in Australia since 1890.

Kanematsu offices published a number of studies on Australia in those years, but none was as encompassing or balanced, though some were rather accurate in their predictions. Antedating by a generation the boom in Australia's mineral resources exports to Japan, Kanematsu's report *Gō shū yushutsu bōeki ni tsuite* (On Australia's export trade), for example, saw with astounding foresight in July 1942 that not only could iron be found in Australia, but also lead, zinc, copper, tungsten, and tantalite, all of which were essential for the building of a new age and needed to be fully exploited. Less accurate was the prognosis that Australian wool and wheat would be sold in decreasing quantities and that in the future the Australian continent would serve as a great whaling base for the Greater East Asia Co-Prosperity Sphere's whale catches in the Antarctic. (Instead, Australia became an important prawning and tuna station for the Japanese fishing industry after the war.)

Finally, the most concrete explanation as to the economic benefits offered by the Co-Prosperity Sphere—often dubbed 'Co-Poverty' or 'No-Prosperity' Sphere in Australia—to the southern continent can be found in Nanpō Sangyō Chōsakai's chapter on the meaning of 'Co-Prosperity' (*kyōeiteki kankei*) in *Gōshū* (Australia). Greater East Asia, it explained, needed Australia as much as Australia needed the Sphere. Without Australia, Greater East Asia would be lacking wool, leather, beef, gold, silver, copper, lead, zinc, iron ore, coal, wheat, and corn. Australia wanted to sell all that Greater East Asia coveted. If Australia stayed outside the Sphere it would benefit no one. It would mean that wool, for example, would have to be provided by Mongolia, but Mongolian sheep were noted only for their leather and the rich meat which the Mongols depended on for their livelihood. Leather would have to be imported from China or India, but it was of low quality. Gold, silver, and copper could be procured from the Philippines, but greater quantities were needed. Iron ore and smokeless coal could be exploited in the *nan'yō* region and in North China, but if Australia added minerals from her neighbouring ports it would be extremely convenient. Wheat could be imported from India, but India's export capacity depended too much on good or bad harvests to be reliable. China's wheat crops could be increased, but the total demand of Greater East Asia was enormous and Australian wheat indispensable.

The chapter ends on the advice that Australia should turn away from the United States and Great Britain and embrace the Sphere. The United States could never be a market for Australian products, because they were producing similar ones. As for Great Britain, previously Australia's best customer: even if she survived the war, she would have lost all her markets, not only in Greater East Asia but also in the Americas and even in Europe. Thus, Britain would not need Australian raw materials, much less be able to pay for them. This was also a war between the countries who wanted to preserve the gold standard and those who opposed it. Gold had already lost much of its value, and silver even more so. It was quite clear who was going to lose the war. But as long as Australia showed signs that she was going to participate in the Greater East Asia Co-Prosperity Sphere, she would be all right and suffer no great damage.

Australia's 'Ideal Future Way'

For as long as it lasted, the idea of the Greater East Asia Co-Prosperity Sphere was a vague concept, and the exact extension of its outer borders remained an obscure line in official as well as civilian minds. This was particularly evident in the case of Australia. In the few surviving documents, policymakers wondered if the fifth continent should be included in the super-sphere structure of the post World War II order. At the outset of the Pacific War, planners had found it easy to include as a prospective Sphere-member any country populated by Asians; they were less sanguine about how to fit a Western culture into the essentially Asian scheme. Significantly, one person well-versed on the Australian situation, Okakura Koshirō, wrote in December 1942: 'It appears an accepted opinion today that Australia is not a part of the Greater East Asia Co-Prosperity Sphere'.

That Australia was not destined to remain forever outside the Sphere, however, can be glimpsed in the scanty adumbrations of a few surviving ministerial research papers. On 24 July 1940, Australia appeared in a Foreign Ministry position paper submitted to the army in preparation for the conclusion of the Axis Pact in September that year. The Ministry was weary of placing Australia in the New World Order. One subparagraph ponders the problem of including India, Australia and New Zealand in the Greater East Asian New Order, but recommends at that stage against designating them as part of the more narrowly defined *nan'yō* region. The Army replied three days later, in what became the blueprint for the Axis Pact of September 1940, that Australia and New Zealand had to be thought of as one corner of the Empire's sphere of existence (*seizonken*); it was in Japan's interest not to see them controlled by a country outside the Sphere.

In a secret planning paper conceived by the Navy General Staff Research Section four months later, Australia appeared in the outermost of the three concentric circles that structured the Greater East Asia Co-Prosperity Sphere. The southern continent was categorized as an independent country linked to Japan only by economic ties and classified as one of 'those outlying areas necessary for the [Sphere's] achievement of absolute economic self-sufficiency'.

This arrangement was obscured again in a later paper on the Essence and Structure of the Nation's Home Defense drafted by the Navy Ministry's Research Section. In defining the extent of the Greater East Asia Co-Prosperity Sphere, all countries located in the Sphere's three concentric belt areas—Japan, Manchukuo, Mongolia, China; the outer *nan'yō* (roughly today's ASEAN region without the Philippines); and Burma, India, Australia, New Zealand—were crossed out with the annotation that actually these countries were not erased but that it was too early to settle the exact limits of the Sphere. Moreover, where it mentioned that the army should play a part in maintaining public peace and in preventing any landing operations by any outside enemy in the outer *nan'yō* and Australian districts, the designation 'outer *nan'yō* and the Australian districts' was crossed out and replaced by the wider designation of 'important regions within the Sphere'.

After Pearl Harbor, with the realization of the Sphere close at hand, plans of how to accommodate Australia became more detailed, if not outright fantastic. The sudden victories of the Japanese army gave the rough forecasts an urgency which revealed the planners' total unpreparedness. 'Pour a million Japanese into Australia after the war' to facilitate postwar management, suggested the 'Land Disposal Plan in the Greater East Asia Co-Prosperity Sphere' (*Daitōa kyōeiken ni okeru tochi shobun an*) conceived by the Army and Overseas Affairs Ministries in December 1941. But not before first settling there three million Chinese immigrants to expel the British through economic competition and to develop the vast land, which the Japanese alone could not do.

'All of Australia, including Tasmania and Lord Howe Island [halfway between Australia and New Zealand], would be put under the provisional control of a Governor-General for Australia', added the accompanying paper, 'Documents relating to fundamental measures to be taken in territories occupied in Southern Asia during the Greater East Asia War' (*Daitōa sensō ni yoru nanpō senkyo shochiiki zengo shori hōsaku taikō*). Although the governor-generalship would be of a civilian nature and enforced not for more than ten years, explained the more concrete 'Land disposal plan', it would be applied forcefully and allow for no autonomy. Two army divisions would keep order, with one mechanized detachment and one unit of the [army's] air force headquartered at Sydney, for despatch to various parts in Australia. A representative government for Australia could be considered only when Japan was in sufficient control of the Australian economy. 'Australia and New Zealand are important raw material countries. If we do not take them, they will in the future pose a danger to our Empire', warned the paper. Primarily targeted in the economic power transfer were British capitalists. The capital rights and interests of British corporations and of individuals who were excessively wealthy would be confiscated, and Australia's rail roads, harbours, mining and iron industries would be managed by Japan under the direct control of the governor-general.

Within the next five years, Darwin—along with the Midway and Howland Islands, New Caledonia, the Bismarck Archipelago, the Sunda, Andaman, Nicobar, and Cocos Islands, Burma, and Far Eastern Russia with Kamchatka—would have to be either 'stabilized' or seized, and Australia and India isolated, advised a singular study paper of the Total War Research Institute in January 1942. It was a preparatory document for the Institute's more elaborate 'Draft of basic plans for the establishment of the Greater East Asia Co-Prosperity Sphere', dated 27 January 1942, which proposed that the East Asiatic Sphere be divided into the Inner Sphere (Japan, Manchukuo, North China—i.e., the regions north of the Yangtze River, the Shanghai, Wuhan, Fukien region, and the coastal provinces of Far Eastern Russia); the Smaller Co-Prosperity Sphere (Eastern Siberia, China, Indochina, the *nan'yō*); and the Greater East Asia Co-Prosperity Sphere (Australia, India, and the Pacific Ocean islands). Alternatively these were called the basic Sphere (*kisoken*), the defence Sphere (*bōeiken*), and the power Sphere (*iryokuken*). The construction of the Smaller Co-Prosperity Sphere was expected to take at least twenty years, after which a gradual expansion toward the construction of the Greater East Asia Co-Prosperity Sphere would take place after recurring war with Great Britain and her allies.

Australia was to be neutralized and liberated from Great Britain without bloodshed. 'Let Australia understand the true intentions of the East Asia Co-Prosperity Sphere. By pointing out her high dependence on the Sphere, let Australia align herself with us', the Total War Research paper urged. Japan would sell Australia her machine products, fish oils, and textiles, and in turn buy Australia's wheat and wool, and offer her good offices for an entrepôt trade via Japan so that Australia would also be able to sell her wool in Russia. Through various peaceful policies Australia was to be guided into joining the Co-Prosperity Sphere. Even in the case of another war with Great Britain, pains should be taken to win Australia over as an ally without resorting to force but through the continued fostering of economic ties as in times of peace.

The draft was written when Japan's war was in full swing, and submitted as 'top secret' to Lieutenant-General Iimura Minoru, the project leader and protégé of Prime Minister Tōjō Hideki. Although Australia is mentioned only at random, together with a number of other countries, this would appear to constitute the most definite and comprehensive plan for her in the surviving official documents. But the source of the scheme must be carefully considered. Although the Total War Research Institute carried the prestige of a cabinet, not a military, organ, the draft was the work of a motley selection of thirty-five 'students' chosen from the ministries' young bureaucrats, the military, industry, shipping and banking houses, the media, and high school teachers, whose age averaged thirty-three. It was not a high-level policy directive, but the product of amateurs, as stands revealed in its unrealistic and often absurd contents. The foreword explains that the 'Draft' was meant as homework to make the students study Sphere problems. It was written under time pressure and printed only for research purposes, with the caveat that many parts were blurry and needed correction.

'Strictly speaking there was little or no Japanese planning for "post war" Asia', writes the historian Akira Iriye before he devotes a chapter to the subject; 'Whatever plans Japanese civilian and military officials developed for Asia during the Second World War were products of strategic and tactical considerations'. In light of this judgement, the ideas of one scholar, Itō Takashi, about the future of Australia, which went far beyond the strategic and expedient, stand out even more.

Itō specialized in British Commonwealth studies. His 343-page book, *Gendai Gōshū ron* (Australia to-day), 1943, was the seventh in a row of economic and political-sociological works about Great Britain, Canada, and India that examined the inner workings of British colonialism and its heritage. After the war, he continued to deepen his research, publishing

Ajia–Taiheiyō to Nihon–Gōshū–Kanada to Nihon keizai (The Japanese economy within the Asia–Pacific Ocean Region and the Japan–Australia–Canada nexus), Hyōgensha, in 1968, and *Ei-renpō shiron* (An historical analysis of the British Commonwealth), Hyōgensha, in 1974.

In the final part of his pre-war book on Australia, he dealt exclusively with the Japan–Australia nexus, predicting that Australia's international position would appreciate if she increased significantly her trade with the East Asian countries. These, in turn, would come to love and respect Australia as an economic power. The Australian–Japanese trade flow with its powerful economic input would be used as the axis of the Sphere, which would encompass all of East Asia and Australia, with India added. Conceptually speaking, this meant tying together the Western Pacific with the East Indian Ocean region, while at the same time combining the Southern Hemisphere and the Northern Hemisphere in one body. If such an economic system were established, the country which stood to profit most would not be Japan, nor China, India, or Indonesia, but Australia with her low population, high production system, and many export possibilities.

If Itō's grand scheme was ahead of its time and reminds us in its regional breadth of the more scientific and detailed visions of Australian and Japanese scholars today, the logic and urgency behind it was that of the 1930s. Itō regretted Australia's unswerving loyalty to the West. 'Without any original ideas of their own, the majority of Australian politicians is following British and U.S. Policy', he lamented: 'Australia is now straying in the most foolish opposite direction from the ideal future way'. The more Australian society tarried in recognizing the necessity for building the Co-Prosperity Sphere, the less would be the profit and the bigger the penalty she would one day have to pay for her ignorance.

In his last chapter on 'Concrete plans for a tie-up with Australia after the completion of the war', he explained that the present war was one of education, to teach the Co-Prosperity Sphere idea: 'We are not picking a quarrel with Australia, all we want is to change the Australians' stubborn attitude'. If they dropped their White Australia policy and recognized man's right for equal opportunity, the problem of good relations and cooperation between the Asia Co-Prosperity Sphere and Australia would work itself out naturally. This could take time. Australians did not yet have the right appreciation of the Co-Prosperity Sphere. Even if Australia was going to be on the loser's side of the war, as was likely, it would be difficult to change her Atlantic outlook to a Pacific Ocean one. Australian goodwill was essential. Without Australian cooperation the ideal of the Greater East Asia Co-Prosperity could not be realized. It was imperative to immediately embark on realistic, positive, and fundamental long-range planning for the postwar era's ultimate structure of an 'Asia–Australia Co-Prosperity Sphere' (*A–Gō kyōeiken*).

With this idea, Itō surpassed his peers on the subject of regional relations. Since the 1920s foreign policy strategists had been nurturing the principle of 'coexistence and cooperation' (*kyōzon kyōei*). Foreign Minister Shidehara Kijūrō had used the slogan to explain his policy of interdependence and mutuality towards China. Later, the concept of regional relations was politically extended by Foreign Ministers Arita Hachirō and Matsuoka Yōsuke who in 1940 first used the phrase 'Greater East Asia Co-Prosperity Sphere'. Even when imbued with the principles of regional economics, it remained largely within the bounds of equatorial Southeast Asia. Now, in 1943, Itō's concrete suggestions for an 'Asia–Australia Co-Prosperity Sphere' to eventually supersede the 'Greater East Asia Co-Prosperity Sphere' stretched to its limits the vision of regional relations. His ideas went far beyond Okakura Koshirō's austere prediction that Australia would end up a totalitarian state in the postwar world; or Wada Shunji's and Madarame Fumio's facile postwar prescriptions to teach Australia Japanese ethics, cane in hand, and thereby turn her into a natural southern appendage of Asia. Itō wearied of linking Australia with the Greater East Asia Co-Prosperity Sphere by making her yield to force. Not coercion but persuasion was to take place on the economic as well as on the cultural level. He not only urged Japan 'to import more than half of Australia's products', but strove to raise mutual cultural respect by making Japan more appealing in the eyes of Australians.

Japan had to inform the world of her true values, he believed. Japanese attempts at cultural promotion had always been piecemeal and regularly failed to reach the hearts of Australians, or any other foreigners for that matter. Itō wondered how the greatest number of Australians could be exposed to the core of Japanese culture in the shortest possible time in order that a lasting understanding grow between the two peoples. He decided that Australia's churchmen and schoolteachers should be targeted, since they were responsible for forming the young minds of Australia's next generation. Itō therefore wanted the Japanese Government to extend group-invitations to the 36,000 Australian clerics and 32,700 primary school teachers over a period of ten years. They would be the guests of Japan for one month and would be provided with free travel passes. While they would be shown Mount Fuji and the sacred shrines, they would be kept away from the geishas, who surely would only evoke their contempt. Itō did not expect the Australians to grasp the Yamato spirit overnight and they would have to be taught patiently, sincerely, and eagerly about things Japanese.

The program's yearly expenditures of around three million yen were to be met by the Japanese Government. Japan's total national budget for 1939 amounted in statistical terms to the spending of one million yen per hour of the year. From this, Itō concluded that the yearly cost of the program would amount to the trifling sum of what the nation spent in three hours. Such postwar promotion was absolutely essential to put the Asia–Australia Co-Prosperity Sphere on a permanent footing and it would open a new page in Japanese–Australian relations.

Not that Japan and Australia had never been friends. In one of his last subchapters entitled 'The consolidation of Japanese–Australian co-operation as a cornerstone for world peace', Itō reminded his readers that in times of peace Australia had been the most desirable country to work with. Australia was rich, close, and their countries had a historical relationship, even if mainly one of trade. Now this relationship was strained but, in the future, positive policies could restore the goodwill and strengthen ties on a mutual, voluntary basis. That would benefit the East Asian Sphere in the narrow sense—and, in a wider one, world peace.

This survey of books and magazines is by no means all-inclusive. Occasionally, Australia appeared in articles of the new journal *Chiseigaku* (Geopolitics) which, for the duration of victory, attracted intellectuals and military minds into the fold of the *Nihon Chiseigaku Kyōkai* (Japan Society of Geopolitics), established in November 1941 under Rear-Admiral Ueda Yoshitake. The first issue was out in January 1942, with a page on the Australasiatic Mediterranean; publication ceased in 1944.

One might also have included *Australia and the South Pacific* (Gōshū oyobi Minami Taiheiyō), June 1943, by Nagakura Kyōsuke, to whom a frustrated section chief in the Foreign Ministry had exclaimed: 'There is not a single book on Australia—write one!'; or Watanabe Chūgo's *Treatise on Colonial Australia* (Gōshū shokumin ron), September 1942, which pointed out that all territories in Southeast Asia were taken; nothing remained except Australia and New Zealand: 'In the north is Manchuria, in the south Australia . . . The Japanese colony in Australia will in the future play an important role'. Or we might have analysed further the slender volume on Australian affairs by an employee of the Mitsubishi trading house who, in July 1942, asked: 'What will the future be? We can not tell. But this much we know: The age of "give-and-take" has now come. There is no more trade conflict. Australia will shake hands with Japan as one of the first countries. Australia will sell wool and wheat to Japan, and Japan its industrial products and textiles to Australia. We should not think that we are strong and rejoice over the bombing of Darwin. We must pay more attention to Australia and not think that we have done well'. But the Japanese writings introduced here are representative of the repetitive major patterns in the *nan'yō*-literature on Australia of the time.

Australian fear of Japan was noted with wonderment in Japan. It led Japanese to think about whether Australia was not part of Asia rather than a continental tributary of far-away Europe? If it was large and underpopulated, Australia was also seen as full of potential for further development, despite its deserts. The great obstacle to its proper development was the White Australia policy. Most Japanese writers saw that policy as an injustice. And as they disputed Europe's sole claim to the Australasian world, they put forward an alternative. Australia should join the Greater East Asia Co-Prosperity Sphere, preferably of the people's own free will but, if not, through pressure and possibly even coercion.

Just how naturally Australia would fit into the Sphere remained a moot point. It was easier to picture the Philippines or Malaya as members of the Greater East Asia Co-Prosperity Sphere—accommodating a white culture in the Sphere demanded more reflection. But there was no such time, as is evident in some 'top secret' documents conceived in early 1942. On the surface these could pass as evidence for the final stage of a Japanese plot that might have embellished any of Australia's traditional threat scenarios. But on closer examination it is clear that they were written in great haste—for example, schoolboy plans that suggested pouring millions of Chinese into Australia first, to pave the way for the Japanese. They reveal how little Japanese had been thinking of Australia all the while. Incorporating Australia into the Sphere presented a challenge that few in the rambunctious years of the Pacific War were intellectually equipped to meet.

Yet ironically, and for all the bizarre plans it produced, the most ardent, crucial, and copious evaluation of Australia by Japanese writers of all shades took place in the early 1940s. Spawned by Japan's comet-like rise in the *nan'yō*, on the outmost fringes of which Australia lay, the Japanese suddenly realized how little they knew about that continent. 'We know nothing about Australia!', was a widely used introductory phrase in those books (incidentally, it often still is today in literature introducing Australia in the wake of the mineral boom of the 1960s and 1970s). However, that ignorance was mutual. While one Japanese writer was appalled to have Japan's northern island of Hokkaido still referred to in a first-rate Melbourne newspaper by its pre-modern name of *Yezo*, Australia specialist Okakura Koshirō would write that Australia federated only in 1904 in response to Japan's victorious war over Russia.

Although it was the growing hegemony of Japan in the Pacific that stimulated all the writing about Australia, jingoism was not the main characteristic in this literature. In fact, such passages as bespoke of growing Japanese puissance and what it had in store for Australia were usually confined to the beginning and end chapters of the books, often giving the blatant impression that they were playing to the war-time censors. The meat of such books was, on the whole, detached pieces of highly informative writing. The volumes composed by the Kanematsu

Trading Company, for example, stand out, as do the various tomes by Itō Takashi, Okakura Koshirō, and Miyata Mineichi.

As the war stretched on, there finally appeared at the end of the long tunnel the first 'good' books on Australia. Ichikawa Taijirō's *Gōshū keizaishi kenkyū* (A study of the economic history of Australia) treated the history of the Australian people, their land, agriculture, and sheep farming in a scholarly way and according to Western historical facts. Though published during the war, it made no reference to the Greater East Asia Co-Prosperity Sphere.

But it was now 1944, the year that Japan's last bastions were falling in the Central Pacific and MacArthur's men were returning to the Philippines. The turn of the tide may explain the tone of Ichikawa's tome. At any rate, his level-headed research served as the basic manuscript for his *Nichigō kankei shi* published in 1953, Japan's first full-length history on Japanese–Australian relations. It would take a further ten to twenty years before writers on both sides of the Western Pacific would pick up the pieces and make a fresh start, writing with renewed vigour about each other's countries along the lines of Ichikawa's objective approach, as the bulk of Japan's prolific 1940s Australia literature sank into oblivion.

Conclusion

JAPANESE had only slowly become aware of Australia, the continent closest to their Asian homeland. For three hundred years they had learned about large and empty *Terra Australis* from Western cartography, which was transmitted first through Portuguese and Spanish mariners and traders, and Jesuit priests in China; then for a long time they were tutored by the Dutch; and finally a set of Russian maps presented to the *bakufu* in 1792 taught them the Australian continent's authentic shape. Because of a strictly enforced policy of isolation, Japanese were late in forming an opinion of Australia based on their own experience. But from the time of Japanese participation in the Melbourne World Exhibition in 1875 until the Sino–Japanese War, great optimism prevailed as to future close relations and a profitable partnership based on economic complementarity.

Japan's victory over China in 1895 marked the beginning of a period of alienation that lasted into the middle of the twentieth century. Issues of racism and imperialism began to taint the relationship, as Australia enforced discriminatory immigration laws in 1901 directed largely at curbing the perceived threat of massive Japanese immigration. After Japan defeated Russia in 1905 and annexed Korea in 1910, Australia began to build its own navy and instituted compulsory military training, essentially in anticipation of a coming clash with Japan. The perceived threat became an even more vexing one when Japan occupied all the Pacific colonies of their common foe, Germany, while at the same time providing Australia with naval protection against their mutual enemy throughout World War I. When Japan occupied Manchuria in 1931, Australian confidence in the League promise of 'collective security' was utterly destroyed, although there was also relief that Japan was advancing northward.

But in 1936, 'southward advance' by immigration and economic development became Japanese government policy. A brainchild of the Japanese navy, it soon escalated into policy-making that concentrated on taking into account the United States Pacific forces. If Japan were to succeed in gaining more control over European colonial territories in the Western Pacific, she would first have to eliminate the rival United States navy in the Pacific. At an opportune moment, when World War II diverted European attention away from the Asia–Pacific region, Japan attacked the United States fleet at Pearl Harbor in December 1941. That attack drew the United States into the war on Britain's side, during which Australia's northeast and northwest coasts became targets of Japanese attacks in 1942. Japanese–Australian relations remained thereafter in the depths of belligerency for ten years, before the 1952 San Francisco Peace Treaty set the groundwork for a new beginning.

This half-century of alienation and of Australia's supreme distrust of Japan's southward advance is the focus of this study. To gauge the rational merit of Australian suspicion suggested a closer look at the history and character of this advance. The southward advance was found never to have been the direct push on to Australian shores so often anticipated in Australian threat-literature. Rather, Japan advanced incrementally to the South whenever she expanded northwards onto the Asian mainland, as happened in the Sino–Japanese War, in World War I, and in World War II.

Japan's wish to expand in the South did not, however, emanate out of the blue. Its emergence in the Western Pacific in the 1870s and 1880s can be seen as a re-emergence. In testing our hypothesis about the forces that produced change and continuity in Japan's southward advance, we have looked to the period before national seclusion, when Japanese were trading and working and settling down in the numerous Japanese quarters that then dotted the Western Pacific from Vietnam to Amboina in the Banda Sea. A proper perspective of Japan's modern history requires a view into the long-past age of Japanese activity in the Western Pacific.

Japan's assertion in the modern period is not only rooted in earlier history, but is strongly linked to a singular event in world history when the authoritarian government of a populous and outgoing island country managed to isolate its subjects for 250 years from much of the course of world history. More fateful in Japan's history than her rapid rise in a series of successful modern wars were the ingenious and insidious tactics of the early Tokugawas and the social circumstances by which the islands of Japan were effectively sealed.

I see the periods of expansion as normal aspects of Japanese history, and the period inbetween as a significant anomaly. Not only did Japan shut herself off from most of the Western and the Southeast Asian world, but she happened to do so just at a crucial time when Europeans were arriving in the Pacific and appropriating neighbouring lands. When again drawn into the mainstream of world history in the 1850s, Japan followed the dictates of the Neo-Imperialistic Age just as, in the evening of the Age of Discoveries, it had embarked on a vigorous course of foreign trading and emigration to the South. Japan expanded, both north and south. This was not surprising. Every powerful country either had already done so, or was doing so—until 1945 definitely curbed conventional expansion with a ghastly, and perhaps providential, invention in modern warfare.

All the while, Japan's southward advance and expansion was part of a larger whole. Its proponents, for example, rarely put their shoulders exclusively to the wheel that moved Japan's fortune south; at other times, they could take a similarly intense interest in the north. Their fervour was for expansionism *per se*. Japan was advancing to regain her place in world history—whether north, south, east, or west—a place lost since the middle of the seventeenth century. Fighting for Asian liberation sometimes offered a pretext, but philanthropy was not the driving motivation. Rather, Japan showed every sign of following the inner law of a resurging country that was wondering why, if strong, it was not doing more in the region whose island territories were all occupied by alien races directing events in the Pacific from twelve thousand miles distance. In this light, Japan's 'southern advance', as well as her advance onto the Asian continent, appear as a late response to fundamental shifts in international relations.

Yet, Japan's southward advance theorists, if they looked to the South Seas, rarely took much notice of faraway Australia. Since the mid-1890s Japanese victories and economic drive were steering national interests in a different direction, toward China and Southeast Asia. In any case, Australian immigration laws effectively prevented Japanese from becoming involved in Australia. As a result, from the late 1890s until the 1930s Australia was placed well outside the ambit of Japanese interests in the *nan'yō*.

Australian strategists may have been haunted for half-a-century by the vision of a Japanese invasion. Yet it is only at the very end of Japan's southward advance, when it peaked in the first half of 1942, that Australia became part of Japanese designs in the *nan'yō*. Navy General Staff officers had made plans to invade Australia in order to deny its use as a base for American forces. But chances were slim that such plans could be realized. The Japanese navy itself was split over the Australia issue.

Combined Fleet was not interested in extending naval battle lines as far south as Australia. The Fleet's Commander-in-Chief, Yamamoto Isoroku, with whom ultimate power of decision for naval war-operations came to lie, consistently spurned Navy General Staff plans that would have involved his navy in the rash adventure of landing marines in Australia. Even had he and his aides, who shared his view, consented, the navy could not have carried out a major landing operation without the support of the army. This certainly was never forthcoming. The Army General Staff firmly and persistently refused to consider any invasion of Australia because it grossly exceeded the limits of national strength and overextended Japan's defence perimeter. Because the army had the final say, the consistent refusal of the generals pulled the rug from beneath the Navy General Staff's feet each time the desk-captains tried to broach the subject.

In the civilian sector, meanwhile, scrutiny of the numerous books that appeared on the South in the early 1940s provides a rare insight into frank Japanese perceptions of Australia. An interesting postscript to that literature is the fact that the main grievances held against Australia for half-a-century were actually repaired in the post-war period. A booklet published by Kanematsu Shōten in July 1942, for example, spells out that, whether Australians liked it or not, the age was fast approaching when their country would become not only a member of the East Asia Co-Prosperity Sphere, but also a place where the people of East Asia would be able to live in peace, and a prime supplier of industrial raw materials for Japan. Indeed, after the Pacific War, not immediately but in time, the obnoxious White Australia policy was dismantled and immigration restrictions eased. Australians gladly started to sell to Japan all they had, feeling themselves more than ever an integral member of the Asia–Pacific region, even as the sphere began to prosper under the golden burden of a healthy Yen. In many ways, Japan's East Asian idyll really emerged: Japanese began to play an active role in developing Australia, dredging its harbours, assisting with expanding the infrastructure to work Australia's mineral resources, developing wide leisure areas, and even jointly establishing Australia's first privately funded university.

Now, there may be some who would draw an easy conclusion from this and say that Japan achieved forty years later what she had set out to do at the beginning of the Pacific War. But to argue as if an unbroken line led from Japan's position in the 1940s to her regained regional prestige in the post-war period is to forget the realities. It was from Japan's thwarted southward advance and the circumstances created by Japan's utter defeat in the Pacific War that conditions for the more mature conduct of international relations in the Asia–Pacific region arose. It is a fact well to remember. Japan's late imperial rise in the Pacific, her downfall and subsequent rise again, without guns, hold an immense lesson. With it lies the hope that war and peace in the Pacific made wiser Japan and

Australia in the postwar period; that their present cooperation afford the two countries insight into the history of their relationship; and that from concord between Japan and Australia will spring inspiration for international relations in Asia and the Pacific as the region braces itself for the twenty-first century.

Notes

Page

1. 'the "Club of 1935"'. Information based on the diary of Foreign Ministry Official Kawamura Shigehisa (16, 31 January 1935), and on his memorandum to Commander Karai Tomeo (28 January 1935) about the participants in the combined army, navy, and foreign ministerial round-table talks. The writer gratefully acknowledges copies of these

documents from Professor Shiozaki Hiroaki. See also, Shiozaki, *Nichi-Ei-Bei sensō no kiro*, p. 301.

1–2. 'E. L. Piesse drew Australian attention to . . . the *nan'yō*': 'If any Australian library has been collecting the books in Japanese on the expansion of Japanese influence and control in Nan-Yo, it must by now have enough to fill a yard or two of shelving'; see Piesse, *Japan and the Defense of Australia*, pp. 12–14.

2. 'close temporarily the Burma Road'. Lord Caldecote, U.K. Secretary of State for Dominion Affairs, to Prime Minister R. G. Menzies; Menzies to Caldecote; 26 and 27 June 1940 (*DAFP*, Vol. 3, Nos 445, 452). Mr S. M. Bruce, High Commissioner in London, to Prime Minister R. G. Menzies; Menzies to Bruce; 6 and 9 July 1940; Memorandum read to War Cabinet by Mr J. Mc Ewen, Australian Minister for External Affairs, Most Secret; 9 July 1940 (*DAFP*, Vol. 4, Nos 14, 20, 22).

2. Neville Meaney contrasts the 'Japanese phase' with the 'British phase' (roughly 1788 to 1904) and the 'American phase' (1945 until today) in Australian foreign policy. He defines each phase by the great power which dominated and conditioned Australian security in the particular periods; Japan became the central factor in Australian foreign policy because of the threat she posed to national interest and survival. See Neville Meaney, ' "Kōka-ron" to "Ōsutoraria no kiki" '.

4–5. 'Honda . . . tells with pride'. See Honda, *Seiiki monogatari*, p.102.

5. 'That memory was also kept in songs'. See Shimizu, 'Nihon-Tōnanajia kankei no bun-meishiteki ichi', pp. 281–2.

9. 'despatching diplomatic missions to Malacca'. See Akiyama, 'Muromachi jidai ni okeru Ryūkyū no Indoshina-shokoku to no tsūkō', pp. 1–21; see also Kobata and Matsuda, *Ryū kyūan Relations with Korea and South Sea Countries* about early embassies to Southeast Asian capitals, and Kerr, *Okinawa*, pp. 91–2.

9. 'the Portuguese "discovered" Japan'. The Portuguese Governor of India, Affonso d'Albuquerque, may have met Japanese already at their conquest of Malacca in 1511, see Boxer, 'Some Aspects of Portuguese Influence', in Moscato, *Papers on Japan*, p. 96.

9. 'The Chinese records tell us'. See Tsunoda and Goodrich, *Japan in the Chinese Dynastic Histories*, pp. 2, 14–15, 22–3; Kurihara, *Jōdai Nihon taigai kankei no kenkyū*, pp. 50–148, 237–80.

9. 'the *Ken-Zui-shi* and *Ken-Tō-shi*'. See Mori, *Kentōshi*; Von Verschuer, *Les Relations Offi-cielles du Japon*.

10. 'Japanese military contacts . . . in Mimana'. According to the traditional Japanese inter-pretation of Chinese annals, the Koreans themselves do not recognize the past existence of a 'Japanese colony' in Mimana in their own historiography, see Hérail, *Histoire du Japon*, p. 46. Recent research has denied the existence of Mimana, see Yamao, *Nihon kokka no keisei*, ch. 1.

10. 'an early seclusion policy'. See Mori, 'The Beginning of Overseas Advance of Japanese Merchant Ships', pp. 5–10.

10. 'the advance of Japanese ships'. See Mori, 'International Relations', p. 85.

10. 'the first organized pirates'. On the formation period of the *wakō* see ibid., p. 90; and Tamura, *Chūsei Nitcho bōeki no kenkyū*, chs 1, 2. Their further development is described in Tanaka, *Chūsei kaigai kōshō shi no kenkyū*; Boxer, *South China in the 16th Century*, pp. xxiv-xxvi, xxxii-iii; Sansom, *A History of Japan 1334–1615*, pp. 265–70, and *The Western World and Japan*, p. 108.

10. 'as far as the Malay Archipelago . . . and Bali'. These countries are mentioned in *Satō Shin'en no shuki* (Memoirs of Satō Shin'en), cited in Takekoshi, *Nihon keizai shi III*, pp. 172–4.

10. '*wakō* crews consisted . . . of Chinese'. See Tanaka, 'Jidai kaisetsu', p. 141; So, *Japanese Piracy in Ming China*.

10–11. For technology transfer via the *wakō*, see Ishii Kenji, 'Fune to kōkai' [I], p. 151; and Mori, 'International Relations', p. 90.

11. 'Mohammedans . . . in Canton'. There are no exact figures; see Hirth and Rockhill, *Chau ju-Kua*, pp. 14–15; Schafer, *The Golden Peaches*, pp. 14–15.

11. On Chinese ship construction and navigation technique, see Ishii Kenji, 'Fune to kōkai' [I], p. 150; Mori, 'International Relations', pp. 79–81, 85; Hirth and Rockhill, *Chau ju-Kua*, pp. 28–9; Mori, *Zoku Nissō-bōeki no kenkyū*, pp. 45–6; Von Verschuer, *Les Relations Offi-cielles du Japon*, pp. 139–41.

11. For Japan adopting Chinese and Western shipbuilding techniques, see Ishii Kenji, 'Fune to kōkai' [I], p. 149; *Kodansha Encyclopedia*, p. 144.
11. 'armour-plated battleships'. Ishii Kenji, 'Fune to kōkai' [II], pp. 148–9.
11. 'Will Adams'. *Kodansha Encyclopedia*, p. 144.
12. 'the monk Bussho Zenji'. Mori, 'International Relations', p. 88. ·
12. 'from Java and Sumatra'. Tanaka Takeo, 'Jidai kaisetsu', p. 139; for turn-of-the-13th-century foreign contacts with Siam, Sumatra, and Java, see also Von Verschuer, *Le commerce extérieur du Japon*, pp. 114–15.
12. 'Nanban, too, must be conquered'. Mori, 'International Relations', pp. 91–3; Kuwata, *Toyotomi Hideyoshi kenkyū*, pp. 251–6; Berry, *Hideyoshi*, pp. 212–13, 278.
12. 'world history might have taken a different course'. See Katō Hidetoshi, *Hikaku bunka e no shikaku*, p. 64.
13. 'Japan's increased interest . . . in the Western Pacific'. Iwao, 'Japanese Foreign Trade', pp. 4–5.
13. 'Silk was being imported'. Katō Eiichi, 'The Japanese-Dutch Trade', p. 46; Iwao, 'Japanese Foreign Trade', p. 2.
13. 'Japan supplied the world with silver'. Iwao, ibid., pp. 5–6, 10; see also Kobata, *Kingin bōekishi no kenkyū*, pp. 7–8.
14. 'Tokugawa Ieyasu . . . encouraged Japanese traders'. Kuno, *Japanese Expansion on the Asiatic Continent*, vol. 2, p. 17.
14. '356 Japanese merchant ships set sail'. Iwao, *Shūinsen bōeki shi*, pp. 184, 127–45, and 'Japanese Foreign Trade', pp. 8–10.
14. 'European merchant vessels'. Hubschmid, *Die Neuzeit*, p. 268.
14. 'Japanese . . . began to reside abroad'. Iwao, *Nan'yō Nihonmachi*, pp. 316–20, 325–6.
14. 'Around 100,000 . . . left Japan'. Ibid., p. 15.
14–15. 'Sumiya Shichirōbei . . . advanced regional map'. A Portolan map with longitudes and latitudes drawn distinctly, it was probably copied from Portuguese sources, but clearly shows Japanese improvement, see *Zusetsu Nihon bunka shi taikei*, p. 107; for Japanese corrections of Portuguese sea maps, see also Boxer, 'Some Aspects of Portuguese Influence', pp. 105–7.
15. 'between 7,000 and 10,000 people'. Iwao, *Nan'yō Nihonmachi*, pp. 15–16.
15. 'Wada Rinzaemon'. Ibid., pp. 289–90.
15. 'Naya "Luzon" Sukezaemon'. The profiles of numerous other Japanese merchant-adventurers of this period can be found in the special issue of *Taiyō*, 'Gōshō hyakunin', pp. 23–8; and in *Zusetsu jinbutsu umi (4)*, pp. 167–72.
15. 'Yamada Nagamasa'. Iwao, *Nan'yō Nihonmachi*, pp. 167–75; Iwao, ed., *Biographical Dictionary of Japanese History*, pp. 271–2. For a critical evaluation of Yamada Nagamasa's place in history, still a subject of dispute, see 'Van Vliet's Historical Account of Siam in the 17th Century', followed by Francis H. Giles, 'A Critical Account of Van Vliet's Historical Account of Siam in the 17th Century', in the Siam Society, *Relationship With Portugal, Holland, and the Vatican*, Bangkok, 1959, pp. 31–136; and H. Carroll Parish, 'The Myth of Yamada Nagamasa and its effect on Thai-Japanese Relations', *Journal of the Siam Society*, 1959, pp. 159–66.
15–16. 'Japanese settlers . . . in Batavia'. See Iwao, *Zoku Nan'yō Nihonmachi*, chs 1–5, 6, 7. The will of Michiel T. Sobei (who died at Batavia in 1663) describing the disposal of his substantial property, is reproduced in Takekoshi, *The Story of the Wakō*.
16. A detailed account in English of the sophisticated lifestyle some Japanese were enjoying in the Dutch East Indies is given in Iwao, 'Japanese Emigrants in Batavia'.
17. 'how the Japanese would have responded to . . . the law of peoples'. See Sansom, *The Western World*, pp. 110–13.
17. 'last Japanese marriage was registered in Batavia'. Iwao, 'Japanese Emigrants in Batavia', p. 17.
17–18. 'Three reasons stand out'. See Katō Eiichi, 'Development of Japanese Studies on Sakoku'; on the *ito wappu* system, see Iwao, 'Japanese Foreign Trade', p. 8.
18. 'The occasional entry on Japan's southern advance'. For example, *Nihon Kingendai shi jiten* (Dictionary of modern Japanese history), 1978, p. 488. *Sekai daihyakkajiten* (Great world encyclopaedia), 1970, vol. 17, p. 97, sketches the history of Japan's southward advance from the 1880s onward; and *Shakai kagaku daihyakkajiten* (Encyclopaedia of social science), 1970, vol. 14, p. 199, from the time of Perry's arrival.

18. 'Japanese and Western studies'. Irie, *Meiji nanshin shikō*, and *Hōjin kaigai hatten shi*; Yano, *'Nanshin' no keifu*, and *Nihon no Nan'yō shikan*. Peattie, 'The Nan'yō', and *Nan'yō*.
19. '"Three Country" view of the world'. See *NKT*, p. 281; for Japanese world-maps fashioned after the traditional Buddhist concept, see plates 3, 6, 8, 18 in this large collection.
19. 'maps and globes brought to Japan'. See Boxer, 'Some Aspects of Portuguese Influence', p. 109. For a detailed chronological account of Western influence on Japanese geography, see Ayusawa , 'Geography and Japanese Knowledge of World Geography'.
19. 'they had inscribed a fifth . . . mass of land'. The various renderings of this Southland relied less on actual Portuguese discoveries than on the works of the sixteenth-century Flemish cartographers, Mercator and Ortelius, who in turn had based themselves on the thirteenth-century traveler Marco Polo and the second-century Greek cartographer Ptolemy. See Wood, *The Discovery of Australia*, pp. 56–71. The first actual sightings of Australia are discussed in Sharp, *The Discovery of Australia*, pp. 1–20.
20. 'Matteo Ricci's Mappa Mundi'. *NKT*, plates 32, 38, 40–2, 44. See also Ikenaga, *Hōsaibanka daihōkan*, plates 127–8, 130, 133; and *NK*, pp. 160–2. For a detailed exposition of the background of Ricci's world map, see D'Elia, 'Recent Discoveries and New Studies'. As regards his rendition of the Southland, Ricci notes, 'I have based everything upon old books printed in my country. As for the whole Southland, since no one has ever been there . . . the facts must be so' (p. 94).
20. 'copies . . . were sent . . . to Japan'. Ricci, *China in the Sixteenth Century*, p. 331. *NKT*, plates 58, 59.
20. 'it reached a wider audience of Japanese intellectuals'. Boxer, *Jan Compagnie in Japan*, p. 12.
20. 'Japan's first printed world-map in 1645'. *NKT*, p. 279, and *NK*, plate 7.
20. 'protrusions . . . repeated on every Ricci-type map'. *NKT*, plates 59–61, 65, 66.
20. 'Into what is Arnhem Land . . . Ricci wrote'. See Lin, Etudes sur l'introduction de méthodes et de connaissances géographiques européennes en Chine, p. 241.
20–1. 'The version of Nagakubo Sekisui'. *NKT*, p. 279 and plate 68.
21. 'Australia . . . explored by the Dutch East India company's servants'. This fascinating chapter is told in Sigmond and Zuiderbaan, *Dutch Discoveries of Australia*.
21. 'François Caron . . . provided the shogun Tokugawa Iemitsu with maps'. Boxer, *Jan Compagnie in Japan*, pp. 4–5.
21. 'the master map of Joan Blaeu'. *NKT*, plates 71, 72.
21. 'Australia became a hallmark'. Some of the better-known works at the turn of the century were those of Hashimoto Sōkichi, 1796; Hayashi Shihei, 1797; and Ishizuka Saikō, 1802: see *NKT*, plates 82, 74 and 83, respectively.
21–2. For Arai Hakuseki and 'Magellanica', see Ishiyama, 'The *Yōgaku* Scholars', pp. 18, 21.
22. '"There is a Southland"'. See Arai, in *Nihon kyōiku shisō taikei*, p. 106.
22. 'Arai . . . had access to Joan Blaeu's world-map'. Ishiyama, 'The *Yōgaku* Scholars', p. 20.
22. 'Nanpō no chi (Southland) is . . . Magellanica'. See Yamamura, *Teisei zōyaku sairan igen*, vol. 2, p. 986.
22. 'two Jesuits in China'. Lin Tong-yang offers a pertinent discussion of the Western transfer of geographical knowledge and its strong impact on the Oriental world-view in the sixteenth century in his dissertation, Etudes sur l'introduction de méthodes et de connaissances géographiques européennes en Chine.
22–3. 'two separate Southlands'. See Yamamura, *Teisei zōyaku sairan igen*, pp. 85, 88, 90, 985–6.
23. 'Shiba Kōkan's celebrated world-map'. *NKT*, plate 79; for a description of this map, see Boxer, *Jan Compagnie in Japan*, p. 21. Although the year 1792 is given on the map, in all probability it was produced in 1793; French, *Shiba Kōkan*, p. 123.
23. 'probably for the first time'. It is possible that a Dutch map bearing the influence of Cook's chartings may have entered Japan after Cook's third Pacific voyage, which ended in 1779, and before the issuing of the Katsuragawa Map in 1794. Such a map might well have depicted Australia's authentic countours. See Unno, 'Tenchi ni kyūyōhō kokumei kō', pp. 128–34.
23. 'It is named after . . . Katsuragawa Hoshū'. The Katsuragawa Map is kept at the Naikaku Bunkozō (Cabinet Library possessions), no. 35245, box 185217. It is depicted in *NKT*, plate

80 and described in *NKT*, appendix, pp. 56–7. Tasmania, however, was still drawn as attached to the mainland; this error was emended only after George Bass and Matthew Flinders discovered the island nature of Tasmania in 1798.

23. 'Kōdayū spent ten years . . . in Russia'. Detailed accounts are given in Lensen, *The Russian Push Toward Japan*, pp. 96–120, and Kamei *Daikokuya Kōdaiyu* , pp. 193–6.

23. 'material . . . from Captain Cook's . . . ships'. Forwarded by rail across Russia via Irkutsk, Cook's latest chartings from his third Pacific voyage were destined for the British ambassador in St Petersburg for quick transmission to London. See Terence Armstrong, 'Cook's Reputation in Russia', in Fisher and Johnston, *Captain Cook and His Times*, pp. 121–8.

24. 'Rezanov . . . gave . . . an older version'. See, for example, the copperplate map *Bankoku yochi zenzu* by Matsubara Uchū: *NKT*, plate 85.

24. 'they were kept . . . secret'. *NKT*, appendix, pp. 56–7.

24. 'Hayashi Shihei arrested'. Boxer, *Jan Compagnie in Japan*, pp. 18–19. The *bakufu*'s restriction of geographical knowledge is described by Shiba Kōkan: 'My world map was printed after I obtained permission from the lord of Shirakawa [Matsudaira Sadanobu] with whom I privately consulted. It cannot be offered for sale. Only important persons are permitted to have it, and the price is therefore irrelevant.' Quoted in French, *Shiba Kōkan*, p. 124.

24. For Takahashi Kageyasu and his official world-map, see *NKT*, plate 87 and appendix, pp. 61–2; Noma, *Chirigaku no rekishi to hōhō*, pp. 71–2.

24–5. For Mitsukuri Shōgo, his new world-map and attention to Australia, see *NKT*, plate 89 and Ishiyama, 'The *Yōgaku* Scholars', pp. 26–9.

25. 'His entries on Australia proper'. In his description of Australia he was indebted to his father-in-law, Mitsukuri Genpo (1799–1863), who had done considerable spadework in his study 'Ausutararia yakusetsu' (Translations on Australia) which based itself on encyclopaedic passages from Jacob Nieuwenhuis, *Algemeen wordenboek van kunsten en wetenschappen* (1822–1829); see Ishiyama, ibid., pp. 29–31; Rangaku Shiryō Kenkyūkai, ed., *Mitsukuri Genpo no kenkyū*, 1978.

25–6. '"Australia is a foreign word"'. These are paraphrased excerpts from Mitsukuri Shōgo, *Kon'yo zushiki*, pp. 1–4.

26. 'Nagakubo Sekisui's . . . world-map was re-issued'. These maps often carried illustrations of ships and peoples from foreign lands. A typical example is Kobayashi Kōhō's world map in *NK*, plate 11; other popularized versions are found in *NKT*, plates 109–13.

26. 'Sydney whaler . . . destroyed . . . Hamanaka'. See Sissons, *Australian-Japanese Relations*, pp. 1–2; and Endō, *Nazo no ikokusen*, p. 47. Toward the end of her 1830–1832 voyage, the Australian whaler was denied provisions at Hamanaka, near present-day Kushiro. The crew thereupon attacked the village on 20, 24, and 26 February 1831, destroying fishing huts and capturing an Ainu and a Japanese soldier of the Matsumae feudal clan. Both men were released at the end of the whaler's two-week stay. Captain Russell issued a letter to the emperor of Japan, warning about European superiority and explaining that the village had been punished for refusing help to his ship in distress. This little-known episode was brought to light by Sissons in his paper, and subsequently Endō made a field trip to the area and published her results in *Nazo no ikokusen*.

26. 'South of Japan . . . lies Australia'. Yoshida, *Yūshūroku*, p. 105.

26–7. 'Yoshida concerned himself . . . with . . . the acquisition of Formosa'. See, for example, ibid., p. 107.

27. '"Magellanica is the fifth of the big continents"'. Satō, *Seiyō rekkoku shiryaku* (Outline of the history of Western nations), in *Satō Nobuhiro kagaku zenshū*, vol. 3, p. 811.

27. 'she was able to colonize . . . New Holland'. Watanabe Kazan, *Gaikoku jijōsho*, p. 158.

27. 'Westerners studied geography'. Fukuzawa, *Fukuzawa Yukichi senshū*, pp. 169–70.

27–8. 'twelve Japanese . . . performed as acrobats'. See Sissons, Australian-Japanese Relations, pp. 12–13.

31–2. 'to keep a "factory" they had to protect it'. See, Parry, *Europe and a Wider World*, pp. 40–3; Sansom, *The Western World*, pp. 65–6.

32. 'The Portuguese soon set up . . . key bases'. See Boxer, *The Portuguese Seaborne Empire*.

32. 'Portugal . . . outdone by Holland'. In the early seventeenth century, the Dutch serviced their far-flung holdings with some 2,000 warships, some 100 of which were stationed in the West Indies, 20 off Guinea, and 40 in Asia. See *The Dutch Seaborne Empire*, p. 69; pp. 14–15 show a useful world-map of the Dutch basing system.

32. 'This assured her . . . a rapid naval deployment system'. See Harkavy, *Great Power Competition*, pp. 47–8.
32. 'dynamic developments under the . . . Tokugawa'. See, for example, Oka, 'Nōzon no henbō to zaigō shōnin'; Yamaguchi, 'Bakuhansei shijō no saihen to shōin seisan'; Wakita, 'Kinsei toshi no kensetsu to gōshō'; Sheldon, *The Rise of the Merchant Class in Tokugawa*, ch. 7.
33. 'the *sankin kōtai* system of "alternate attendance"'. It forced the feudal lords and their retinue to spend abundantly on their processions to Edo and their costly stay there. It also generated the growth of Osaka as the commercial centre of the nation, where most of the lords converted their rice revenues into money for their *sankin* expenses; see Tsukahira, *Feudal Control in Tokugawa Japan*, pp. 2–3.
33. 'Prolonged peace . . . spawned a peculiar culture'. See Tsunoda, *Sources of the Japanese Tradition*.
33–4. 'Japan . . . established . . . settlements'. Chief among these were Ayuthia near Bangkok with an estimated Japanese population of 8,000, three settlements at Tourane, Kang-an, and Faifo in Annam (Vietnam), one near the river Mekong north of Phnom Penh, one each in Java, Cochin-China, and Tong-King, and a large settlement near Manila; the latter grew from around 300 Japanese traders and settlers in 1593 to 1,000 in 1595 under the early international trade initiatives of Toyotomi Hideyoshi, and reached a steady population of around 3,000 in the 1620s; see Kuwata, *Toyotomi Hideyoshi kenkyū*, p. 256.
34. 'Fukuzawa Yukichi's call to civilize Korea'. See the daily which Fukuzawa edited, *Jiji shimpō* (News of the times) [*JS*], 1 June 1883, in *Fukuzawa Yukichi zenshū* (The complete works of Fukuzawa Yukichi; 1958–64) [*FZ*], vol. 9, pp. 5–7; *JS*, 11 October 1883, in *FZ*, vol. 10, pp. 69–70; and *JS*, 11 December 1882, in *FZ*, vol. 8, p. 437.
34. 'letters to Formosa and the Philippines'. See Hideyoshi's letters to India (25 July 1591), the Philippines (15 September 1591), and Formosa (5 November 1593) in Tsuji, *Kaigai kōtsu shiwa*, pp. 421–6, 429–35, 442–3.
34. 'Hideyoshi issued orders again in 1597'. Tokutomi, *Kinsei Nippon kokumin shi*, vol. 9, pp. 441–6, 649–53, 707. Sansom, *A History of Japan 1334–1615*, pp. 352–61, 373, 379.
34. 'Ieyasu ordered . . . Murayama Tōan to invade Formosa'. Tokutomi, *Kinsei Nippon kokumin shi*, vol. 13, pp. 373–4.
34. 'Iemitsu . . . on record to conquer the Philippines'. Ibid., vol. 14, pp. 257–61; Aoki, *Dai-Nippon rekishi shūsei*, vol. 3, pp. 460–1; Tsuji, *Kaigai kōtsu shiwa*, pp. 541–2, 620–1; Ōkuma, *Kaikoku gojūnen shi*, p. 277.
35. 'Russian ships . . . appear off the Japanese east coast'. Tokutomi, *Kinsei Nippon kokumin shi*, vol. 23, p. 142.
35. For Mitsukuni, Riken, and Shihei on Hokkaido, see Tokugawa, *Dai Nihon shi*, vol. 5, pp. 580–9, Index-vol. pp. 58–9; and Tokutomi, *Kinsei Nippon kokumin shi*, vol. 25, pp. 326–9, 331–4.
35. 'Kudō Heisuke . . . argued forcibly'. See Kudō, *Aka Ezo fūsetsu kō*, pp. 29–39.
35. 'Kudō . . . influenced Hayashi Shihei'. Iwao, *Biographical Dictionary of Japanese History*, p. 208.
35. 'Hayashi strongly urged . . . to absorb Ezo'. Hayashi, *Sangoku tsūran zusetsu*, pp. 55–81.
35–6. 'Those are the latitudes of London and Paris'. See Honda, *Seiiki monogatari*, p. 133.
36. 'Satō Nobuhiro . . . an early advocate of Greater Japan'. See Satō, *Satō Nobuhiro kagaku zenshū*, vol. 3, pp. 821–2, 824–5.
36. 'Japan must . . . conquer Manchuria'. In a letter to Kido Takayoshi (19 February 1856), Yoshida suggested that Takejima Island near Korea be converted into a military base for operations on the mainland; *NST*, vol. 54, pp. 224–5.
36. 'it will surely be destroyed'. Yoshida, *Yūshūroku*, p. 107.
36. 'Yoshida's companion in death'. They were beheaded on the same site and on the same day for speaking out against the government.
36. 'he called for the annexation of . . . Santang'. Sanai shokan (Letters of Sanai [to Tamiya Jōun, 28 November 1857]), in *NST*, vol. 55, pp. 567–8.
37. 'Yamagata Aritomo . . . reminisced'. See Ōyama, *Yamagata Aritomo ikensho*, pp. 229–30.
37. 'Oda Nobunaga . . . iron-clad warships'. See Ishii Kenji, 'Fune to kōkai' [II], pp. 148–9.
37–8. 'Tokugawa Ieyasu . . . invited . . . Spanish naval architects'. Ibid., p. 402; a galliot-type ship in the 500-gross-ton class was actually built under the direction of the Spaniard

Sebastian Viscano, see *Kodansha Encyclopedia*, 1983, vol. 7, p. 144. Japanese were also in possession of a book that contained the whole body of navigation techniques then known to the Portuguese. Entitled *Genna kōkaisho*, the Genna Nautical Book was a compilation of navigational knowledge with a foreword by Ikeda Kōun who had copied it from Manoel Goncalvez, a Portuguese captain, during their voyage to Manila in 1619. The book treats topics such as distance tables of longitude and latitude; methods for judging latitude from the height of the sun; techniques for reading a compass and the thirty-two direction markings; plummet sounding; navigation chart of the waters between Siam and Japan; and necessary knowledge for navigators and pilots. It furthermore introduced navigational instruments such as the quadrant and the astrolabe. See Arima, 'The Western Influence on Japanese Military Science', pp. 118–19; Hirose, 'The European Influence on Japanese Astronomy', p. 64.

38. For annotated illustrations of these converted war ships, see *Zusetsu jinbutsu umi (3)*, pp. 125–30.
38. 'fighting patterns developed . . . under Oda Nobunaga'. See Ishii Kenji, in ibid., p. 152 and *Zusetsu jinbutsu umi (4)*, pp. 145–7; see also illustration of the Japanese naval fighting formation, ibid., pp. 50–1.
38. 'Japanese shipping declined'. The 49-ton restriction was, however, soon lifted to accommodate the need for large-scale coastal vessels which grew in capacity to 147–96 gross tons, see *Kodansha Encyclopedia*, p. 145.
38. 'Matsudaira Shungaku . . . induced a reform'. Tsukahira, *Feudal Control in Tokugawa Japan*, pp. 129–31.
38. 'in September 1853 the law was relaxed'. In November the shogunate ordered the Mito clan to build a Western-style warship. The clan opened a ship construction site at Ishikawajima in Edo, the Satsuma clan did likewise in Sakurajima on Kyūshū, and the Chōshū clan followed suit; all produced warships by the middle of that decade. By May 1866 the Japanese built their own first screw- equipped steam warship without foreign assistance; the *Chiyodagata Maru* with a displacement of 136 tons was launched from the Ishikawajima Shipbuilding Factory; see Arima, 'Western Influence on Japanese Military Science', pp. 131–2, 136.
38. 'Japanese . . . ignored the Dutch'. See Ericson, 'The Bakufu Looks Abroad', pp. 388–9.
38–9. 'Douglas arrived with 33 officers'. Ōkuma, *Kaikoku gojūnen shi*, pp. 301–3; Marder, *Old Friends, New Enemies*, pp. 3–5; Ikeda, *Kaigun to Nihon*, pp. 146–56.
39. 'On the eve of the Sino-Japanese war'. Rawlinson, *China's Struggle for Naval Development*, pp. 168–9.
39. 'the *Tsukuba* as far as Australia'. See Sawa, *Kaigun shichijūnenshi dan*, pp. 257–8; Ōkuma, *Fifty Years of New Japan*, vol. 1, p. 227.
39. 'Shiga . . . requested permission'. See Miwa, Crossroads of Patriotism in Imperial Japan, p. 142. Shiga had also gained the sympathy of the captain of the *Tsukuba* with whom he had sailed in the previous year to Korea and who supported his application to travel on the next voyage; Hijikata, 'Shiga Shigetaka to "Nan'yō jiji"', p. 128.
39. 'he sought to add a new dimension'. For an analysis of the book's intellectual framework, see Miwa, 'Shiga Shigetaka'.
40. 'This southern group of islands'. Hattori, *Nan'yōsaku*, p. 142.
40. 'Japan should . . . stand up [and] occupy the Solomons'. Nozawa, *Nan'yō shi*, pp. 102–4.
40. 'raw materials from Australia'. See Inagaki, *Tōhōsaku*, pp. 113–19.
40. 'We have to think about that'. Inagaki, *Nan'yō chōsei dan*, p. 79.
40. 'the latter has rated poorly'. See Yano, 'Nanshin' no keifu, pp. 48–9.
41. 'create a militarily strong country'. Yoshida, *Yūshūroku*, pp. 105, 107.
41. 'obtain the nan'yō'. Watanabe Shūjirō, *Sekai ni okeru Nihonjin*, pp. 2, 4, 386.
41. 'Honda . . . prescribed a . . . scheme'. Honda, *Seiiki monogatari*, pp. 133, 138, 142–3, 162–3.
41. 'islands . . . for Japan's criminal population'. Irie, *Meiji nanshin shikō*, pp. 73–7.
41. 'prisoners to develop . . . islands'. See Satō, *Bōkaisaku*, in *Satō Nobuhiro kagaku zenshū*, vol. 3, p. 826.
41. 'go south . . . to defend the sea lanes'. See Satō, *Kondō hisaku*, in ibid., vol. 2, p. 199.
42. 'Japan must send her soldiers to Luzon'. Ibid., vol. 3, p. 826.
42. 'tie the Philippines . . . to Japan'. Hattori, *Nan'yōsaku*, pp. 4, 80–2.
42. 'give the Eta new-found glory'. Sugiura, *Hankai yume monogatari*, pp. 18–28. On the

emancipation of the Eta class, see de Vos and Wagatsuma, *Japan's Invisible Race*, pp. 34, 63.

42. For Suganuma on the Philippines, see his 'Shin Nippon no zūnan no yume', pp. 659, 681, 689; and his correspondence 'Manira tsūshin' (Communications from Manila) in *Nippon*, 22, 27, 28 July 1889.

43. '*Datsu-A-Ron*'. Fukuzawa, *Jiji shimpō*, 16 March 1885, in *FZ*, vol. 10, pp. 238–40.

43. 'Let us change our empire'. Jansen, *Japan and Its World*, p. 69.

43. 'dreamstories'. Sugiura's *Hankai no yume monogatari* (Story of Hankai's dream), Suganuma's *Shin Nippon no zūnan no yume* (Dream of New Japan's expansion to southern lands), and Shiga's seventh chapter in *Nan'yō jiji* 'Gōshū yume monogatari' (An Australian dream story).

43–4. 'Tangaroa'. See Shiga, *Nan'yō jiji*, ch. 15, 'Tangaroa shinrei no yume monogatari' (Dream story of the Samoan god, Tangaroa).

44. 'Prince Kitashirakawa's words'. See *Yūbin hōchi shinbun*, 19 March, 29 April 1879, p. 3.

44. 'the *Tōhō Kyōkai*'. See 'Tōhō kyōkai setchi no shushi' (The objectives of the East Asian Society) in each issue of *Tōhō kyōkai hōkoku* (Transactions of the East Asian Society), at the back of the table of content page.

44. 'the most pressing tasks for Japan'. 'Shokumin kyōkai setsuritsu shuisho' (The aims of the Colonization Society), in *Shokumin kyōkai hōkoku*, vol. 1, pp. 109–11.

45. 'hoist the Rising Sun'. *Nihonjin*, 3 April 1890, p. 12; Shiga suggests starting with rocks and islands nearest to Japan, and mentions Lare Rock, Pinnacle Islands, Four Pins Island, Channel Rock, and Chausse Island, all located in the East China Sea.

45. 'Taguchi Ukichi . . . believed in 1890'. See Taguchi, 'Nan'yō keiryakuron', pp. 372–3. Despite his optimistic assessment, Taguchi had run into difficulties himself, when he sailed to Micronesia to set up Japan's first South Seas Trading company (*Nantō Shōten*) in 1890. Off Guam, the crew members were at first not allowed to go ashore because they lacked the required health certificates issued by the Spanish consul in Yokohama; after four days they were permitted to land and fined 50 yen for violating harbour regulations, which were later waived when Taguchi pleaded ignorance. At Ponape, Spanish officials again gave them a hard time with landing rights, but after prolonged negotiations they allowed Taguchi and his team to set up a store at Santiago harbour. Taguchi's six-and-a-half month trip on the 90-ton vessel *Tenyū Maru* is described in Irie, *Meiji nanshin shikō*, pp. 102–10.

45. 'Miyake Setsurei . . . reminisced'. In Miyake, *Daigaku konjaku tan*, pp. 142–3; see also Irie, *Meiji nanshin shikō*, pp. 116–17.

46. 'New Zealand's destiny . . . emporium of the South Pacific'. See Barclay, *A History of the Pacific*, pp. 145, 149.

46. 'Western colonies' stringent immigration . . . laws'. Mizutani Shinroku, for instance, who stands at the beginning of Japanese commercial relations with Micronesia, was immediately apprehended by Spanish officials when he arrived on his 45-ton vessel, the *Sōyō Maru*, at Ponape, his first stop in the Carolines, where he sought to trade. Informed that it was illegal, he was told to proceed to Santiago harbour for inspection of his ship; there he was promptly fined and ordered to leave. On his return trip he managed to trade secretly with the natives of the Mokil islands in items such as food, lamps, kerosene, and hardware, before he reached his home in the Bonin Islands in October 1887; see Gō, *Nan'yō bōeki gojūnen shi*, pp. 3–4.

46. 'Ōishi Masami urged . . . peaceful expansion'. Ōishi, *Fukyōsaku*, pp. 41–2, 50, 59, 64–71, 91, 102–3, 123–4, 144, 152.

46. 'colonization did not mean territorial annexation'. Tsuneya, *Kaigai shokumin-ron*, pp. 1–3, 68, 78–88; Australia is given considerable space in pp. 187–250.

46–7. 'Iriye . . . suggested'. Iriye, *Pacific Estrangement*, p. 38.

47. 'There will be established new Japans'. See Tokutomi, *Dai-Nihon bōchōron*, pp. 5–6, 17, 66–72, 147–8.

48. 'Japanese sailors, acrobats, and pearlers'. D. C. S. Sissons, who has pioneered studies in the history of Australian-Japanese relations, has done extensive research on these first Japanese visitors to Australia; see his 'Immigration in Australian-Japanese Relations'; 'Karayuki-San'; 'The Early Japanese Influence on the Northern Territory'; 'The Japanese in the Australian Pearling Industry'; Australian-Japanese Relations: The First Phase, 1859–91.

48. 'Nonami Kojirō'. Hattori Tōru describes 'Japanese Nona' in *Nankyū no shin shokumin*, pp. 9–10, as a 42-year-old successful pearler and the distinguished leader of the Japanese community on Thursday Island.
48. 'Their early impressions'. See Sissons, 'The Japanese in the Australian Pearling Industry', pp. 11–12.
49. 'Hashimoto was accompanied'. See Hashimoto, *Fu Gōshū Meruborun hakurankai kikō*, vol. 1, p. 1.
49. 'Hashimoto's reaction to . . . the Aborigines'. Ibid., p. 8; see also Williams, 'Far More Happier than We Europeans', pp. 499–501.
49. For Hashimoto's experiences in Melbourne, see Hashimoto, *Fu Gōshū Meruborun hakurankai kikō*, vol. 1, pp. 12–18, 30–2; vol. 2, pp. 116–22.
49. 'Vice-Ambassador Muragaki Awaji no Kami'. Yoshida Tsunekichi, ed., *Kōkai nikki: Nichibei ryōkoku kankeishi (chū)* (Ocean diary: A history of Japanese-American relations; 1958). There is also an English translation: Helen Uno, ed., *Kōkai Nikki: The Diary of the First Japanese Embassy to the United States of America*, Tokyo, Foreign Affairs Association of Japan, 1958.
50. For Sakata's comments on the exhibition and trade with Australia, see Sakata, *Gōshū Shidoni fu bankoku hakurankai hōkokusho*, part 1 (the Garden Palace was burned to the ground three years after Sakata's visit); and part 2, pp. 16–18, 26–7, 63, 157–9, 162–4.
51. 'Alexander Marks . . . installed . . . in 1879'. See JFMA, File 6.1.5.9–7.
51. 'Sakata criticizes this step'. See Sakata, *Gōshū Shidoni fu bankoku hakurankai hōkokusho*, part 2, pp. 160–1.
51. 'Japan's lowest social class'. See Shiga, *Nan'yō jiji*, p. 30. Shiga probably ran into Pemberton Willard's Japanese troupe, hired in early 1886 in Japan for an Australian tour as 'The Japanese Village'; see also Sissons, Australian-Japanese Relations, pp. 22–4.
52. 'Australians are the bravest . . . Anglo-Saxons'. See Shiga, *Nan'yō jiji*, p. 30.
52. 'Only Japan can benefit'. Ibid., pp. 32, 37.
52. 'they will be hailed'. Ibid., p. 31.
52. 'Shiga . . . at his most prophetic'. Ibid., pp. 31, 36.
52–3. On Japanese imports and exports from and to Australia, see ibid., pp. 32–8.
53. 'the twentieth century's most significant . . . event'. Ibid., pp. 39–41. Shiga was not far off the mark, for Australian federation took place fifteen years later in 1901, although federation was neither an overwhelming event in the south Pacific, nor did it weaken Australia's ties with Britain. As regards the establishment of a joint capital, the first Federal Parliament met at Canberra on 9 May 1927, twenty-six years after the publication of Shiga's report.
54. 'Shiga's penchant for social Darwinism'. Ibid., pp. 41–5, 48–9. Shiga refers to the first-cited political party as the Dokuritsutō, and then adds in Roman letters, 'National Party'; the opposing party he calls Honkokutō, followed by 'Imperialistic'. 'Australia for Australians' is also printed in Roman letters. In Chapter 9, Shiga attributes the large inflow of immigrants from Europe to the scourge of communism, nihilism, and anarchy, which, according to him, had impoverished many parts of the Old World—'Australia was one solution to the poor Europeans' plight'.
54. 'my southerly neighbours, my good brothers'. Ibid., p. 46.
54. 'the *Tsukuba* . . . to rendezvous . . . with the . . . Japanese'. See Marks to Vice Foreign Minister, 2 October 1885, *Nihon gaikō bunsho*, 1885, p. 543; Vice Foreign Minister to Marks, 19 February 1886, *Nihon gaikō bunsho*, 1886, p. 507.
54. 'the key to Pacific trade'. See Inagaki, *Tōhōsaku*, p. 108.
55. 'Australia . . . a huge trade center'. See Mishima, *Gōshū oyobi Indo*, pp. 78, 84–9, 91–2, 147–53. For a modern account of the strike, see Fitzpatrick and Cahill, *The Seamen's Union of Australia*, pp. 19–23.
55. 'What position are we going to adopt?' See Hirose Takeo, *Kōnan Shiki*, pp. 120–1. The book was published posthumously, after Hirose's bravery in the Russo-Japanese war had made him a national hero.
55. For Hirose on the Australian military, see ibid., pp. 113–20.
56. 'a man set out'. See Watanabe Kanjūrō, *Gōshū tanken hōkokusho*, pp. 1–5. Watanabe was recruited from outside the Foreign Ministry for the task. 'Mr Kanjūrō Watanabe . . . will soon proceed to Australia in the capacity of a private individual . . . whose service this Department has decided to avail of in collecting reports on the subject of emigration to that continent': Foreign Ministry to Marks, 26 July 1893, in JFMA, File 6.1.6.17.

57. 'Japanese did not understand the foreign way of trading'. See Watanabe, *Gōshū tanken hōkokusho*, pp. 78, 80–2. Kanematsu went on to found Kanematsu Gōshō, a leading *sōgō shōsha* (general trading company) which still controls a major marketing share in Japan's textile industry.

57–8. 'two profitable areas'. Ibid., pp. 283–7.

58. 'Japanese contract labour in Queensland'. Ibid., pp. 74–5, 288–9.

58. 'five hundred Japanese ... on Thursday Island'. See Hattori, *Nankyū no shin shokumin*, pp. 1–2, 6, 14–15.

59. 'Christmas plum pudding'. *Gōshū sanbutsu kōtei daikahyō*, p. 3.

63. 'Australia ... had invited Chinese immigrants'. Roberts, 'History of Contacts between the Orient and Australia', p. 3. See Choi, *Chinese Migration and Settlement in Australia*, for a detailed description of the beginning of Chinese immigration to Australia.

65. 'A strong Japanese navy might ... constitute a menace'. British Minister Le Poer Trench to Earl of Kimberley, British Foreign Office, 12December 1894; and Foreign Office to Colonial Office, 27 April 1895 (in Stargardt, *Australia's Asian Policies*, pp. 114–15).

65. 'Australia now had at her door a maritime power'. Hutton to the New South Wales Colonial Secretary, 12 March 1895, and copies of letter to Duke of Cambridge and George H. Reid, Premier of New South Wales, 22 April and 27 July 1895 (in Meaney, *The Search for Security*, p. 29).

65. 'Craig studied ... Japan's occupation of Taiwan'. Quoted in DA, pp. 18–19.

65. 'military exercises in 1895'. Shepherd, *Australia's Interests and Policies in the Far East*, p. 5.

66. The Katsura, Kodama, and Gotō comments are in Tsurumi, *Gotō Shimpei*, pp. 414, 417–23, 426.

67. 'a brake on her southward advance'. See Shimizu, 'Taishō shoki ni okeru "Nanshin ron"', pp. 2–9. See also his abridged and translated version '*Nanshin-ron*: Its Turning Point in World War I', pp. 386–402.

67. 'Japan ... talked about in the Australian parliament'. Meaney, *The Search for Security*, pp. 137–8, 140, 146–7.

68. 'does any power go with it?'. Uchida, *Kokumin kaigai hatten saku*, p. 1. For an appraisal of Japanese psychological constraints about being a first-class power in the *nan'yō* at that time, see Shimizu, 'Taishō shoki ni okeru "Nanshin ron"', pp. 30–4.

68. 'Japan should ... expand ... with money'. See his speech of 8 September 1913, 'Hokushū nanshin-ron' (On defending the north and advancing south) in Inukai, *Kokubō oyobi gaikō*, pp. 82–7.

68. Nitobe rejoices over annexation of Korea. See Miwa, 'Nitobe Inazō and the Development of Colonial Theories and Practices in Prewar Japan', p. 12.

68. 'Momotarō ... as a tool ... to stir ... the southward advance'. See Nitobe, *Nitobe hakushi bunshū*, pp. 408–9. A full treatment of Momotarō and Japanese attitudes toward expansion can be found in Miwa, *Crossroads of Patriotism in Imperial Japan*, pp. 343–8. See also Shimizu, '"Ware wa umi no ko" kara "yashi no mi"', pp. 14–17.

68–9. For Fukuzawa on Momotarō, see Storry, *Japan and the Decline of the West*, p. 14.

69. 'Momotarō Doctrine ... of aggression'. Kamishima, *Kindai Nippon no seishin kōzō*, pp. 202, 204–5.

69. 'Momotarō ... as a propaganda piece'. Momotarō symbolized Japan, and his three companions: Taiwan, Korea, and Manchukuo. The ogres were Churchill, Roosevelt, and Chiang Kai-Shek. For the full dialogue, photos of rehearsals and performances, and the background of 'Momotarō' as a propaganda piece in occupied territories, see Koide, *Nanpō engeiki*, pp. 209–64.

69. For Takekoshi's comments on the South, see Takekoshi, *Nangokuki*, pp. 1–15, 337–8; *Taiyō* (The Sun), June 1911, pp. 82–3.

69. 'a voluntary expression of friendship'. For Japan's decision to join the war, see Takeuchi, *War and Diplomacy*, p. 169; Clyde, *Japan's Pacific Mandate*, p. 268; Ikeda, *Nihon no kaigun*, Vol. 2, pp. 28–9; and Peattie, *The Nan'yō*, pp. 38, 324.

70. 'suffused with pan-Asianist thought'. See Shimizu, 'Taishō shoki ni okeru "Nanshin ron"', p. 27. For an early version of the regional *tōyō* concept, see Jimbo Bunji, *Tōsa kenkyū nan'yō no hōko* (A treasure house of the South Seas), Tokyo, Jitsugyo-no-Nihon-sha, 1915, pp. 10–27.

70–1. For Asianists' and Tokutomi Sohō's influence on the *nanshin-ron*, see Shimizu, 'Taishō shoki ni okeru "Nanshin ron"', pp. 34–6, 41, 44, 47, 50–1.

71. 'numerous books on the *nanshin-ron'*. This ideology was particularly strong during and just after World War I. Major works written at that time included Yamada Kiichi, *Nan'yō angya shi* (A walking tour in the South Seas), 1910; Shiomi Heinosuke, *Nan'yō hatten* (Development of the South Seas), 1912; Inoue Kiyoshi, *Nan'yō to Nihon* (The South Seas and Japan), 1913; Egawa Kaoru, *Nan'yō o mokuteki ni* (Aiming at the South Seas), 1913; Sano Minoru, *Nan'yō shotō junkōki* (A cruise in the South Sea Islands), 1913; Nakai Kinjo, *Nan'yō dan* (An account of the South Seas), 1914; Soejima Yasoroku, *Teikoku nanshin saku* (An Imperial southward advance policy), 1916; Yamada Kiichi, *Nanshin saku to Ogasawara guntō* (The policy of southward advance and the Ogasawara Islands), 1916; and Matsumoto Takayuki, *Nanpō teikoku ron* (An Imperial southern region), 1918. For a schematic analysis of the political, geographical, and economic topics treated in most of these books, see Table 2 in Shimizu, 'Taishō shoki ni okeru "Nanshin ron"', pp. 20–1.
71. 'the South Seas . . . a boundless treasure house'. Nan'yō Kyōkai, *Nan'yō Kyōkai nijūnen shi*, pp. 5–6.
72. 'a *nanshin-ron* void of military aggression'. See Tsurumi, *Nan'yō yūki*, especially his final comments on 'capitalistic southward advance' and 'Imperialism and the South Seas', pp. 643–53.
72. For Yamamoto on the South, see Yamamoto Teijirō, 'Nan'yō shisatsu dan', pp. 7–8, 19–20, 23.
72. 'Australia in . . . literature on the *nan'yō'*. For example, Tanaka, *Gōshū shisatsu fukumeisho*, 653 pages with many accurate maps of each state, it treats Australia's geography, farming, politics, fishery, and especially her forestry with lots of statistics and photos of trees; Osaka Shōsen, *Gōshū jijō*, on shipping trade. During and after World War I appeared: Jose's history of Australia, *Gōshū oyobi sono shotō*, with the translator's comment: 'Although allied to Great Britain, we know geographically very little about Australia. Presently and in the future Australia will enter an important relationship with Japan. We translated this book to throw light on the subject of Australia'; Tsuchiya, *Gōshū (Nanpō tairiku) oyobi Shinseiran (Chōhakuun)*, 80 pages of photos about Australia precede this Japanese appraisal of Australia in mid-war; Anzai, *Gōshū no sangyō kin'yū oyobi bōeki*, mainly statistics with relevant figures for the Japanese-Australian trade-flow during the war (pp. 705–36); Koide 's postwar report, *Gōshū yōgyō chōsa hōkokusho*, on Australia's geography, history, real estate, industries, and all about sheep.
73. '"outer" South Seas'. The Japanese used the term 'Southeast Asia' already in World War I (the West adopting it only in World War II); its evolution from the *nan'yō* concepts is described in Shimizu, 'Kindai Nihon ni okeru "Tōnanajia" chiiki gainen no setsuritsu (1)', pp. 2–15, 22–38.
73. 'According to a 1933 source'. See Matsumura, *Minami ni mo seimeisen ari*, p. 2, with folding map.
74. 'Japanese Foreign Ministry . . . negotiated'. *Nihon Gaikō Bunsho*, 1883, p. 440–9.
74. 'most pearlers did well'. See Sissons, 'The Early Japanese Influence on the Northern Territory', p. 16; and The Japanese in the Australian Pearling Industry, p. 1.
74. 'Marks . . . warned the Japanese Vice Foreign Minister'. Marks to Hayashi, 2 April 1894, JFMA File 3.8.2.33, Vol. 1.
75. '*Kongo* could not be despatched'. Marks to Hayashi and Hayashi to Marks, 9 May, 18 August 1894, JFMA File 3.8.2.33, Vol. 1.
75. 'Japanese numbers had not increased particularly'. Sissons, 'The Early Japanese Influence on the Northern Territory', p. 19. In 1893, 21 Japanese men and 12 women lived at Darwin. They were from the prefectures of Wakayama, Nagasaki, Fukuoka, and Miyazaki; see Watanabe Kanjūrō, *Gōshū tanken hōkokusho*, pp. 279–81.
75. 'small number . . . a threat'. Alexander Marks to Vice Foreign Minister, 4 October 1893, JFMA File 3.8.2.33, Vol. 1; Sissons, 'The Early Japanese Influence on the Northern Territory', p. 19.
75. On warning the Queensland and South Australian Parliaments, see ibid., pp. 19–20.
75. 'Willis asked . . . in the Legislative Assembly'. 8 May 1895, see New South Wales, *Votes and Proceedings of the Legislative Assembly*, 1895–1896 Session, Vol. 6, pp. 1320–5, (AWD, p. 108).
75. 'Griffith led a debate'. See Sissons, 'The Early Japanese Influence on the Northern Territory', p. 20.
76. 'Kingston . . . had played a leading part'. See Norris, *The Emergent Commonwealth*, pp. 54–5.

76. 'Kingston was the driving force'. See Sissons, 'The Early Japanese Influence on the Northern Territory', p. 20; see also Takeda, Australia-Japan Relations, pp. 17–18.
76. 'colonies . . . none too enthusiastic about the summoning of an Intercolonial Conference'. See Kathleen J. Melhuish quoted in Takeda, Australia-Japan Relations, p. 18.
76. 'Hanihara would tell an Australian government official'. PM's Department file SC234/42, Piesse Papers, File 'Eastern Tour 1919–20' (DA, pp. 28–9).
77. On Marks trying to obtain an island for a Japanese colony, see Marks to Japanese Foreign Minister, 20 March 1896, and Jacob Goldstein to Marks, 14 May 1896, JFMA File 3.8.2.33, Vol. 1.
77. 'Its most important points for Australia'. The text of the treaty appears in AWD, pp. 109–10.
77–8. 'Japanese coolies stick together'. Straits Times, 15 November 1895.
78. 'one overall conclusion'. In Sissons, Attitudes to Japan, p. 19.
79. 'White Australia policy . . . a national security policy'. H. I. London, for example, writes in Non-White Immigration and the 'White Australia' Policy, Sydney, Sydney University Press, 1970: 'To a very great extent Australian defense policy was nothing but a disguise for the protection of White Australia against "the yellow peril". The White Australia immigration policy had been elevated to a national faith on which it was believed self-preservation depended.' According to Yarwood, the Immigration Restriction Bill of 1896 was presented as part of an Australia-wide plan to bring to logical completion the defence against coloured immigration; see Yarwood, Asian Migration to Australia, p. 11. Indeed, Attorney-General Alfred Deakin declared on 12 September 1901 that the White Australia policy was the Australian version of 'the Monroe doctrine' in the Pacific, CPD, 1901–2 Session, Vol. 4, p. 4807, in Takeda, Australia-Japan Relations, p. 53.
79. 'the speeches of the Grand Old Man'. For Sir Henry Parkes's speeches in New South Wales, see Parliamentary Debates, Legislative Assembly, 1887–1888 Session, Vol. 32, pp. 3787–8, 4781–7 (3 April, 16 May 1888), and Sydney Morning Herald, 9 April 1888, 25 October 1889 (in AWD, pp. 93–104).
79. 'the new form of warfare from which we may suffer'. Official Report of the National Australasian Convention Debates, Sydney, 2 March-9 April 1891 (New South Wales Government Printer, 1891), 13 March 1891, pp. 316–17 (in AWD, p. 105).
79. 'argument by men like Reid or Homburg'. See Yarwood, Asian Migration to Australia, p. 8; Sissons, Attitudes to Japan, pp. 13–15.
80. 'an often ridiculously phrased dictation'. Sample of a dictation test from a Sydney newspaper cutting, in JFMA File 3.8.2.33, Vol. 6.
80. For Hugh Nelson's opportunism, see Takeda, Australia-Japan Relations, pp. 37–43.
80. 'influx of Japanese labourers', see Yarwood, Asian Migration to Australia, p. 16.
81. 'they do not mean to hide their light under a bushel'. Brisbane Courier, 12 May 1897.
81. 'an appanage of the Mikado'. North Queensland Register, 5 May 1897.
81. 'the Scotchmen of the East'. Brisbane Courier, 21 July 1897.
82. 'Having learnt through England'. Torres Straits Pilot, 22 June 1897. A Wakayama man, Satō Torajirō, had graduated in law from Michigan University. He sailed with youths he recruited to Thursday Island in 1893, amassed there a small fortune in the pearling industry, and lost it by 1900. Then he stood successfully for the House of Representatives for Gumma prefecture from 1903 to 1909, and died in a bomb attack when he was mistaken for the governor-general in Korea in 1928. See Episodes: A Glimpse of Australia-Japan Relations 1859–1979, produced under the auspices of the Embassy of Japan in Australia, [1979], pp. 27–8.
83. 'Immigration of Japanese . . . has been suspended'. Japanese Consul at Townsville Nakagawa to Ōkuma, and Ōkuma to Morikawa, 7, 9 June 1897, JFMA File 3.8.2.33, Vol. 1.
83. 'Japanese immigration [to] . . . Queensland . . . continued unabated'. See Yarwood, Asian Migration to Australia, pp. 16–18.
83. 'more stringent than originally conceived'. For a detailed study of the diplomatic aspects of the immigration issue in London and Australia, see Takeda, Australia-Japan Relations, pp. 11–59; Meaney, The Search for Security, pp. 107–19; Yarwood, Asian Migration to Australia, pp. 12–18; and Willard, History of the White Australia Policy.
83. 'Alliance . . . a check against a Russian fleet'. Sydney Morning Herald, 14 February 1902 (in AWD, pp. 125–8).
83. For Suttor in Kobe, see Takeda, Australia-Japan Relations, pp. 74–105.

84. 'Deakin [in] direct talks with . . . Iwasaki'. Ibid., pp. 162–70; Meaney, *The Search for Security*, pp. 129–32. Australia differed here significantly from Canada. The Canadian Government had not signed the treaty in 1894 for similar reasons and despite growing trade relations with Japan; in 1906, however, it accepted the treaty without changing the article that gave full privilege to the subjects of each country in each other's territories.

84. 'travellers are carried . . . according to the race'. Tayui Rinzaburō to Tramway Company, 13 June 1904, JFMA File 3.8.22.33, Vol. 9.

84. 'Tayui . . . advised . . . Komura'. Tayui to Komura, confidential despatch, No. 3, *Nihon Gaikō Bunsho,*10 June 1905, Vol. 38–2, No. 1139, pp. 237–41.

84. 'withdrawal of Britain's five battleships in the Pacific'. This took place during the first drafting for the renewal of the Anglo-Japanese alliance designed to strengthen British security in India and Japan's hand in Korea. The Japanese stipulated that Britain and Japan maintain naval forces superior to the fleet of any third power. Britain left this responsibility for the Pacific region entirely to Japan after the destruction of the Russian squadron, when she immediately withdrew her battleships to reinforce the Channel fleet; see Nish, *The Anglo-Japanese Alliance in Decline*, pp. 353–8.

85. 'be ready . . . to give and . . . receive . . . blows'. *Commonwealth Parliamentary Papers*, 1905 Session, Vol. 11, No. 31 (in *AWD*, pp. 154–8).

85. 'Allan McLean . . . warned'. *Herald*, 13 June 1905 (in Meaney, *The Search for Security*, p. 126).

85. 'Japan . . . is an aggressive nation'. *CPD*, 1905 Session, Vol. 29, p. 5346, 22 November 1905 (in ibid., p. 127).

85. 'danger of invasion . . . from Asia'. *The Call*, II November 1906, (in ibid., p. 127).

85. 'Let us make any sacrifice'. Ibid. pp. 127–8, and *Sydney Morning Herald*, 8 August 1905 (in *AWD*, p. 161).

86. 'Pearce . . . demolished Pulsford's motion'. *CPD*, 1905 Session, Vol. 27, pp. 2788–9, September 1905, in Takeda, *Australia–Japan Relations*, pp. 176–7.

86. 'I am prepared to write articles'. See E. H. Foxall to Foreign Minister Viscount Hayashi, 2 December 1907, JFMA File 3.8.2.33, Vol. 8.

87. 'Deakin became the prime mover'. See Meaney, *The Search for Security*, pp. 186–91; Sissons, *Attitudes to Japan*, pp. 48–60.

87. 'we have slammed the door of Australia right in their faces'. *CPD*, 1903 Session, Vol. 14, p. 2056, 14 July 1903 (in *AWD*, pp. 134–5).

87. 'to keep Australia intact'. Sissons, *Attitudes to Japan*, p. 53.

87. 'twenty million . . . behind the guns'. Senator Pearce's 'Eight Hour Day' address at Horsham (reported in the *Argus*, 26 April 1909) (in ibid., p. 55).

87. 'surrounded by nations hungering for room'. *CPD*, 1909 Session, Vol. 51, pp. 3613–19, 21 September 1909 (*AWD*, p. 185).

87–8. 'Both Houses passed with little debate'. See Meaney, *The Search for Security*, pp. 188–9, 191; Sissons, *Attitudes to Japan*, p. 58.

88. 'Is not Japan an ally'. 2 April 1909. In the event, Pearce seems to have suffered for his indiscretion as a minister; he was described as foolish, childish to have believed in such rubbish, and should have shut up, *Daily Telegraph*, 6 April and *Evening News*, 2 April.

88. 'If the Japanese . . . were . . . to rise to-morrow'. *Sun*, 6 March 1911.

88. '"It has occurred to me"'. Japanese Consul-General to Frey, 6 March 1911, JFMA File 3.8.2.33, Vol. 8.

88–9. 'the titles speak for themselves'. *Lone Hand*, May 1907, August-December 1908, December 1910 (in Meaney, *The Search for Security*, pp. 159–60).

89. 'Other stories about Japanese'. See Sissons, *Attitudes to Japan*, pp. 68–70.

89. '"I am genuinely surprised"'. The background of *The Australian Crisis* has been researched and discussed in Meaney, *The Search for Security*, pp. 159–63; see also Sissons, *Attitudes to Japan*, pp. 68–70. Excerpts of C. H. Kirmess, *The Australian Crisis*, are in *AWD*, pp. 176–80.

89. 'Churchill asked for Australian . . . Dreadnoughts'. See Great Britain, *Parliamentary Debates*, House of Commons, 1914 Session, Vol. 59, cols. 1931–3, 17 March 1914 (in *AWD*, pp. 205–6).

89. 'Australian leaders . . . flabbergasted'. See Meaney, *The Search for Security*, p. 250.

89. 'well-informed and sophisticated opinion'. See Ball, *Australia and Japan*, p. 5, and Meaney, *The Search for Security*, pp. 251, 258–61.

90. 'there is nothing in the Anglo-Japanese treaty'. *Argus*, 31 March 1914 (in *AWD*, pp. 208–9);

see also Eggleston's 'Naval Policy and the Pacific Question', with its unmistakable racist sentiments, in *Round Table*, Vol. 4, June 1914, pp. 394–403.

90. 'continuing bonds of interest'. *Commonwealth Paliamentary Papers*, 1914 Session, Vol. 11, No. 33 (in *AWD*, pp. 212–13).

91. 'gigantic convoy'. For the preparations of this massive operation, see Jose, *Official History*, pp. 72, 82–100, 150–64.

91. 'passing the Cocos Island'. On previous day, the leading British vessel *Minotaur* had been called away for another operation. For an account of the sea battle at Cocos Island, with illustrations and positions shown, see ibid., pp. 179–207; see also Bean, *The Official History*, Vol. 1, pp. 101–8.

91–2. '*Emden* . . . a dangerous ship'. See Jose, *Official History*, pp. 164–78.

92. 'Goodwill . . . slightly strained'. Captain Katō Kanji communicated to Captain Silver after the battle: 'Hearty congratulations on success of "Sydney" . . . I would venture to request that should similar occasion again arise, you will inform me of the number, disposition, course, name, position etc., of the enemy, & what you intend doing; otherwise misunderstandings may arise and co-operation become ineffective.' Silver answered: 'I feel very pleased at your congratulations & I much regret any misunderstanding . . . I did not think it wise to detach you & lessen strength of escort', in Kaigun daijin kanbō kiroku (Navy Ministry, record office), '*Ibuki senji nisō*', entries made on 9 November 1914 at 1.30 p.m. and 3.30 p.m., respectively. It is possible that such minor grievances, accumulated by a reluctant Japanese navy under British naval command, hardened Katō Kanji's attitude toward the West and turned him into an obstinate opponent of Anglo-Saxon naval hegemony during the interwar years (see Chapter 9).

92. 'patrolling the Australian coastline'. See Jose, *Official History*, pp. 340–2.

92–3. The *Yahagi* incident is documented in Kaigun Gunreibu, *Taishō yonen*, pp. 57–65.

93. 'things are *not* going well here'. Letter, Hughes to Pearce, 21 April 1916, Australian War Memorial, Pearce Papers, Bundle 3, folder 3 (in *AWD*, pp. 234–5).

94. 'Hunt . . . twice had talks with the Japanese Consul-General'. Letter, Hunt to Hon. H. Mahon, Minister for External Affairs, 9 February 1918, Papers 1913–30 and Special Subjects Misc. II, File 'Hon. H. Mason' (in *DA*, pp. 11–13).

94. 'Suttor . . . in favour of . . . Anglo-Japanese Commercial Treaty'. See Takeda, *Australia-Japan Relations*, pp. 96–9.

94. For Canada's gentleman agreements with Japan, see Iino, 'Nichi-Ei tsūsan kōkai jōyaku to Kanada no Nihonjin imin mondai', pp. 1–18; see also Pringsheim, *Neighbors Across the Pacific*, pp. 1–30.

94–5. For Count Ishii's explanation of the controversy, see Ishii Kikujirō, *Diplomatic Commentaries*, pp. 96–104, and 'Daisensō gaikō no issetsu'.

95. 'Hughes in "a state of some alarm"'. Sissons, *Attitudes to Japan*, p. 79; E. L. Piesse, 'Japan and Australia' address to the 'Boobooks' at Melbourne, 15 May 1925, in *DA*, p. 48.

95. 'Hughes's suspicion . . . fueled the Labor Party's attitude'. Sissons, *Attitudes to Japan*, pp. 79–83; Clark, *A Short History of Australia*, pp. 204–7.

95. 'references to Japan are . . . unpleasant'. *Argus*, 21 October 1916 (in *AWD*, pp. 240–1).

95. 'the yellow journalism of . . . Kayahara Kazan'. Kayahara, 'Nihon kokumin o jisatsu seshimuru mono wa Ei-Bei de aru', pp. 8–9; see also Sissons, *Attitudes to Japan*, pp. 83–4.

95. 'latent Australian northward advance'. The story of Australia's drive for island acquisitions in the Pacific is described in Thompson, *Australian Imperialism in the Pacific*.

96. 'feeding the inhabitants'. Jose, *Official History*, p. 72.

96. 'Had the Australians . . . gone northward right away'. Ibid., pp. 132–3. See also Hirama, 'Kaigunshiteki ni mita nanshin no ichi dammen', p. 95; 'Daiichiji sekai taisenchū', pp. 64–5.

96. 'George Pearce was . . . mistaken'. See Hirama, 'Daiichiji sekai taisenchū', pp. 64–5.

96–7. 'They are . . . out of our beat'. Hunt to Glynn, 12 October 1914, File Hon. P. McM. Glynn, in *DA*, p. 11.

97. 'down to the printing of postage-stamps'. Jose, *Official History*, pp. 136–7.

97. 'Britain asked Australia not to proceed'. Ibid., pp. 135–6.

97. 'question of future to be settled at the end of the war'. Telegram (secret), Harcourt to Ferguson, 3 December 1914, AA, CP, 78/23, item 89/68 (in *AWD*, p. 222).

97. 'My dear Ronald'. Harcourt to Ferguson, 6 December 1914, National Library of Australia, Munro Ferguson Papers 696/1306–09 (in *AWD*, pp. 223–4).

97–8. 'We have not . . . good grounds for objecting'. Letter (Private and Personal), Ferguson to Andrew Fisher, Prime Minster, 24 January 1915, ibid., 696/3863 (in *AWD*, p. 225).

98. 'Ferguson assured Harcourt''. Cablegram, Ferguson to Harcourt, 19 May 1915, ibid., 696/6629 (in *AWD*, p. 229).

98. 'consider favourably the Equator'. Hughes to Pearce, 21 April 1916, Australian War Memorial, Pearce Papers, Bundle 3, Folder 3 (in *AWD*, p. 234).

98. 'Britain bartered post-war assurances'. Telegram (Secret), Long to Ferguson, 1 February 1917, AA, CP 447/2, item SC472 (in *AWD*, pp. 241–2).

98. 'Hughes's unequivocal consent'. Telegram, Ferguson to Long, 10 February 1917, PRO, CO 532/91/232 (in *AWD*, p. 243).

98. 'His Majesty's Government accede with pleasure'. Despatch, Long to Ferguson, 2 March 1917, AA, CP 447/3 (in *AWD*, p. 244).

98. 'It is necessary to remind you'. Letter, Hughes to Lloyd George, 4 November 1918, House of Lords Library, Lloyd George Papers, Box 38, Folder 5 (in *AWD*, pp. 260–2).

99. 'if you wish any further discussion'. Letter, Lloyd George to Hughes, 31 December 1918, ibid. (in *AWD*, pp. 263–4).

99. 'Holman enclosed . . . a long memorandum'. Holman to Shimizu, 29 July 1919, JFMA File 1.1.4.1, Vol. 10.

99. 'Baron Makino Shinken's three proposals'. Scott, *The Official History*, pp. 791–2.

99. 'How much better . . . to accept the Japanese amendment'. Copy of letter, Piesse to Lt. Commander J. G. Latham, Member of Australian Delegation to the Paris Peace Conference, 7 May 1919, NLA, Piesse Papers (in *AWD*, p. 283).

100. 'Pacific Islands encompass Australia like fortresses'. U. S., *Foreign Relations*, 'The Paris Peace Conference, 1919', Vol. 3, pp. 720–2 (in *AWD*, p. 265).

100. 'Wilson told a Conference member'. David Hunter Miller, *My Diary at the Conference of Paris*, 21 vols, New York, 1924, Vol. 1, pp. 99–100 (in *AWD*, pp. 272–3).

100–1. 'Matsuoka challenged . . . the right to claim'. Japan, Navy Ministry, 'Nan'yō shin senryō chi no shōrai'.

101. 'starting with a clean slate'. Doc. SC374/122, NLA, Piesse Papers, file 'Peace Conference' (in Sissons, Attitudes to Japan, pp. 90, 98).

101. 'Immigration Restriction Law . . . on grounds of defence'. In July 1918, for example, the Chief of the General Staff recommended that a European be refused admission to New Guinea 'because other aliens perhaps Japanese might follow'. The Defence Department thereafter prohibited admission to all aliens. Memo, Piesse to Secretary, P.M.'s Department, 23 July 1920, 'Admission of Aliens to German New Guinea', NLA, Piesse Papers, file 'New Guinea' (in ibid., p. 37, fn. 13).

101. 'an "incident" might occur'. Latham's memorandum to Joseph Cook (in ibid., p. 90).

101. 'C-type Mandate, thrashed out by the Australian delegation'. See Scott, *The Official History*, pp. 785–6.

101–2. Japan's loss of rights in Australian Melanesia is detailed in Sissons, Attitudes to Japan, pp. 94–9, based on U. S., *Foreign Relations*, 'The Paris Peace Conference, 1919', Vol. 9, pp. 641 ff., and *CPD*, Vol. 103, p. 4454, 14 September 1920.

102. 'Hughes . . . called for an Australian Monroe Doctrine'. See *CPD*, 1919 Session, Vol. 89, pp. 12171–2, 10 September 1919 (in *AWD*, p. 289).

103. 'Jellicoe . . . volunteered his opinion'. See Hamill, *The Strategic Illusion*, p. 19.

103. 'Jellicoe never . . . appreciated . . . Japan . . . as an ally'. Nish, *Alliance in Decline*, p. 203.

103. 'Japan as a future source of danger'. See the Jellicoe Report on Naval Defence, Vol. 4 (secret), pp. 221–3, AA, Commonwealth Record Series, A65/2 (in *AWD*, pp. 290–1).

103. For the results of the two conferences in January and February, see Memorandum, Lieutenant-General H. G. Chauvel, Chairman of the Conference of Senior Officers, to Senator George Pearce, Minister for Defence, 6 February 1920, enclosing 'Report of the Conference of Senior Military Officers, constituted by the Minister for Defence on 22 January 1920, to advise upon the Military Defence of Australia', AA, MP, 729/2, File 1855/1/42 and File 1856/4/472 (in *AWD*, pp. 292–6).

103. 'to give Australia a "sporting chance"'. 'Minutes of a Special Meeting of the Council of Defence', 12 April 1920, AA, MP 104 9/1, File 19/016 (in *AWD*, pp. 298–9).

103–4. 'Spy stories blossomed'. See 'Japanese Espionage in Australia in Its Relation to Japanese Policy', address by E. L. Piesse for a conference of intelligence officers, Australian Military Forces, 17 April 1924, NLA, Piesse Papers (in *DA*, p. 42).

104. 'to haunt impressionable Australians'. See Walton, 'Feeling for the Jugular', pp. 23–5. Walton's 'pioneering piece', as he calls it, shows that the bogey of the 1920s is still alive in Australia. His article bases itself entirely on the unreliable data collected in the paranoia of those years without Japanese material to back his descriptions of what he terms Japanese 'high tempo, low tempo', etc. espionage on the New South Wales littoral.

104. 'Piesse . . . played down the Japanese spy-scare'. See DA, pp. 43, 46, and Piesse, 'Japan and Australia', p. 479.

104–5. 'no . . . more faithful friend . . . than Japan'. Sydney Morning Herald, 4 February 1921.

105. 'I . . . express my deep . . . shame'. Sydney Morning Herald, 1 November 1920.

105. 'my intention to give a dinner'. Bainbridge to Watt, 2 June 1919, JFMA File 3.8.2.33, Vol. 9.

106. 'thank you for your kind present'. Receipts of 16, 26 June and 14, 15, 23, 25 July 1919, JFMA File 3.8.2.33, Vol. 9.

106. 'let us coquette with . . . Australia'. Hornabrook to the Times (he enclosed an article for publication, 'The Anglo-Japanese Alliance: An Australian View'), to Stead's Review, and to Prime Minister Hughes, 26, 29 March and 28 April 1921, respectively, in JFMA File 1.1.4.1, Vol. 10.

107. 'the words of Hornabrook'. Hornabrook to Acting Consul-General Tamaki, 30 March and 11, 12, 27 April 1921, in JFMA File 1.1.4.1, Vol. 10.

107. 'This gives us breathing time'. Argus, 18 July 1911 (in Meaney, The Search for Security, p. 225).

107. 'the Treaty with Japan should be renewed'. 'Stenographic Notes of a Meeting of Representatives of the United Kingdom, the Dominions and India', PRO, British Cabinet Papers 32/2, Part 1, Vol. 1, pp. 2–19 (in AWD, pp. 316–18).

107. 'no better way than having the Japanese as an ally'. Empire Weekly (Vancouver), 16 September 1921.

107. 'Hughes's speeches created very friendly sentiments in Japan'. Daily Telegraph, 11 October 1921.

107–8. 'Alliance . . . to be modified'. CPD, 1921 Session, Vol. 94, pp. 7262–70, 7 April 1921 (in AWD, p. 314).

108. On the background of the Washington Conference, see W. M. Hughes's report to Parliament about the summoning of the Washington Conference, 30 September 1921, CPD, 1921 Session, Vol. 97, pp. 11630–3 (in AWD, pp. 319–21); see also Nish, Alliance in Decline, pp. 333–53.

108. 'Piesse . . . valued the Four Power Treaty'. 'The Quadruple Pacific Treaty', a paper by Piesse, NLA, Piesse Papers (in AWD, p. 321).

108. 'This Treaty establishes an equilibrium'. CPD, 1922 Session, Vol. 99, pp. 786–93, 26 July 1922 (in AWD, pp. 323–6).

108–9. 'We have been nervous'. Ibid., pp. 821–3, 27 July 1922 (in AWD, pp. 326–9).

109. 'defence expenditures were cut'. Sissons, Attitudes to Japan, pp. 121–2.

109. 'Australia's first embryonic foreign office'. Edwards, Prime Ministers & Diplomats, pp. 52–4, 58.

109. 'study of Japanese affairs . . . "quite unnecessary"'. See Sissons, Attitudes to Japan, pp. 123–4.

113. 'Japan has paid Australia a . . . compliment'. Sydney Morning Herald, 2 December 1925.

113. 'Viscount Kato desires' and 'The beginning of our history'. Kato to Bruce, and Bruce to Kato, 15, 16 December 1925, in JFMA File 1.1.4.1, Vol. 10.

114. 'Mitsui . . . on a tour of Australia'. See Mitsui, Gōshū ryōkōki, pp. 1–2, 13–16.

114. 'Piesse . . . dismissed Japan . . . as a threat to Australia'. Piesse, 'Japan and Australia', pp. 475, 487–8.

115. 'Nitobe . . . supported by intellectual retainers'. Nakami, International Thought of the Japanese Intellectuals, pp. 1–3.

115. 'Australian delegations . . . led by Frederic Eggleston'. Edwards, Prime Ministers & Diplomats, pp. 94–5.

115. 'Japanese . . . unconcerned about the White Australia policy'. Nakami, International Thought of the Japanese Intellectuals, pp. 5–6.

115. 'Japanese residents in Australia dropped'. See Shimizu, 'Nihon-Tōnanajia kankei to "Nanshin-ron"', pp. 19–20 (Table 4).

116. In the new, large influx of Japanese immigrants into the Southeast Asian region, those engaged in the trading profession were the most visible group, accounting for 31.2 per cent, while farmers took second place with 25.8 per cent. For a comparison of southward protagonists in the seventeenth century, the 1860s, and the1920s, see Shimizu, 'Nihon-Tōnanajia kankei no bunmei shiteki ichi', pp. 298–302, 304–6.
117. 'Japanese immigrants [in] Batavia'. See Iwao, *Zoku Nanyō Nihonmachi*, chs 1–3.
118. 'Japanese . . . in Davao'. See Hashiya, 'Senzenki Fuiripin ni okeru hōnin keizai shinshutsu no keitai', pp. 33–51.
119. 'the Nan'yō-chō was established'. Clyde, *Japan's Pacific Mandate*, pp. 78–82.
119. 'Australia's civil administrative center remained at Rabaul'. See Radi, 'New Guinea Under Mandate', p. 77.
119. 'Japanese . . . stood at 944'. Yanaihara, *Pacific Islands Under Japanese Mandate*, pp. 259, 262.
119. 'six men of ability'. Clyde, *Japan's Pacific Mandate*, p. 79.
120. 'no steady . . . Australian administrative influence'. Radi, 'New Guinea Under Mandate', pp. 95, 97.
120. 'Japan's . . . management-by-delegation style'. Yanaihara, *Pacific Islands Under Japanese Mandate*, pp. 262–3.
120. 'no rule at all'. Radi, 'New Guinea Under Mandate', p. 97.
120. 'police functions . . . were dominant'. Ibid., pp. 97, 99.
120. 'Ainsworth's recommendations were ignored'. Ibid., pp. 76, 98–9.
120. 'Japan . . . developed tremendously its agricultural-industrial potential'. This and the following two paragraphs rely on Peattie, *Nan'yō*, ch. 4.
121. 'John Alvin Decker protested'. Decker, *Labor Problems in the Pacific Mandates*, p. 51; see also chs 5, 6.
121–2. 'Australia's mandate problems . . . produced similar ill-effects'. Radi, 'New Guinea Under Mandate', pp. 82,109–13.
122. 'New Guinean labourers had the lowest wages'. Decker, *Labor Problems in the Pacific Mandates*, p. 190.
122. 'Ruthless recruiters . . . caused social discord'. See Radi, 'New Guinea Under Mandate', pp. 89–90, 92–4, 132–4.
122. 'headmen . . . compensated for each volunteer'. Peattie, *Nan'yō*, ch. 4; Decker, *Labor Problems in the Pacific Mandates*, pp. 130–50; Yanaihara, *Pacific Islands Under Japanese Mandate*, pp. 278–80.
122. 'Lugard . . . castigated Australia'. See Hudson, *Australia and the League of Nations*, p. 147.
122. 'making the territories . . . pay for themselves'. See Radi, 'New Guinea Under Mandate', pp. 80, 82; see also Sir Joseph Cook's statement in 1919: 'I hope that we shall be able by good and judicious management to make them pay the cost of their own development', in Hudson, ed., *New Guinea Empire*, p. 4.
122–3. 'Japan's exports to Australia had risen . . . to 65 million yen in 1934'. See Narita, *Nichigō tsūshō gaikō shi*, pp. 101–3. W. R. Purcell gives a more detailed account of Japanese trade activities in Australia during the interwar period in his absorbing study on 'The Nature and Extent of Japanese Commercial and Economic Interests in Australia,1932–1941'.
123. 'the depression . . . reinforced their . . . two-way trade pattern'. See Shepherd, *Australia's Interests*, pp. 20–8.
123–4. 'Frank Anstey denounced in Parliament'. 27 June, 16 July 1924, *CPD*, 1924 Session, Vol. 107, pp. 1702–3, 2115–17 (in *AWD*, pp. 346–50).
124. 'Bruce was forced to reduce defence expenditure'. Summary of Proceedings of General Meeting of the Council of Defence, 8 July 1924, AA, MP1049/9, File 1851/4/17 (in *AWD*, pp. 368–9).
124. 'Scullin further curtailed defence expenditures'. Ibid., 12 November 1929 (in *AWD*, pp. 369–71, 373).
124. 'the Antarctic region and . . . the New Hebrides'. A Statement on Australia's "Foreign Policy and Relations" by Keith Officer, External Affairs Section, Prime Minister's Department, 8 August 1930, AA, CRS A981, item Imperial 126 (in *AWD*, p. 373–4).
124. 'Australia . . . not apprehensive of . . . Japan'. Ian Hamill, *The Strategic Illusion*, p. 188.
125. 'it upset the Australian government'. Cablegram, J. G. Latham to S. M. Bruce, High Commisssioner in London, and Bruce to Latham 2 and 3 March 1933, AA, CRS A981, item China 114 ('old') pt 5 (in *AWD*, pp. 386–7).

125. 'Latham urged that a formula be sought'. 'Report upon the International Position in the Far East', in secret letter, Latham, to Lyons, 3 July 1934, NLA, Papers of Sir Earle Page, Ms. 1633/288 (in *AWD*, pp. 388–9).

125–6. 'a long conversation with Foreign Minister Hirota Kōki'. Ibid., pp. 389–90; on the 'Question of Bases', see for example Peattie's careful evaluation in *Nan'yō*, pp. 230–56.

126. 'Menzies . . . took his minister's concerns . . . to London'. Notes of the Third Meeting of British Commonwealth Prime Ministers, held in the Prime Minister's Room at the House of Commons on 9 May 1935, AA, CRS A981, item Imperial Relations 135 (in *AWD*, pp. 394–5).

126. 'to rejoice . . . every time Japan advanced'. Nancy H. Hooker, ed., *The Moffat Papers*, Cambridge, Mass., Harvard University Press,1956, pp. 126–30 (in *AWD*, pp. 396–7).

127. 'Hughes . . . sounded a loud warning'. pp. 118–19, 122–4 (in *AWD*, pp. 387–99).

127. 'The air arm has all the attractions of novelty'. 'Albatross' [E. L. Piesse], *Japan and the Defence of Australia*, pp. 17–18, 20–1, 47–8.

127–8. 'Japan was likely to extend her Empire towards Australia'. Ibid., pp.17–21.

131. 'Port Darwin'. Darwin, Australia's northern gateway, was first investigated in 1839 by Captain John L. Stokes in the *Beagle*. In 1869 a settlement was established there called Palmerston and the harbour named Port Darwin, in honour of Charles Darwin with whom Stokes had sailed on an earlier voyage in the *Beagle*. Only Port Darwin survived as place name after 1911, when the administration of the Northern Territory was transferred from the South Australian to the Federal Government.

131. 'Ishimaru's plot'. See Ishimaru, *Nichi-Ei hissen ron*, Ch. 12. The writer has come across no other raid-scenario involving Australia in the Japanese pre-war literature.

132. 'History has no experience'. See *CPD*, Vol. 152, pp. 1549, 1553 (in A. W. Stargardt, *Australia's Asian Policies* (1977), pp. 158–60).

132. The building of defences for Darwin began in the early 1930s with the raising of barracks and the stationing of a garrison. In connection with the Singapore strategy, the construction of oil storage tanks had taken place already between 1924 and 1928. An official United States naval observer, Commander Marshall Collins, was despatched to Darwin in March 1941. At the time of attack, United States naval and air force units were stationed in Darwin for action in the Netherlands East Indies, Borneo, and the Philippines region and to reinforce the Australian air force and army in the North. Despite direct warnings before the raid, Darwin was taken by surprise.

For an excellent detailed account of army, navy, and civilian life in Darwin before and during the Pacific War, see the definite study by Powell, *The Shadow's Edge*. For a critical appraisal of the Japanese raid on Darwin, the bravery of some, and the mistakes of many, see Lockwood, *Australia's Pearl Harbour*, and Hall, *Darwin 1942*. For low troop morale at Darwin, see also Horner, *Crisis of Command*, pp. 68–72. A comprehensive view of the impact of United States forces in Australia is given in Potts, *Yanks Down Under 1941–45*.

132. 'off the face of the earth'. Hall, *Darwin 1942*, p. 77.

132. 'panic'. Lockwood, *Australia's Pearl Harbour*, pp. 143–6; ibid., pp. 79–84.

133. 'fifty-eight subsequent attacks'. Lockwood, *Australia's Pearl Harbour*, p. 223; Hall, *Darwin 1942*, pp. 164–5. For the fierce attack on Broome, see Prime, *WA's Pearl Harbour*, and Tyler, *Flight of Diamonds*. See also the Japanese time-table of bombing events on Australia's north coast for the days from 19 February to 16 June1942, based on the *Dōmei Tsūshin* (News service), listed in Kanematsu Shōten Kabushikigaisha, *Daitōa senboppatsu go no Gōshū no ugoki*, pp. 26–8.

133. 'Darwin attack . . . in . . . war histories'. Australia's official war history gives it only the barest outline; the Japanese official history of the Pacific War, in more than a hundred volumes, allows it a tiny paragraph in BBS, *Daihon'ei kaigunbu rengōkantai*, Vol. 2, pp. 191–2.

133. 'more news concerning horse-racing'. Hurley to General Marshall, 21 February 1942. Hurley, a former Secretary of War and old friend of General MacArthur, had been sent to Australia to lend his 'energetic support' to get supplies to MacArthur in the Philippines; see Horner, *Crisis of Command*, pp. 47, 330.

133. 'the first Australian flag damaged'. Abbott, *Australia's Frontier Province*, pp. 81–2.

133. About the looting, see Hall, *Darwin 1942*, pp. 127–39; Lockwood, *Australia's Pearl Harbour*, pp. 169–71, 202; Powell, *The Shadow's Edge*, pp. 239–40; and Abbott, who was the Administrator at that time, *Australia's Frontier Province*, p. 94.

133. 'Japan's . . . punitive expedition to Taiwan'. Under the leadership of Saigo Tsugumichi, 3,658 troops descended on Taiwan in one British, one French, and four Japanese vessels; they landed on 22 May 1874 and, after chastising natives for having ill-treated Japanese subjects, withdrew on 3 December the same year. The Japanese sustained 572 casualties (12 died in action, 560 through illness); total war expenses amounted to 7,700,010 yen; see Yasuoka, 'Taiwan shuppei'; Iechika Yoshiki, ' "Taiwan shuppei" hōshin no tenkan to chō shū ha no hantai undō'.

135. 'the Australian Government . . . started a trade war'. By 1935, Australian imports of Japanese cotton-piece goods had risen more than 350 per cent above the 1926 figure. A dramatic shift was taking place in the Australian textile market away from Great Britain and toward Japan. It was mainly to counteract Japan's huge textile sales that on 22 May 1936 Australia raised stiff tariffs on imports. Japan immediately retaliated by boycotting Australian wool, shifted her patronage to South Africa, New Zealand, and South America, and turned to staple fiber as a substitute for Australian wool. See Shepherd, Australia's Interests, Ch. 3; Bruno, 'The "Trade Diversion" Episode of the Thirties'; Sissons, 'Manchester v. Japan'; Fukushima, ' "Bōeki tenkan seisaku" '.

135. 'None of us can imagine'. Nichigō Kyōkai, Nichigō kyōkai sōkai kaimu hōkoku, Vol. 9, p. 6.

135. 'visits of your [Navy] are entirely appreciated'. Ibid., Vol. 8, p. 27.

136. 'the Five Ministers' Conference'. The attending ministers were the Prime Minister, Foreign Minister, Finance Minister, Army Minister, and Navy Minister; the Four Ministers' Conference, later in the day, took place without the Finance Minister.

136. 'We must plan to develop . . . the outer Southern area'. (The 'outer southern area' was practically identical with today's South East Asian region.) See Gendai-shi shiryō, Vol. 8, Tome 1, p. 361; for an English translation of 'Fundamentals of National Policy', see Joyce C. Lebra, Japan's Greater East Asia Co-Prosperity Sphere, pp. 62–3.

136. 'indispensable for . . . defence'. Gendai-shi shiryō, Vol. 8, Tome 1, p. 365.

137. 'protégé Takahashi Sankichi'. In a polemical book of his, Nanpō kyōeiken o kataru (About the Southern Co-Prosperity Sphere, May 1941), Takahashi denounced the White Australia policy which kept the continent underpopulated: even though families received five pound allowances from the government for each child born, a hundred years would not suffice to relieve the labour shortage and develop the country's natural resources. The new geopolitical concept of the Austral–Asian Mediterranean (i.e., the notion that Australia's fate was inextricably entwined with that of Asia) would have to open their eyes and infuse them with the vitality of a new civilization. Australia was said to be locked in secret military agreement with the United States, and thereby constituted a direct threat to the establishment of the Greater East Asia Co-Prosperity Sphere (pp. 31–5).

137. 'Katō's influence . . . among the cadets'. See Asada, 'The Japanese Navy and the United States'; Marder, Old Friends, New Enemies, p. 100.

137. 'important factors [for] . . . seizing Manchuria'. See, for example, Clyde and Beers, The Far East, pp. 325–9.

138. 'the so-called "Ōsumi purge" '. Asada, 'The Japanese Navy and the United States', pp. 225–32.

138. 'The Japanese press . . . made it clear'. For example, Japan Chronicle, 6 April 1933, in Clyde, Japan's Pacific Mandate, p. 186.

138. 'Palau, Tinian, and Saipan . . . militarily strengthened'. See BBS, Chūbu Taiheiyō hōmen kaigun sakusen, pp. 60–2.

138. 'plans for harbour extensions'. Suikō kai hen, 'Moto kaigun chūjō Sōka Ryūnosuke danwa shūroku', p. 127.

138. 'the building of a Fourth Fleet'. See BBS, Daihon'ei, kaigunbu, Vol. 1, pp. 254–5; it was completed in 1937 as a unit attached to the China Fleet (p. 358); on 15 November 1939, it became completely independent (pp. 431–3) with its regional task duties focusing on the nan'yō area, including Australia (p. 392).

138. 'Stockpiling 10 million tons became the navy's ambition'. Ibid., pp. 381–3. Japan's oil self-supply (mainly from Niigata) peaked in 1915. Although in the early 1930s the world prices of oil production dropped, the dollar rose against the yen, so that oil imports became expensive. A conference of various ministries convened on the initiative of the navy to discuss the oil shortage Japan was facing; it issued a policy for oil stockpiling in 1934. (The writer gratefully acknowledges the explanations of Hatano Sumio at the War History Office.) On Japan's oil problems, see Matsumoto, 'Nihon teikokushugi no shigen mondai',

pp. 119–23; Yanagihara, *Sekiyū zuisō*, pp. 8–24; and Willmott, *Empires in the Balance*, pp. 68–71.

138. 'Suetsugu stepped up pressure on Ōsumi'. See Asada, 'The Japanese Navy and the United States', p. 241.

139. 'First Committee . . . established in March 1936'. *Gendai-shi shiryō*, Vol. 8, Tome 1, pp. 351–3.

139. 'promotion of Manchuria's industrial potential'. BBS, *Daihon'ei rikugunbu*, Vol. 1, pp. 376–8.

139. 'Japan's future depended . . . on . . . oil, rubber, and tin'. Shiozaki, *Nichi-Ei-Bei sensō no kiro*, p. 302.

139. 'vehemently defied the counsel of Ishihara'. See Hirota Kōki Denki Kankōkai, *Hirota Kōki*, p. 204.

139. 'Japan's main hypothetical enemy'. See BBS, *Daihon'ei rikugunbu*, Vol. 1, pp. 159, 244–7, 395.

139. 'Manchurian and southern questions . . . inseparable'. See Hatano, 'Nihon kaigun to "nanshin"', p. 240.

139–40. 'The Emperor showed surprise'. BBS, *Daihon'ei kaigunbu, rengōkantai*, Vol. 1, pp. 321, 325. The complete text of the new Imperial National Defence Policy is reproduced on pp. 318–20.

140. For the 'Shōwa Ten Club' deliberations, see Shiozaki, *Nichi-Ei-Bei sensō no kiro*, p. 301; he bases himself on the diary entries of Kawamura Shigehisa.

140. 'First Committee produced . . . "General Plan for National Policy"'. See *Gendai-shi shiryō*, Vol. 8, Tome 1, pp. 354–5; Lebra, *Japan's Greater East Asia Co-Prosperity Sphere*, pp. 58–60.

141. 'the Army . . . had drawn up its own study paper'. See *Gendai-shi shiryō*, Vol. 8, Tome 1, p. 357.

141. 'its title changed . . . to "Fundamentals of National Policy"'. See Hirota Kōki Denki Kankō kai, *Hirota Kōki*, pp. 206–8; *Gendai-shi shiryō*, Vol. 8, Tome 1, pp. 361–2; Lebra, *Japan's Greater East Asia Co-Prosperity Sphere*, pp. 62–3.

141. 'a *supplementary* policy paper'. See BBS, *Gendai-shi shiryō*, Vol. 8, Tome 1, pp. 363–5.

142. For the Pakhoi Incident, see BBS, *Daihon'ei rikugunbu*, Vol. 1, pp. 417–18; *Gendai-shi shiryō*, Vol. 8, Tome 1, pp. 194–286; and Akagi Kanji's detailed study, 'Nihon kaigun to Hokkai jiken', pp. 138–40.

142. 'restraint was urged by the Japanese army'. 12 September 1936, Army General Staff Operations Division, in *Gendai-shi shiryō*, Vol. 8, Tome 1, p. 227; and Hatano, 'Nihon kaigun to "nanshin"', p. 224.

142. 'every potential for . . . war between Japan and China'. Akagi Kanji stresses this point in his full discussion of the Pakhoi Incident in 'Nihon kaigun to hokkai jiken', pp. 133–45; see also *Gendai-shi shiryō*, Vol. 8, Tome 1, pp. 194–286.

143. 'war in July 1937 . . . brought the navy and the army together'. See Hatano, 'Nihon kaigun to "nanshin"', pp. 228–31.

143. 'the navy . . . began to curb its own interests'. See Kaigunshō Shiryō, *Shōwa shakai keizai shiryō shūsei*, Vol. 5, pp. 29–31.

143. 'Yonai Mitsumasa enforced the dispatch of three divisions'. See Crowley, 'A Reconsideration of the Marco Polo Bridge Incident', p. 290; Marder, *Old Friends, New Enemies*, p. 106; Asada, 'The Japanese Navy and the United States', p. 245.

143. 'Hainan . . . put under the control of . . . Taiwan'. Two weeks after the invasion, Taiwan offered to assist in the exploitation of iron mining. Commanding Admiral Shimada Shigetarō congratulated himself in September: 'The Hainan operation went smoothly'; see Hatano, 'Nihon kaigun to "nanshin"', p. 226.

144. 'the Nanpō sōtokufu'. See *Gendai-shi shiryō*, Vol. 10, Tome 3, pp. 464–5, xci-xcii.

144. 'Hainan . . . pilot base for future operations'. See Hatano, 'Nihon kaigun to "nanshin"', p. 226; see also Izawa, *Nanshin seisaku*, p. 226.

144. 'Japan to appropriate Indonesia's oil fields'. See, Gunreibu (Navy General Staff, First Section of Operations), 'Taifutsuin hōsaku ni kansuru kenkyū (1940.8.5.)' (Study of policy toward French Indochina), in *Gendai-shi shiryō*, Vol. 10, Tome 3, pp. 369–71.

144. 'no chance would be missed to recover ground lost since . . . 1639'. A common critique of European in-roads into the Asia–Pacific region since the sixteenth century can be found in the sweeping article by Rear-Admiral Ueda Yoshitake, 'Taiheiyō no sōha o ronzu'.

145. 'a concrete schedule for military operations in the South'. Navy General Staff, Nakahara chūjō nisshi, 1/11, entry for 9 September 1939.
145. 'Nakahara's schedule was acted on'. See *TSM*, Vol. 7, pp. 17–18.
145. For naval preparations to seize the Dutch East Indies in May 1940, see ibid., pp. 18–19, 44, and *Bekkan*, p. 322.
145. 'Outline of the Main Principles'. See *TSM*, Vol. 7, pp. 22–3, and *Bekkan*, pp. 317–18.
146. 'scrap . . . army plan for . . . invasion of the Dutch East Indies'. *TSM*, Vol. 7, p. 44.
146. 'The navy . . . refused to yield to . . . General Koiso'. Ibid., pp. 44–5.
146. 'The navy knew from large-scale map exercises'. Ibid., pp. 19–20.
146. 'The army yielded'. *TSM, Bekkan*, p. 323.
146. 'The navy received a further concession'. *TSM*, Vol. 7, pp. 50–1, 80; Asada, 'The Japanese Navy and the United States', p. 251.
147. 'An American embargo . . . a matter of life and death'. See *Gendai-shi shiryō*, Vol. 10, Tome 3, pp. 369–71.
147. 'the navy . . . took its first step towards war with the United States'. See *TSM*, Vol. 7, pp. 47, 51–2, 80–1.
148. 'to secure permanent bases near Saigon'. According to a communication from the Operations Section to their counterparts in the Army General Staff on January 24; see ibid., p. 86.
148. 'a new "Outline of Policy toward French Indochina and Thailand"'. Reproduced in *TSM, Bekkan*, pp. 359–60.
148. 'the South could be won without having to fight the United States'. *TSM*, Vol. 7, p. 112.
148. 'prepare for war against the United States'. Ibid., p. 113.
148. 'the army . . . accepted . . . military operations . . . only if "absolutely unavoidable"'. Ibid., p. 116.
148. 'new "Outline of Policy toward the South"'. In ibid., p. 117; see also Japan, Foreign Ministry, *Nihon gaikō nempyō narabini shuyō bunsho* (Chronology and major documents of Japanese foreign relations), 1965, Vol. 2, pp. 495–6.
149. For Tomioka, Ishikawa, and Maeda comments, see Asada, 'The Japanese Navy and the United States', pp. 252–3.
149. 'it recommended an armed advance into Indochina'. See *TSM, Bekkan*, p. 436. About the important role played by the middle-echelon officers, especially of the navy, in the decision to go to war with America, see also Asada and Hatano, 'The Japanese Decision to Move South', pp. 395–9; Hosoya, 'Japan's Decision for War in 1941', pp. 48–9.
149. 'break the "ABCD encirclement"'. Asada, 'The Japanese Navy and the United States', p. 253.
149. 'We must build bases in French Indochina'. See Ike, *Japan's Decision for War*, pp. 50–1.
149. 'he was heard muttering'. In Asada, 'The Japanese Navy and the United States', p. 253.
150. For the establishment of the Tainanken, see *Gendai-shi shiryō*, Vol. 8, Tome 1, pp. 361–2.
150. For the central figures in the Tainanken, see Hatano, 'Shōwa kaigun no nanshin-ron', pp. 278–81.
150. 'the Tainanken planned . . . Japan's thrust'. See Kaigunshō Shiryō, *Shōwa shakai keizai shiryō shūsei*, pp. 294–305, 339–43.
150–1. 'the Committee paid special attention to two points'. See Hatano, 'Nihon kaigun to "nanshin"', pp. 217–18.
151. 'Nan'yō Kōhatsu . . . accounted for more than 60 per cent of the Nan'yō-chō's revenues'. See Peattie, 'The Nan'yō', pp. 192–6; Matsue, *Nan'yō kaitaku jūnenshi*.
151. 'Matsue visited the Vice Chief of the Navy General Staff'. See BBS, *Daihon'ei kaigunbu, rengōkantai*, Vol. 1, pp. 296–7.
151–2. 'We shall use the good offices of the *Nan'yō Kōhatsu*'. See 'Poryō "Tchimooru" ni tai suru shinshutsu hōshin ni kan suru ken oboe' (Memorandum for the planned advance into Portuguese Timor), in Kaigunshō Shiryō, *Shōwa shakai keizai shiryō shūsei*, pp. 261–2.
152. 'Fitzmaurice . . . warned Australia'. Lt. Col. W. R. Hodgson, Secretary of Department of External Affairs, to Department, 24 April 1937; Fitzmaurice to A. Eden, U.K. Secretary of State for Foreign Affairs, 17 June 1937 (*DAFP*, Vol. 1, Nos 18, 51).
152. 'As you rightly surmise'. Pearce to Fitzmaurice, 18 August 1937 (*DAFP*, Vol. 1, No. 59).

152. 'Wittouck . . . a most unscrupulous financier'. Memorandum by J. K. Waller, Department of External Affairs, 9 July 1937 (*DAFP*, Vol. 1, No. 49).

152. 'Wittouck . . . cannot obtain Lisbon confirmation'. Department of External Affairs, to Fitzmaurice, 8 December 1938 (*DAFP*, Vol. 1, No. 332).

152. From 'Oil Search' to 'Companhia Ultramarina de Petroleo', see A. T. Stirling, Australia's External Affairs officer in London, to Department of External Affairs, 20 November 1939 (*DAFP*, Vol. 2, Nos 377, 349).

152–3. 'oil concessions . . . granted'. Sir Walford Selby, U.K. Ambassador to Portugal, to Commonwealth Government, 25 November 1939 (*DAFP*, Vol. 2, No. 387).

153. 'cross-examining the Portuguese Vice-Minister'. In A. T. Stirling to Department of External Affairs, 13 December 1939 (*DAFP*, Vol. 2, No. 417).

153. 'Nippon Mining Company . . . began to develop the costly project'. Wakamatsu Torao, Japanese Consul-General in Sydney, to J. A. Lyons, Prime Minister,·5 April 1938 (*DAFP*, Vol 1, No. 178). For details of the financing, see Purcell, 'Japanese Commercial and Economic Interests in Australia', pp. 36–7.

153. 'not anti-Japanese in intention'. See Shepherd, *Australia's Interests*, pp. 90, 97.

153. 'iron ore . . . less . . . than previously supposed'. Prime Minister's Department to E. E. Longfield Lloyd, Australian Government Commissioner in Japan, 17 March 1938 (*DAFP*, Vol. 1, No. 140).

153–4. 'geographical–political changes . . . an important catalyst'. Frei, 'Ōsutoraria kara mita Nihon no chiseigakuteki kyōi', pp. 118–20.

154. 'Already in Spring 1937'. Major B. Combes, General Staff, Army Headquarters, to H. A. Peterson, Department of External Affairs, 29 April 1937 (*DAFP*, Vol. 1, No. 21).

154. 'The use of Japanese capital'. See Longfield Lloyd to J. F. Murphy, Secretary of Department of Commerce, 6 October 1937 (*DAFP*, Vol. 1, No. 111).

155. 'We are getting increasing evidence'. See Lyons to Bruce, 17 March, 7 April 1938 (*DAFP*, Vol. 1, Nos 141, 181).

155. 'letters from the Japanese Consul-General'. Wakamatsu to Lyons, 24 May, 14 June 1938 (*DAFP*, Vol. 1, Nos 208, 216).

155. 'Yoshida . . . conferred with . . . Bruce'. Bruce to Lyons, Enclosure II: *Note verbale* handed to Bruce by Yoshida, 18 June 1938 (*DAFP*, Vol. 1, No. 225).

155. 'depriving a "have not" power of iron ore'. Craigie to U.K. Foreign Office, 24 June 1938 (*DAFP*, Vol. 1, No. 222).

155. 'Itō . . . visited Longfield'. Longfield Lloyd to Prime Minister's Department, 15, 17 June 1938 (*DAFP*, Vol. 1, Nos 217, 218).

155–6. 'British Government . . . vexed by . . . Australia's export policy'. See Bruce to Prime Minister's Department, 31 March 1938, and Craigie to U.K. Foreign Office, 25 June 1938 (*DAFP*, Vol. 1, Nos 175, 223).

156. 'the Australian Government . . . strengthened its resolve'. See Lt. Col. W. R. Hodgson, Secretary of Department of External Affairs, to F. Strahan, Secretary of Prime Minister's Department, 'Memorandum on Silver Lead Deposits in Western Australia and Japanese Activities', 8 March 1940 (*DAFP*, Vol. 3, No. 94).

156. 'The Japanese Government . . . began to press the Portuguese Government'. R. G. Casey, Australia's Minister to the United States, to Department of External Affairs, most secret cablegram (51), 1 April 1940 (*DAFP*, Vol. 3, No. 122).

156. 'Machado agreed at first with Holland'. Memorandum by T. Elink Schuurman, Netherlands Consul-General in Australia, 2 April 1940 (*DAFP*, Vol. 3, No. 123).

156. 'Nomura . . . suggested "hinting in a roundabout way"'. A. T. Stirling, Australia's External Affairs officer in London, to Department of External Affairs, most secret cablegram, 9 January 1940 (*DAFP*, Vol. 3, No. 9).

156. 'they would make trouble at Macao'. Bruce to Robert G. Menzies, Prime Minister, 5 April 1940 (*DAFP*, Vol. 3, No. 127).

156. 'Portugal's Minister . . . had come round to welcome Japan'. A. T. Stirling to Department of External Affairs, most secret cablegram, 23 April 1940 (*DAFP*, Vol. 3, No. 171).

157. 'Fitzmaurice . . . informed England and Australia'. Fitzmaurice to A. Eden, U.K. Secretary of State for Foreign Affairs, 2 September 1937, and Fitzmaurice to W. M. Hughes, Minister for External Affairs, 5 January 1938 (*DAFP*, Vol. 1, Nos 68, 119).

157. 'they all dismissed the run'. Fitzmaurice to Hughes, ibid.; F. G. Shedden, Secretary of Department of Defence, to Lt. Col. W. R. Hodgson, Secretary of Department of External Affairs, 29 March 1938 (*DAFP*, Vol. 1, No. 172).

157. 'Thorby raised the matter again'. A. T. Stirling, Australia's External Affairs officer in London, to Department of External Affairs, 20 March 1939 (*DAFP*, Vol. 2, No. 44).
157. 'The possibility of Japanese penetration'. Cabinet submission by H. V. C. Thorby, 14 March 1939 (*DAFP*, Vol. 2, No. 38).
158. 'the Portuguese Government . . . gave its . . . approval . . . in December 1940'. Prime Minister's Department to Bruce, 18 March 1940 (*DAFP*, Vol. 3, No. 104; Vol. 4, p. xv).
158. 'Japan was planning . . . a consulate in Dilli'. See Menzies to Lord Cranborne, U.K. Secretary of State for Dominion Affairs, 30 December 1940 (*DAFP*, Vol. 4, No. 241).
158. 'Ross . . . would . . . monitor . . . Japanese activities'. Full Cabinet Submission by Sir Frederick Stewart, Minister for External Affairs, 25 January 1941 (*DAFP*, Vol. 4, No. 257).
158. 'the Japanese have stolen a march on us'. David Ross, Department of Civil Aviation Representative in Dilli, to Hodgson, 30 September 1941 (*DAFP*, Vol. 5, No. 74).
158. 'the Australian Government urged Ross to stay on'. Cranborne to Commonwealth Government, 17 October 1941 (*DAFP*, Vol. 5, No. 89).
158. 'Ross was recognised as Consul for Great Britain'. Dr H. V. Evatt, Minister for External Affairs, to M. de A. Ferreira de Carvalho, Governor of Portuguese Timor, 5 November 1941 (*DAFP*, Vol. 5, No. 99, fn. 3).
158–9. 'Consul Kuroki and an entourage of seven officials'. Cranborne to Commonwealth Government, 17 October 1941 (*DAFP*, Vol. 5, No. 89).
159. 'stand by for joint action with Dutch forces'. Cranborne to John Curtin, Prime Minister, 11 December 1941 (*DAFP*, Vol. 5, No. 186).
159. 'to liquidate the Japanese'. Commonwealth Government to Cranborne, 12 December 1941 (*DAFP*, Vol. 5, No. 187).
159. 'forty thousand Timorese were to die'. In terms of relative loss of life, it was one of the great, yet never properly acknowledged, catastrophes of World War II; see Dunn, *Timor*; Jill Jolliffe, *East Timor: Nationalism & Colonialism*, Brisbane, University of Queensland Press, 1978, pp. 44–7.
160. 'not on the list of . . . Japan's basic war plan'. Army General Staff, 'Nihon no shoki senryaku ni okeru kōryaku han'iki no kettei ni kan suru chinjutsusho'.
160. 'A meticulous schedule . . . for this first stage'. Tomioka, *Kaisen to shūsen*, p. 116. BBS, *Daihon'ei, kaigunbu, rengōkantai*, Vol. 2, p. 5.
161. '"Where shall we go from there?"'. BBS, *Minami Taiheiyō rikugun sakusen*, Vol. 1, p. 123. From 1938 to 1941, Ugaki headed the First Department of the Navy General Staff, with its First Section responsible for longterm strategic planning; in August 1941 he joined Combined Fleet to become Yamamoto Isoroku's Chief of Staff.
161. '"It might be . . . "'. See Stargardt, *Australia's Asian Policies*, p. 159.
162. 'what I worried about most was Australia'. Tomioka, *Kaisen to shūsen*, pp. 116–17.
162. '"We must think quickly"'. BBS, *Nantō hōmen kaigun sakusen*, Vol. 1, p. 354.
162. '"The Army General Staff opposes navy"'. Army General Staff, Tanaka Shin'ichi chūjō gyōmu nisshi.
163. 'the Navy General Staff sought . . . control over all of Australia'. BBS, *Daihon'ei kaigunbu, rengōkantai*, Vol. 2, pp. 307–8; BBS, *Nantō hōmen kaigun sakusen*, Vol. 1, pp. 353–4.
163. 'Naval plans to invade Australia'. BBS, *Daihon'ei rikugunbu*, Vol. 3, pp. 471–2.
163. '"We respect the plans of the navy"'. Ibid., pp. 510–11.
163. 'The army wished . . . to defend, not increase'. BBS, *Minami Taiheiyō rikugun sakusen*, Vol. 1, p. 125.
163. 'war in March . . . with the Soviet Union'. Ibid., p. 122.
163–4. 'The Navy General Staff calculated . . . three divisions'. In his post-war recollections, Captain Tomioka mentions five to six divisions as the figure used by the army in their discussions, see Tomioka, *Kaisen to shūsen*, p. 117.
164. 'to secure the . . . Australian coastlines'. BBS, *Daihon'ei kaigunbu, rengōkantai*, Vol. 2, pp. 312–13; BBS, *Nantō hōmen kaigun sakusen*, Vol. 1, p. 353.
164. 'John Curtin cabled'. Horner, *Crisis of Command*, p. 37.
164. 'We are now . . . beset grievously'. Urgent message to Roosevelt in January 1942, in ibid., p. 39.
164. 'Australia reinforced with 40,000 to 50,000 United States troops'. See ibid., p. 38. Even in her gravest hour, though, Australia wanted racial purity preserved: the Australian Government immediately opposed the U.S. proposal to include 2,000 black troops in the despatch of U.S. anti-aircraft ground troops. Later it withdrew its veto on the assumption that 'the U.S.A. Authorities being aware of our views, will have regard to Australian

susceptibilities in the numbers they decide to despatch'; see R. G. Casey, Minister to the United States, to Department of External Affairs, 9, 10 January 1942; Department of External Affairs to Casey, 13 January 1942; Dr H. V. Evatt, Minister for External Affairs, to Casey, 21 January 1942 (*DAFP*, Vol. 5, Nos 264, 269, 290).

164. 'Australian naval and air forces were almost non-existent'. See Horner, *Crisis of Command*, pp. 33–4, 39; Robertson, *Australia at War*, pp. 100–1. For an informed discussion that negates the existence of the controversial 'Brisbane Line', see Chapman, *Iven G. Mackay Citizen and Soldier*, pp. 283–92.

164. 'at least ten divisions'. The ten divisions were calculated in the belief that Australia had 600,000 men under arms; see BBS, *Daihon'ei rikugunbu*, Vol. 3, p. 474; BBS, *Daihon'ei kaigunbu, rengōkantai*, Vol. 2, p. 314; and BBS, *Minami Taiheiyō rikugun sakusen*, Vol. 1, p. 123.

164. 'twenty-five divisions to defend Australia'. Appreciations by the Chiefs of Staff, 11 December 1941, 27 February 1942, in Horner, *Crisis of Command*, p. 45.

164. 'it wanted to withdraw 200,000 troops'. BBS, *Minami Taiheiyō rikugun sakusen*, Vol. 1, p. 122.

164–5. '"Should Japan secure complete freedom of the seas"'. Curtin to Churchill, 21 January 1942 (*DAFP*, Vol. 5, No. 287).

165. 'The Japanese Army General Staff calculated'. BBS, *Minami Taiheiyō rikugun sakusen*, Vol. 1, pp. 123–4; BBS, *Daihon'ei rikugunbu*, Vol. 3, pp. 472, 510.

165. '"Break them with what?"'. See Horner, *Crisis of Command*, p. 47.

165. 'once the war had started'. Tomioka, *Kaisen to shūsen*, pp. 117–18.

165. 'a bigger slice of the military budget'. BBS, *Daihon'ei rikugunbu*, Vol. 3, p. 510.

165. 'introduced its plan formally'. See Japan, Army General Staff, Daihon'ei kimitsu sensō nisshi, entry for 6 February 1942.

166. 'the army would only disagree'. Ibid., entry for 9 February 1942.

166. 'Blinded by victory'. BBS, *Daihon'ei rikugunbu*, Vol. 3, p. 471.

166. 'Yamamoto . . . called for energetic offensives against Hawaii, Australia'. Army General Staff, Imoto Kumao chūsa gyōmu nisshi.

166. 'At the next Saturday Conference on 14 February'. Ibid., entry for 20 February 1942.

166. 'so much gibberish'. Army General Staff, Daihon'ei kimitsu sensō nisshi, entry for 14 February 1942, p. 50.

166–7. 'Sugiyama Gen moderated the cantankerous dispute'. See BBS, *Daihon'ei rikugunbu*, Vol. 3, p. 470.

167. 'India . . . a matter for the army . . . Australia for the navy'. Sugiyama, *Sugiyama memo*, Vol. 2, pp. 5–6; BBS, *Minami Taiheiyō rikugun*, Vol. 1, p. 124.

167. 'Tanaka . . . cabled from Java'. Ibid., p. 128.

168. 'The army looked . . . west'. There, also, lured the prospect of linking up with the German army expected to come marching down from the far Caucasus into the Near East at some future point in the war; see BBS, *Nantō hōmen kaigun sakusen*, Vol. 1, pp. 352–3.

168. 'Combined Fleet . . . looked east'. 'Eastern Operations' had a longer history. For a study of Hawaii in Japanese war plans, see Stephan, *Hawaii Under the Rising Sun*, esp. chs 5, 6, 7.

168. 'Yamamoto concentrated . . . on western operations'. BBS, *Daihon'ei kaigunbu*, Vol. 2, pp. 309, 320, 322; BBS, *Nantō hōmen kaigunbu sakusen*, Vol. 1, p. 353.

168. 'acting in concert with the German and Italian navies'. Ibid.; BBS, *Daihon'ei kaigunbu*, Vol. 2, pp. 309, 322, 339; German and Italian submarines were then believed to be sinking British aircraft carriers and battleships in the Mediterranean and their armies charging onwards to Egypt.

168. 'invasion plans . . . to which all services agreed'. BBS, *Nantō hōmen kaigun sakusen*, Vol. 1, p. 353.

168. 'Yamamoto . . . not interested in an invasion of Australia'. See BBS, *Daihon'ei kaigunbu, rengōkaitai*, Vol. 2, p. 309; and BBS, *Nantō hōmen kaigun sakusen*, Vol. 1, p. 355.

168. 'One, invade Ceylon'. See BBS, *Nantō hōmen kaigun sakusen*, Vol. 1, p. 355.

169. 'they strongly pressed for an invasion of . . . northeastern parts of Australia'. See ibid., p. 354.

169. 'defence of Timor . . . closely bound up with the defence of Darwin'. Curtin to Cranborne, 6 January 1942 (*DAFP*, Vol. 5, No. 258).

169. 'the liquidating of Japanese in Portuguese Timor'. Cranborne to Curtin, 11 December 1941 (*DAFP*, Vol. 5, No. 186).

169. 'only if Japanese aggression had already taken place'. Cranborne to Curtin, 28 December 1941 (*DAFP*, Vol. 5, No. 234).
169. 'aggression . . . by Dutch and Australian forces'. Ferreira de Carvalho, Governor of Portuguese Timor, to Curtin, 18 December 1941 (*DAFP*, Vol. 5, No. 200, fn. 2).
169. 'imminent German invasion of the Iberian Peninsula'. S. M. Bruce, High Commissioner in London, to Curtin, 27 December 1941 (*DAFP*, Vol. 5, No. 232).
169. 'Lord Cranborne . . . implored Curtin not to mention Britain's complicity'. Cranborne to Curtin, 27 December 1941 (*DAFP*, Vol. 5, No. 233).
169. 'He suggested that Australian troops replace the Dutch troops'. The Dutch had already agreed to withdraw, and in their role as scapegoat submitted an official regret to Lisbon, which stated clearly that action had been necessitated 'in view of the Japanese submarine activity off Portuguese Timor'. Cranborne to Curtin, 17 December 1941 (*DAFP*, Vol. 5, No. 202).
169. 'Curtin expressed his anger'. Curtin to Cranborne, 26 December 1941 (*DAFP*, Vol. 5, No. 225).
169–70. 'the Australian Government agreed to move . . . infantry . . . to Dilli'. Commonwealth Government to Cranborne, 29 December 1941, 7 February 1942 (*DAFP*, Vol. 5, Nos 235, 320).
170. 'The army pleaded for withdrawal . . . but the navy wanted to retain Portuguese Timor'. See BBS, *Daihon'ei kaigunbu, rengōkantai*, Vol. 2, p. 190; Army General Staff, Daihon'ei kimitsu nisshi, 24 January 1942, p. 38.
170. 'Tōjō strongly insisted'. See ibid., 24, 28 January, pp. 38, 40.
170. 'the parties reached an agreement of sorts'. BBS, *Daihon'ei kaigunbu, rengōkantai*, Vol. 2, p. 190. Japanese landings took place at dawn on 20 February. The A.I.F. (Australian Infantry Battalion) and the 2/2nd Independent [commando-type] company of some 330–350 men stood no chance against the superior Japanese numbers. The Tasmanian battalion resisted for three days before 1,137 went into captivity. A few escaped to Australia. In June 1942, 5,000–6,000 Japanese troops were reported in the island as against some 400 Australian and 200 Dutch troops in the mountains; see Commonwealth Government to Clement Atlee, U.K. Secretary of State for Dominion Affairs, 18 June 1942 (*DAFP*, Vol. 5, No. 527); Robertson, *Australia at War*, p. 94. The independent company took to the hills and harassed the Japanese for one year, inflicting losses, but without ever seriously challenging Japanese control of Timor; their story is told in Horton, *Ring of Fire*, pp. 112–40.
170. 'elimination of the "Port Darwin-Timor-Bali" line'. BBS, *Daihon'ei kaigunbu rengōkantai*, Vol. 2, pp. 187–8.
170. 'Japanese forces left Palau'. Ibid., p. 191; Robertson, *Australia at War*, p. 94.
170. 'to annihilate enemy strength in the Port Darwin area'. Lockwood, *Australia's Pearl Harbour*, p. 6, according to information given to him by the Japanese historian, Tsunoda Hitoshi.
170. 'a study concerning the feasibility of destroying Darwin'. Army General Staff, Tanaka Shin'ichi chūjo gyōmu nisshi, entry for 18 February 1942, p. 195.
171. 'At a meeting . . . on 27 February'. Navy General Staff, Sanagi memo, Vol. 3, entry for 27 February 1942.
171. 'At a further significant conference'. Meeting in the morning at the Navy Ministry's official residence, the chiefs of the War Operations Sections and the Military Affairs Bureaux, Tanaka Shin'ichi and Fukutome Shigeru for the army, and Mutō Akira and Oka Takazumi for the navy, coordinated in lengthy and strenuous debate the next objects of war for stage two; see BBS, *Daihon'ei rikugunbu*, Vol. 3, pp. 512–22.
171. 'the army even allowed inclusion in the text'. It is reproduced in BBS, *Daihon'ei kaigunbu, rengōkantai*, Vol. 2, pp. 337–8.
171. 'Consequences of cutting the communication lines'. See BBS, *Daihon'ei rikugunbu*, Vol. 3, p. 478; and Army Ministry, Bei-Gō narabini Ei-In-Gō kan.
171–2. 'Combined Fleet abandoned its plan to invade Ceylon'. BBS, *Daihon'ei kaigunbu, rengō kantai*, Vol. 2, p. 335.
172. For Tōjō's appeals, see Army General Staff, Daihon'ei kimitsu sensō nisshi, 21 January 1942, p. 36; and BBS, *Minami Taiheiyō rikugun sakusen*, Vol. 1, pp. 124,126–8.
172. 'The dates for the invasion of New Caledonia, Fiji, and Samoa were firmly set'. See BBS, *Daihon'ei kaigunbu, rengōkantai*, Vol. 2, p. 384.
172. 'Army and navy leaders were already squabbling'. The dispute was settled in favour of

army rule and joint army-navy management of the mineral deposits. Some 2,000 tons of nickel were to be shipped to Japan in the first year together with a large amount of cobalt; see BBS, *Minami Taiheiyō rikugun sakusen*, Vol. 1, pp. 142–4.

172. 'Psychological warfare against Australia was to be stepped up'. See ibid., pp. 144–5.
172. 'change in dates to July'. Ibid., pp. 129–30.
173. 'Yamamoto . . . informed the Navy General Staff'. See Kawakami and Pineau, *Midway— the Battle that Doomed Japan*, p. 54.
173. 'Navy General Staff . . . studying the approaches to . . . New Guinea'. Tanaka, *Imperial Japanese Armed Forces in Papua New Guinea*, pp. 5–8.
173. 'a meeting . . . close to tears'. See Kawakami and Pineau, *Midway—the Battle that Doomed Japan*, pp. 56–7; BBS, *Daihon'ei kaigunbu, rengōkantai*, Vol. 2, pp. 342–4; BBS, *Middowee kaisen*, pp. 42–4; Stephan, *Hawaii Under the Rising Sun*, pp. 111–12; Agawa, *The Reluctant Admiral*, pp. 295–7.
173. 'It is probably this dispute'. See Tomioka, *Kaisen to shūsen*, p. 118.
173. 'Admiral Yamamoto Isoroku threatened by phone to resign'. BBS, *Middowee kaisen*, p. 44.
173. 'the Doolittle raid'. Sixteen B-25 bombers, launched from the carrier *Hornet*, dropped their explosives over Tokyo, Yokohama, Nagoya, and Kobe on 18 April. Most of them escaped to China and the U.S.S.R.
173. 'the army . . . was won over'. See Stephan, *Hawaii Under the Rising Sun*, pp. 113–15.
173. 'unless one takes at face-value the headlines'. See *Australasian Post*, 14 March 1985, pp. 2–5; *Age*, 21 February 1985; Yamamoto and Mizuno, 'Warera Gōshū hondo ni jōriku seri'.
173–4. 'a living shield of ten Timorese youth'. This and the remaining passages are based on interviews with Mizuno Suzuhiko in Nagoya, 26 March 1986, and Yamamoto Masayoshi in Tokyo, 17 May 1986.
179. 'Australia . . . kept a low profile'. See Shepherd, *Australia's Interests*, pp. 36–7; Tyler, 'Australia's Defense Problem', p. 119; Mansergh, *Survey of British Commonwealth Affairs*, p. 149; Millar, *Australia in Peace and War*, p. 99.
179. 'The main paper read'. See Melbourne, 'A Foreign Policy for Australia', p. 36.
179. 'the Manchurian problem had nothing to do with Australia'. According to Debuchi Katsuji's confidential report on his mission to the South Pacific, JFMA File L.3.3.0.14 .
179. 'Casey kept up his broker services'. Hasluck, *The Government and the People*, pp. 549–50, 552.
180. 'Inoue Shōzō . . . was perplexed'. See Inoue Shōzō, *Ugoku Gōshū*, pp. 1–3, 68–9, 129–31.
180–1. 'Hayashi Sōtarō . . . noticed a growing Australian preoccupation'. Hayashi Sōtarō, *Nichi-Gō tsūshō mondai*, pp. 14–15.
181. 'Takagi Saburō . . . defined Australia's feelings'. Takagi, *Taiyōshū no genjō ni tsuite*, pp. 23, 25, 28–30.
181. 'Japan . . . stretching her hands toward New Guinea'. Watanabe Izō, *Taisen to Nan'yō guntō*, pp. 15–16.
182. 'The puzzle that Japan posed'. See Matsunaga, *Gōshū inshōki*, pp. 357–8.
182–3. "How long will it be". Ibid., pp. 341–9.
184. 'our geography teacher did not tell us'. Ibid., pp. 355–6. The first Japanese Minister to Australia, Tatsuo Kawai, had made a vexing start on 14 March 1941 when Japan was refused permission to appoint supplementary service attaches to Canberra, see *DAFP*, Vol. 6, p. xii.
184. 'I may with respect suggest'. Nichigō Kyōkai, *Sōkai kaimu hōkoku*, Vol. 13, p. 20.
184. 'The Far East is our far-North'. See House of Representatives, *Debates*, Vol. 49, p. 822 (in *AWD*, pp. 326–9).
184. 'what the "Far East" is to Europe'. See House of Representatives, *Debates*, Vol. 44, pp. 327–38 (in *AWD*, pp. 390–1).
184. 'the "Far East" as Australia's "Near North"'. *Sydney Morning Herald*, 27 April 1939. (*AWD*, pp. 450–1).
185. 'A new geography was needed'. See Hatano, '"Tōa shinchitsujo" to chiseigaku', pp. 33–4.
185. 'geopolitical principles . . . discussed in Japan'. Ibid., pp. 17–18.
185. 'not one invented by the Japanese'. See Haushofer, *Geopolitik des Pazifischen Ozeans*, pp. 144–55. He mentions as his sources Lautensach's article in the German journal *Zeit-*

schrift für Geopolitik, Heft 1, "Die Mittelmeere als geopolitische Kraftfelder" and Kurt Wiersbitzky's article "Politische Geographie des Australasiatischen Mittelmeeres", in Ergänzungs Heft 227 zu *Petermann's Geographische Mitteilungen*, (1936).

185-6. 'The islands had once been connected'. See Iimoto, 'Nan'yō no chiseigaku'.

186. 'Kawanishi . . . saw world affairs differently'. See Hatano, '"Tōa shinchitsujo" to chiseigaku', p. 33.

186. '"Austral" means . . . Southland of Asia'. Kaneko and Kiyokawa, *Nanpō keizai shigen soran*, p. 2.

186. 'told . . . to write a book about Australia'. Okakura, *Gōshū no shakai to keizai*, pp. 305-6; interview with Okakura, 2 July 1985.

187. 'Australia . . . part of Asia'. Kanematsu Shōten, *Gōshū yushutsu bōeki ni tsuite*, p. 8.

187. 'Australia . . . one of the South Asian countries'. Miyata, *Gōshū renpō*, p. 347.

187. 'Madarame . . . urged Australia to "return"'. Madarame, *Gōshū shinryaku shi*, pp. 269, 272.

187. 'Inoue . . . offered a syllogism'. Inoue Shōzō, *Ugoku Gōshū*, p. 292.

187. '(inner) nan'yō'. '*Uchi*' means 'inside'; it is written with the same Chinese character as the more colloquial form of '*ie*', 'household' or 'family', which connotates easily with all that '*uchi*' stands for as the basic principle of unity in the Japanese social structure; see Nakane, *Japanese Society*, pp. 3-7. Common alternatives for '*uchi*' and '*soto*' nan'yō were '*ura*' and '*omote*' nan'yō.

187. 'Japanese generally placed Australia in neither'. Nitobe Inazō, for example, excludes it in his definition of the *nan'yō* in 'Nan'yō no keizaiteki kachi (I)', pp. 1596-600.

187-8. 'Australia . . . in the Japanese living sphere'. It appears that already since June 1940, under the influence of Germany's victory over France and to forestall a German territorial grab in the Pacific, the Japanese Government began to regard the French and British islands in the South Pacific—'Oceania', including Australia—as part of the Japanese sphere; see Miwa, *Nihon*, pp. 5-14. The author explains how the Japanese Government resurrected seventh century terminology from the Classics, especially *Hakkō-ichi-u* (The World under the roof of eight corners), as a smoke-screen to manipulate opinion and shroud in obscurantist language Japanese hegemonial claims for the undefined limits of the Greater East Asia Co-Prosperity Sphere.

188. 'one of the world's virgin continents'. Murobuse, *Nanshinron*, p. 223.

188. 'a region without people'. Matsunaga, *Gōshū inshōki*, pp. 55-6.

188. 'a widespread . . . interest in population problems'. See Bailey, 'Public Opinion and Population Problems', p. 72.

189. 'carry up to two hundred million people'. Borrie, *Immigration, Australia's Problems and Prospects*, p. 8.

189. 'Australia could comfortably support twenty million people'. Taylor, *Australia*, p. 444.

189. 'It still is today'. 'Australia's population will be about 20 million at the turn of the century', see Australian Information Service, *Australia: Current Report* (Canberra, 1982); see also Department of Immigration and Ethnic Affairs, *1788-1978 Australia and Immigration* (Canberra, 1978), p. 46; Australian Government Public Service, *Issues in Immigration* (Canberra, 1980), p. 48.

189. 'the low population level thwarted any hope'. Kaigun, *Taiheiyō 2600 nenshi*, pp. 768-9, 786-7.

189. 'new relationship of give-and-take'. Okakura, *Gōshū no shakai to keizai*, p. 297.

189. 'Iron Knob . . . almost inaccessible'. Ibid., p. 133.

189. 'not . . . without the Asian worker'. Nanpō Sangyō Chōsakaihen, *Gōshū*, pp. 155-6.

189. 'idly hoarding . . . raw materials'. Kaigun, *Taiheiyō 2600 nenshi*, p. 768.

189-90. 'failed to develop their country'. According to the diary entry in Brown, *Suez to Singapore*, p. 390.

190. 'Australians had needed Asian help before'. See Kawaji, 'Gōshū no chiseigakuteki kō satsu', pp. 264-6.

190. 'the case of Takasuka'. See Sissons, An Immigrant Family.

190. 'Australia was saddled with two big problems'. See Kaigun, *Taiheiyō 2600 nenshi*, pp. 786-7

190. 'Asia had no claim to admission'. See Gregory, *The Menace of Colour*, pp. 125, 172.

190-1. For Konoe's comments, see his 'Eibei hon'i no heiwashugi o haisu', pp. 23-6; and 'Sekai no genjō o kaizō seyo', pp. 58, 60.

191. For Yanaihara's comments, see his 'Nan'yō seisaku o ronzu', pp. 39–43; and 'Taiheiyō no heiwa to Eikoku', pp. 15–16.
191. 'cruelly closed to Japan'. Ishibashi, 'Eikoku wa Nihon no tachiba o ryōkai subeshi', p. 44.
191. 'intellectual heir apparent to Nitobe Inazō'. See Tōno, 'Shōwa shoki no "jiyū shugisha"', pp. 64–5.
191–2. 'the keynote chapter'. See Tsurumi Yūsuke, 'Sōron' (Introduction) in Taiheiyō, *Gōshū no shizen to shakai*, pp. 1–18.
192. '10 million farmers to Australia'. Ibid., pp. 16–18.
192. 'settle one million farm families in Manchuria'. Sakurai, *Nihon nōgyō no saihensei*, p. 30.
192. 'Katō's narrow and militant agrarianist views'. See Tsukuba Hisaharu, *Nihonjin no shisō: nōhonshugi no sekai* (Agrarianism in Japanese thought), Tokyo, San'ichi Shobo, 1961 p. 183–4; Havens, *Farm and Nation in Modern Japan*, pp. 277, 283.
192. 'Australia [not] . . . the domain solely of the Yamato farmer'. Tsurumi, in Taiheiyō, *Gōshū no shizen to shakai*, pp. 17–18.
192. For Hack's proposals, see Roberts, 'History of Contacts between the Orient and Australia', pp. 18–20.
192–3. 'send thither a large body of Japanese settlers'. See Williams, *Foreigners in Mikadoland*, p. 277; and South Australian Parliamentary Paper No. 37, 1898, in Sissons, 'The Early Japanese Influence on the Northern Territory', January 1978, pp. 14–16.
193. 'the Hack and the Parsons proposals lived on'. See, e.g., Izumi, *Gōshū shi*, p. 69; Itō, *Gendai Gōshū ron*, p. 1; Kanematsu Shōten Chōsabusha, *Gōshū*, p. 536.
193. 'Hack's blueprint . . . in Tsurumi's book'. Taiheiyō, *Gōshū no shizen to shakai*, pp. 252–4.
193. 'their corrections admit'. See Sissons, 'The Early Japanese Influence on the Territory' December 1977, pp. 18–21; he also mentions the publication of a more accurate interpretation by J. Cross in 1960.
193. 'an insufficient number to develop the Australian continent'. Wada, *Ōsutoraria*, p. 34; Nan'yō Keizai Kenkyūjo, *Gōshū jinkō no kōsei*, pp. 33–5.
193–4. 'a typical chapter entitled "Hakugō shugi"'. See Miyata, *Gōshū renpō*, pp. 310–21.
194. 'nothing but a crafty British plot'. Wada, *Ōsutoraria*, pp. 32–41.
194–5. 'semi-official and governmental books'. For example, Nan'yō Keizai Kenkyūjo, *Gōshū jinkō no kosei*; and Nōrinshō Sōmukyoku Nanpō Shigen Chōsashitsu, *Gōshū oyobi Shinseiran ni okeru hakujin ni kansuru chōsa*.
195. 'the White Australia policy was an economic . . . problem'. Okakura, *Gōshū no shakai to keizai*, p. 248.
195. 'Three conditions'. Izumi, *Gōshū shi*, pp. 262–3.
195. 'Crawford . . . said as much'. Crawford, 'Australia as a Pacific Power', p. 70.
196. 'his remedial treatise'. Madarame, *Gōshū shinryaku shi*, pp. II-III, 1–2, 270–1, 273.
196. From the 'New Order in East Asia' to the 'Greater East Asia Co-Prosperity Sphere'. For an analysis that shows that the two public statements of 1938 and 1940 reflect not similarity or continuity, but rather intellectual dissimilarity and discontinuity, see Miwa, 'Japanese Policies and Concepts for a Regional Order in Asia, 1938–1940', pp. 2–3, 7. For the Japanese version, see his '"Tōa shinchitsujo" sengen to "Dai Tōa kyōeiken" kōsō no dansō', p. 197. For another incisive study on the development of Greater East Asia Co-Prosperity Sphere policy-making, see Berger, 'The Three-dimensional Empire'. The workings of the Shōwa Kenkyū Kai and its main actors are described in Fletcher, *The Search for a New Order*.
196. 'first officially used by . . . Matsuoka'. *Tokyo Asahi Shimbun*, 2 August 1940.
196. '"Greater Asianism"'. For example, it promoted an 'agrarianist' response to the social ills of Japan and a return to the classical ways of East Asia as an anti-thesis to the modern industrial society of the West; see Nakayama, *Tai shi seisaku no honryū*, pp. 49–50; Nakayama is said to have drafted the proclamation for the 'New Order in East Asia' in 1938; see Miwa, 'Japanese Policies', p. 10.
196–7. 'an open-ended regionalism'. See Rōyama, *Tōa to sekai*.
197. 'Asia's Australia'. Madarame, *Gōshū shinryaku shi*, p. 276.
197. 'the land's original tribes'. Miyata, *Gōshū Renpō*, p. 359.
197. 'how to integrate the Southeast Asian economy into the Sphere'. See Rōyama, 'Daitōa kōiki ken ron: Chiseigakuteki kōhatsu'. In title and text, Royama characteristically stresses

the dimensional aspect of *kōikiken* (an *extended* sphere) rather than playing on the emotional aspect of *kyōeiken* (a *co-prosperity* sphere).

197. 'writing at a time of boom and victory'. See for example Shillony, *Politics and Culture in Wartime Japan*, especially Chs 4, 5; and Keene, 'Japanese Writers and the Greater East Asia War'.

197. 'no reason to doubt the doom of White Australia'. See Madarame, *Gōshū shinryaku shi,* p. 276.

197–8. 'a . . . factual book on Australia'. Interview with Okakura Koshirō, 2 July 1985.

198. 'not the special sphere . . . of white people'. Miyata, *Gōshū Renpō,* pp. 213–14; Yoneda Makoto, 'Daitōasen to Ni-Shi jin Gōshū ishokuken mondai'.

198. 'imperialistic . . . since the 1880s'. Miyata, *Gōshū Renpō,* p. 2, 323–4, 351.

198. 'Japan was simply too strong'. Nanpō Sangyō Chōsakai, *Gōshū,* p. 151.

198. 'Matsunaga Sōtoo in Melbourne's Botanic Gardens'. Matsunaga, *Gōshū inshōki,* p. 366.

198. 'on the same boat'. The last repatriation boat to leave was the *Kamakura maru,* reserved for higher officials such as Ambassador Kawai Tatsuo. It also carried home the dead bodies of the four Japanese naval officers who had attacked Sydney and Newcastle in their midget submarines. The ship arrived back at Yokohama on 9 October 1942. See Matsunaga, *Gō shū inshōki,* p. 1; and Nichigō Kyōkai, *Nichigō kyōkai gojūnen,* p. 52.

198–9. 'Australians are haughty'. See Nishikawa, *Saikin no Gōshū jijō,* pp. 20–1, 337–42.

199. '"Australia, orphan of the South Pacific"'. See Madarame, *Gōshū shinryaku shi,* p. 275; Kanematsu Shōten Chōsabusha, *Gōshū,* p. 1; Tokyo Nichi-Nichi Shimbun Tōahen, *Daitōa sen ni okeru Jūkei, Indo, Gōshū,* p. 9.

199. 'free of any pangs'. See Hamill, *The Strategic Illusion,* p. 313.

199. 'help the Orphan of the Pacific'. Okakura, *Gōshū no shakai to keizai,* pp. 1, 263.

199. 'utterly forsaken Australia'. Matsunaga, *Gōshū inshōki,* pp. 391–2.

199. 'the British had been trying to do a bolt'. Kanematsu Shōten Chōsabusha, *Gōshū,* p. 558.

199. 'heed the warm-hearted counsel of Prime Minister Tōjō'. Ibid., p. 558; Matsunaga, *Gōshū inshōki,* p. 393.

199. 'Is there not a Prime Minister like Pibun'. Matsunaga, *Gōshū inshōki,* pp. 393–4.

200. 'they . . . would always have to fear the Sphere'. Nanpō Sangyō Chōsakai, *Gōshū,* p. 150.

200. 'news received with great emotion'. Miyazaki, 'Daitōa sensō no daini dankai to Gōshū', pp. 24, 33.

200. 'embraced by the Japanese war flame'. Tōkyō Nichi Nichi Shinbun Tōabu, *Daitōasen ni okeru Jūkei, Indo, Gōshū,* p. 12.

200. the 'British triangle' and . . . 'United States triangle'. Ibid., pp. 312–13.

200–1. 'The Arafura Sea would . . . turn into a bridge'. Iguchi Ichirō, *Chisei dōtairon,* pp. 189–247.

201. 'close to the level of German geopolitical scholarship'. Haushofer, *Geopolitik des Pazifischen Ozeans,* Introduction.

201–2. 'to render more clearly in Japanese'. Kunimatsu, *Chiseigaku to wa nani ka?,* pp. 6–7.

202. 'European law of geopolitics'. See Cohen, *Geography and Politics,* p. 45; Whittlesey, *Germany Strategy of World Conquest,* p. 170.

202. 'making Australia's northern desert zone bloom'. Itō, *Gendai Gōshū ron,* p. 321.

202. 'The ultimate solution of Japan's problem'. Haushofer in *Zeitschrift für Geopolitik,* 1930, p. 961, as quoted in Hans W. Weigert, 'Haushofer and the Pacific', *Foreign Affairs,* July 1942, p. 741.

202. 'his troupe of German geopoliticians'. See also Pahl, *Das Politische Antlitz der Erde,* pp. 9, 21; Richard Hennig, *Geopolitik,* Leipzig, Teubner Verlag, 1931, pp. 60, 185, 272; März, 'Das Schicksal überseeischer Wachstumsspitzen', p. 341.

202. 'The Japanese are tropical colonizers'. See Bowman, *The New World,* p. 614.

202. 'overcrowded Japan . . . could make good use of Australia'. See Van Valkenburg, *Elements of Political Geography,* pp. 291–301.

202–3. 'Australia . . . will cease to be white man's [country]'. See Spykman, *America's Strategy in World Politics,* pp. 131, 154–5.

203. 'Mishima . . . was re-published'. *Gōshū oyobi Indo tanken shi,* pp. 341–2.

203. 'Shiga . . . was particularly distorted'; especially Shiga's concept of *kokusui hozon shugi* (preservation of nationality), which was later corrupted by the ultranationalists into a

mysterious belief in the essence of the 'Japanese race'. See Miwa, 'Shiga Shigetaka', pp. 1–3, 7–8.

203. *'Nan'yō jiji* . . . depicted as a blueprint for Japanese expansion'. See, e.g., Hijikata, 'Shiga Shigetaka to "Nan'yō jiji"', pp. 127–33.

203. 'expansion by commerce . . . within the defence system of British naval strength'. See Miwa, 'Shiga Shigetaka', p. 37, and Crossroads of Patriotism in Imperial Japan, p. 152.

203–4. 'Fukuzawa . . . [has] . . . flair for geopolitics'. Nishikawa, *Saikin no Gōshū jijō*, p. 7.

204. 'Yoshida Shōin and . . . Mitsukuri Shōgo . . . too'. See Komaki, 'Daitōa no chiseigakuteki gaikan', pp. 3–4. Iguchi Ichirō, 'Kita Gōshū no chiseigakuteki kōsatsu'.

204. 'Other articles covered'. The April and May numbers of *Taiheiyō* ran special issues on Australia; see also March issue 1943; and Maida Minoru in *Shina*, May 1942.

204. 'settling Australia's tropical north has failed'. Wada, 'Nettai Gōshū kaihatsu mondai', p. 37.

204. 'All the oceans are . . . recognized as the Great Japanese Sea'. Komaki, 'Daitōa no chiseigakuteki gaikan'; Fifield and Pearcy, *Geopolitics in Principle and Practice*, p. 20.

204. 'the Pacific Ocean . . . "an Anglo-Saxon sea"'. Josiah Strong, *Expansion*, 1900, in Irye, *Pacific Estrangement*, p. 70.

204. 'one Empire . . . one Navy'. Minutes of Proceedings of the Colonial Conference, 1907, (Command Paper) Cd. 3523 (in Hamill, *The Strategic Illusion*, p. 12).

204. 'Japanese literature on Hawaii'. See Stephan, *Hawaii Under the Rising Sun*, pp. 55–68.

205. 'last line of defence . . . across Eastern Australia'. Navy General Staff, Nakahara chūjō nisshi, entry for 2–4 August 1940.

205. 'Australia . . . veering towards extreme autarky'. Kawaji, 'Gōshū no chiseigakuteki kō satsu', pp. 227, 253, 264.

205. 'the Ottawa agreements'. To remedy the desparate economic conditions of the great Depression, the British Commonwealth countries met at Ottawa in 1932. The general objective of their conference was to lower the trade barriers between the several members of the Empire according to the principle 'the home producer first, empire producers second, and foreign producers last'.

205. 'We shall not force her'. Kawaji, 'Gōshū no chiseigakuteki kōsatsu', pp. 253, 264.

205. 'Australia to sell . . . in the Greater East Asia Co-Prosperity Sphere'. Ibid., pp. 264–5.

205. 'They were a materialistic people'. Okakura, *Gōshū no shakai to keizai*, pp. 308–10.

205. 'Australia [had] three choices'. Ibid., p. 263.

205–6. 'As an affiliated Sphere member'. Ibid., pp. 289–312, 317, 321.

206. 'the Australian continent would serve as a great whaling base'. In Kanematsu Shōten, *Gōshū yushutsu*, p. 8.

207. 'the meaning of "Co-Prosperity"'. See Nanpō Sangyō Chōsakaihen, *Gōshū*, pp. 152–4.

208. 'Australia is not a part of the Greater East Asia Co-Prosperity Sphere'. Okakura, *Gōshū no shakai to keizai*, p. 289.

208. 'Australia appeared in a Foreign Ministry position paper'. Foreign Ministry, Sōri, riku-kaigai yonshō kaigi kettei an (Gaimushō an), p. 478.

208. 'Australia . . . as one corner of the Empire's sphere'. Army General Staff, Nichi-Doku-I teikei kyōka ni kan suru ken (rikugun an), p. 463.

208. 'Australia appeared in the outermost of the three concentric circles'. Navy General Staff, Operational Section, Daitōa kyōeiken kensetsu taikō (shian), pp. 2–3, 5; see also Stephan, *Hawaii Under the Rising Sun*, pp. 79–80.

208. For Australia in the paper on Essence and structure of the Nation's Home Defense, see Navy Ministry, Kaigunshō Chōsaka, Kokubō kokka no honshitsu to kōzō, pp. 228–9.

209. 'Pour a million Japanese into Australia'. Army and Colonial Affairs Ministry, Daitōa kyō eiken ni okeru tochi shobun an, pp. 17, 24, 26.

209. For Australia under a Japanese Governor-General, see Army and Colonial Affairs Ministry, Daitōa sensō ni yoru nanpō senkyo shochiiki zengo shori hōsaku taiko, pp. 14–26.

209. 'Two army divisions would keep order'. In comparison, half a division with a mechanical detachment was believed sufficient for Manila, and the same with an additional 5,000 soldiers for Hawaii; see Army and Colonial Affairs Ministry, Daitōa kyōeiken ni okeru tochi shobun an, p. 18.

209. 'Darwin . . . would have to be . . . "stabilized" . . . and Australia . . . isolated'. Total War Research Institute, Daitōa kyōeiken kensetsu gen'an oyobi Tōa kensetsu daiichiki sōryoku

senhō ryaku ni kansuru yobi kenkyū tōshin. See also Kawahara, *Shōwa seiji shisō kenkyū,* pp. 306–7.

209–10. For Australia in the draft of basic plans for the establishment of the Greater East Asia Co-Prosperity Sphere, see Total War Research Institute, Daitōa kyōeiken kensetsu gen'an (sōkō), pp. 2–4, 149, 152, 158–9.

210. 'the product of amateurs'. See Kawahara, *Shōwa seiji shisō kenkyū,* pp. 303–5.

210. 'Strictly speaking'. See Iriye, 'Wartime Japanese Planning for Post-War Asia', p. 177.

211. 'The Australian-Japanese trade flow . . . as the axis of the Sphere'. Itō, *Gendai Gōshū ron,* pp. 315–16.

211. 'visions of Australian and Japanese scholars today'. See, e.g., Miller, *India, Japan, Australia,* John Crawford & Saburo Okita, *Australia, Japan and Western Pacific Economic Relations* (1976); Crawford and Okita, *Raw Materials and Pacific Economic Integration,* Canberra, Australian National University Press,1978; Peter Drysdale and Hugh T. Patrick, 'Evaluation of a Proposed Asian–Pacific Regional Economic Organisation', *Australia-Japan Economic Relations Research Paper,* No. 61, Canberra, Australian National University, 1979; Drysdale, 'An Organisation for Pacific Trade, Aid, and Development'.

211. 'Australia is now straying . . . from the ideal future way'. Itō, *Gendai Gōshū ron,* p. 316.

211. 'the postwar era's ultimate structure of an "Asia-Australia" Co- Prosperity Sphere"'. Ibid., pp. 319–24.

212. 'Okakura Koshirō's austere prediction'. Okakura, *Gōshū no shakai to keizai,* p. 312.

212. 'to teach Australia Japanese ethics, cane in hand'. See Wada, *Ōsutoraria,* p. 79; Madarame, *Gōshū shinryaku shi,* p. 273.

212. 'import more than half of Australia's products'. Itō, *Gendai Gōshū ron,* p. 342.

212. 'Australia's churchmen and schoolteachers should be targeted'. Ibid., pp. 334–6.

213. Japanese-Australian co-operation as 'a cornerstone for world peace'. See ibid., pp. 322–4.

213. 'write one!'. Nagakura, *Gōshū oyobi Minami Taiheiyō,* preface.

213. 'The Japanese colony in Australia'. Watanabe Chūgo, *Gōshū shokumin ron,* pp. 163, 167.

213. 'We should not . . . rejoice over the bombing of Darwin'. Shirani, *Gōshū jijō,* p. 73.

214. 'Hokkaido . . . referred to [as] . . . Yezo'. Inoue Shōzō, *Ugoku Gōshū,* p. 130.

214. 'Australia federated only in 1904'. Okakura, *Gōshū no shakai to keizai,* p. 290.

215. 'the first "good" books on Australia'. See Ichikawa, *Gōshū keizai shi kenkyū.* The study was conceived as the first in a series of three volumes—the other two were to treat Australia's industries, banking and financial institutions and her administration. Ichikawa had worked for three years at the Sydney consulate and was repatriated on the *Kamakura* in October 1942.

219. 'A booklet . . . spells out'. See Kanematsu Shōten, *Gōshū yushutsu,* p. 18.

Bibliographic Essay

This book's long time-frame and its mooring between three fields of study, those of Japan's history of southern interests and Japanese and Australian diplomatic history, call for a note on the main sources that guided my research. The following comments on the character and limitations of the sources used are arranged by subjects in the marching order of the text. All specific publishing data can be found in the Bibliography which also gives a more complete list of sources used.

Japan in the Western Pacific before the 1630s

A useful, illustrated guide to the evolution of Japanese shipbuilding from the Muromachi period to the early seventeenth century, is Ishii Kenji, 'Fune to kōkai no rekishi' (A history of ships and navigation), Parts I and II, in *Zusetsu jinbutsu umi no Nihon shi (3 and 4)* (An illustrated Japanese history of personalities and the sea), 1979. Iwao Seiichi's thorough *Shuinsen bōeki shi no kenkyū* (Study of the red seal ship trade), 1958, describes how Japanese ship-technique was used for expansion by trade and emigration that flourished under Tokugawa Ieyasu in the early seventeenth century. It cites the routes of the ships, their cargoes and purposes, their network in the Western Pacific, down to the ships' speed with which they reached their destinations in the region.

Iwao's histories on the Japanese settlements in the Western Pacific region before seclusion strongly moulded the argument for my study's point of departure, particluarly his *Nan'yō Nihonmachi no kenkyū* (Study of Japanese settlements in the South Seas), 1966. Based on original Western language documents of the colonies where once the Japanese mingled with Europeans in the Southeast Asian region, it describes the region's major towns and their administration, and explains the characteristics of the Japanese settlements that developed in the South and the causes for their decline. Rare maps show the locations of Japanese quarters reconstructed according to contemporary maps. More detailed is the author's careful follow-up *Zoku Nan'yō Nihonmachi no kenkyū: Nan'yōtō shochiiki bunsan Nihonjin imin no seikatsu to katsudō* (A second study of Japanese settlements in the South Seas: life and occupations of the Japanese immigrants in Island Southeast Asia in the sixteenth and seventeenth centuries), 1987. In this final tome, Iwao focuses on Batavia where, thanks to meticulous Dutch colonial archivists, knowledge of the elevated life-styles, which many Japanese led in the Dutch East Indies, survived in documentary testimony on their marriages, control and administration of their settlements, their activities in financial business, commerce and slave trade, and on their testimonies at court in wills and testaments. It has appended seventy-three translated sources and four indexes for peoples' names, place names, subjects, and documents.

Earliest Geographical Notions of Australia

My search for Australia in Japanese maps was guided primarily by the superbly illustrated works on the evolution of Japanese world geography edited by Namba Matsutarō, Muroga Nobuo, and Unno Kazutaka, such as *Nihon no kochizu* (Old Japanese maps), 1969. An extended version edited by Oda Takeo, Muroga Nobuo, and Unno Kazutaka, *Nihon kochizu taisei: sekaizu-hen* (The world in Japanese maps until the mid-19th century), 1975, features reprints of 138 colour maps and 127 black and white maps; an appendix describes the background and special points of each map, and tells where the maps can be found. With this reliable guide, it is easy to look for the originals dispersed throughout Japan. Many can be located at the Ueno Museum in Tokyo, or in Kyoto. Valuable and accessible original maps are at the Cabinet Library.

The emergence of Australia in the Japanese world view can also be gauged by consulting Japanese geographies of the Tokugawa period. Three of them stand out. Arai Hakuseki's *Sairan igen* (Review of foreign testimony), 1713, is the earliest useful commentary on world geography and contains an entry on 'Magellanica'. A fuller treatment with maps of that 'South Land', then partially navigated by the Dutch, is given in the corrective work by Yamamura Shōei, *Teisei zōyaku sairan igen* ('Sairan igen' revised and enlarged), 1979. The most complete discussion of Australia appears in Mitsukuri Shōgo's *Kon'yo zushiki* (Explanatory notes on the world map), 1846; section five devotes itself entirely to Australia and the South Pacific islands. See also his father-in-law, Mitsukuri Genpo's translations on Australia from Dutch sources in *Mitsukuri Genpo no kenkyū* (The research of Mitsukuri Genpo), 1978.

Japan's Re-emergence 1850s–1923

A good first source for late Tokugawa thinkers on renewed Japanese expansion is still Tokutomi (Sohō) Iichirō, *Kinsei Nippon kokumin shi* (A history of the Japanese people in modern times), 1934, a set of fifty volumes. Each contains around 500 pages based on an extensive use of primary sources produced in the declining years of the *bakufu*.

The writings of familiar late Tokugawa thinkers such as Honda Toshiaki, *Seiiki monogatari* (Stories about Western lands), 1798, Satō Nobuhiro, or Yoshida Shōin can be studied in greater detail in the convenient *Nihon shisō taikei* series, or of course in the collected works of the individual writers themselves. Some, like Hayashi Shihei's *Sangoku tsūran zusetsu* (An illustrated survey of three countries), 1785, or Kudō Heisuke's *Aka Ezo fūsetsu-kō* (Reports of the Red Ezo), 1781, have been reprinted in new editions such as *Hoppō mikōkai kobunsho shūsei* (A collection of rare old texts on the northern region), 1978, with reproductions of the writers' original maps and illustrations.

Irie Toraji did considerable spade work on early Japanese thinkers and their southern interests in his two scholarly books *Hōjin kaigai hatten shi* (A history of Japanese overseas development), 1936, and *Meiji nanshin shikō* (A short history of southward expansion in the Meiji Era), 1943. The two consummate works are invariably the first to which Japanese writers turn for reference on the *nanshin*. The former includes South and North America, Hawaii, Manchuria, and the South Seas, with a chapter on the 'Establishment of rubber enterprises and South Seas emigration'; the latter describes with much detail Japanese early ventures into Micronesia from 1868 until the month of publication in March 1943, when Japan was seriously threatening Australia and the Dutch East Indies.

After this introduction one may want to peruse for oneself the writings of Meiji *nanshin-ron sha*. Probably the most representative to start off with are the books by Suzuki Tsunenori, *Nantō junkōki* (Record of a cruise in the southern islands), 1893, and *Nan'yō tanken jikki* (A true story of exploration in the South Seas), 1892; or by Hattori Tōru, *Nihon no Nan'yō* (Japan's South Seas), 1888; *Nan'yōsaku* (Policy toward the South), 1891; *Nankyū no shin shokumin* (A new colony in the southern hemisphere), 1894—which treats the growing Japanese presence on Thursday Island. The often-cited article by Taguchi Ukichi, 'Nan'yō keiryakuron' (22 March 1890), in *Teiken Taguchi Ukichi zenshū* (Collected works of Teiken Taguchi Ukichi), 1928, is disappointingly short, but it is worthwhile perusing the numerous articles on the South Seas in the influential journal *Tōkyō keizai zasshi* (Tokyo Economic Review) which he edited. The spate of information appeared in 1890–1891, when he was involved in establishing the Nantō Shōkai (South Sea Islands Company) and spent seven months in the Micronesian islands.

A useful overview on the literature of the *'nanshin'* from the mid-Meiji to the Shōwa period can be found in Yano Tooru's similar two books, *"'Nanshin' no keifu* (Genealogy of 'southward advance'), 1975, and *Nihon no Nan'yō shikan* (Japanese historical view of the South Seas), 1979. They offer an admirable collection of literature on the *nanshin* compressed into the size of a paperback. But they are no substitute for perusing for oneself such representative works as Takekoshi Yosaburō's *Nangokuki* (Account of southern countries), 1910, or Tsurumi Yūsuke's *Nan'yō yūki* (Travel sketches of the South Seas), 1917, to catch the mood of the times and form one's own judgment as to the meaning and significance of *nanshin* in Japanese history.

Those who want to read farther can consult the studies by Shimizu Hajime. His 'Taishō shoki ni okeru "Nanshin ron" no ichikōsatsu: sono Ajia shugiteki henyō o megutte' (A study of the 'southward advance' in the early Taishō period: its changes under the impact of Asianism), 1983, for example, brings out in greater detail the changes that began to occur in the *nanshin-ron* literature at an important time before and during World War I. The article is available in English as *'Nanshin-ron*: Its Turning Point in World War I', 1987. In another article which pays attention to the continuity factor in the 'southward advance': 'Nihon-Tōnanajia kankei no bunmei shiteki ichi' (The situation of Japanese-Southeast Asian relations in the history of civilization), 1986, the author compares, in an original way, similarities between Japanese going South in the 1600s and in the 1920s.

Other occasional articles on the *nanshin* theme include Ōhata Tokushirō's ' "Nanshin" no shisō to seisaku no keifu' (The idea of southward advance and the genealogy of the policy), 1983. Whereas Yano approaches the Japanese southern drive since the early Meiji period mainly from the people's (*minkan*) level, Ōhata sees the 'southern advance' almost purely from the perspective of government policy; he prefers to emphasize the more significant 'go-north' policy which enjoyed the firm support of the government.

Balancing these two views is an interesting paper by Shiozaki Hiroaki, who pays equal attention to the *nanshin-ron* and the *hokushin-ron* in 'Gunbu to Nanpō shinshitsu' (The military and the southern advance),

1983. Crediting the 'go-north' and 'go-south' policies equally, he perceives the two antipodal drives as narrowing in the 1930s until they are accommodated, at first in the national policy plans of August 1936, then in the New Order proclamation (1938), and finally in the Greater East Asia Co-Prosperity Sphere policy (1940). This approach is close to Hatano Sumio's mentioned further on.

Earliest Japanese Visitors' Perceptions of Australia

Some intellectuals who early prompted Japanese to expand in the South devoted space to Australia in their works. Although Inagaki Manjirō's comments on Australia are limited in *Tōhōsaku* (Eastern policy), 1891, what he says is full of foresight as to the complementary partnership in trade which he envisages. That work is a translated version of his Cambridge thesis published by T. Fisher Unwin as *Japan and the Pacific and A Japanese View of the Eastern Question,* 1890. Shiga Shigetaka, free-trader and doyen-advocate of southern exploration, devoted five chapters to Australia in his epochal *Nan'yō jiji* (Current affairs in the South Seas), 1887. Equally absorbing are the passages in Mishima Kazuo's, *Gōshū oyobi Indo* (Australia and India), 1891, two-thirds of which cover Australia.

For books exclusively on Australia written before the Sino–Japanese War, one can consult Watanabe Kanjūrō's, *Gōshū tanken hōkokusho* (Report on the exploration of Australia), 1894. Commissioned by the Japanese Foreign Ministry, Watanabe introduces there land and society in a systematic way, based on half a year of personal observations between Darwin and Melbourne. Of further interest are the official books on Australia written by two Japanese bureaucrats who represented Japan at intercolonial and world expositions in Australia. Sakata Haruo's *Gōshū Shidonifu bankoku hakurankai hōkokusho* (A report on Sydney's world exhibition), 1881, is filled with statistics, while Hashimoto Masato's two-volume diary, *Fu Gōshū Meruborun hakurankai kikō* (An account of the trip to the Melbourne exhibition), 1876, vividly describes his delegation's voyage to the South and their experiences in Australia. As an original contribution to earliest Japanese appreciations of Australia, a full translation of Hashimoto's diary into English would be of interest.

In English are available the absorbing and carefully researched studies by D. C. S. Sissons, which contribute to a detailed understanding of earliest Japanese migration to Australia. Particularly noteworthy are his 'Immigration in Australian-Japanese Relations, 1871–1971', 1972; 'The Japanese in the Australian Pearling Industry', 1979; and 'Karayuki-San: Japanese Prostitutes in Australia, 1887–1916', 1977.

White Australia, and Relations During and After World War I

The eight volumes of collected documents, Gōshū ni oite honpō imin tokō seigen ikken (On overseas immigration restriction of Japanese in Australia), at the Japanese Foreign Ministry Archives are a useful primary source for Japanese–Australian relations from 1893 to 1921. They contain numerous Australian newspaper cuttings of the period, long passages from Hansard, and a wealth of letters, telegrams, and memorandums that went back and forth between Tokyo and the colonial and Commonwealth governments on the subject of the White Australia policy, prior to and after its establishment. Narita Katsushirō, a former ambassador to Australia, offers a basic and useful chronological introduction arranged by topics on Japanese immigrants, diplomacy, and trade in Japanese–Australian relations before World War II, in the first two parts of his *Nichigō tsūshō gaikōshi* (A diplomatic history of commercial relations between Japan and Australia), 1971.

For those without ready access to Australian diplomatic archives, Neville Meaney's wide collection of important diplomatic documents in *Australia and the World: A Documentary History from the 1870s to the 1970*, 1985, is of great value, especially for its meticulous information on source location. The same can be said of his *The Search for Security in the Pacific, 1901–14*, 1976, a carefully annotated history of Australian defence and foreign policy. The documentary appendix of D. C. S. Sissons's M.A. thesis, Attitudes to Japan and Defence 1890–1923 (1956), can also be used with profit as a guide to important documents in Japanese–Australian relations in that period. Details on the Australian navy in World War I can be found in Arthur W. Jose, *Official History of Australia in the War of 1914–18: The Royal Australian Navy*, 1937. For a well researched and candid study on Australia's 'northward advance', see Roger C. Thompson, *Australian Imperialism in the Pacific: The Expansionist Era 1820–1920*, 1980.

Consolidation in the Western Pacific Mandates

Useful contemporary accounts on Japanese mandate rule are Yanaihara Tadao's detailed study *Pacific Islands Under Japanese Mandate*, 1939; and *Japan's Pacific Mandate*, 1935, by Paul H. Clyde, an American historian who received rare permission to travel freely in Micronesia. Fifty years later, a comprehensive study has appeared by Mark R. Peattie, *Nan'yō: The Rise and Fall of the Japanese in Micronesia 1885–1945*, 1988. It covers the entire evolution of Japanese settlement of the central Pacific Islands, from the days of the first trading pioneers, such as Mori Koben who settled in Truk in the 1890s, to the economic, political, and social developments in the Japanese Mandates until their utter destruction in the Pacific War. It is richly illustrated with photographs of colonial Japan and many reproduced maps of the Japanese towns in Micronesia.

Australian mandate rule is discussed in books edited by W. J. Hudson, such as *New Guinea Empire: Australia's Colonial Experience*, 1974, and *Australia and Papua New Guinea*, 1971. A scholarly assessment in the latter, Heather Radi's 'New Guinea Under Mandate 1921–41' is particularly honest and useful. For a documented contemporary critique of occidental and oriental mandate power abuse, see also J. A. Decker, *Labor Problems in the Pacific Mandates*, 1940.

The Japanese Navy's Southward Advance and Australia, 1936–1942

Two articles stand out as good introductions to the responsibilities which the navy must assume for the Pacific War. The diplomatic historian, Tsunoda Jun's 'Nihon no tai Bei kaisen (1940 nen–1941 nen)' (Japan's opening of war against the United States, 1940–1941), 1963, traces the navy's initiative in planning for southern advance to a 1936 draft plan concerning the critical problem of oil resources in the Dutch East Indies (Tsunoda's significant discussion of the navy's role in southern strategy is available in an abridged translation in William Morley, ed., *The Fateful Choice: Japan's Advance into Southeast Asia, 1938–1941*, New York, Columbia University Press, 1980). Asada Sadao's 'The Japanese Navy and the United States', in Dorothy Borg and Shumpei Okamoto, eds, *Pearl Harbor as History: Japanese–American Relations 1931–1941*, 1973, points out the crucial role of the disciples of Katō Kanji's 'Fleet Faction'.

The Japanese navy's *nanshin* enthusiasm is further revealed in new research along the same line by younger scholars, such as Hatano Sumio in 'Shōwa kaigun no nanshin ron' (The Navy's southward advance in the Shōwa period), 1984, and 'Nihon kaigun to "nanshin": sono seisaku to riron no shiteki tenkai' (The Japanese Navy and the southward advance: the historical development of its policies and theory), 1986. Hatano also shows that the Navy's *nanshin* and the Army's *hokushin* policies were beginning to converge much earlier than the generally accepted years of 1940–1941, namely from 1936–1937 onward. His article, 'The Japanese Decision to Move South (1939–1941)', written with Asada Sadao in Esmonde M. Robertson and Robert Boyce, eds, *Paths to War: New Essays on the Origins of the Second World War*, 1989, further lays bare the important role which the navy played in bringing Japan into World War II. More documentary evidence on the power of the middle-echelon naval officers, such as Ishikawa Shingo, is evinced in the work of Kudō Michihiro, *Nihon Kaigun to Taiheiyō sensō* (The Japanese Navy and the Pacific War), 2 Vols, Iwamura Seiro, 1982.

But these works say little about Australia and her place in Japanese war plans in the first year of the Pacific War. The first source to consult is the War History issued by the Bōei-chō, Bōeikenshūjo, Senshishitsu (Self-defense Agency, National Defense College, War History Office). This comprehensive series owes its existence to the decision in 1955 by Japan's Military War History Department to write an official war history under the direction of Colonel Nishiura Susumu. Documents were collected and interviews conducted in a ten-year preparatory program. The series' first volume appeared in 1966; today it numbers 104 volumes. The initial idea had been to combine army and navy testimony in well-digested joint works of war history. But the notorious intraservice feud, carried over into the post-war period, dashed any such hope: army and navy each went their own way to assemble the facts according to their service colours. Their accumulated amount of overlapping evidence can now draw-out research to tedious length; but plodding through army and navy testimony allows one to hear both sides and so draw closer to the truth.

Of greatest use to learn about Australia's place in the war stages were the two volumes *Daihon'ei kaigunbu, rengōkantai* (Imperial Headquarters, Navy General Staff, Combined Fleet), 1975. The entire series is well footnoted and the facts therein gathered can be further pursued in position papers and individual diaries, most of which can be seen freely at the War History Office archives, National Defense College, Tokyo—though several are still closed or require a special permission.

Some of this invaluable primary source material, such as the Army General Staff's, *Daihon'ei kimitsu sensō nisshi* (The secret war diary of Imperial Headquarters), deposited in War History Office, National Defense College, Tokyo, has been edited and published as *Daihon'ei kimitsu nisshi*, 1952, by Tanemura Sakō. Other servicemen, who were once involved in plans concerning Australia, later published studied reminiscences about the opening of the war. For example, Tomioka Sadatoshi, *Kaisen to shūsen: hito to kikō to keikaku* (The opening and closing of the war: the people, the mechanism, and the planning), 1968; and Ishikawa Shingo, *Shinjuwan made no keii: kaisen no shinsō* (The circumstances leading to Pearl Harbor: the real facts about the opening of the war), 1960. These hold a certain interest, but one must exercise caution with their post-war accounts; their real voice rings truest in documents one can gather on them before 1945.

For documentary evidence on Australian foreign policy in this period, this study relied most of all on *Documents on Australian Foreign Policy, 1937–1949* (Australian Government Publishing Service), Vols 1–5 (1937–June 1942). The series contains large numbers of the documents that concern Japan. It is well indexed and has a useful subject table, which makes for easy research when investigating, for example, 'Japan and Portuguese Timor', or 'Japan and the Yampi Sound Iron Mine'. Published in progress since 1975, they reached Vol. 7 (1944) in 1988.

Another diplomatic source of reference was the Nichigō Kyōkai's (Japan–Australia Society), *Nichigō Kyōkai sōkai kaimu hōkoku* (Working report of the general meeting of the Japan–Australia Society), Vols 8–14. The Society was founded in 1928, amid strengthening trade and diplomatic relations between Japan and Australia in the early Shōwa years; these seven slim volumes of annual reports cover the years from 1936 to March 1942. They reproduce the usual allocutions of dignitaries uttered at receptions in Tokyo and Canberra, some of which are even interesting. The Society was a perceptive organ that tried to remedy the steady decline in relations after the trade war in 1936. One of its last acts was in 1941 when, on the eve of the Pacific War, Japan suggested the construction of a genuine Tea House for the Sydney Chapter to celebrate the 2600th year of the Japanese Empire, 'now that relations are becoming closer'. When New Zealand joined the Society after the war, it became the Japan–Australia–New Zealand Society. In 1980 it published a commemorative volume, *Nichigō Kyōkai gojū nen, Nihon Nyūjirando Kyōkai nijūhachi nen shi* (Historical records of the Japan–Australia Society— 50 years, and the Japan–New Zealand Society—28 years. The first two parts provide a useful summary of the Society's pre-war activities with photographs of its past presidents, such as Prince Tokugawa Iemasa, Viscount Sakatani Yoshiro, and former Ambassador to Australia Kawai Tatsuo.

Australia in the Nan'yō Literature 1940–1944

The final chapter is itself a long note on Japanese sources which treat Australia in the early 1940s, and self-explanatory. Practically all the books are available at the Japanese Diet Library in Tokyo. A complete guide for much of that literature, at least for the length of a year, is Amano Keitarō's *Daitōashiryō Sōran* (Survey of documents on Greater East Asia), 1944; it offers data on a vast collection of Japanese source materials on the Asia–Pacific region published in the crucial period between 8 December 1941 and December 1942 (see pp. 348–63).

Finally, the section dealing with Japan's vision of Australia in the post-war era relied on primary Army, Navy, and Foreign Ministry position papers from the Bōeichō archives of the War History Office, National Defense College, Tokyo, and from the Oriental Institute of the Eastern Culture University (Daitō Bunka Daigaku Tōyō kenkyūjo Zō) with its valuable naval history documents. Of further special interest were the documents of the Total War Research Institute (Sōryokusen Kenkyūjo), Daitōa kyōeiken kensetsu gen'an (sōkō) (Draft of basic plans for the establishment of the Greater East Asia Co-Prosperity Sphere), 27 January 1942, and Daitōa kyōeiken kensetsu gen'an oyobi Tōa kensetsu daiichiki sōryoku senhō ryaku ni kansuru yobi kenkyū tōshin (Report on the preliminary study of the plans for the establishment of the Greater East Asia Co-Prosperity Sphere, and on the strategy for the first period of the total war for the construction of a 'New East Asia'), 14 January 1942. Both documents are best studied with the critical comment provided in Kawahara Hiroshi's *Shōwa seiji shisō kenkyū* (A study of political thought in the Shōwa period), 1979, and the background offered in Morimatsu Toshio's incisive study, *Sōryokusen Kenkyūjo* (The Total War Research Institute), 1983.

Bibliography

UNPUBLISHED SOURCES IN JAPANESE

Foreign Ministry Archives (Gaimushōkan Gaikō Shiryōkan), Tokyo

Documents relating to staff employment, File 6.1.6.17.

Gōshū ni oite honpō imin tokō seigen ikken 濠洲ニ於テ本邦移民渡航制限一件 (On overseas immigration restriction of Japanese in Australia), File 3.8.2.33, Vols 1–8.

Honpō meishi no shogaikoku hōmon kankei zakken本邦名士ノ諸外国訪問関係雑件 (Documents on the visits of Japanese dignitaries to various countries), Debuchi Katsuji's confidential report on his mission to the South Pacific, File L.3.3.0.14, Vol. 1.

Kakkoku chūzai teikoku meiyoryōji ninmen zakken (Meruborun bu) 各国駐在帝国名誉領事任免雑件 (メルボル゛ン部) (Documents on appointments and dismissals of Japanese honorary consuls: Melbourne section), File 6.1.5.9-7.

Sōri, rikukaigai yonshō kaigi kettei an (Gaimushō an) 総理陸海外四相会議決定案 (外務省案) (Plans for decisions of Four Ministerial Conference of the Prime Ministry, and the Army, Navy, and Foreign Ministry (The Foreign Minister's plan), 24 July 1940, in Kaigun shiryō (Ōshū sensō) 9 海軍史料 (欧州戦争)9 (Naval history documents [European War] 9). Deposited at Daitō Bunka Daigaku Tōyō Kenkyūjo Zō 大東文化大学東洋研究所蔵 (Oriental Institute of the Eastern Culture University).

Teikoku shogaikoku kan gaikō kankei zassan (Nichi-Gō kan) 帝国諸外国間外交関係雑纂 (日濠間) (Miscellaneous diplomatic documents on Empire relations with various countries: Japan and Australia), File 1.1.4.1, Vol. 10.

War History Office, National Defense College, Tokyo

Army General Staff (Daihon'ei rikugunbu sensō shidō han 大本営陸軍部戦争指導班)

Daihon'ei kimitsu sensō nisshi 大本営機密戦争日誌 (The secret war diary of Imperial Headquarters), Vol. 5, 8 December 1941–1 April 1942.

Imoto Kumao chūsa gyōmu nisshi 井本熊男中佐業務日誌 (Working diary of Lieutenant-Colonel Imoto Kumao), Vol. 15/23.

Nichi-Doku-I teikei kyōka ni kan suru ken (rikugun an) 日独伊提携強化ニ関ス件 (陸軍案) (Proposal for strengthening cooperation between Japan, Germany, and Italy (Army plan), 27 July 1940, in Kaigun shiryō (Ōshū sensō) 9 海軍史料 (欧州戦争) 9 (Naval history documents [European war] 9). Deposited at Daitō Bunka Daigaku Tōyō Kenkyūjo Zō 大東文化大学東洋研究所蔵 (Oriental Institute of the Eastern Culture University).

Nihon no shoki senryaku ni okeru kōryaku han'iki no kettei ni kan suru chinjutsusho 日本の初期戦略に於ける攻略範域の決定に関する陳述書 (Written declaration concerning the delimitations of conquest in the early stage of Japan's war strategy), 3 May 1949.

Tanaka Shin'ichi chūjō gyōmu nisshi 田中新一中将業務日誌 (The working diary of Lieutenant-General Tanaka Shin'ichi, 14 January–26 April 1942, Vols 2/7).

Tanaka Shin'ichi chūjō shuki 田中新一中将手記 (Memoirs of Lieutenant-General Tanaka Shin'ichi).

Army Ministry (Rikugunshō 陸軍省)

Bei-Gō narabini Ei-In-Gō kan no sōgō izon kankei narabini kore ga shadan ni yoru eikyō 米豪並英印豪間／相互依存関係並之カ゛遮断ニ依ル影響 (The consequences of cutting the communication lines between the United States and Australia, and between England, India, and Australia), Microfilm (of old documents concerning Army-Navy relations), reel T. 1108, t. 31205–31219. Deposited at Waseda University, Tokyo.

Army and Colonial Affairs Ministry, Research Section (Gun-Takumusho, Chōsa Bu 軍・拓務省調査部)

Dai Tōa kyōeiken ni okeru tochi shobun an 大東亜共栄圏ニ於ル土地処分案 (Land disposal plan in the Greater East Asia Co-Prosperity Sphere), IPS-

DOC, IMT (International Prosecution Section-Document, International Military Tribunal) 295.

Dai Tōa sensō ni yoru nanpō senkyo shochiiki zengo shori hōsaku taikō 大東亜戦争⊆依ル南方占拠諸地域善後処理方策大綱 (Documents relating to fundamental measures to be taken in territories occupied in southern Asia during the Greater East Asia War), IPS-DOC, IMT 295.

Total War Research Institute (Sōryokusen Kenkyūjo 総力戦研究所)

Daitōa kyōeiken kensetsu gen'an (sōkō) 大東亜共栄圏建設原案(草稿) (Draft of basic plans for the establishment of the Greater East Asia Co-Prosperity Sphere), 27 January 1942.

Daitōa kyōeiken kensetsu gen'an oyobi Tōa kensetsu daiichiki sōryoku senhō ryaku ni kansuru yobi kenkyū tōshin 大東亜共栄圏建設原案及東亜建設第一期　総力戦方略⊆関ル予備研究答申 (Report on the preliminary study of the plans for the establishment of the (Greater East Asia Co-Prosperity Sphere, and on the strategy for the first period of the total war for the construction of a 'New East Asia'), 14 January 1942, IPS-DOC IMT 492.

Navy General Staff (Kaigun gunreibu 海軍軍令部)

Miwa nisshi 三和日誌 (Diary of Captain Miwa Yoshitake).

Nakahara chūjō nisshi 中原中将日誌 (Diary of Vice Admiral Nakahara).

Operational Section (Sakusen ka 作戦課), Dai Tōa kyōeiken kensetsu taikō (shian) 大東亜共栄圏建設大綱 (試案) (Draft outline for the construction of the Greater East Asia Co-Prosperity Sphere), 29 November 1940. Deposited in the East Asian Library, Hoover Institution on War, Revolution, and Peace, Stanford, California. [The writer gratefully acknowledges a copy thereof from Professor John J. Stephan.]

Sanagi memo 佐薙メモ (Notes of Commander Sanagi Tsuyoshi).

Navy Ministry (Kaigunshō 海軍省)

Kaigun daijin kanbō kiroku 海軍大臣官房記録 (Record office), *Ibuki* senji nisō 伊吹戦時日そう (The war-logbook of the *Ibuki*).

Kaigunshō Chōsaka 海軍省調査課 (Research Section), Kokubō kokka no honshitsu to kōzō 国防国家の本質と構造 (Essence and structure of national defence), Kokubō kokka ni kansuru kenkyū kōzō 国防国家⊆関ル研究構造 (Organizing research related to national defence), 19 February 1941, in Kaigun shiryō fuzoku shiryō (A). Sōgō kenkyū kai 海軍史料付属資料(A)綜合研究会 (Naval history documents and appended papers [A]. Composite research meetings). Deposited at Daitō Bunka Daigaku Tōyō Kenkyūjo Zō 大東文化大学東洋研究所蔵 (Oriental Institute of the Eastern Culture University).

Nan'yō shin senryō chi no shōrai 南洋新占領地ノ将来 (The future of the newly occupied territories in the South Seas), in Senji shorui 戦時書類 (Wartime documents), Vol. 18.

Naval Association (Suikō kaihen 水交会編)

Moto kaigun chūjō Kusaka Ryūnosuke danwa shūroku 元海軍中将草麗龍之 介談話収録 (The collected memories of former Vice-Admiral Sōa Ryū-nosuke), Vol. 1, February 1960.

PUBLISHED SOURCES IN JAPANESE
(All publishers are in Tokyo unless otherwise indicated)

Akagi Kanji 赤木完爾, 'Nihon kaigun to Hokkai jiken' 日本海軍と北海事件, in Keio Gijuku Daigaku Daigakuin Hōgaku Kenkyū Ka (Keio University Law School), *Shōwa gojūnendo ronbun shū* 昭和五十年度論文集 (Thesis collection of 1977), Keiō Daigaku, 1977, pp. 133–45.

Akima Ryōichi 秋間良一,'Gōshū, Nan'yō no keizai jijō' 濠洲南洋の経済事情 (The economic situation of Australia and the South Pacific) in *Gōshū, Nan'yō ni okeru orimono no jukyū jōkyō* 濠洲南洋に於ける織物の需給状況, (Supply and demand of textiles in Australia and the South Pacific), Yushutsu Shinkō Chōsakai.

Akioka sekai kochizu shūsei 秋岡コレクション世界古地図集成 (Akioka collection: old world-maps, 16th-19th centuries; Kawadeshobo shinsha, 1988).

Akiyama Kenzō 秋山謙蔵, 'Muromachi jidai ni okeru Ryūkyū no Indoshina-shokoku to no tsūkō' 室町時代に於ける琉球の印度支那諸国との通交 (Traffic between the Ryuukyuu islands and the countries of Indochina in the Muromachi period), in *Rekishi-chiri* 歴史地理 (History-Geography), Vol. 56, December 1930, pp. 1–21.

Amano Keitarō 天野敬太郎, *Daitōashiryō sōran* 大東亜資料総覧 (General survey of documents on Greater East Asia), Kyoto: Taigadō, 1944.

Anzai Chikao 安西千賀夫, *Gōshū no sangyō kin'yū oyobi bōeki* 濠洲ノ産業金融及貿易 (Trade and industrial finance in Australia), 1920.

Aoki Busuke 青木武助, *Dai-Nippon rekishi shūsei* 大日本歴史集成 (A comprehensive history of Great Japan), Ryubun-kan, 3 vols, 1915–1917.

Arai Hakuseki 新井白石, *Sairan igen* 采覧異言 (Review of foreign testimony), 1713, [from *Arai Hakuseki zenshū*, Vol. 2, 1905], in *Nihon kyōiku shisō taikei* 日本教育思想大系 *(Outline of Japanese thought on education), Vol. 10, Nihon Tosho Sentaa, 1979, [Vol. 2], pp. 73–115.

Bōei-chō, Bōeikenshūjo, Senshishitsu [BBS] 防衛庁、防衛研修所、戦史室 (Self-defense Agency, National Defense College, War History Office), *Minami Taiheiyō rikugun sakusen: Pooto Moresubi-Gatō shoki sakusen* 南太平洋陸軍作戦:ポ‐トモレスビ‐カ゛島初期作戦 (Army operations in the South Pacific: the early stage from Port Moresby to Guadalcanal), Vol. 1, Asagumo Shinbunsha, 1968.

———, *Chūbu Taiheiyō hōmen kaigun sakusen* 中部太平洋方面海軍作戦

(Naval operations in the central Pacific theater), Vol. 1, Asagumo Shin-bunsha, 1970.

———, *Daihon'ei rikugunbu* 大本営陸軍部 (Imperial Headquarters, Army General Staff), Vols 1, 3, Asagumo Shinbunsha, 1967, 1970.

———, *Middowee kaisen* ミッドウェー海戦 (The battle of Midway), Asagumo Shinbunsha, 1971.

———, *Nantō hōmen kaigun sakusen: Gatō dakkai sakusen kaishi made* 南東方面海軍作戦:ガ島奪回作戦開始まで (Naval operations in the southeastern theater: until commencement of the recapture of Guadalcanal), Vol. 1, Asagumo Shinbunsha, 1971.

———, *Daihon'ei kaigunbu, rengōkantai* 大本営海軍部・連合艦隊 (Imperial Headquarters, Navy General Staff, Combined Fleet), 2 vols, Asagumo Shinbunsha, 1975.

Endō Masako 遠藤雅子, *Nazo no ikokusen* 謎の異国船 (Mystery-ships from strange lands), Bunka Shuppan Kyoku, 1981.

Frei, Henry, 'Ōsutoraria kara mita Nihon no chiseigakuteki kyōi: 1931 nen —1941 nen' オーストラリアから見た日本の地政学的脅威ー1931年ー1941年ー (The Japanese geopolitical threat as seen from Australia, 1931–1941), in Miwa Kimitada 三輪公忠, ed., *Nihon no 1930 nendai: kuni no uchi to soto kara* 日本の1930 年代ー国の内と外からー (Japan in the 1930s: an inside and outside view of the country), Saikōsha, 1980, pp. 103–34.

Fukushima Teruhiko 福島輝彦, '"Bōeki tenkan seisaku" to Nichigō bōeki funsō (1936 nen)' 「貿易転換政策」と日豪貿易紛争 (1936 年) (The Japa-nese-Australian trade dispute and the Trade Diversion Policy of 1936), in *Kokusai seiji* 国際政治 (International politics), Journal of the Japan Associ-ation of International Relations, Vol. 68, 1981, pp. 59–78.

Fukuzawa Yukichi 福沢諭吉, *Fukuzawa Yukichi zenshū* 福沢諭吉全集 (The complete works of Fukuzawa Yukichi), ed. Keio University, Iwanami Shoten 1958–1964, Vols 8–10.

———, *Fukuzawa Yukichi senshū* 福沢諭吉選集 (Selected works of Fu-kuzawa Yukichi), Iwanami, 1981.

Gaimushō hen 外務省編 (Japanese Foreign Ministry), *Nihon gaikō nenpyō narabini shuyō bunsho, 1840–1945* 日本外交年表並びに主要文書, 1840— 1945 (Chronology and major documents of Japanese foreign relations, 1840–1945), 2 vols, Hara Shobō, 1965.

Gendai-shi shiryō 現代史資料 (Source material on contemporary history), Vol. 8: *Nitchū sensō* 日中戦争 (The Sino-Japanese war), Tome 1; Vol. 10: *Nitchū sensō*, Tome 3, Misuzu Shobō, 1964.

Gō Takashi 郷隆, *Nan'yō bōeki gojūnenshi* 南洋貿易五十年史 (History of fifty years of South Seas trade), Nan'yō Bōeki Kabushiki Kaisha, 1942.

Gōshū sanbutsu kōtei daikahyō 濠洲産物公定代価表 (Official pricelist of Aus-tralian products), Tōkyō Shōgyō Kaigijo, 1895.

Hashimoto Masato 橋本正人, *Fu Gōshū Meruborun hakurankai kikō* 赴豪洲咩厘呅府博覧会紀行 (An account of the trip to the Melbourne exhibition), Kangyōryō 勧業寮 (Department for Industrial Promotion), 1876, 2 vols.

Hashimoto Sanai 橋本左内, *Sanai shokan* 左内書簡 (Sanai's letters), 1857, in *Nihon shisō taikei* 日本思想大系 (An outline of Japanese thought), Vol. 55, Iwanami Shoten, 1971.

Hashiya Hiroshi 橋谷弘, 'Senzenki Fuiripin ni okeru hōjin keizai shinshutsu no keitai: shokugyō betsu jinkō chōsa o chūshin toshite' 戦前期フィリピンにおける邦人経済進出の形態 ： 職業別人口調査を中心として (The nature of Japanese economic advance in the prewar Philippines: according to occupation and population patterns), in *Ajia keizai* アジア経済 (Asian economies), Vol. 26, No. 3, 1985.

Hatano Sumio 波多野澄雄, '"Tōa shinchitsujo" to chiseigaku' 東亜新秩序と地政学 (Geopolitics and the New Order in East Asia), in Miwa Kimitada, ed., *Nihon no 1930 nen dai: kuni no uchi to soto* (Japan in the 1930s: an inside and outside view of the country), Saikōsha, 1980, pp. 14–47.

———, 'Nichi-Doku-I sangoku dōmei ni kansuru jakkan no shiryō', 日独伊三国同盟に関する若干の資料 (Some historical documents relating to the tripartite pact of Japan, Germany, and Italy), in *Gunji shigaku* 軍事史学 Vol. 20, no. 1, 1984, pp. 51–62.

———, 'Shōwa kaigun no nanshin ron' 昭和海軍の南進論 (The Navy's southward advance in the Showa period), in *Zōkan rekishi to jinbutsu: hishi-Taiheiyō sensō* 増刊歴史と人物：秘史・太平洋戦争 (Special issue of 'History and personalities': hidden episodes of the Pacific War), Chūōkōron, December 1984, pp. 277–85.

———, 'Nihon kaigun to "nanshin": sono seisaku to riron no shiteki tenkai' 日本海軍と「南進」―その政策と理論の史的展開― (The Japanese Navy and the southward advance: the historical development of its policies and theory), in Shimizu Hajime 清水元, ed., *Ryō taisenkanki Nihon-Tōnan'ajia kankei no shosō* 両大戦間期日本・東南アジア関係の諸相 (Various aspects of Japanese-Southeast Asian relations between the two World Wars), Ajia Keizai Kenkyūjo, 1986, pp. 207–36.

Hattori Tōru 服部徹, *Nihon no Nan'yō* 日本の南洋 (Japan's South Seas), Nan'yōdō, 1888.

———, *Nan'yōsaku* 南洋策 (Policy toward the South), Muraoka Genba, 1891.

———, *Nankyū no shin shokumin* 南球の新殖民 (A new colony in the southern hemisphere), Hakubunsha, 1894.

Hayashi Shihei 林子平, *Sangoku tsūran zusetsu* 三国通覧図説 (An illustrated survey of three countries), 1785, in *Hoppō mikōkai kobunsho shūsei* 北方未公開古文書集成 (A collection of rare old texts on the northern region), Vol. 3, Sōbunsha, 1978, pp. 55–109.

Hayashi Sōtarō 林荘太郎, *Nichi-Gō tsūshō mondai* 日豪通商問題 (The Japanese-Australian trade problem), No. 95, Kabushiki Kaisha Kanematsu Shōten, 1936.

Hijikata Teiichi 土方定一, 'Shiga Shigetaka to "Nan'yō jiji"' 志賀重昂と「南洋時事」 (Shiga Shigetaka and his 'Conditions in the South Seas'), in *Shin Ajia* 新亜細亜 (New Asia), March 1942.

Hirama Yōichi 平間洋一, 'Daiichiji sekai taisenchū ni shōjita gōgaku (kai-shaku) jō no mondai ten' 第一次世界大戦中に生じた語学 (解釈) 上の問題点 (Problems of mistranslation in diplomatic documents during W.W. I), in *Gaikō jihō* 外交時報 (Diplomatic review), No. 1240, July/August 1987, pp. 60–71.

————, 'Kaigunshiteki ni mita nanshin no ichi dammen: Nihon kaigun o Mikuroneshia senryō ni fumikiraseta haikei' 海軍史的に見た南進の一断面：日本海軍をミクロネシア占領に踏み切らせた背景 (One aspect of Japan's southward advance from the viewpoint of naval history: background of the Japanese navy's occupation of Micronesia), in *Seiji keizai shigaku* 政治経済史学 (Politics, economics, and history), Vol. 250, February 1987, pp. 85–100.

Hirose Takeo 広瀬武夫, *Kōnan shiki* 航南私記 (Personal record of a southern voyage), Shutokuenzo, 1904.

Hirota Kōki Denki Kankōkai 広田弘毅伝記刊行会 (Committee to publish a biography of Hirota Kōki), ed., *Hirota Kōki* 広田弘毅, 1966.

Hokkaidō Chō 北海道庁 (The Government Office of Hokkaido), *Gōbei shi-satsu fukumeisho* 濠米視察復命書 (Inspection report on Australia and America), Hokkaidō, 1907.

Honda Toshiaki 本多利明, *Seiiki monogatari* 西域物語 (Stories about Western lands), 1798, in *Nihon shisō taikei*, Vol. 44, Iwanami Shoten, 1970, pp. 88–163.

Ichikawa Taijirō 市川泰治郎, *Gōshū keizaishi kenkyū* 濠洲経済史研究 (A study of the economic history of Australia), Shōsankaku, 1944.

————, *Nichi-Gō kankeishi* 日濠関係史 (A history of Japanese-Australian relations), Nichigō Kyōkai-Nihon Nyūjirando Kyōkai, 1953.

Iechika Yoshiki 家近良樹, '"Taiwan shuppei" hōshin no tenkan to Chōshū ha no hantai undō' 「台湾出兵」方針の転換と長州派の反対運動 (The conversion of the policy of the dispatch of troops to Formosa and the opposition of the Chōshū faction) in *Shigaku zasshi* 史学雑誌 (Historical review), Vol. 92, No. 11, 1983, pp. 55–77.

Iguchi Ichirō 井口一郎, 'Kita Gōshū no chiseigakuteki kōsatsu' 北濠洲の地政学的考察 (A geopolitical analysis of North Australia), in *Taiheiyō* 太平洋 (Pacific Ocean), Vol. 5, March, April, May, 1942.

————, *Chisei dōtairon: gendai chiseigaku no shomondai* 地政動態論：現代地政学の諸問題 (A theory of geopolitical movements: geopolitical problems of to-day), Teikoku Shōin, March 1943.

Iimoto Nobuyuki 飯本信之, 'Nan'yō no chiseigaku' 南洋の地政学 (The geo-politics of the Nan'yō), in *Nan'yō chiri taikei* 南洋地理大系 (Outline of the geography of South Asia, 8 vols, April 1942), Vol. 1, Daiamondosha, 1942, pp. 29–123.

Iino Masako 飯野正子, 'Nichi-Ei tsūsan kōkai jōyaku to Kanada no Nihonjin imin mondai' 日英通産航海条約とカナダの日本人移民問題 (The Anglo-Japanese Treaty of Commerce and Navigation and the Japanese Immigration Problem in Canada) in *Kokusai seiji* 国際政治 (International politics), Vol. 79, 1985, pp. 1–18.

Iizawa Shōji 飯沢章治, *Nanshin seisaku no saininshiki* 南進政策の再認識 (The new consciousness of the southward advance policy), Takayama Shoin, 1939.

Ikeda Kiyoshi 池田清, *Nihon no kaigun* 日本の海軍 (The Japanese navy), 2 vols, Shiseido, 1966,1967.

———, *Kaigun to Nihon* 海軍と日本 (The navy and Japan), Chūō Kōronsha, 1981.

Ikenaga Takeshi 池長孟, *Hōsaibankaku daihōkan* 邦彩鸞革大宝鑑 (Great pictorial dictionary of Japanese reforms), Osaka: Sōgensha, 1933.

Inagaki Manjirō 稲垣満次郎, *Tōhōsaku* 東方策 (Eastern policy), Kassei Kaisha, 1891.

———, *Nan'yō chōsei dan* 南洋張征談 (Talk on an exploration deep into the South Seas), Yasui Hidema, 1892.

Inoue Shōzō 井上昇三, 'Gōshū to Tōyō' 濠洲と東洋 (Australia and the East Asian region) in *Tōyō* 東洋 (Oriental Review), Vol. 44, No. 9, 1941.

———, *Ugoku Gōshū* 動く濠洲 (Australia on the move), Hōunkai, 1942.

Inoue Takeo 井上武夫, *Gōshū no unmei* 濠洲の運命 (The destiny of Australia), Hajime Shobō, October 1943.

Inukai Tsuyoshi 犬養毅, *Kokubō oyobi gaikō* 国防及外交 (Japan's defence and diplomacy), Dai Nippon Seinen Kyōkai, 1914.

Irie Toraji 入江寅次, *Meiji nanshin shikō* 明治南進史考 (A short history of southward expansion in the Meiji Era), Iwanami Shoten, 1943.

———, *Hōjin kaigai hatten shi* 邦人海外発展史 (A history of Japanese overseas development), Ida Shōten, 1948.

Ishibashi Tanzan 石橋湛山, 'Eikoku wa Nihon no tachiba o ryōkai subeshi' 英国は日本の立場を了解すべし (England must understand Japan's viewpoint), *Tōyō Keizai Shinpō* 東洋経済新報 (Oriental economist), March 1938, in *Ishibashi Tanzan zenshū* 石橋湛山全集 (The complete works of Ishibashi Tanzan), Vol. 11, Tōyō Keizai Shinpōsha, 1912, pp. 42–5.

Ishii Kenji 石井謙治, 'Fune to kōkai no rekishi' [I] 船と航海の歴史 (A history of ships and navigation), in *Zusetsu jinbutsu umi no Nihon shi (3): Kenminsen to wakō* 図説人物海の日本史 (3): 遣明船と倭寇 (An illustrated Japanese history of personalities and the sea [3]: ships despatched to China and the *wakō*), Mainichi Shinbunsha, 1979, pp. 143–52.

———, 'Fune to kōkai no rekishi' [II] (A history of ships and navigation), in *Zusetsu jinbutsu umi no Nihon shi (4): Tenkajin to Nanbansen* 図説人物海の日本史4天下人と南蛮船 (An illustrated Japanese history of personalities and the sea [4]: potentates and southern ships), Mainichi Shinbunsha, 1979, pp. 145–54.

Ishii Kikujirō 石井菊次郎, 'Daisensō gaikō no issetsu' 大戦争外交の一節 (An instance in the diplomacy of the Great War), in *Gaikō jihō* 外交時報 (Diplomatic review), No. 551, 1928, pp. 24–30.

Ishikawa Shingo 石川信吾, *Shinjuwan made no keii: kaisen no shinsō* 真珠湾ま
での経緯－開戦の真相－ (The circumstances leading to Pearl Harbor: the
real facts about the opening of the war), Jiji Tsūshin Sha, 1960.

Ishimaru Tōta 石丸藤太, *Nichi-Ei hissen ron* 日英必戦論 (Japan must fight
Britain), Shunjū Sha, September 1933.

Itō Takashi 伊東敬, *Gendai Gōshū ron* 現代濠洲論 (Australia to-day), San-
shōdōkan, February 1943.

Iwao Seiichi 岩生成一, *Shuinsen bōeki shi no kenkyū* 朱印船貿易史の研究
(Study of the red-seal ship trade), Kōbundō, 1958.

──, *Nan'yō Nihonmachi no kenkyū* 南洋日本町の研究 (Study of Japanese
settlements in the South Seas), Iwanami Shoten, 1966.

──, *Zoku Nan'yō Nihonmachi no kenkyū: Nan'yōtō shochiiki bunsan Nihon-
jin imin no seikatsu to katsudō* 続南洋日本町の研究－南洋島嶼地域分散日
本人移民の生活と活動 (A second study of Japanese settlements in the
South Seas: life and occupations of the Japanese immigrants in Island
Southeast Asia in the sixteenth and seventeenth centuries), Iwanami
Shoten, 1987.

Izumi Shinsuke 泉信介, *Gōshū shi* 濠洲史 (A history of Australia), May
1942.

Jose, Arthur W., *Gōshū oyobi sono shotō* 濠洲及其諸島 (A history of Australasia: from the earliest times to the present), tr. by Inoue Tomijirō, Dai
Nihon Bunmei Kyōkai Jimusho, May 1914.

Kaigun Gunreibu 海軍軍令部 (Navy General Staff), *Taishō yonen oyobi itaru
kyū nen kaigun senshi* 大正四年及至九年海軍戦史 (The naval war history
from 1915 to 1920), Vol. 2, 1924.

Kaigunshō Shiryō 海軍省資料 (Documents of the Navy Ministry), *Shōwa
shakai keizai shiryō shūsei* 昭和社会経済史料集成, II, (A collection of historical material on the society and economy of the Showa period), Vol. II,
Daitō Bunka Daigaku Tōyō Kenkyūjo (Oriental Institute of the Eastern
Culture University), 1980.

Kaigun Yūshū Kaihen 海軍有終会編, *Taiheiyō 2600 nenshi* 太平洋二千六百年
史 (The Pacific: a history commemorating 2600 years), August 1943.

Kamei Takayoshi 亀井高孝, *Daikokuya Kōdaiyu* 大黒屋光太夫, Yoshikawa
Kōbunkan, 1975.

Kamishima Jirō 神島二郎, *Kindai Nippon no seishin kōzo* 近代日本の精神構造
(The spiritual structure of modern Japan), Iwanami, 1961.

Kaneko Takanosuke 金子鷹之助 and Kiyokawa Masaji 清川正二, *Nanpō
keizai shigen sōran: Ōsutoraria/Nyūjirando no keizai shigen* 南方経済資源総
覧：オーストラリア・ニュージーランドノ経済資源 (Survey of economic resources of the
southern region: the economic resources of Australia and New Zealand),
Vol. 12, Tōa Seikeisha, February 1943.

Kanematsu Shōten 兼松商店, *Gōshū yushutsu bōeki ni tsuite* 濠洲輸出貿易に
ついて (Australia's exports), Kabushiki Kaisha Kanematsu Shōten, No. 15,
July 1942.

Kanematsu Shōten Chōsabu 兼松商店調査部, *Gōshū* 濠洲 (Australia), Kokusai Nihon Kyōkai, February 1943.

Kanematsu Shōten Kabushikigaisha 兼松商店株式会社, *Daitōa senboppatsu go no Gōshū no ugoki* 大東亜戦勃発後の豪州の動き (Activities regarding Australia after the outbreak of the Greater East Asia War), Sōgōshōsha, July 1942.

Katō Hidetoshi 加藤秀俊, *Hikaku bunka e no shikaku* 比較文化への視角 (Towards a viewpoint of comparative culture), Chūōkōronsha, 1968.

Katō Kanji 加藤完治, *Nihon nōson kyōiku* 日本農村教育 (Japanese farm village education), Tōyō Tosho, 1943.

Kawahara Hiroshi 河原宏, *Shōwa seiji shisō kenkyū* 昭和政治思想研究 (A study of political thought in the Shōwa period), Waseda Daigaku Shuppanbu, 1979.

Kawaji Kanichi 河地貫一, 'Gōshū no chiseigakuteki kōsatsu: hakugōshugi o chūshin to shite' 濠洲の地政学的考察：白濠主義 を中心として (The geopolitical structure of Australia: focusing on White Australia), in Komaki Saneshige 小牧実繁, ed., *Daitōa chiseigaku shinron* 大東亜地政学新論 (New geopolitical theory of Greater East Asia), Kyoto: Hoshino Shoten, 1943.

Kayahara Kazan 茅原華山, *Tōhoku taiseiron* 東北大勢論 (On conditions in northeastern Japan), Yamagata, 1895.

———, 'Nihon kokumin o jisatsu seshimuru mono wa Ei-Bei de aru' 日本国民を自殺せしむるものは英米である (England and America are driving the Japanese people toward suicide), in *Dai san teikoku* 第三帝国 (The third empire), No. 53, October 1915, pp. 4–9.

Kimiya Yasuhiko 木宮泰彦, *Nihon minzoku to kaiyō shisō* 日本民族と海洋思想 (The Japanese people and their notions of foreign lands), Tōkō Shoin, 1942.

Kobata Atsushi 小葉田淳, *Kingin bōekishi no kenkyū* 金銀貿易史の研究 (A historical study of the gold and silver trade), Hōsei Daigaku Shuppankyoku, 1976.

Koide Hideo 小出英男, *Nanpō engeiki* 南方演芸記 (Memories of entertainment in the southern region), Shin Kigen Sha, 1943.

Koide Mitsuji 小出満二, *Gōshū yōgyō chōsa hōkokusho* 濠洲羊業調査報告書 (Report on the Australian sheep farming industry), 1920.

Kojima Masanori 小島昌憲, *Gōshū no rigen* 濠洲の利源 (Australia's profitable resources), Hōkōkai, 1915.

Komaki Saneshige 小牧実繁, 'Daitōa no chiseigakuteki gaikan' 大東亜の地政学的概観 (A geopolitical overview of Greater East Asia), in *Chirigaku* 地理学 (Geography), April 1942, pp. 1–8.

———, *Daitōa chiseigaku shinron* 大東亜地政学新論 (New geopolitical theory of Greater East Asia), Kyoto: Hoshino Shoten, 1943.

Konoe Fumimaro 近衛文麿, 'Eibei hon'i no heiwashugi o haisu' 英米本位の平和主義を排す (Down with the Anglo-American peace principles), in

Nihon oyobi Nihonjin日本及日本人(Japan and the Japanese), No. 746, December 1918, pp. 23–6.

———, 'Sekai no genjō o kaizō seyo: gizenteki heiwaron o haigekisu' 世界の現状を改造せよー偽善的平和論を排撃す (Restructure the status quo in the world! Reject hypocritical Pacificism), in KING キング, February 1933, pp. 58–60.

Kudō Heisuke 工藤平助, *Aka Ezo fūsetsu-kō* 赤蝦夷風説考 (Reports of the Red Ezo), 1781, in *Hoppō mikōkai kobunsho shūsei* 北方未公開古文書集成 (A collection of rare old texts on the northern region), Vol. 3, Sōbunsha, 1978, pp. 29–51.

Kudō Michihiro 工藤美知尋, *Nihon kaigun to Taiheiyō sensō* 日本海軍と太平洋戦争 (The Japanese Navy and the Pacific War), 2 Vols, Iwamura Seiro, 1982.

Kunimatsu Hisaya 国松久弥, *Chiseigaku to wa nani ka?* 地政学とは何か？ (What is geopolitics?), Kajitani Shōin, 1942.

Kurihara Tomonobu 栗原朋信, *Jōdai Nihon taigai kankei no kenkyū* 上代日本対外関係の研究 (Studies on the external relations of ancient Japan), Yoshikawa Tōbunkan, 1978.

Kuwata Tadachika 桑田忠親, *Toyotomi Hideyoshi kenkyū* 豊臣秀吉研究 (Studies on Toyotomi Hideyoshi), Kadokawa Shoten, 1975.

Madarame Fumio 班目文雄, *Gōshū shinryaku shi* 濠洲侵略史 (A history of the invasion of Australia), Ōbunsha, June 1942.

Maida Minoru 米田実, 'Daitōasen to Ni-Shi jin Gōshū ishokuken mondai' 大東亜戦と日支人濠洲移植権問題 (The Greater East Asia War and the problem of Australian naturalization of Japanese and Chinese), in *Shina* 支那 (China), Vol. 33, May 1942, pp. 1–16.

Matsue Haruji 松江春次, *Nan'yō kaitaku jūnenshi* 南洋開拓十年史 (History of ten years of South Seas Development), Nan'yō Kōhatsu Kabushiki Kaisha, 1932.

Matsumoto Toshirō 松本俊郎, 'Nihon teikokushugi no shigen mondai' 日本帝国主義の資源問題 (Japanese imperialism and the problem of raw materials), in *Taikei Nihon gendai shi* 体系・日本現代史 (A systematic history of modern Japan), Vol. 4, Nihon Hyōronsha, 1979, pp. 94–123.

Matsumura Kanesuke 松村金助, *Minami ni mo seimeisen ari: Nichi-Man-Nan keizai burokku no teishō* 南にも生命線ありー日・満・南・経済ブロックの提唱 (The south offers a life-line, too: proposing an economic block of Japan, Manchuria, and the South), Rinsan Shoten, 1933.

Matsunaga Sotoo 松永外雄, *Gōshū inshōki* 濠洲印象記 (Impressions of Australia), Wani Shoten, December, 1942.

Matsuzaki Manojō 松崎万之噵, *Gōshū shi* 濠洲史 (History of Australia), Seikokan Shoten, 1907.

Meaney, Neville, '"Kōka-ron" to "Ōsutoraria no kiki": Ōsutoraria gaikō seisaku shi ni okeru Nihon, 1905–1941 nen' 「黄禍論」と「オーストラリアの危機」ーオーストラリア外交政策史における日本、1905—1941 年 — ('The Yellow

Peril' and 'The Australian Crisis': The Japanese phase in the history of Australian foreign policy, 1905–1941), in *Kokusai seiji* 国際政治 (International politics), Vol. 68, 1981, pp. 5–22.

Mishima Kazuo 三嶋一雄, *Gōshū oyobi Indo* 濠洲及印度 (Australia and India), Mainichi Shimbunsha, 1891.

———, *Gōshū oyobi Indo tanken shi* 濠洲及印度探検誌 (Record of an expedition to Australia and India), Nihon Kōen Kyōkai, 1943 (reprint of 1891 ed.).

Mitsui Takasumi 三井高維, *Gōshū ryōkōki* 濠洲旅行記 (Travelogue of Australia), 1924.

Mitsukuri Genpo, see Rangaku Shiryō Kenkyūkai.

Mitsukuri Shōgo 箕作省吾, *Kon'yo zushiki* 坤輿図識 (Explanatory notes on the world map), Mimasaka: Mukarō Zōban, 1846.

Miwa Kimitada 三輪公忠, ed., *Nihon no 1930 nendai: kuni no uchi to soto kara* 日本の 1930 年代―国の内と外から― (Japan in the 1930s: an inside and outside view of the country), Saikōsha, 1980.

———, '"Tōa shinchitsujo" sengen to "Dai Tōa kyōeiken" kōsō no dansō' 「東亜新秩序」宣言と「大東亜共栄圏」構想の断層 (The declaration of the 'New Order in East Asia' and the shift to the 'Greater East Asia Co-Prosperity Sphere' concept), in Miwa Kimitada, ed., *Saikō: Taiheiyō sensō zenya: Nihon no 1930 nendai ron to shite* 再考太平洋戦争前夜：日本の 1930 年代論 として (A reconsideration of the eve of the Pacific War: Japan in the 1930s), Sōseiki, 1981, pp. 196–231.

———, *Nihon: 1945 nen no shiten* 日本：1945 年の視点 (Japan: in the perspective of the year 1945), Tokyo University Press, 1987.

Miyake Masaki 三宅正樹, chief ed., *Shōwa shi no gunbu to seiji* 昭和史の軍部 と政治 (Military and politics in Showa history), 5 vols, Daiichi Hōki Shuppansha, 1983.

Miyake Setsurei 三宅雪嶺, *Daigaku konjaku tan* 大学今昔譚 (A talk on the universities past and present), Gakkansha, 1946.

Miyata Mineichi 宮田峯一, *Gōshū Renpō* 濠洲聯邦 (The Commonwealth of Australia), Kōbunshaka, September 1942.

Miyazaki Akira 宮崎亮, 'Daitōa sensō no daini dankai to Gōshū' 大東亜戦争 の第二段階と濠州 (Australia and the second stage of the Greater East Asian War), in *Shin Ajia* (New Asia), March 1942.

Mori Katsumi 森克巳, *Kentōshi* 遣唐使 (Diplomatic envoys to the T'ang court), Nihon Rekishi Shinsho Zōhoban, 1966.

———, *Zoku Nissō-bōeki no kenkyū* 続日宋貿易の研究 (Continuing research on Japan-Sung trade), Kokusho Kankōkai, 1975.

Morimatsu Toshio 森松俊夫, *Sōryokusen Kenkyūjo* 総力戦研究所 (The Total War Research Institute), Hakuteisha, 1983.

Murobuse Kōshin 室伏高信, *Nanshinron* 南進論 (On the southward advance), Nihon Hyōron Sha, July 1936.

NK, see Namba *et al.*

NKT, see Oda *et al.*

Nagakura Kyōsuke 長倉矯介, *Gōshū oyobi Minami Taiheiyo* 濠洲及び南太平洋 (Australia and the South Pacific), Nihon Shobō Kan, 1943.

Nakamura Hiroshi, ed., with Unno Kazutaka 海野一隆, Oda Takao 織田武雄, and Muroga Nobuo 室賀信夫, *Nihon kochizu taisei* 日本古地図大成 (The world in Japanese maps until the mid-19th century), Kōdansha, 1972.

Nakayama Masaru 中山優, *Tai shi seisaku no honryū* 対支政策の本流 (Main currents of Japanese politics towards China), Ikusei Sha, 1937.

Namba Matsutarō 南波松太郎, Muroga Nobuo 室賀信夫, Unno Kazutaka 海野一隆, eds, [*NK*] *Nihon no kochizu* 日本の古地図 (Old Japanese maps), Osaka: Sōgensha, 1969.

Nanpō Sangyō Chōsakaihen 南方産業調査会編, *Gōshū* 濠洲 (Australia), Nanshinsha, July 1942.

Nan'yō Keizai Kenkyūjo 南洋経済研究所 (South Seas Economic Institute), *Gōshū jinkō no kōsei* 濠洲人口の構成 (The organization of the Australian people), Nan'yō shiryō, No. 192, January 1943.

———, *Gōshū jinmei jiten* 濠洲人名字典 (A directory of Australian personalities), Vol. I, Nan'yō shiryō No. 468, May 1944.

Nan'yō Kyōkai 南洋協会, *Nan'yo Kyōkai nijūnenshi* 南洋協会二十年史 (Twenty years of the South Seas Society), 1935.

Narita Katsushirō 成田勝四郎, *Nichigo tsūshō gaikōshi* 日豪通商外交史 (A diplomatic history of commercial relations between Japan and Australia), Shinheiron, 1971.

Nichigō Kyōkai 日豪協会 (Japan-Australia Society), *Nichigō Kyōkai sōkai kaimu hōkoku* 日豪協会総会会務報告 (Working report of the general meeting of the Japan-Australia Society), Vols 8–14, Japan-Australia Society, 1936–1942.

Nichigō Kyōkai 日濠協会, Nihon Shinseiran Kyōkai 日本新西蘭協会, *Nichigo Kyōkai gojū nen, Nihon Shinseiran Kyōkai nijūhachi nen shi* 日濠協会五十年日本新西蘭協会二十八年史, (Historical records of the Japan-Australia Society—50 years, and the Japan-New Zealand Society—28 years), Japan-Australia Society, 1980.

Nihon gaikō bunsho 日本外交文書 (Diplomatic documents of Japan), 1883, 1885, 1886, 1905, Vols 16,18,19, 38–2, Nihon Kokusai Kyōkai, 1936–1954.

Nihonjin 日本人 (The Japanese) No. 44, 3 April 1890.

Nihon Kokusai Seiji Gakkai 日本国際政治学会 (Japanese Association of International Politics), *Taiheiyo senso e no michi: kaisen gaikō shi* 太平洋戦争への道：開戦外交史 (The road to the Pacific War: the diplomatic history of the opening of the war), Vol. 7; *Bekkan shiryō hen* 別巻資料編 (Supplementary volume of documents), Asahi Shimbunsha, 1963.

Nihon shisō taikei 日本思想大系 (An outline of Japanese thought), Vols 54, 55, Iwanami Shoten, 1971.

Nihon Takushoku Kyōkaihen 日本拓殖協会編, *Nanpō bunken mokuroku* 南方

文献目録 (A bibliography on documents of the southern region), September 1942.

Nippon 日本, July, August, 1889.

Nishikawa Chūichirō 西川忠一郎, *Saikin no Gōshū jijō* 最近の濠洲事情 (The recent situation of Australia), Sanyōdō Shoten, 1942.

Nitobe Inazō 新渡戸稲造, 'Nan'yō no keizaiteki kachi (I)' 南洋の経済的価値 (The economic value of the Nan'yō [I]), in *Kokka gakkai zasshi* 国家学会雑誌 (Journal of the Association of Political and Social Sciences), Tokyo University, October 1916, pp. 1592–1606.

———, *Nitobe hakushi bunshū* 新渡戸博士文集 (Selections from Inazo Nitobe's writings), Nitobe Memorial Fund, 1936.

Noma Saburō 野間三郎 *et al.*, *Chirigaku no rekishi to hōhō* 地理学の歴史と方法 (The history and method of geography), Taimeidō Hakkan, 1970.

Nōrinshō Sōmukyoku Nanpō Shigen Chōsashitsu 農林省総務局南方資源調査室 (Ministry of Agriculture and Forestry Research Section for Southern Natural Resources), *Gōshū oyobi Shinseiran ni okeru hakujin ni kansuru chōsa* 濠洲及新西蘭ニ於ケル白人ニ関スル調査 (A study of white people in Australia and New Zealand), January 1943.

Nōshōmushō Shōmukyoku 農商務省商務局 (Office for trade and agriculture), *1911 nen ni okeru Nichigō bōeki no gaikyō* 1911 年ニ於ケル日濠貿易ノ概況 (Outline of Japanese-Australian trade in 1911), Shōmushūsan No. 11, 1913.

Nozawa Tōkichi 野沢藤吉, *Nan'yō shi* 南洋志 (Thoughts on the South Seas), as dictated by Suzuki Tsunenori, Saitō Iwajirō, 1890.

Oda Takeo 織田武雄, Muroga Nobuo, and Unno Kazutaka, [*NKT*] *Nihon kochizu taisei: sekaizu-hen* 日本古地図大成：世界図編 (The world in Japanese maps until the mid-19th century; the collection includes reprints of138 colour maps and 127 black and white maps), Kōdansha, 1975.

Ōhata Tokushirō 大畑篤四郎, '"Nanshin" no shisō to seisaku no keifu' (The idea of southward advance and the genealogy of the policy), in *Nihon gaikō seisaku no shiteki tenkai: Nihon gaikōshiteki kenkyū* 日本外交政策の史的展開：日本外交史的研究 (Studies on Japanese diplomatic history: the historical development of Japanese diplomacy), Vol. 1, Seibundō, 1983.

Ōishi Masami 大石正己, *Fukyōsaku* 富強策 (On enriching and strengthening the nation), Hakubundō, 1891.

Oka Mitsuo 岡光夫, 'Nōson no henbō to zaigōshōnin' 農村の変貌と在郷商人 (Rural district traders and the transfiguration of farm villages), in *Iwanami kōza Nihon rekishi* 岩波講座日本歴史, (The Iwanami lectures in Japanese history), Vol. 12, Iwanami Shoten, 1976, pp. 45–88.

Okakura Koshirō 岡倉古志郎, *Gōshū no shakai to keizai* 濠洲の社会と経済 (Economy and society of Australia), Dentsu Shuppan Bu, February 1943.

Ōkuma Shigenobu 大隈重信, *Kaikoku gojūnenshi* 開国五十年史 (Fifty years of New Japan), Kaikoku gojūnen shi, 1907, 2 vols.

Osaka Shōsen Kabushiki Kaisha 大阪商船株式会社 (Osaka shipping company), *Gōshū jijō* 濠洲事情 (Condition of Australia), 1913.

Ōyama Azusa 大山梓, ed., *Yamagata Aritomo ikensho* 山形有友意見書 (The written opinions of Yamagata Aritomo), Hara Shobō, 1966.

Rangaku Shiryō Kenkyūkai 蘭学資料研究会, ed., *Mitsukuri Genpo no kenkyū* 箕作阮甫の研究 (The research of Mitsukuri Genpo), Shibunkaku, 1978.

Rōyama Masamichi 蝋山政道, *Tōa to sekai* 東亜と世界 (East Asia and the world), Kaizō Sha, 1941.

———, 'Daitōa kōiki ken ron: chiseigakuteki kōsatsu' 大東亜広域圏論：地政学的考察 (An extended regionalism of Greater East Asia: a geopolitical analysis), in Taiheiyō Kyōkai 太平洋協会 (Pacific Society), *Taiheiyō mondai no saikentō* 太平洋問題の再検討 (A reconsideration of the issues of the Pacific Ocean), Asahi Shinbun Sha, 1941, pp. 2–57.

Sakata Haruo 坂田春雄, *Gōshū Shidonifu bankoku hakurankai hōkokusho* 濠洲悉徳尼府万国博覧会報告書 (A report on Sydney's world exhibition), 1881.

Sakurai Takeo 桜井武雄, *Nihon nōgyō no saihensei* 日本農業の再編成 (The reorganization of Japanese agriculture), Chūō Kōronsha, 1940.

Satō Nobuhiro 佐藤信淵, *Satō Nobuhiro kagaku zenshū* 佐藤信淵家学全集 (The collected works of Satō Nobuhiro), 3 vols, Iwanami Shoten, 1925–1927.

Sawa Kannojō 沢鑑之丞, *Kaigun shichijūnenshi dan* 海軍七十年史談, (Conver- sing on the seventy-year history of our navy), Bunsei Dōshisha, 1943.

Seisan Chōsakai 生産調査会 (Investigation committee on products and industry) Nōshōmushō (Ministry for Agriculture & Commerce), *Gōshū oyobi Nyūshiirando shisatsu fukumeisho* 豪州およびニュー・ジーランド視察復命書 (Inspection report on Australia and New Zealand), 1911.

Shepaado Jakku シエパート・ジャック, Tōa ni okeru Gōshū no rieki to seisaku 東亜に於ける濠洲の利益と政策 (Australia's interests and policies in the Far East), Gōshū Kenkyū Kai Yaku, December 1943.

Shiga Shigetaka 志賀重昂, *Nan'yō jiji* 南洋時事 (Current affairs in the South Seas), Maruzen, 1887.

———, *Shiga Shigetaka zenshū* 志賀重昂全集 (The collected works of Shiga Shigetaka), Vol. 3, Shiga Shigetaka Zenshū Hakkōkai, 1927.

Shimizu Hajime 清水元, 'Taishō shoki ni okeru "Nanshin-ron" no ichikōsatsu: sono Ajia shugiteki henyō o megutte' 大正初期における「南進論」の一考察：そのアジア主義的変容をめぐって (A study of the 'southward advance' in the early Taishō period: its changes under the impact of Asianism), in *Ajia kenkyū* アジア研究 (Research on Asia), Ajia Seikei Gakkai アジア政経学会, Vol. 30, No. 1, 1983.

———, '"Ware wa umi no ko" kara "Yashi no mi" made: shōka ni miru "nanshin ron"'「われは海の子」から「椰子の実」まで―唱歌にみる「南進」論 (From 'We are the children of the sea' to 'The coconut': Japan's 'southward advance' seen through songs), in *UOC FORUM*, Union Overseas Corp., No. 1, 1983, pp. 6–21.

————, 'Nihon-Tōnanajia kankei to "Nanshin-ron"' 日本東南アジア関係と南進論 (The southern advance and Japan-Southeast Asia relations) in *Senzenki Nihon to dai san sekai* 戦前期日本と第三世界 (Japan and the Third World in the pre-war period), Ajia Keizai Kenkyūjo, 1983.

————, 'Nihon-Tōnanajia kankei no bunmei shiteki ichi' 日本東南アジア関係の文明史的位置 (The situation of Japanese-Southeast Asian relations in the history of civilization), in Hara Yōnosuke 原洋之介, ed., *Tōnanajia kara no chiteki bōken: shinboru, keizai, rekishi* 東南アジアからの知的冒険：シンボール・経済・歴史, (Intellectual adventures in Southeast Asian studies: symbolism, economics, history), Libro, 1986.

————, 'Kindai Nihon ni okeru "Tōnanajia" chiiki gainen no seiritsu (1): shō chū gakkō chiri kyōkasho ni miru' 近代日本における「東南アジア」地域概念の成立 (1)：小・中学校地理教科書にみる (The formation of the concept of 'Southeast Asia' in modern Japan based on a study of geography textbooks used in primary and junior-high schools), in *Ajia keizai* アジア経済 (Asian economy), Vol. 28, Nos 6, 7, 1987, pp. 2–15, 22–38.

Shiozaki Hiroaki 塩崎弘明, 'Gunbu to Nanpō shinshutsu' 軍部と南方進出 (The military and the southern advance), in Miyake Masaki 三宅正樹, chief ed., *Shōwa shi no gunbu to seiji* 昭和史の軍部と政治 (Military and politics in Showa history), Vol. 3, Daiichi Hōki Shuppansha, 1983.

————, *Nichi-Ei-Bei sensō no kiro: Taiheiyō no yūwa o meguru sei senryaku* 日英米戦争の岐路：太平洋の宥和をめぐる政戦略 (The turning point of the Japanese-Anglo-American War: Japan's political strategy concerning appeasement in the Pacific), Yamakawa Shuppansha, 1984.

Shirani Yasushi 白仁泰, *Gōshū jijō* 濠洲事情 (Conditions in Australia), Ritsumeikan Shuppanbu, July 1942.

Shokumin Kyōkai hōkoku 殖民協会報告 (Transactions of the Colonization Society), 1893, reprinted Vol. I, Fuji Shuppan, 1986.

Suganuma Teifu 菅沼貞風, 'Shin Nippon no zunan no yume' 新日本の図南の夢 (Dream of New Japan's expansion to southern lands), in *Dai Nippon shōgyō shi*, Iwanami Shoten, September 1940 (reprint), pp. 635–92.

————, *Dai Nippon shōgyō shi* 大日本商業史 (A comprehensive commercial history of Japan), Iwanami Shoten, 1940.

Sugiura Jūgo 杉浦重剛, *Hankai yume monogatari* 半壊夢物語 (The dream story of Hankai), Sawaya Hatsuda, 1886.

Sugiyama Gen, 杉山元 *Sugiyama memo* 杉山メモ (Notes of Field Marshal Sugiyama Gen), Rikugun 陸軍, Sanbō honbu 参謀本部 (Army General Staff), 2 vols, Hara Shobō, 1967.

Sukotto E. スコット イ E., tr. Yamakawa Toshio 山川敏夫 *Osutoraria shi* オーストラリア史 (History of Australia), Tōkadō Kan, July 1943.

————, tr. Gōachōsajo 濠亜調査所, *Gōshū shi* 濠洲史 (History of Australia), Kasumigaseki Shobō, October 1944.

Suzuki Tsunenori 鈴木経勳, *Nan'yō tanken jikki* 南洋探検実記 (A true story of exploration in the South Seas), Hakubunkan, 1892, 2 vols.

———, *Nantō junkōki* 南島巡航記 (Record of a cruise in the southern islands), Keizai Zasshi Sha, 1893.

Taguchi Ukichi 田口卯吉, 'Nan'yō keiryakuron' 南洋経略論 (How to expand into the South Seas), 22 March 1890, in *Teiken Taguchi Ukichi zenshū* 鼎軒田口卯吉全集 (Collected works of Teiken Taguchi Ukichi), Vol. 4, Teiken Taguchi Ukichi Hakkōkai, 1928, pp. 372-3.

Taiheiyō Kyōkaihen 太平洋協会編, *Gōshū no shizen to shakai* 濠洲の自然と社会 (Australia's resources and society), Chūo Kōron Sha, January 1943.

Taiwan Ginkō Chōsa Bu 台湾銀行調査部, *Gōshū renpō no sangyō gaiyō* 濠洲聯邦の産業概要 (Production outline of the Australian Commonwealth), October 1942.

Taiyō 太陽, 'Nanshin ka Hokushin ka' 南進か北進か (Southward or northward advance?), November 1913.

———, 'Gōshō hyaku nin' 豪商百人 (One hundred wealthy merchants), Heibonsha, Special issue, No. 17, Winter 1976.

Takagi Saburō 高木三郎, *Taiyōshū no genjō ni tsuite* 大洋洲の現状について (On the conditions in Oceania), Kaigai Kōgyō Kyōkai, October 1941.

Takahashi Sankichi 高橋三吉, *Nanpō kyōeiken o kataru* 南方共栄圏を語る (About the Southern Co-Prosperity Sphere), Dai Nippon Yūbenkai Kōdansha, May 1941.

Takekoshi Yosaburō 竹越与三郎, *Nangokuki* 南国記 (Account of southern countries), Niyūsha, 1910.

———, in *Taiyō*, Vol. 17, June 1911, pp. 82-5.

———, *Nihon keizai shi, III* 日本経済史 (The history of Japanese economy, III), Heibonsha, 1935.

———, *Wakōki* 倭冦記 (A history of the *wakō*), Hakuyōsha, 1939.

Tamura Hiroyuki 田村洋幸, *Chūsei Nitchō bōeki no kenkyū* 中世日朝貿易の研究 (A study of the trade between Japan and Korea in medieval times), Sanwa Shobō, 1967.

Tanaka Takeo 田中健夫, *Chūsei kaigai kōshō shi no kenkyū* 中世海外交渉史の研究 (Historiography of overseas negotiations in the Middle Ages), Tokyo Daigaku Shuppankai, 1959.

———, 'Jidai kaisetsu' 「時代解説」(Commentary on the age) in *Zusetsu jinbutsu umi no Nihon shi (3): Kenminsen to wakō* 図説人物海の日本史 (3): 遣明船と倭冦 (An illustrated Japanese history of personalities and the sea [3]: ships despatched to China and the *wakō*), Mainichi Shinbunsha, 1979.

Tanaka Yoshijūrō 田中由十郎, *Gōshū shisatsu fukumeisho* 濠洲視察復命書 (Inspection report on Australia), Nōshōmushō Sanrinkyoku, 1913.

Tanemura Sakō 種村左孝 *Daihon'ei kimitsu sensō nisshi* 大本営機密戦争日誌 (The secret war diary of Imperial Headquarters), Daiamondo Sha, 1952.

Tōa Kenkyūjo 東亜研究所, *Nichigo bōeki gaikan* 日濠貿易概観 (Outline of Japanese-Australian trade), November 1939.

————, *Ōsutorarashia no chiri* オーストララシアの地理 (The geography of Australasia), 1942.

Toho Kyokai hokoku 東方協会報告 (Transactions of the East Asian Society), No. 6, November 1891.

Tokugawa Mitsukuni 徳川光国, *Dai Nihon shi* 大日本史 (A comprehensive history of Japan), Vol. 5, Yoshikawa Kōbunkan, 1911.

Tokutomi Iichirō 徳富猪一郎, *Dai-Nihon bōchoron* 大日本膨脹論 (On the expansion of Japan), Minyū Sha, 1894.

————, *Kinsei Nippon kokumin shi* 近世日本国民史 (A history of the Japanese people in modern times), Minyū Sha: Vol. 9, *Toyotomi shi jidai* 豊臣氏時代 (The Toyotomi period), 1922; Vol. 13, *Ieyasu jidai gaikan* 家康時代概観 (A general view of the Ieyasu period), 1924; Vol. 14, *Tokugawa bakufu kamiki* 徳川幕府上期 (The early Tokugawa Bakufu period), 1924; Vol. 23, *Tanuma jidai* 田沼時代 (The Tanuma period), 1927; Vol. 25, *Bakufu bunkai sekkin jidai* 幕府分解接近時代 (The period approaching the final decline of the Bakufu), 1927.

Tōkyō Asahi Shimbun 東京朝日新聞, 2 August 1940.

Tōkyō Kōgyō Daigaku Kōgyō Chōsabu 東京工業大学工業調査部, *Nichigo bōeki no hatten to sono shōrai sei* 日濠貿易の発展と其将来性 (Development and future prospects of the Japan-Australia trade), August 1936.

Tōkyō Nichi Nichi Shinbun Tōabuhen 東京日日新聞東亜部編, *Daitōasen ni okeru Jūkei, Indo, Gōshū* 大東亜戦に於ける重慶・印度・濠洲 (Chungking, India, and Australia in the Greater East Asia War), Daidō Shuppansha, December 1942.

Tomioka Sadatoshi 富岡定俊, *Kaisen to shūsen: Hito to kikō to keikaku* 開戦と終戦：人と機構と計画 (The opening and closing of the war: the people, the mechanism, and the planning), Mainichi Shinbunsha, 1968.

Tōno Tadashi 藤野正, 'Shōwa shoki no "jiyū shugisha": Tsurumi Yūsuke o chūshin toshite' 昭和初期の「自由主義者」ー鶴見祐輔を　中心としてー (Liberalism in the early Shōwa period: The case of Tsurumi Yūsuke), in *Nihon rekishi* 日本歴史 (Japanese history), No. 415, 1982.

Tsuchiya Gensaku 土屋元作, *Gōshū (Nanpō tairiku) oyobi Shinseiran (Chōhakuun)* 濠洲 (南方大陸) 及新西蘭 (長白雲) (Australia [the southern country] and New Zealand [the long white cloud country]), Asahi Shinbunsha, 1916.

Tsuji Zennosuke 辻善之助, *Kaigai kōtsū shiwa* 海外交通史話 (A historical account of the communications of Japan with nations beyond the seas), Naigai Shoseki Kabushiki Kaisha, 1930.

Tsuneya Seifuku 恒屋盛服, *Kaigai shokumin-ron* 海外植民論 (On overseas colonization), Hakubunsha, 1891.

Tsunoda Jun 角田順, 'Nihon no tai Bei kaisen (1940 nen-1941 nen)' 日本の対米開戦 [1940年—1941年) (Japan's opening of war against the United

States (1940–1941), in Nihon Kokusai Seiji Gakkai, *Taiheiyō sensō e no michi* 太平洋戦争への道, Vol. 7, Asahi Shimbunsha, 1963, pp. 1–387.

Tsurumi Yūsuke 鶴見祐輔, *Nan'yō yūki* 南洋遊記 (Travel sketches of the South Seas), Dai Nihon Yūbenkai Kōdansha, 1917.

———, *Gotō Shinpei* 後藤新平 (Biography of Gotō Shinpei), Vol. 2, Keisō Shobō Press, 1965.

Uchida Kakichi 内田嘉吉, *Kokumin kaigai hatten saku* 国民海外発展策 (Overseas development policies for the people), Takushoku Shimpōsha, 1914.

Ueda Yoshitake 上田良武, 'Taiheiyō no sōha o ronzu' 太平洋の争覇を論ず (Discussing the struggle for supremacy in the Pacific), in Ueda Yoshitake, ed., *Chiseigaku ron* 地政学論 (Theories of geopolitics), 1942, pp. 195–219.

Unno Kazutaka 海野一隆, 'Tenchi ni kyūyōhō kokumei kō' 天地に球用法国名考 (A list of country names on the globe), in *Arisaka Takamichi* 有坂隆道, ed., Nihon Yōgakushi no kenkyū 日本洋学史の研究 (Study of the history of Western learning), Osaka: Sōgensha, 1974, pp. 113–37.

Wada Shunji 和田俊二, *Ōsutoraria* オーストラリア, Asahi Shimbun Sha, 1942.

———, 'Nettai Gōshū kaihatsu mondai' 熱帯濠洲開発問題 (The problem of developing Australia's tropics), in *Chirigaku* 地理学 (Geography), April 1942, pp. 25–37.

Wakita Osamu 脇田修, 'Kinsei toshi no kensetsu to gōshō' 近世都市の建設と豪商 (The wealthy merchants and the establishment of towns in the modern period), in *Iwanami kōza Nihon rekishi* 岩波講座日本歴史 (The Iwanami lectures in Japanese history), Vol. 9, Iwanami Shoten, 1975, pp. 155–94.

Watanabe Chūgo 渡辺忠吾, *Gōshū shokumin ron* 濠洲植民論 (Treatise on colonial Australia), Hikarigaoka Shobō, September 1942.

Watanabe Izō 渡辺鏡蔵, *Taisen to Nan'yō guntō* 大戦と南洋群島 (The Great War and the South Sea Islands), Series No. 70, Watanabe Keizai Kenkyū jo, 1941.

Watanabe Kanjūrō 渡辺勘十郎, *Gōshū tanken hōkokusho* 濠洲探検報告書 (Report on the exploration of Australia), Gaimushō Tsūshōkyoku, 1894.

Watanabe Kazan 渡辺華山, *Gaikoku jijōsho* 外国事情書 (Document on foreign affairs), in Satō Shōsuke 佐藤昌介, tr., *Nihon no meicho* 日本の名著 (Famous Japanese books), Chūōkōronsha, 1972, pp. 83–257.

Watanabe Shūjirō 渡辺修次郎, *Sekai ni okeru Nihonjin* 世界における日本人 (The Japanese in the world), 1893, reprinted by Keio Shobō, November 1942.

Yamaguchi Tetsu 山口徹, 'Bakuhansei shijō no saihen to shōhin seisan' 幕藩制市場の再編と商品生産 (Commodity production and market reorganization under the shogunate and clan systems), in *Kōza Nihon rekishi* 講座日本歴史 (Lectures in Japanese history), Vol. 6, Tokyo Daigaku Shuppan Kai, 1985, pp. 229–65.

Yamamoto Masayoshi 山本正義 and Mizuno Suzuhiko 水野鈴彦, 'Warera Gōshū hondo ni jōriku seri' われら豪州本土に上陸せり (We landed on the Australian mainland), in *Rekishi to jinbutsu* 歴史と人物 (History and personalities), Chūō Kōronsha, August 1985, pp. 112–31.

Yamamoto Teijirō 山本悌二郎, 'Nan'yō shisatsu dan' 南洋視察談 (An informal inspection report on the South Seas), in *Seiyūkai* 政友会, 25 September 1918.

Yamamura Shōei 山村昌永, *Teisei zōyaku sairan igen* 訂正増訳采覧異言 ('Sairan igen' revised and enlarged), 2 vols, 1802, [Vol. 9 in the series of: Rangaku shiryō sōsho I, sakuin-kaisetsu hen: Hirano Mitsuru hen, 12 vols], Seishisha, 1979.

Yamao Yukihisa 山尾幸久, *Nihon kokka no keisei* 日本国家の形成 (The formation of the Japanese state), Iwanami Shoten, 1977.

Yanagida Izumi 柳田泉, *Seiji shōsetsu kenkyū* 政治小説研究 (A study of political novels), Vol. 2, Shinjūsha, 1939.

Yanagihara Hiromitsu 柳原博光, *Sekiyu zuisō* 石油随想 (Random thoughts on oil), Hara Shobō, 1952.

Yanaihara Tadao 矢内原忠雄, 'Nan'yō seisaku o ronzu' 南洋政策を論ず (Debating the South Seas policy), in *Kaizō* 改造 (Reconstruction), June 1936, pp. 25–43.

———, 'Taiheiyō no heiwa to Eikoku' 太平洋の平和と英国 (England and peace in the Pacific), in *Kaizō*, July 1937, pp. 2–16.

Yano Tooru 矢野暢, *'Nanshin' no keifu* 「南進」の系譜 (Genealogy of 'southward advance'), Chūō Shinsho, 1975.

———, 'Taishō ki "nanshin-ron" no tokushitsu' 大正期「南進論」の特質 (Japanese views on the southward advance during the Taishō period), in *Tōnanajia Kenkyū* 東南アジア研究, Vol. 16, No. 1, 1978, pp. 5–31.

———, *Nihon no Nan'yō shikan* 日本の南洋史観 (Japanese historical view of the South Seas), Chūō Shinsho, 1979.

Yasuoka Akio 安岡昭男, 'Taiwan shuppei: seihan to tai shin kaisen junbi' 台湾出兵－征藩と対清開戦準備 (The despatch of troops to Taiwan: the punishing of the natives as a prologue to the opening of war with China), in *Gunji shigaku* 軍事史学 (Military history), Vol. 10, Nos 1, 2, 1974, pp. 98–107.

Yokohama Shōkin Ginkō Tōdoriseki Chōsabu 横浜正金銀行頭取席調査部, *Gōshū keizai mondai* 濠洲経済問題 (Australia's economic problems), No. 132, August 1942.

Yoshida Shōin 吉田松陰, *Yūshūroku* 幽囚録 (A prison notebook), in *Yoshida Shōin zenshū* 吉田松陰全集 (The complete works of Yoshida Shōin), Vol. 2, Yamato Shobō, 1973, pp. 76–133.

Yūbin hōchi shinbun 郵便報知新聞 (The post), March, April 1879.

Zusetsu jinbutsu umi no Nihon shi (3): Kenminsen to wakō 図説人物海の日本史 (3): 遣明船と倭冦 (An illustrated Japanese history of personalities and the sea [3]: ships despatched to China and the *wakō*), Mainichi Shinbunsha, 1979.

Zusetsu jinbutsu umi no Nihon shi (4): Tenkajin to Nanbansen 図説人物海の日本史4天下人と南蛮船 (An illustrated Japanese history of personalities and the sea [4]: potentates and southern ships), Mainichi Shinbunsha, 1979.

Zusetsu Nihon bunka shi taikei 図説日本文化史大系 (An illustrated outline of the history of Japanese culture), *Edo jidai* 江戸時代 (The Edo period), I, Vol. 9, Shōgakkan, 1967.

PUBLISHED SOURCES IN WESTERN LANGUAGES

Abbott, C. L. A., *Australia's Frontier Province*, Sydney: Angus & Robertson, 1950.

Agawa Hiroyuki, *The Reluctant Admiral: Yamamoto and the Imperial Navy*, tr. John Bester, Tokyo: Kodansha International, 1979.

'Albatross', see Piesse, E. L.

Arima Seiho, 'The Western Influence on Japanese Military Science, Shipbuilding, and Navigation', in *Monumenta Nipponica*, Vol. 19, 1964, pp. 118–45.

Asada Sadao, 'The Japanese Navy and the United States', in Dorothy Borg and Shumpei Okamoto, eds, *Pearl Harbor as History: Japanese-American Relations 1931–1941*, New York: Columbia University Press, 1973, pp. 225–59.

—— and Sumio Hatano, 'The Japanese Decision to Move South (1939–1941)', in Esmonde M. Robertson and Robert Boyce, eds, *Paths to War: New Essays on the Origins of the Second World War*, London: Macmillan, 1989, pp. 383–407.

Australasian Post, 'The Soldier Who Invaded Australia', 14 March 1985.

Ayusawa Shintarō, 'Geography and Japanese Knowledge of World Geography', in *Monumenta Nipponica*, Vol. 19, 1964, pp. 275–93.

Bailey, K. H., 'Public Opinion and Population Problems', in P. D. Phillips, ed., *et al.*, *The Peopling of Australia: Further Studies*, Melbourne: Melbourne University Press, 1933.

Ball, W. Macmahon, *Australia and Japan: Documents and Readings in Australian History*, Melbourne: Thomas Nelson, 1969.

Barclay, Glen, *A History of the Pacific from the Stone Age to the Present Day*, London: Futura Publications, 1978.

Bean, C. E. W., *The Official History of Australia in the War of 1914–1918: The Story of ANZAC From the Outbreak of War to the End of the First Phase of the Gallipoli Campaign, May 4, 1915*, Vol. 1, Brisbane: University of Queensland Press, 1981 [1st ed. 1921].

Berger, Gordon, 'The Three-dimensional Empire: Japanese Attitudes and the New Order in Asia, 1937–1945', in *Japan Interpreter*, Vol. 12, 1979, pp. 355–83.

Berry, Mary Elizabeth, *Hideyoshi*, Cambridge, Mass.: Harvard University Press, 1982 (Harvard East Asian series 97).

Borg, Dorothy and Shumpei Okamoto, eds, *Pearl Harbor as History: Japanese-American Relations 1931–1941*, New York: Columbia University Press, 1973.

Borrie, W. D., *Immigration, Australia's Problems and Prospects*, London: Angus & Robertson, 1949.

Bowman, Isaiah, *The New World*, New York: World Book Co., 1928.

Boxer, Charles R., *Jan Compagnie in Japan, 1600–1817*, The Hague: Martin Nijhoff, 1950.

———, *South China in the 16th Century: Being the Narrative of Galeote Pereira. . .1550–1575* , London: Hakluyt Society, 1953.

———, *The Dutch Seaborne Empire 1600–1800*, London: Hutchinson, 1965.

———, *The Portuguese Seaborne Empire*, New York: Knopf, 1969.

———, 'Some Aspects of Portuguese Influence in Japan, 1542–1640' in Michel Moscato, comp., *Papers on Portuguese, Dutch, and Jesuit Influences in 16th- and 17th-Century Japan: Writings of Charles Ralph Boxer*, Washington, D.C.: University Publications of America, Inc., 1979.

Brown, Cecil, *Suez to Singapore*, Garden City, N. Y.: Halycon House, 1943.

Bruno, Herbert, 'The "Trade Diversion" Episode of the Thirties', in *Australian Outlook*, Journal of the Australian Institute of International Affairs, Vol. 22, 1968, pp. 7–14.

Campbell, David A. S., 'A Foreign Policy for Australia', in W. G. K. Duncan, ed., *Australia's Foreign Policy*, Sydney: Angus & Robertson, 1938, pp. 163–210.

Chapman, Ivan, *Iven G. Mackay Citizen and Soldier*, Melbourne: Melway Publishing, 1975.

Choi, C. Y., *Chinese Migration and Settlement in Australia*, Sydney: Sydney University Press, 1975.

Clark, Manning, *A Short History of Australia*, London: Heinemann, 1977. [1st ed. 1963].

Clyde, Paul H., *Japan's Pacific Mandate*, New York: Macmillan, 1935.

——— and Burton F. Beers, *The Far East: A History of the Western Impact and the Eastern Response, 1830–1970*, New Jersey: Prentice-Hall, 1971.

Cohen, Saul B., *Geography and Politics in a World Divided*, 2nd ed., New York: Oxford University Press, 1975.

Cooper, Michael, S.J., ed., *They Came to Japan: An Anthology of European Reports on Japan, 1543–1640*, Berkeley: Univ. of California Press, 1965.

———, ed., *The Southern Barbarians: The First Europeans in Japan*, Tokyo: Kodansha International, 1971.

Craig, G. C., *The Federal Defence of Australia*, London, 1897.

Crawford, John G., 'Australia as a Pacific Power', in W. G. K. Duncan, ed.,

Australia's Foreign Policy, Sydney: Angus & Robertson, 1938, pp. 69–121.

―――― and Okita Saburo, *Australia, Japan, and Western Pacific Economic Relations*, Canberra: Australian Government Publishing Service, 1976.

Crowley, James B., 'A Reconsideration of the Marco Polo Bridge Incident', in *Journal of Asian Studies*, Vol. 22, 1963, pp. 277–91.

Decker, J. A., *Labor Problems in the Pacific Mandates*, Shanghai: Kelly & Walsh, 1940.

D'Elia, Pasquale, 'Recent Discoveries and New Studies (1938–1960) on the World Map in Chinese of Father Matteo Ricci, S.J.', in *Monumenta Serica*, Vol. 20, 1961, pp. 82–164.

Detwiler, Donald S. and Ch. B. Burdick, eds, *War in Asia and the Pacific 1937–1949: The Southern Area*, Part II, Vol. 7, New York and London: Garland Publishing, 1980.

de Vos, George and Wagatsuma Hiroshi, *Japan's Invisible Race: Caste in Culture and Personality*, Berkeley and Los Angeles: University of California Press, 1967.

Documents on Australian Foreign Policy, 1937–1949, Canberra: Australian Government Publishing Service, 1975–1982. Vol. 1, 1937–1938; Vol. 2, 1939; Vol. 3, January 1940-June 1940; Vol. 4, July 1940-June 1941; Vol. 5, July 1941-June 1942.

Drysdale, Peter, 'An Organisation for Pacific Trade, Aid and Development: Regional Arrangements and the Resources Trade', *Australia-Japan Economic Relations Research Paper*, No. 49, Canberra, Australian National University, 1978.

Dunn, James, *Timor: A People Betrayed*, Brisbane: Jacaranda Press, 1983.

Edwards, P. G., *Prime Ministers & Diplomats: The Making of Australian Foreign Policy 1901–1949*, Melbourne: Oxford University Press, 1983.

Ericson, Mark D., 'The Bakufu Looks Abroad: The 1865 Mission to France', in *Monumenta Nipponica*, Vol. 34, 1979, pp. 383–407.

Ezawa Joji, 'Geopolitical Unity in the Australasian Seas', in *Geopolitische Untersuchungen*, Nihon-Hyōronsha Verlag, 1942, pp. 1–7.

Fifield, R. H. and G. E. Pearcy, *Geopolitics in Principle and Practice*, Boston: Ginn & Co., 1944.

Fisher, Robin and Hugh Johnston, eds, *Captain Cook and His Times*, Canberra: Australian National University Press, 1979.

Fitzpatrick, Brian and Rowan J. Cahill, *The Seamen's Union of Australia, 1872–1972*, Sydney: Seamen's Union of Australia, 1981.

Fletcher, William Miles, *The Search for a New Order: Intellectuals and Fascism in Prewar Japan*, Chapel Hill, Ill.: University of North Carolina Press, 1982.

French, Calvin L., *Shiba Kōkan*, New York: Weatherhill, 1974.

Fujimura Michio, 'Japan's Changing View of Asia', in *Japan Quarterly*, Vol. 24, 1977, pp. 423–31.

Gregory, J. W., *The Menace of Colour: A Study of the Difficulties Due to the*

Association of White & Coloured Races, with an Account of Measures Proposed for Their Solution & Special Reference to White Colonization in the Tropics, London: Seeley, Service & Co., 1925.

Hall, Timothy, *Darwin 1942: Australia's Darkest Hour*, Sydney: Methuen, 1980.

Hamill, Ian, *The Strategic Illusion: The Singapore Strategy and the Defense of Australia and New Zealand*, Singapore: Singapore University Press, 1981.

Harkavy, Robert E., *Great Power Competition for Overseas Bases: The Geopolitics of Access Diplomacy*, Elmsford, N.Y.: Pergamon Press, 1982.

Hasluck, Paul, *The Government and the People 1939–1941*, Vol. I, Series 4 in the series *Australia in the War of 1939–1945*, Canberra: Australian War Memorial, 1952.

Haushofer, Karl, *Geopolitik des Pazifischen Ozeans: Studien über die Wechselbeziehungen zwischen Geographie und Geschichte*, 3rd ed., Berlin: Kurt Vowinckel Verlag, 1938 [1st ed., 1924].

Havens, Thomas, *Farm and Nation in Modern Japan: Agrarian Nationalism 1870–1940*, Princeton: Princeton University Press, 1974.

Hérail, Francine, *Histoire du Japon: Des Origines à la Fin de Meiji*, Paris: Publications Orientalistes de France, 1986.

Hill, Friedrich and W. W. Rockhill, trs (of Chau Ju-kua) *Chu-fan-chi: On the Chinese and Arab Trade in the Twelfth and Thirteenth Centuries*, Taipei: Ch'eng-wen Publishing, 1967 [1st pub. 1911].

Hirose Hideo, 'The European Influence on Japanese Astronomy', in *Monumenta Nipponica*, Vol. 19, 1964, pp. 295–314.

Horner, David M., *Crisis of Command: Australian Generalship and the Japanese Threat, 1941–1943*, Canberra: Australian National University Press, 1978.

———, *High Command: Australia & Allied Strategy 1939–1945*, Sydney: George Allen & Unwin, 1982.

Horton, Dick, *Ring of Fire: Australian Guerrilla Operations Against the Japanese in World War II*, Melbourne: Macmillan, 1983.

Hosoya Chihiro, 'Japan's Decision for War in 1941', in *Peace Research in Japan*, Japan Peace Research Group, 1967, pp. 41–51.

Hubschmid, Hans, *Die Neuzeit: Von der Renaissance bis zum Beginn der Aufklärung*, Erlenbach-Zürich und Stuttgart: Eugen Rentsch Verlag, 1961.

Hudson, W. J., ed., *Australia and Papua New Guinea*, Sydney: Sydney University Press, 1971.

———, ed., *New Guinea Empire: Australia's Colonial Experience*, Melbourne: Cassell, 1974.

———, *Australia and the League of Nations*, Sydney: Sydney University Press, 1980.

Ike Nobutaka, ed., *Japan's Decision for War: Records of the 1941 Policy Conferences*, Stanford: Stanford University Press, 1967.

Iriye Akira, *Pacific Estrangement: Japanese and American Expansion, 1897–1911*, Cambridge, Mass.: Harvard University Press, 1972.

———, 'Wartime Japanese Planning for Post-War Asia', in Ian Nish, ed., *Anglo-Japanese Alienation 1919–1952*, Cambridge: Cambridge University Press, 1982, pp. 177–97.

Ishii Kikujirō, tr. William R. Langdon, *Diplomatic Commentaries*, Baltimore: John Hopkins Press, 1936.

Ishiyama Hiroshi, 'The Yōgaku Scholars' Awareness of the Outer World: Japanese World Geography in the Tokugawa Period', in *Acta Asiatica*, Bulletin of the Institute of Eastern Culture, Tokyo: Tōhō Gakkai, February 1982, No. 42, pp. 18–40.

Iwao Seiichi, 'Japanese Emigrants in Batavia During the 17th Century', in *Acta Asiatica*, No. 18, 1970, pp. 1–25.

———, 'Japanese Foreign Trade in the 16th and 17th Centuries', in *Acta Asiatica*, No. 30, 1976, pp. 1–18.

———, ed., *Biographical Dictionary of Japanese History*, Tokyo: Kodansha International, 1978.

Jansen, Marius, B., *Japan and Its World: Two Centuries of Change*, Princeton: Princeton University Press, 1980.

Jose, Arthur W., *Official History of Australia in the War of 1914–18: The Royal Australian Navy*, Vol. 9, Sydney: Angus & Robertson, 1937.

Katō Eiichi, 'Development of Japanese Studies on Sakoku (Closing the Country): A Survey', in *Acta Asiatica*, No. 22, 1972, pp. 84–103.

———, 'The Japanese-Dutch Trade in the Formative Period of the Seclusion Policy: Particularly on the Raw Silk Trade by the Dutch Factory at Hirado 1620–1640', in *Acta Asiatica*, No. 30, 1976, pp. 34–84.

Kawakami, Clarke H. and Roger Pineau, eds, *Midway–the Battle that Doomed Japan: The Japanese Navy's Story* by Mitsuo Fuchida and Masatake Okumiya, Annapolis: Naval Institute, 1955.

Keene, Donald, 'Japanese Writers and the Greater East Asia War', in Donald Keene, *Appreciations of Japanese Culture*, Tokyo: Kodansha International, 1981 [1st ed. 1971], pp. 300–21.

Kerr, George H., *Okinawa: The History of an Island People*, Tokyo: Charles E. Tuttle, 1958.

Kobata Atsushi and Matsuda Mitsugu, *Ryuukyuuan Relations with Korea and South Sea Countries*, Kyoto: Atsushi Kobata, 1969.

Kodansha Encyclopedia of Japan, Vol. 7, Tokyo: Kodansha International, 1983.

Kuno, Yoshi S., *Japanese Expansion on the Asiatic Continent: A Study in the History of Japan with Special Reference to Her International Relations with China, Korea, and Russia*, Berkeley and Los Angeles: University of California Press, vols 1 and 2, 1937 and 1940.

Lebra, Joyce C., *Japan's Greater East Asia Co-Prosperity Sphere in World War II*, London: Oxford University Press, 1975.

Lensen, George A., *The Russian Push Toward Japan*, Princeton: Princeton University Press, 1959.

Lockwood, Douglas, *Australia's Pearl Harbour: Darwin 1942*, Adelaide: Rigby, 1966.

Mansergh, Nicholas, *Survey of British Commonwealth Affairs: Problems of External Policy, 1931–1939*, London: Oxford University Press, 1952.

Marder, Arthur J., *Old Friends, New Enemies: The Royal Navy and the Imperial Japanese Navy, Strategic Illusions 1936–1941*, Oxford: Oxford University Press, 1981.

März, Josef, 'Das Schicksaal überseeischer Wachstumsspitzen', in Haushofer-März, *Zur Geopolitik der Selbstbestimmung*, München: Rosl, 1923, pp. 165–456.

Meaney, Neville, *The Search for Security in the Pacific, 1901–14*, Sydney: Sydney University Press, 1976.

——, *[AWD] Australia and the World: A Documentary History from the 1870s to the 1970s*, Melbourne: Longman Cheshire, 1985.

Melbourne, A. C. V., 'A Foreign Policy for Australia', in H. Dinning and J. G. Holmes, eds, *Australian Foreign Policy 1934*, Melbourne: Melbourne University Press, 1935, pp. 22–47.

Millar, T. B., *Australia in Peace and War: External Relations 1788–1977*, Canberra: Australian National University Press, 1978.

Miller, J. D. B., ed., *India, Japan, Australia: Partners in Asia?* Papers from a Conference at the Australian National University, September 1967, Canberra: Australian National University Press, 1968.

Miwa Kimitada, 'Fukuzawa Yukichi's "Departure from Asia": A Prelude to the Sino-Japanese War', in Edmund Skrizypczak, ed., *Japan's Modern Century*, Tokyo: Sophia University, 1968.

——, 'Shiga Shigetaka (1863–1927): A Meiji Japanist's View of and Actions in International Relations', *Research Papers*, Series A-3, Tokyo: Institute of International Relations, Sophia University, 1970.

——, 'Japanese Policies and Concepts for a Regional Order in Asia, 1938–1940', *Research Papers*, Series A-46, Tokyo: Sophia University, 1983.

——, 'Nitobe Inazō and the Development of Colonial Theories and Practices in Prewar Japan', *Research Paper*, Series A-50, Tokyo: Institute of International Relations, Sophia University, 1987.

Mori Katsumi, 'International Relations Between the 10th and the 16th Century and the Development of the Japanese International Consciousness', in *Acta Asiatica*, No. 2, 1962, pp. 69–93.

——, 'The Beginning of Overseas Advance of Japanese Merchant Ships', in *Acta Asiatica*, No. 23, 1972, pp. 1–24.

Moscato, Michel, comp., *Papers on Portuguese, Dutch, and Jesuit Influences in 16th- and 17th-Century Japan: Writings of Charles Ralph Boxer*, Washington, D.C.: University Publications of America, 1979.

Nakane Chie, *Japanese Society*, Berkeley: Univ. of California Press, 1970.

Nish, Ian, *The Anglo-Japanese Alliance in Decline: The Diplomacy of Two Island Empires 1894-1907*, London: Athlone Press, 1966.

———, *Alliance in Decline: A Study in Anglo-Japanese Relations 1908-23*, London: Athlone Press, 1972.

Norris, R., *The Emergent Commonwealth: Australian Federation: Expectations and Fulfilment 1889-1910*, Melbourne: Melbourne University Press, 1975.

Okuma Shigenobu, *Fifty Years of New Japan (Kaikoku gojūnen shi)*, English version edited by Marcus B. Huish, 2 vols, London: Smith, Elder & Co., 1909.

Pahl, Walther, *Das Politische Antlitz der Erde*, Leipzig: Goldmann Verlag, 1938.

Parry, J. H., *Europe and a Wider World, 1415-1715*, London: Hutchinson's University Library, 1949.

Peattie, Mark R., 'The Nanyō: Japan in the South Pacific, 1885-1945', in Ramon H. Myers and Mark R. Peattie, eds, *The Japanese Colonial Empire, 1895-1945*, Princeton: Princeton University Press, 1984, pp. 172-210.

———, *Nan'yō: The Rise and Fall of the Japanese in Micronesia 1885-1945*, Honolulu: Hawaii University Press, 1987.

Piesse, E. L., 'Japan and Australia', *Foreign Affairs*, Vol. 4, 1926, pp. 475-88.

——— ['Albatross'], *Japan and the Defence of Australia*, Melbourne: Robertson & Mullens, 1935.

Potts, Daniel E. and Annette, *Yanks Down Under 1941-45*, Melbourne: Oxford University Press, 1985.

Powell, Alan, *The Shadow's Edge: Australia's Northern War*, Melbourne: Melbourne University Press, 1988.

Prime, Mervyn W., *WA's Pearl Harbour: The Japanese Raid on Broome*, Bullcreek, W.A.: Royal Australian Air Force Association, 1985.

Pringsheim, Klaus H., *Neighbors Across the Pacific*, Westport, Conn.: Greenwood, 1983.

Purcell, W. R., 'The Nature and Extent of Japanese Commercial and Economic Interests in Australia, 1932-1941', *Australia-Japan Economic Relations Research Paper*, No. 53, Canberra, Australian National University, 1978.

Purser, Frank, *The Story of Corunna Downs: W.A.'s Secret Wartime Air Base*, Bullcreek, W.A.: Royal Australian Air Force Association, n.d.

Pyle, Kenneth E., *The New Generation in Meiji Japan: Problems of Cultural Identity, 1885-1895*, Stanford, Calif.: Stanford University Press, 1969.

Radi, Heather, 'New Guinea Under Mandate 1921-41', in W. J. Hudson, ed., *Australia and Papua New Guinea*, Sydney: Sydney University Press, 1971, pp. 34-137.

Rawlinson, John L., *China's Struggle for Naval Development 1839-1895*, Harvard East Asian Series 25, Cambridge, Mass: Harvard University Press, 1967.

Ricci, Matteo, *China in the Sixteenth Century*, tr. Louis Gallagher, New York: Random House, 1953.

Roberts, S. H., 'History of Contacts between the Orient and Australia', in I. Clunies Ross, ed., *Australia and the Far East*, Sydney: Angus & Robertson, 1936.

Robertson, Esmonde. M., *The Origins of the Second World War*, 2nd ed., London: Macmillan, 1988.

Robertson, John, *Australia at War, 1939–1945*, Melbourne: William Heinemann, 1981.

Saniel, Josefa M., *Japan and the Philippines 1868–1898*, Quezon City: University of the Philippine Press, 1969.

Sansom, George B., *A History of Japan to 1867*, 3 vols, Tokyo: Charles E. Tuttle, 1974 [1st pub. 1958, 1961, 1963].

————, *The Western World and Japan: A Study in the Interaction of European and Asiatic Cultures*, Tokyo: Charles E. Tuttle, 1977 [1st pub. 1950].

Schafer, Edward H., *The Golden Peaches of Samarkand*, Berkeley: University of California Press, 1981 [1st pub. 1963].

Scott, Ernest, *The Official History of Australia in the War of 1914–1918: Australia During the War*, Vol. 11, Sydney: Angus & Robertson, 1936.

Sharp, Andrew, *The Discovery of Australia*, Oxford: Oxford University Press, 1963.

Sheldon, Charles D., *The Rise of the Merchant Class in Tokugawa Japan, 1600–1868: An Introductory Survey*, Monographs of the Association for Asian Studies, 5, Locust Valley, N.Y.: J. J. Augustin, 1958.

Shepherd Jack, *Australia's Interests and Policies in the Far East*, New York: Institute of Pacific Relations Inquiry Series, 1939.

Shillony, Ben-Ami, *Politics and Culture in Wartime Japan*, Oxford: Clarendon Press, 1981.

Shimizu Hajime, '*Nanshin-ron*: Its Turning Point in World War I', in *Developing Economies*, Vol. 25, 1987, pp. 386–402.

Sigmond, J. P. and L. H. Zuiderbaan, *Dutch Discoveries of Australia*, The Hague: Martin Nijhoff, 1950.

Sissons D. C. S., 'Immigration in Australian-Japanese Relations, 1871–1971', in J. A. A. Stockwin, ed., *Japan and Australia in the Seventies*, Sydney: Angus & Robertson, 1972, pp. 193–210.

————, 'Manchester v. Japan: The Imperial Background of the Australian Trade Diversion Dispute with Japan, 1936', in *Australian Outlook*, Vol. 30, 1976, pp. 480–502.

————, 'Karayuki-San: Japanese Prostitutes in Australia, 1887–1916', 2 parts, in *Historical Studies*, Vol. 17, Nos 68 and 69, 1977, pp. 323–41, 474–88.

————, 'The Early Japanese Influence on the Northern Territory', in *Northern Territory Newsletter*, Nov., Dec.,1977, Jan. 1978, pp. 15–21, 16–21, 13–16.

————, 'The Japanese in the Australian Pearling Industry', in *Queensland Heritage*, Vol. 3, 1979.

So, Kwan-wai, *Japanese Piracy in Ming China During the 16th Century*, Michigan: Michigan State University Press, 1975.

Spykman, Nicholas J., *America's Strategy in World Politics*, New York: Harcourt & Brace, 1942.

Stargardt, A. W., *Australia's Asian Policies: The History of a Debate 1839–1972*, Institute of Asian Affairs in Hamburg, Wiesbaden: Otto Harrassowitz, 1977.

Stephan, John J., *Hawaii Under the Rising Sun: Japan's Plans for Conquest After Pearl Harbor*, Honolulu: University of Hawaii Press, 1984.

Storry, Richard, *Japan and the Decline of the West in Asia 1894–1943*, London: Macmillan, 1979.

Takegoshi Yosaburo, *The Story of the Wako: Japanese Pioneers in the Southern Region*, tr. Hideo Watanabe, Tokyo: Kenkyusha, 1940.

Takeuchi Tatsuji, *War and Diplomacy in the Japanese Empire*, Tokyo: Tuttle, 1935.

Tanaka Kengoro, *Operations of the Imperial Japanese Armed Forces in the Papua New Guinea Theater During World War II*, Tokyo: Japan-Papua New Guinea Goodwill Society, 1980.

Taylor, Griffith, *Australia*, London: Methuen, 1940.

Thomas, Alan, 'The Politicisation of the ABC in the 1930s: A Case Study of "The Watchman"', in *Politics*, Vol. 13, 1978, pp. 286–95.

Thompson, Roger C., *Australian Imperialism in the Pacific: The Expansionist Era 1820–1920*, Melbourne: Melbourne University Press, 1980.

Toby, Ronald P., *State and Diplomacy in Early Modern Japan: Asia in the Development of the Tokugawa Bakufu*, Princeton: Princeton University Press, 1984.

Tsukahira Toshio G., *Feudal Control in Tokugawa Japan: The Sankin Kōtai System*, Harvard East Asian Monographs, Cambridge, Mass.: Harvard University Press, 1966.

Tsunoda Ryusaku and L. Carrington Goodrich, *Japan in the Chinese Dynastic Histories: Later Han Through Ming Dynasties*, South Pasadena: P. D. and Ione Perkins, 1951.

————, William Theodore de Barry, and Donald Keene, eds, *Sources of the Japanese Tradition*, New York: Columbia University Press, 1958.

Tyler, Dennet, 'Australia's Defense Problem', in *Foreign Affairs*, Vol. 18, 1939, pp. 116–26.

Tyler, William H., *Flight of Diamonds: The Story of Broome's War and the Carnot Bay Diamonds*, Perth, W.A.: Hesperian Press, 1987.

Van Valkenburg, Samuel, *Elements of Political Geography*, New York: Prentice-Hall, 1943.

Von Verschuer, Charlotte, *Les Relations Officielles du Japon avec la Chine aux VIIIe et IXe siècles*, Genève: Librairie Droz, 1985.

————, *Le Commerce Extérieur du Japon: Des Origines au XVIe Siècle*, Paris: Maisonneuve & Larose, 1988.

Walton, R. D., 'Feeling for the Jugular: Japanese Espionage at Newcastle 1919–1926', in *Australian Journal of Politics and History*, Vol. 32, 1986, pp. 20–38.

Weigert, Hans W., 'Haushofer and the Pacific', in *Foreign Affairs*, Vol. 20, 1942, pp. 732–42.

Whittlesey, Derwent, *Germany Strategy of World Conquest*, New York: Farrar and Rinehart, 1942.

Willard, Myra, *History of the White Australia Policy to 1920*, Melbourne: Melbourne University Press, 1923 (reprinted 1974).

Williams, Glyndwr, 'Far More Happier than We Europeans: Reactions to the Australian Aborigines on Cook's Voyage', in *Historical Studies*, University of Melbourne, Vol. 19, October 1981.

Williams, Harold S., *Foreigners in Mikadoland*, Tokyo: Charles E. Tuttle, 1963.

Willmott, H. P., *Empires in the Balance: Japanese and Allied Pacific Strategies to April 1942*, Annapolis: Naval Institute Press, 1982.

Wood, G. Arnold, *The Discovery of Australia*, Melbourne: Macmillan, 1922 (revised by J. C. Beaglehole and reissued in 1969).

Yanaihara Tadao, *Pacific Islands Under Japanese Mandate*, London: Oxford University Press, 1940.

Yarwood, A. T., *Asian Migration to Australia: The Background to Exclusion, 1896–1923*, Melbourne: Melbourne University Press, 1967.

UNPUBLISHED SOURCES IN WESTERN LANGUAGES

Lin, Tong-yang, Etudes sur l'Introduction de Méthodes et de Connaissances Géographiques Européennes en Chine (1583- 1718), Thèse de Doctorat, Université de Paris-Sorbonne, 1982.

Miwa Kimitada, Crossroads of Patriotism in Imperial Japan: Shiga Shigetaka (1863–1927), Uchimura Kanzō (1861–1930), and Nitobe Inazō (1862–1933), Doctoral Dissertation, Princeton: Princeton University, 1967.

Nakami Mari, International Thought of the Japanese Intellectuals within the Institute of Pacific Relations, Paper read at the 31st International Congress of Human Sciences in Asia and North Africa, 2 September 1983, Tokyo.

Shimizu Hajime, Southeast Asia in Modern Japanese Thought: The Development and Transformation of 'Nanshin Ron', Paper deposited at the Department of Pacific and Southeast Asian History, Research School of Pacific Studies, Australian National University, June 1980, pp. 1–56.

Sissons, D. C. S., Attitudes to Japan and Defence 1890–1923, M.A. thesis, University of Melbourne, 1956.

————, An Immigrant Family, Paper deposited at the Department of International Relations, Research School of Pacific Studies, Australian National University, Canberra, 12 April 1977.

————, The Japanese in the Australian Pearling Industry, Paper deposited at the Department of International Relations, Research School of Pacific Studies, Australian National University, Canberra, June 1978, pp. 1–41.

————, Australian-Japanese Relations: The First Phase, 1859–91, Paper deposited at the Department of International Relations, Research School of Pacific Studies, Australian National University, October 1978.

Takeda Isami, Australia-Japan Relations in the Era of the Anglo-Japanese Alliance, 1896–1911, Ph.D. thesis, University of Sydney, 1984.

Index